Foundations for Mental Health and Community Counseling

An Introduction to the Profession

Foundations for Mental Health and Community Counseling

An Introduction to the Profession

Mark S. Gerig

Hiawatha Behavioral Health

PEARSON

Merrill
Prentice Hall

Upper Saddle River, New Jersey
Columbus, Ohio

Library of Congress Cataloging-in-Publication Data

Gerig, Mark S.
  Foundations for mental health and community counseling : an introduction to the profession / Mark S. Gerig.
    p. ; cm.
  Includes bibliographical references and index.
  ISBN 0-13-117800-8
  1. Mental health counseling. 2. Mental health counseling--Practice. 3. Mental health services.   I. Title.
  [DNLM: 1. Counseling. 2. Community Mental Health Services.
  WM 55 G369f 2007]
  RC466.G47 2007
  362.2'04256—dc22

                                    2006013075

Vice President and Executive Publisher: Jeffery W. Johnston
Publisher: Kevin M. Davis
Editorial Assistant: Sarah N. Kenoyer
Production Editor: Mary Harlan
Production Coordinator: John Shannon/Laserwords
Design Coordinator: Diane C. Lorenzo
Text Design and Illustrations: Laserwords Private Limited
Cover Design: Candace Rowely
Cover Image: SuperStock
Production Manager: Laura Messerly
Director of Marketing: David Gesell
Marketing Manager: Autumn Purdy
Marketing Coordinator: Brian Mounts

This book was set in Berkeley by Laserwords Private Limited. It was printed and bound by R. R. Donnelley & Sons Company. The cover was printed by R. R. Donnelley & Sons Company.

Pearson Education Ltd.   Pearson Education Australia Pty. Limited
Pearson Education Singapore Pte. Ltd.   Pearson Education North Asia Ltd.
Pearson Education Canada, Ltd.   Pearson Educación de Mexico, S.A. de C.V.
Pearson Education–Japan   Pearson Education Malaysia Pte. Ltd.

10 9 8 7 6 5 4
ISBN: 0-13-117800-8

Dedication

I dedicate this book to my colleagues at Hiawatha Behavioral Health. Their innovative service to consumers and dedication to the mental health field are testimony to the greatness of the counseling profession.

Mark S. Gerig is the Manager of Crisis and Elderly Services at Hiawatha Behavioral Health (HBH) in Sault Ste. Marie, Michigan. He is a Licensed Mental Health Counselor and Licensed Psychologist and is former Associate Professor, Chair of the Department of Counseling, and Coordinator of the Mental Health Counseling Specialization at Bethel College, Mishawaka, Indiana. In addition to his present responsibilities at HBH, Dr. Gerig serves as an adjunct professor at Algoma University College, Sault Ste. Marie, Ontario, Canada.

Dr. Gerig has been a leader in state and national professional associations. He has served as the President and Chair of Professional Development of the Indiana Mental Health Counselors Association (IMHCA) and presently serves on the Professional Issues Committee of the American Mental Health Counselors Association (AMHCA). In recognition of his professional service, he has been named recipient of the 2005 American Mental Health Counselors Association Counselor Educator of the Year, 2003 Indiana Mental Health Counselors Association Mental Health Counselor of the Year, and a 2002 American Mental Health Counselors Association Service Award.

Dr. Gerig resides in Sault Ste. Marie, Michigan, with his wife, Michelle, and daughter, Laurén. His son, Brandon, attends Lake Superior State University. In addition to his professional activities, Mark enjoys hiking, biking, fishing, and ice hockey.

The allied mental health professions have undergone dramatic changes over the past several decades. Economic, sociohistorical, and political forces have altered boundaries and scopes of practice among the traditional people-helping professions. Thus, contemporary mental health and community counselors look on a horizon that is ever changing.

My primary purpose in writing *Foundations for Mental Health and Community Counseling: An Introduction to the Profession* is to provide a text that paints an accurate picture of the profession of mental health counseling in this contemporary environment. Its content is flavored by my years of experience as a counselor educator; as a practitioner, supervisor, and manager in agency and behavioral health settings; and as a leader in professional associations. The reader will discover a fresh perspective that reflects a professional view from the trenches that is academically well informed.

The title of the text reflects its underlying orientation. Mental health counseling and community counseling are identified as distinct specializations by the Council for the Accreditation of Counseling and Related Educational Programs (CACREP). Furthermore, persons graduating with a Master of Arts degree in Counseling receive graduate training in the related but distinct specializations of mental health and community counseling. Yet these entry-level counseling professionals compete for similar positions in the workplace. Thus, although the training models reflect distinct emphases or specializations, significant overlap exists in the professional practice of these graduates. Thus, it is accurate to speak of mental health and community counselors as taking their place in a single profession. That is the primary audience to which I write.

As I write this preface, CACREP has issued the proposed revisions for its 2008 standards (Council for the Accreditation of Counseling and Related Educational Programs, 2005). Interestingly, it is being proposed that the mental health and community counseling specializations be merged. You will not find a political agenda within the pages that follow. That is not my intent. In some ways I anticipate this debate, but it is not my purpose to take a specific position on the proposed merger. Rather, it is my intent to write this text for counselor-trainees who will work in the mental health professions. This text provides detailed coverage of content viewed as foundational to the training of mental health and community counselors as identified by CACREP.

ORGANIZATION AND SPECIAL FEATURES OF THE TEXT

The text consists of three parts. In Part 1, historical and theoretical foundations are explored. Chapter 1 defines mental health and community counseling, the nature of the profession, and how it relates to both other counseling specializations and the allied mental health professions. Chapter 2 broadens the reader's understanding of these distinctions by investigating the historical development of the mental health professions, with special focus on professional counseling and its evolution. Chapter 3 discusses the theoretical foundations of the profession and introduces readers to a comprehensive model of mental health counseling. This model is a synthesis of the basic theoretical foundations, establishes the unique character of the profession, and describes how it can expressed in assessment and treatment. It also presents an organizational rubric around which research and programs can be developed that uniquely reflect the mental health counseling perspective. Chapter 4 provides an overview of the traditional and contemporary theories and techniques of counseling.

Part 2 focuses on the professional practice and work settings of mental health and community counselors. Chapter 5 takes an in-depth look at the education and credentialing of mental health and community counselors. The CACREP model and process of attaining professional licensure and certification are clearly described. Chapter 6 examines what mental health and community counselors do and where they work. Attention is given to the specific processes and modalities of counseling. This includes motivational interviewing, assessment and diagnosis, mental status exams, and treatment planning. The chapter concludes with the first-hand descriptions of professional practice in several specific settings. Chapter 7 addresses the important skills of assessment and research, while taking a scientist-practitioner perspective. Chapter 8 discusses the contemporary multicultural context in which counseling occurs. The professional necessity and ethical mandate to be multiculturally competent counselors is emphasized. Chapter 9 focuses on the ethical and legal issues that arise in mental health counseling. The 2005 American Counseling Association *Code of Ethics* is fully integrated throughout this discussion.

Part 3 focuses on contemporary issues and trends in the mental health counseling profession. These topics include managed care (chapter 10), community mental health (chapter 11), and future directions of the profession (chapter 12). Part 3 enables the reader to see professional life from the trenches. I believe you will find that this text accurately conveys the excitement, opportunities, and challenges of the mental health counseling profession.

ACKNOWLEDGMENTS

Many persons have made direct and indirect contributions to the content and production of this text. I must recognize the important role certain counselor educators played in my own professional development. My deep gratitude is extended to Martin Ritchie, Nick Piazza, Bob Wendt, and Gary R. Collins. Each played key roles in introducing me to the profession. Special thanks are directed to Bill King, whose mentoring cleared a path for me to assume leadership positions in state professional associations.

Several persons played critical roles in the production of this text. I thank my graduate assistants, Sam Augsburger and Sarah Shannon, who proofed the manuscript and assisted in putting together some of the tables, figures, and appendixes. The editorial assistance and support of Kevin Davis, Publisher, and his assistant, Sarah Kenoyer, helped me find my way through the writing process. In addition, I greatly appreciate the comments of the following reviewers, whose input enabled me to bring particular topics into better focus: G. Michael Arciniega, Arizona State University; Jeremy Blowers, Plattsburgh State University; Judith A. Burnett, Stetson University; Jeffrey Cornelius-White, Texas A&M International University; Chris D. Erickson, The George Washington University; Jerome M. Fischer, University of Idaho; Irene Houston, Auburn University; Todd F. Lewis, University of North Carolina, Greensboro; Chris

McCarthy, University of Texas at Austin; Norman D. Rice, University of Memphis; Bonnie A. Rudolph, Texas A&M International University; Eric A. Schmidt, Texas State University–San Marcos; Simeon Schlossberg, McDaniel College; Thomas Scofield, University of Nebraska at Kearney; I. Michael Shuff, Indiana State University; Margery Shupe, Xavier University; and Joshua C. Watson, Mississippi State University–Meridian.

Finally, this undertaking is truly made possible through the support of my wife, Michelle, and our children, Brandon and Laurén. Their loving support and encouragement enabled me to keep on task, especially at those times when I would have rather been fishing!

THE PRENTICE HALL COMPANION WEBSITE:
A VIRTUAL LEARNING ENVIRONMENT

Technology is a constantly growing and changing aspect of our field that is creating a need for content and resources. To address this emerging need, Prentice Hall has developed an online learning environment for students and professors alike—Companion Websites—to support our textbooks.

In creating a Companion Website, our goal is to build on and enhance what the textbook already offers. For this reason, the content for each user-friendly website is organized by topic and provides the professor and student with a variety of meaningful resources. Common features of a Companion Website include:

- **Counseling Topics**—17 core counseling topics representing the diversity and scope of today's counseling field.
- **Annotated Bibliography**—Seminal foundational works and key current works
- **Web Destinations**—Significant and up-to-date practitioner and client sites
- **Professional Development**—Helpful information regarding professional organizations and codes of ethics
- **Electronic Blue Book**—Send homework or essays directly to your instructor's email with this paperless form
- **Chat**—Real time chat with anyone who is using the text anywhere in the country—ideal for discussion and study groups, class projects, etc.

To take advantage of these and other resources, please visit the *Foundations for Mental Health and Community Counseling* Companion Website at

www.prenhall.com/gerig

RESEARCH NAVIGATOR: RESEARCH MADE SIMPLE!

www.ResearchNavigator.com

Merrill Education is pleased to introduce Research Navigator—a one-stop research solution for students that simplifies and streamlines the entire research process. At www.researchnavigator.com, students will find extensive resources to enhance their understanding of the research process so they can effectively complete research assignments. In addition, Research Navigator has three exclusive databases of credible and reliable source content to help students focus their research efforts and begin the research process.

HOW WILL RESEARCH NAVIGATOR ENHANCE YOUR COURSE?

- Extensive content helps students understand the research process, including writing, internet research, and citing sources.
- Step-by-step tutorial guides students through the entire research process from selecting a topic to revising a rough draft.
- Research Writing in the Disciplines section details the differences in research across disciplines.
- Three exclusive databases—EBSCO's ContentSelect Academic Journal Database, *The New York Times* Search by Subject Archive and "Best of the Web" Link Library—allow students to easily find journal articles and sources.

WHAT'S THE COST?

A subscription to Research Navigator is $7.50 but is available at no additional cost when ordered in conjunction with this textbook. To obtain free passcodes for your students, simply contact your local Merrill/Prentice Hall sales representative, and your representative will send you the Evaluating Online Resource Guide, which contains the code to access Research Navigator as well as tips on how to use Research Navigator and how to evaluate research. To preview the value of this website to your students, please go to www.educatorlearningcenter.com and use the Login Name "Research" and the password "Demo."

BRIEF CONTENTS

CONTENTS

Part 3: **CONTEMPORARY ISSUES AND TRENDS**   **201**

Note: Every effort has been made to provide accurate and current Internet information in this book. However, the Internet and information posted on it are constantly changing, so it is inevitable that some of the Internet addresses listed in this textbook will change.

Part 1

Theoretical and Historical Foundations

1

What Is a Licensed Mental Health or Professional Counselor?

OUTLINE

I was a young counselor freshly groomed and searching for my first professional position. With a Master of Arts degree in counseling in hand, I began to wade through the classified ads in several newspapers, seeking to find a job where I could engage in the professional practice. First, I looked under Administration and Professional and, then, to the Medical and Dental section. Finally, I looked over the General Help Wanted category.

To my chagrin, I did not find any advertisements using the professional titles of mental health or community counselors. In fact, the term *counselor* did not appear in any mental health–related advertisement. What I did find surprised me greatly! One entry was titled, "Counselor Needed," but went on to describe an opening for a person to work behind a cosmetics counter at a local department store and provide counsel to its customers regarding the relative benefits of the store's products. In another advertisement, the employer sought experienced loan officers to provide credit counseling at a mortgage company. A large grocery store was looking to hire a counselor to work in the fresh meats department and assist customers in selecting the proper cut of meat. Since I didn't have meat-cutting experience, I didn't qualify!

Yes, I did find classified ads that related to the mental health profession. However, they were seeking therapists, psychologists, psychiatric nurses, and social workers. Most of these positions required at least two years of experience and an appropriate license. Discouraged, I persisted in sending out resumes to a variety of human service organizations and mental health centers.

This true story does have a happy ending. I did find a position! Interestingly, the position I accepted was in response to an advertisement that had not even mentioned the term *counselor*. Rather, the small, private not-for-profit agency had a job opening for an individual, group, and family therapist. The official job description noted that an MSW (Master's in Social Work) was required and an ACSW (Academy of Certified Social Workers) was preferred. I had neither! But I did have entry-level knowledge and skills in doing individual, group, and family counseling. The director of the agency, who held the ACSW credential, was unfamiliar with the training model of graduate programs in counseling and was impressed with the broad-based, skill-oriented approach to training. Once she understood the training model of the counseling profession, she became very open to hiring other appropriately trained counselors for positions that had formerly been reserved for persons who had graduated from master's-level programs in social work or psychology.

Mental health counseling is the "new kid" setting up residence on the block where the other mental health professions have lived. While we share many things in common with our neighbors, our profession possesses a unique identity that sets us apart from those professions. The identity of mental health counselors is rooted in a unique historical and philosophical tradition. In addition, mental health counseling draws from a specific training model where specialization builds on a common core of curricular experiences that links us with closely related counseling professions. Certainly, the profession has come a long way since the days of my first job search.

This book is written to serve as an introduction to the profession of mental health counseling, one of the most exciting and upcoming professions in the field of mental health. Licensed Mental Health Counselors (LMHCs), who are also referred to as Licensed Professional Counselors (LPCs), currently number 80,000 and are recognized as licensed practitioners in 48 states and the District of Columbia (American Counseling Association, 2003; American Mental Health Counselors Association, 2004). Persons entering into this profession receive their academic training from graduate programs in counseling. Such programs typically offer specializations in mental health or community counseling that are designed to prepare students to fulfill licensure requirements for licensure as an LMHC or LPC.

This book is titled *Foundations for Mental Health and Community Counseling: An Introduction to the Profession* with this background in mind. My goal in writing this text is to explore the foundations of the mental health and community counseling specializations, as identified by the Council for the Accreditation of Counseling and Related Educational Programs (CACREP). While two unique specializations are accredited by CACREP, students who graduate from one or the other often compete for the same positions and seek to meet requirements for the same license types (e.g., Licensed Professional Counselor, Licensed Professional Clinical Counselor, or Licensed Mental Health Counselor). Thus, we may speak of mental health and community counseling as two separate specializations in the academic training of counselors who work under numerous licensed titles. The realities of the contemporary mental health delivery system clearly demonstrate that persons graduating from these respective specializations and holding counseling-related licenses work in similar settings and provide similar services. They direct their services to individuals, groups, families, and organizations who seek to enhance their level of mental health or treat pathology.

Throughout this text, I will use the terms *mental health and community counseling* or *mental health and community counselors* to refer to persons who have received academic training from programs either accredited by or tailored after the CACREP model. Although acknowledging that numerous professional titles accompany the license types attained by these professions, I will refer to the licensed professionals as *licensed mental health and/or professional counselors* throughout the text. Finally, recognizing that licensed mental health and professional counselors provide a similar range of services, I will use the term *mental health counseling* when referring to their general professional identity. A unifying model for the profession, which I have titled the *comprehensive model of mental health counseling*, is presented in chapter 3. I hope that the chapters that follow provide a voice of unity, clarity, and inspiration to those seeking to join a profession that is increasingly viewed as a major player in the mental health delivery system (Ivey, 1989).

WHAT IS A COUNSELOR? ENTER A LAND OF CONFUSION!

The words *counselor* and *counseling* are commonly used but often misunderstood terms. Seiler (1990) notes that the term *counseling* is used by business and government to describe occupations ranging from retail sales counselors to the tax counselors of the Internal Revenue Service. These words are used in so many ways that it becomes difficult to understand their specific meanings apart from context in which the words appear. And, even then, confusion can reign.

There are several reasons for this confusion and ambiguity. First, to *counsel* commonly refers to activities such as deliberating, consulting, guiding, or advising. Numerous professions engage in activities that fall under the rubric of counseling when the word is used in this general way. Attorneys, car salespersons, and, yes, even meat cutters can be described as being counselors to their respective clientele. Thus, the word *counsel* can refer to a very broad range of helping processes in which one person provides assistance to others in a particular manner.

Second, mental health and licensed professional counselors are not the only mental health-related professionals who counsel. Professional counseling is a basic role that is part of a wide range of mental health professions (Hanna & Bemak, 1997). Psychiatrists, psychologists, social workers, marriage and family therapists, psychiatric nurses, and pastors rightfully describe their professional roles as counselors. In addition, these mental health professions sometimes utilize theories and techniques of counseling. These are not the property of any given profession but are processes of facilitating change that may be used by each of the professions. Furthermore, a number of professional organizations and accrediting bodies use the term *counseling* as well (e.g., American Counseling Association [ACA], Division 17 of the American Psychological Association [APA], or the American Association of Pastoral Counselors [AAPC]).

Third, the counseling profession itself unintentionally contributes to the confusion. The term *counselor* is used as a generic title that follows the areas of specialty within the profession. Thus, *school, gerontological, career, marriage and family, mental health,* and *college* are all qualifying terms that specify counseling specialties. While persons in these specialties correctly view themselves as being professional counselors, the title *licensed professional counselor* relates to a statutory credential used to regulate a specific mental health profession.

Confused? If so, you are in the company of many persons who, in the process of applying for admission into graduate programs in the counseling-related disciplines, experience uncertainty regarding which specific discipline and program to choose. I have directed a graduate program in counseling, and have found that the most frequently asked question prospective students pose to me is, "What is the difference between being a mental health counselor and a social worker or marriage and family therapist?" The uncertainty experienced by such inquirers in part reflects the identity confusion that plagues the mental health professions. The remainder of this chapter provides a response to such questions and dispels confusion by clarifying what it means to call oneself a licensed mental health or professional counselor. In addition, the professional organizations that represent counselor interests are identified and described briefly. Finally, similarities and differences among the mental health counseling profession, other counseling specializations, and related professions are discussed.

WHAT IT MEANS TO BE A MENTAL HEALTH, COMMUNITY, OR LICENSED PROFESSIONAL COUNSELOR: SOME HELPFUL DEFINITIONS

The definition of *counseling* has evolved in response to forces both from within the profession and from the contemporary mental health care environment (Nugent, 2000). The American Counseling Association defines *professional counseling* as follows: "the application of mental health, psychological, or human development principles, through cognitive, affective, behavioral, or systemic intervention strategies that address wellness, personal growth, or career development, as well as pathology" (ACA Governing Council, 1997, p. 8).

The definition developed by the ACA (1997) relates very closely to an earlier and more detailed definition of mental health counseling put forth by the American Mental Health Counselors Association (AMHCA) in 1987:

> Mental Health Counseling is the provision of professional counseling services, involving the application of principles of psychotherapy, human development, learning theory, group dynamics, and the etiology of mental illness and dysfunctional behavior to individuals, couples, families, and groups, for the purposes of treating psychopathology and promoting optimal mental health.
>
> The practice of Mental Health Counseling includes, but is not limited to diagnosis and treatment of mental and emotional disorders, psychoeducational techniques aimed at the prevention of such disorders, consultation to individuals, couples, families, groups, organizations, and communities and clinical research into more effective psychotherapeutic treatment modalities. (Mental Health Counseling Training Standards, 1987, p. 6)

Lewis, Lewis, Daniels, and D'Andrea (1998) provide additional clarification by defining *community counseling* as "a comprehensive helping framework of intervention strategies and services that promotes the personal development and well-being of all individuals and communities" (p. 5). Their model contains four categories of service components provided by community counselors: (a) direct client services,

(b) indirect client services, (c) direct community services, and (d) indirect community services.

Historically, community counseling was a specialization for training counselors whose primary focus was on community interventions and agency work settings. In contrast, mental health counselors, while frequently working in agency settings, had interests in private practice. Thus, the mental health counseling specialization had an increased emphasis on diagnosis, treatment planning, third-party reimbursement, and psychopharmacology. However, in recent years, the boundary between community and mental health counseling has become blurred, as graduates from either specialization tend to work in similar settings. In addition, mental health counselors and community counselors are eligible for similar license types (i.e., LPC, Licensed Professional Clinical Counselor (LPCC), LMHC). The most apparent difference lies in academic requirements. According to CACREP standards (CACREP, 2001), community counseling requires 48 semester hours of graduate study, whereas mental health counseling requires 60 semester hours.

When these definitions are considered together, several major themes emerge that help us to understand better what it means to be a licensed mental health or professional counselor. First, LMHCs and LPCs possess knowledge and skills for the promotion of wellness *and* treatment of pathology. Such training is foundational as they work with client systems in their quest to move toward optimal human functioning as well as away from emotional distress, dysfunction, and mental illness (Bloom et al., 1990). As Hill (1991) noted, "Such terms as *personal empowerment, competencies,* and *positive health* (wellness) may be new to psychology, but they are integral to the very heritage of our profession" (p. 47).

Second, wellness and pathology are understood within the framework of normal human development. This points to the application of human development principles, psychoeducation, and strength-based interventions in addition to the traditional techniques of psychotherapy as primary tools of intervention for the LMHC and LPC. Van Hesteren and Ivey (1990) note that counseling and development go hand in hand. And from this positive developmental orientation, mental health counselors find a theoretical base from which to view presenting issues related to mental health promotion as well as remediation of psychopathology (Ivey & Rigazio-DiGilio, 1991). Clients are understood as having the capacity to learn and apply skills taught rather than being seen as patients (Dinkmeyer, 1991). Furthermore, it has been established that psychoeducation can accelerate and add depth to the counseling process (Guerney, 1977).

Third, an ecological model (Bronfenbrenner, 1979) provides the theoretical foundation for guiding both the assessment and intervention strategies implemented by mental health counselors. Case conceptualization, when conducted by mental health counselors, considers the multiple levels of the client's environment. Individuals are not assessed or treated as if they are isolated or autonomous from the larger social system. Services provided may address presenting issues by using direct or indirect approaches and may be directed to multiple levels of the client system (Lewis et al., 1998). In this way, interventions capitalize on the strengths and resources that are available within the social milieu of the client. In addition, this framework enables mental health counselors to respond to the needs of individuals, couples, families, groups, and organizations in ways that are culturally sensitive.

Fourth, the preceding definitions clearly communicate the multidisciplinary nature of the profession (Pistole & Roberts, 2002). Weikel and Palmo (1989) note that the profession of mental health counseling was born as a hybrid, with psychology and education as the uneasy bed partners. Much of the theoretical foundation on which the profession stands is not of its own origin. The disciplines of education, psychology, cognitive science, philosophy, and the medical sciences have made important contributions to our knowledge base. In addition, LMHCs and LPCs frequently work as members of a multidisciplinary treatment team (Weikel & Palmo, 1989, 1996). It is logical and even essential that training should, therefore, include the best of scientific information from the other mental health professions (Seiler & Messina, 1979). The professional benefit from such collaboration is that counselors are able to provide more comprehensive interventions and treatment services for their clients. Furthermore, treatment teams benefit from the unique perspective of prevention, wellness, and personal growth provided by mental health counselors.

RELEVANT PROFESSIONAL ORGANIZATIONS

Four organizations are very important in understanding the professional identities of licensed mental health and professional counselors. These include the American Counseling Association (ACA), American Mental Health Counselors Association (AMHCA), National Board of Certified Counselors (NBCC), and Council for the Accreditation of Counseling and Related Educational Programs (CACREP).

The ACA is the organization that represents the interests of professional counselors in general. Founded in 1952, nearly 60,000 members call the ACA their professional home. The organization was originally known as the American Personnel and Guidance Association (APGA) and was formed through the alliance of four smaller groups: the National Vocational Guidance Association, American College Personnel Association, National Association of Guidance Supervisors, and Student Personnel Association for Teacher Education (Myers, 1995). These smaller groups, representing the specializations of career counseling, student development, counselor education and supervision, and teacher education, formed the original four divisions of the association. This historical tradition continues, with the ACA presently serving as the home for 18 divisions. These divisions are identified and described briefly in Table 1.1.

The AMHCA was founded in 1976 as a professional association representing the interests of professional counselors having the following characteristics in common: They were (a) academically prepared at either the master's or doctoral level; (b) working in community mental health, private practice, or agency settings; (c) delivering a

TABLE 1.1

Divisions of the American Counseling Association

American College Counseling Association (ACCA)
Promotes student development in colleges, universities, and community colleges.

American Mental Health Counselors Association (AMHCA)
Promotes advocating for client access to quality services within the health care industry.

American Rehabilitation Counseling Association (ARCA)
Promotes the enhancement of people with disabilities as well as excellence within the rehabilitation counseling profession in practice, research, consultation, and professional development.

American School Counselor Association (ASCA)
Promotes school counseling professionals and interest in activities that affect the personal, educational, and career development of students. ASCA members also work collaboratively with parents, educators, and community members to provide a positive learning environment.

Association for Adult Development and Aging (AADA)
Promotes information sharing, professional development, and advocacy related to adult development and aging issues as well as addresses counseling concerns across the lifespan.

Association for Assessment in Counseling and Education (AACE)
Promotes the effective use of assessment within the counseling profession.

Association for Counselor Education and Supervision (ACES)
Emphasizes the need for quality education and supervision of counselors for all work settings.

Association for Counselors and Educators in Government (ACEG)
Promotes counseling clients and their families in local, state, and federal government or in military-related agencies.

Association for Creativity in Counseling (ACC)
Promotes awareness, advocacy, and understanding of the diverse and creative approaches to counseling.

Association for Gay, Lesbian and Bisexual Issues in Counseling (AGLBIC)
Promotes awareness of the unique needs of client identity development and provides a nonthreatening counseling environment by aiding in the reduction of stereotypical thinking and homoprejudice.

Association for Multicultural Counseling and Development (AMCD)
Promotes cultural, ethnic, and racial empathy and understanding through programs that advance and sustain personal growth.

Association for Specialists in Group Work (ASGW)
Promotes professional leadership in the field of group work, establishes standards for professional training, and supports research and the dissemination of knowledge.

Association for Spiritual, Ethical, and Religious Values in Counseling (ASERVIC)
Promotes spiritual, ethical, religious, and other human values that are essential to the full development of the person as well as the discipline of counseling.

TABLE 1.1 (Continued)	**Counseling Association for Humanistic Education and Development (C-AHEAD)** Provides a forum for the exchange of information about humanistically oriented counseling practices and promotes changes that reflect the growing body of knowledge about humanistic principles applied to human development and potential. **Counselors for Social Justice (CSJ)** Promotes equity and ending oppression and injustice affecting clients, students, counselors, families, communities, schools, workplaces, governments, and other social and institutional systems. **International Association of Addiction and Offender Counselors (IAAOC)** Promotes the development of effective counseling and rehabilitation programs for people with substance abuse problems, other addictions, and adult and/or juvenile public offenders. **International Association of Marriage and Family Counselors (IAMFC)** Promotes the development of healthy family systems through prevention, education, and therapy. **National Career Development Association (NCDA)** Promotes career development for all people across the lifespan through public information, member services, conferences, and publications. **National Employment Counseling Association (NECA)** Provides professional leadership to people who counsel in employment and/or career development settings.

wide range of mental health services similar to those offered by more established mental health care professions; and, up to 1976, (d) had no professional home due to their uniqueness (Smith & Robinson, 1995). In 1978, the AMHCA became a division of the APGA. Its membership grew quickly, and it soon became the largest division of the umbrella association. The relationship of AMHCA and ACA has frequently been "stormy and fraught with miscommunication and misinformation" (Smith & Robinson, 1995, p. 159). Currently, while still a division of the ACA, AMHCA operates in an autonomous manner. Its finances are separate from the ACA and its members can join AMHCA independently of the ACA. The AMHCA offers a variety of member benefits, such as liability and group health insurance, annual conferences, newsletters, and journals that supplement those benefits provided by the ACA. In addition, its relationship to the ACA is better described as collaborative than affilliative (Pistole & Roberts, 2002). The primary agenda of AMHCA includes professional credentialing and recognition, right to practice, legislative activity, and third-party reimbursement.

Both the ACA and AMHCA have chapters at the state level. State chapters provide numerous services for the profession. These include the development of continuing education opportunities presented through state conventions and regional workshops. State chapters also serve as advocates for the consumers of mental health services in their respective states. In addition, licensure of the profession involves a statutory process that is specific to each state. State associations work closely with state licensure boards through consultation and advocacy for the development and implementation of licensure laws. Finally, issues concerning reimbursement for services typically have regional dimensions. While ACA and AMHCA advocate for the profession at the national level, state chapters are called on to respond to policy and practice concerns that affect mental health counselors of their respective states. Examples include Medicaid reimbursement, professional recognition and panel membership, and right to practice and scope of practice issues. Therefore, many professionals become members of both national and state professional organizations.

The National Board of Certified Counselors (NBCC) is an independent corporation whose purpose is to certify professionals who meet standards to qualify as certified counselors or specialists. Since its establishment in 1981, the NBCC has certified more than 50,000 counselors who have demonstrated knowledge and skills at a minimum competency level in specific areas of study deemed foundational for all professional counselors regardless of specialization. Upon certification as a National Certified Counselor (NCC), professionals can qualify for specialty certification in three areas: mental health counseling, school counseling, or addictions counseling. The following titles are granted:

- Certified Clinical Mental Health Counselor (CCMHC)
- National Certified School Counselor (NCSC)
- Master Addictions Counselor (MAC)

National certification is a voluntary, nonstatutory credential that verifies that the professional has met certain professional standards. The certifications most frequently sought by LMHCs and LPCs are the NCC and CCMHC.

The Council for the Accreditation of Counseling and Related Educational Programs (CACREP) was also established in 1981 and is the accrediting arm of the ACA (CACREP, 2001). It is an independent organization that was created by the ACA and its divisions to "develop, implement, and maintain standards of preparation for the counseling profession's graduate-level programs" (p. 15). CACREP accomplishes this mission by developing academic training standards for the counseling professions, encouraging excellence in program development, and granting accreditation of professional preparation programs. The standards identify specific objectives for the following areas within an academic program (CACREP, 2001):

- the institution
- program objectives and curriculum
- clinical instruction
- faculty and staff
- organization and administration
- evaluation in the program
- program area standards

Master's- and doctoral-level programs in counseling that demonstrate that they meet or exceed these standards are granted accreditation. The following master's-level program areas may be accredited by CACREP:

- career counseling
- college counseling
- community counseling
- gerontological counseling
- marital, couples, and family counseling/therapy
- mental health counseling
- school counseling
- student affairs

CACREP also grants accreditation to doctoral programs in counselor education and supervision.

Thus, CACREP sets the national standard by which the quality of all counselor education programs can be assessed. Most LMHCs and LPCs graduate from counselor education programs that are either accredited by CACREP or whose objectives mirror the standards set for the specializations of mental health or community counseling. In addition, the educational requirements specified in most state licensure laws have integrated CACREP standards. Graduates from CACREP-approved programs, therefore, are at an advantage when applying for professional licensure. A more detailed discussion of the training models for community and mental health counselors along with their relationship to certification and licensure is provided in chapter 5.

OTHER SPECIALTIES WITHIN THE COUNSELING PROFESSION

According to the ACA Policies and Procedures Manual (American Counseling Association, 1995, as cited in Myers, 1995), specialties are recognized when specialty accreditation or certification processes are established by CACREP, NBCC, the Council on Rehabilitation Education (CORE), or the Commission on Rehabilitation Counselor Certification (CRCC). Based on these criteria, recognized specialties in addition to mental health counseling include addictions counseling, career counseling, gerontological counseling, marriage and family counseling, rehabilitation counseling, and school counseling. Each of these is discussed briefly next.

ADDICTION COUNSELING

Addiction counselors assist persons who have problems with alcohol, narcotics, and other harmful or addictive substances; gambling; or eating disorders. They find employment in chemical abuse treatment facilities, chemical abuse/dependence programs housed within community mental health centers, outpatient clinics, or employee assistance programs.

The National Association of Alcohol and Drug Abuse Counselors (NAADAC) has developed a three-tier certification system based, in part, on academic degree requirements. Criteria for National Certified Addiction Counselor I and II do not require the master's degree. The highest level of certification granted is the Master Addictions Counselor (MAC).

Addiction counselors possess skills in a variety of intervention strategies and can use individual, group, and family modalities of treatment. Increasingly, clients are being seen who present with substance abuse/dependence disorders and co-occurring mental illness. To provide optimal care for such clients, addiction counselors become integral parts of a multidisciplinary approach to treatment.

CAREER COUNSELING

Career counselors work primarily with persons who seek help in the processes of career planning and decision making. Such issues have lifespan implications and occur in an ecological context. Thus, in addition to helping persons match personal characteristics to specific job requirements, career counselors frequently address personal, family, and social factors that influence or are influenced by career-related decisions and stressors. Social roles, discrimination, stress, sexual harassment, bias, stereotyping, pay inequities, or tokenism can be aspects of the presenting problem (Engels, Minor, Sampson, & Splete, 1995).

GERONTOLOGICAL COUNSELING

As the aging of the U.S population continues, counselors are called on to provide specialized services for older persons. Gerontological counselors possess general competencies to empower older persons and facilitate wellness. They possess a working knowledge of specific conditions, such as Alzheimer's disease, chronic and terminal illness, substance abuse and complications due to polypharmacy, and life transitions that affect the quality of life of older persons. They must keep abreast of new state and federal legislation as well as other organizational policies that influence the daily lives of their clientele. In addition to traditional techniques of counseling, gerontological counselors have skills in the use of life review, resocialization therapies, bereavement counseling, community assessment and intervention, advocacy, and consultation.

MARRIAGE AND FAMILY COUNSELING

Marriage and family counselors work in private practice and agency settings and possess skills in family systems assessment and treatment. The family unit, often viewed as a three-generational system, is recognized as the most basic emotional entity and becomes the focus of treatment. In contrast to marriage and family therapists, marriage and family counselors receive training in the core areas of counseling as specified by CACREP and complete a set of courses that relate to the treatment of family dysfunction and promotion of family wellness. Thus, couples, premarital, marriage, family, and divorce counseling are all important skills that marriage and family counselors use to enhance the quality of life in families as they progress through the family life cycle.

REHABILITATION COUNSELING

Rehabilitation counselors are prepared to assist persons with disabilities in adapting to environments as well as assist environments in adapting to the specific needs of the disabled person. They work in an ever-expanding number of traditional and nontraditional employment settings. These include public and private rehabilitation centers, employee assistance programs, disability management programs, school-based transition programs, university programs for students with disabilities, and hospitals (Leahy & Szymanski, 1995). General counseling skills are essential for adequate performance in these settings. In addition, rehabilitation counselors must be knowledgeable in current rehabilitation-related legislation, federally funded programs, and the organizational structures and processes of the rehabilitation service system. Vocational evaluation, assessment, and work adjustment techniques are used by rehabilitation counselors to help clients reach their full potential of productivity.

SCHOOL COUNSELING

School counselors are employed in elementary, middle/junior high, senior high schools, and postsecondary settings. They work with the full range of students, including at-risk and special needs populations. Overall, the primary goal of school counselors is to facilitate the whole-person development of all students.

A variety of approaches are used, including individual, small- and large-group counseling, as well as advocacy and consultation. Individual and small-group counseling are used to help students develop and implement effective stratigies for coping with and resolving a variety of personal problems and developmental concerns. Career and social development guidance is also offered to larger groups using psychoeducational techniques. Frequently, school counselors consult with educational specialists, including school psychologists, administrators, and medical professionals, to facilitate the development and implementation of individualized educational plans. In such roles, they may serve as a type of case manager who oversees the networking of services to ensure that the specific needs of the students are being met. Clearly, school counselors must possess a working knowledge of human development principles in order to develop and implement preventive and remedial programs that meet the needs of a culturally diverse student population.

MENTAL HEALTH COUNSELING AND THE ALLIED MENTAL HEALTH PROFESSIONS

As noted earlier, the profession of mental health counseling is multidisciplinary at its foundation and in practice. And this contributes to some of the identity confusion that exists in the profession as well as among consumers. In order to clarify the place of LMHCs and LPCs among other contemporary mental health providers, it is useful to describe other professions that license and certify practitioners who also deliver mental health care to individuals, groups, couples, and families. These are psychiatrists, psychologists, social workers, and marriage and family therapists. A list of the professional organizations that represent these various mental health professions is presented in Appendix A.

Psychiatrists are physicians, typically holding doctorates in medicine (M.D.), who specialize in the diagnosis, treatment, and prevention of mental illness. They must graduate from medical school and then complete up to 4 years of residency training in psychiatry. Frequently, additional training is acquired so that the practitioner can specialize in such areas as child or geriatric psychiatry, psychopharmacology, or a specific mode of therapy. Given their extensive medical training, psychiatrists are qualified to understand the complex relationship between psychological disorder and physical illness. They are the mental health professionals who can prescribe medications. In addition, certification by psychiatrists is often required for involuntary admission of patients for inpatient hospitalization. The American Psychiatric Association is the professional organization that represents and supports the interests, practice, and research of psychiatrists.

Psychologists are doctorally trained professionals who assess, diagnose, and treat mental illness and emotional distress. Clinical psychology is the subdiscipline that is primarily focused on the study, assessment, treatment, and prevention of abnormal behavior (Carson & Butcher, 1992). In contrast, counseling psychologists have focused traditionally on the presenting problems of relatively normal populations. However, this distinction has become less pronounced in recent years. Typically, state licensure laws for psychologists utilize the generic title of psychologist and rarely make any distinctions among the specializations within the discipline. Psychologists have the statutory right to diagnose and treat mental illness. In addition, psychologists are highly trained in the administration, scoring, and interpretation of psychological tests. Recently, psychologists have been seeking drug prescription privileges, particularly with neuroleptic or psychotropic medications (Cummings, 1990). The American Psychological Association represents the professional interests of psychologists.

Social work has a long and distinguished history among the allied mental health professions. It can be defined as "the professional activity of helping individuals, groups, or communities to enhance or restore their capacity for social functioning and creating societal conditions favorable to this goal" (Barker, 1987, p. 154).

Social workers provide important services to individuals, groups, and families by doing one or more of the following: assisting in linking people to tangible services, providing counseling, helping communities to provide and improve health and social services, and advocating for the inclusion of social work principles and values in relevant legislative processes.

The profession and practice of clinical social work are regulated by licensure laws in all 50 states. In addition, the Academy of Certified Social Workers (ACSW) grants certification to social workers who hold regular membership of the National Association of Social Workers (NASW), the national organization that represents the professional interests of social workers. In order to apply for certification, social workers must hold a master's degree from a graduate school of social work (i.e., the MSW), must have accumulated 2 years or 3,000 hours of postgraduate degree experience in an agency setting under qualified supervision, and must pass the ACSW written exam.

Marriage and family therapy can be viewed both as a professional orientation and specific vocation within the mental health professions. As a professional orientation, marriage and family therapy is a theoretical lens and set of techniques used by trained mental health professionals in the treatment of emotional disorders and relational problems. The presenting issues are viewed from a family systems perspective (Commission on Accreditation for Marriage and Family Therapy Education, 1997). This systems orientation is applicable to the treatment of individuals, couples, and family disorders or problems. In contrast, *marriage and family therapists* are members of a distinct profession who diagnose and treat a wide range of human conditions, including individual psychopathology, parent-child problems, and marital distress and conflict. Based on a systems orientation, the family is viewed as the most basic emotional unit and therefore becomes the target of assessment and intervention. In order to be licensed as a marriage and family therapist, the practitioner must have earned either a master's or doctoral degree in marriage and family therapy and have at least 2 years of clinical experience conducted under qualified supervision (e.g., an AAMFT Clinically Approved Supervisor). The American Association of Marriage and Family Therapists (AAMFT) is the professional organization that represents the professional interests of marriage and family therapists.

CONCLUSION: THE PROCESS OF CONSOLIDATING PROFESSIONAL IDENTITY

It is useful to view the process of consolidating a professional identity in mental health counseling as a developmental process. Students entering counseling programs as well as recent graduates often wrestle with their own set of "who am I" questions. They may not see clear distinctions between who they are relative to the other mental health professions. Or they continue to feel uncomfortable performing in their professional roles despite adequate levels of skill and training.

Be patient. In many ways, the process of attaining a stable professional identity can be likened to the adolescent process of attaining *identity achievement* (Marcia, 1966, 1980). Explore alternatives and ask questions that enable you to see the "lay of the land" more clearly. Proceed down the path with trusted peers and a knowledgeable mentor to walk alongside. Fully invest yourself in your training experience.

Friedman and Kaslow (1986) postulated a six-stage developmental model for counseling professionals that starts with an anticipatory stage, in which new counselors learn they will be meeting with clients. This stage ends when counselors start to meet with their clinical supervisors. Stage 2, the dependency stage, is where novice counselors rely heavily on supervisors for answers. In stage 3, counselors continue to rely on their supervisors but are beginning to move toward independent activity. At stage 4, counselors experience the excitement that comes with initiating autonomous counseling interventions and seeing clients' positive responses. Counselors develop a sense of identity and autonomy in stage 5. In the final stage, counselors have settled in to their profession and exhibit calmness and collegiality. Kral and Hines (1999) found that it takes from 5 to 6 years before new counseling professionals gain a stable sense of identity and competence.

In addition, establishing a sense of professional identity involves integrating the sense of belonging to the mental health counseling profession and comfort with the professional roles performed into one's overall sense of self. This is a dynamic process that occurs within an ecological context. The counselor is a person who takes on a particular set of roles that involves specific intra- and interpersonal processes regulated by the profession. The unique shape of these factors and how they integrate into a coherent professional identity depend on forces external to both the person and the profession. Thus, the development of professional identity is a function of a person-environment interaction. Figure 1.1 illustrates this developmental process.

FIGURE 1.1 Developing Professional Identity: A Person-Environment Interaction

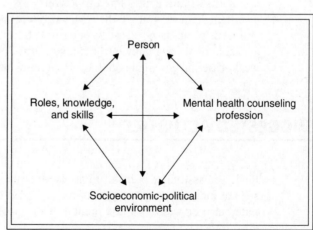

Achieving a coherent professional identity as a professional mental health counselor has much to do with who you are as a person and your personal developmental context and history. The shape that your professional identity takes is influenced by your ongoing interaction with a number of sociocultural forces. These include the economic system; societal and cultural values, mores, and beliefs; governmental policies and funding; the nature of public and private institutions; and related mental health professions.

This chapter has provided you with foundational information to help you see more clearly what it means to be an LMHC or LPC. Through the consolidation of professional identity, you will experience a sense of well-being and congruity as you move through time as well as the comfort and security of knowing where you are going. It is only by possessing a clear view of who you are and where you are going that you can be a helpful facilitator, guide, or anchor for those you serve. Ultimately, your personal satisfaction and survival in the profession depend on it.

DISCUSSION QUESTIONS

1. On page 17, a six-stage developmental model for counseling professionals is described briefly. What specific personal characteristics or experiences might facilitate one's positive professional development? What specific personal characteristics or experiences might hinder one's professional development?
2. Given that the development of a professional identity is a developmental process, suppose you are in your first year of professional practice and a client challenges your competency. What would be your internal experience in such a situation? How would you respond?
3. From a consumer point of view, is it possible to clearly differentiate the specific roles or strengths of the various mental health professions? What specific recommendations would you make to increase the visibility and accurate perception of the mental health counseling profession?
4. To what extent do you see the various counseling specializations as constituting a common profession? Identify potential strengths and resources that are made available by having *unity* in the midst of this *diversity?* Can you see any potential weaknesses or potential conflicts of interests? Be specific.

SUGGESTED ACTIVITIES

1. Review classified ads from a variety of sources (e.g., local newspapers, Web sites of mental health organizations, etc.) and identify how employers differentiate between or among the mental health professions in the postings. Discuss your findings.

2. Explore the Web sites of the professional associations representing the interests of community and mental health counselors. Investigate and report on the types of information and varieties of services provided by them.
3. You might want to learn more about the similarities and differences among mental health counselors and the allied mental health professions. What similarities do you detect as you compare the Web sites of these organizations? What distinct emphases do you detect through the materials found on their Web sites?
4. Upon hearing that you are training to become a mental health counselor, your friend states, "Oh, so you are going to be one of those 'shrinks' who treats crazy people!" How would you respond? Practice your response by doing role-plays with members of your class.
5. In this chapter, the common practice of working as part of a multidisciplinary team was discussed briefly. Design your ideal multidisciplinary team whose goal is to provide an effective and efficient wrap-around mental health service to persons with chronic mental illness living in the community.

2 The Counseling Professions in Historical Perspective

OUTLINE

When gathering information about clients in initial sessions, I find it useful to utilize genograms. These are structural diagrams that describe a family's three- or four-generational relationship system (Sherman & Fredman, 1986). As I gather verbal information regarding clients' families of origin, I diagram not only the connectedness among blood relatives, but also key events, roles, and communication patterns existing within the family over three or more generations. This technique provides a tool for efficient documentation of individual and family history, and it also helps clients better understand who they are by placing them within the context of those from whom they came.

In this chapter, you will learn more about the professional identity of LMHCs and LPCs in a developmental and ecological context. For the purpose of establishing a relatively secure professional identity, history is necessary and relevant. With regard to the discipline of psychology, Leahey (1980) notes,

> The events of today are influenced by the historical past and will influence the historical future. To understand what we are doing and why we are doing it, we need to understand what psychologists did before us as well as the nature of historical change. To ignore the past is to cut off a source of self-understanding. (p. 14)

Our professional identity, which might, at times, appear overly confusing when viewed in the isolation of the here and now, takes on a distinct appearance when viewed in its historical context. In the pages that follow, you will see how each of the various mental health professions emerged. As a profession evolves, new or existing professions step in and provide unique services that either complement the services of existing professions or fill gaps by meeting identified yet unfulfilled needs of certain populations.

In reading this chapter, you will gain a more complete understanding of the profession. But beyond that, you might be able to capture a glimpse of the passion and vision that was part of the founding of the profession. This understanding of the profession will contribute to your sense of professional pride, which is helpful in developing professional identity and integrity.

EARLY VIEWS AND TREATMENT OF MENTAL HEALTH AND ILLNESS

Archeological discoveries yield clues to the earliest views of humanity regarding health and mental illness. Discovery of human skulls in which crude holes appear to have been created by chipping away bony material leads to the hypothesis that ancient people recognized the source of abnormal behavior as being within the person's head. The hole, referred to as a trephine, was made to provide an exit for the source of the symptoms. In addition, ancient papyri have been discovered that indicate belief that the brain was the site of mental functions. These papyri also show that early humans relied on magic and incantations for the cure of disease (Carson, Butcher, & Mineka, 1996).

Incised bones discovered in archeological excavations tell us little about earliest perspectives on the nature of persons, views of wellness and mental disorder, and treatment. Useful sources of information are the study of comparative religion, myth, and the writings of early philosophers. For example, the Old Testament of the Christian bible contains references to madness and confusion of the mind. King David, for example, feigns madness as he allows a flow of saliva to run down his beard. In the biblical context, madness is distinguished from folly, which seems to be contrasted with wisdom. Madness was seen as being the consequence of evil spirits or an angry God, whereas folly or foolish behavior stemmed from choices made by persons who lacked wisdom. Thus, we see that early distinctions were made between those behavioral conditions that were essentially beyond human control and those related to poor judgment and faulty decision making.

Early Greek philosophy provides additional insight into early views of mental health/illness and its treatment. Hippocrates (460–377 B.C.), who is referred to as the father of medicine, related general behavioral tendencies to the relative balance of four bodily fluids—blood, black bile, yellow bile, and phlegm. Significant imbalances were expressed behaviorally as overt expressions of temperament. For example, the underlying cause of melancholia was considered to be an excess of black bile. To treat melancholia, Hippocrates recommended a tranquil lifestyle, sobriety, abstinence from all excesses, vegetable diets, strenuous exercise (but not to the point of fatigue), and blood-letting (Viney & King, 2003). Plato (428–348 B.C.) contended that aberrant behaviors resulting from madness were a societal issue that required community response (Plato, n.d.).

Promotion of happiness and wellness also found expression in the philosophies of early Greeks and Romans. Epicurius (341–270 B.C.) advocated hedonism but recognized that such an approach to life carried with it a risk for pain if the pleasures were withdrawn. Epictetus (50–138 A.D.) advocated peace of mind. He believed that people were disturbed not by things, but by the view they took of those things. The treatment recommendations of Galen (130–200 A.D.) included massage and drinking chilled wines while reclining in a warm bath (Carson, Butcher, & Mineka, 2002).

The Middle Ages were marked by both cruel and humane treatments of persons who displayed deviant behaviors. Those behaviors that could not be explained readily were attributed to supernatural causes. Humans were thought to be the site where the ultimate battle between "good" and "evil" took place. Thus, "water tests" were used to determine whether or not a person was in league with the devil. In contrast, centers for the humane treatment of the mentally disturbed arose in Baghdad and Damascus in the ninth and tenth centuries (Polvan, 1969). Beginning in the 1300s, the Colony of Gheel, located in Belgium, became a center of care for the mentally ill that was characterized by love and kindness.

However, by the 16th century, a system of hospitals, known as asylums, was developed in Europe to provide shelter for persons unable to care for themselves. Conditions in many of these institutions were deplorable, with residents frequently kept in restraints and left to lie in their waste. By the late 1700s, voices of reform were being heard from advocates such as Phillipe Pinél, William Tuke, and Benjamin Rush (Carson et al., 1996). This resulted in a more humane approach, referred to as "moral treatment." The primary goal of moral treatment was to provide respite for both the mentally ill and for society. The regimen of treatment included organized schedules of productive labor, spiritual and cultural improvement, socializing, entertainment, education, nutrition, and exercise (Fancher, 1995).

In summary, we can see that throughout recorded history there has been a basic distinction between healthy and unhealthy forms of behavior. Furthermore, some of these forms of behavior were considered to be under the person's conscious control whereas other forms of behavior not easily explained were viewed as being beyond one's personal control. As will be seen in the sections that follow, this basic framework remains relatively intact as various mental health professions emerge and seek either to treat pathology or enhance human functioning. As Fancher (1995) notes, "Professional care for mental health has evolved from giving 'moral treatment' to the clearly deranged to claiming to offer, in the name of scientific advance, access to life reasonably free from emotional distress" (p. 53).

THE EMERGENCE OF PSYCHIATRY

The application of moral treatment was far removed from the application of medical science. However, members of the medical profession served as supervisors for these institutions. This group of medical professionals, seeking to apply humanitarian ideals to the condition of the mentally ill, became the foundation of psychiatry.

In 1844, thirteen asylum supervisors gathered to form the Association of Medical Superintendents of American Institutions for the Insane (AMSAII) (McGovern, 1985). Predating the formation of the American Medical Association by 2 years, the AMSAII became the first organized medical specialty society in America (Fancher, 1995). Thus, it became a primary force in the treatment of the insane. Advocating moral treatment, which did not require significant medical knowledge, the AMSAII upheld its standards while keeping such well-known advocates as Dorothea Dix from becoming members of the organization.

However, science advanced and new approaches for the treatment of mental illness were being discovered. A second generation of medical doctors emerged—neurologists— who had more interest in science and its application to the mentally ill. In contrast to the asylum superintendents, neurologists were more scientifically minded and were eager to apply their specialization to the treatment of persons with nervous conditions. These doctors were not welcome in the AMSAII. However, they were successful in exerting pressure on the AMSAII to endorse a policy that did not challenge the authority of the superintendents but called for all future superintendents to be competent scientists. In 1892, the organization changed its name to the American Medico-Psychological Association, which in 1927 became the American Psychiatric Association (Fancher, 1995).

Several milestones came out of this tradition. First, the physiological cause for paresis (syphilis of the brain) was discovered. This was one of the most serious forms of mental illness of the day. Now, for the first time, brain pathology was demonstrated to be the cause of the illness. In 1917, a cure was found. This led to an expectation that many other forms of mental illness had biological roots that could be treated successfully. Thus, the medical model was applied to the treatment of mental disorders.

Second, a neurologist by the name of Sigmund Freud began to treat a range of nervous conditions, referred to as neuroses, using hypnosis and talking therapies. He soon discovered that hypnosis was unnecessary as he reported that his female patients improved through a talking-out and working-through process. Believing that the root of neuroses resided deep within the person's psyche, Freud developed a theory of mental and emotional functioning that captured the attention of young psychiatrists and neuologists. Rather than train psychoanalysts in universities, Freud established the Institute of Psychoanalysis in Vienna. Thus, the model was formed whereby psychiatrists would be trained in rigorous residencies at training centers apart from colleges and universities.

Third, a German psychiatrist named Emil Kraepelin (1856–1926) developed the first major classification system of all mental illnesses. He based his system on thousands of case studies. His work made an important contribution to the medical model and laid the foundation for the modern-day *Diagnostic and Statistical Manual, Fourth Edition, Text Revision* (DSM-IV-TR).

ROOTS OF THE COUNSELING-RELATED PROFESSIONS

The historical antecedents of psychology lie in philosophy (Cangemi & Kowalski, 1993; Resnick, 1997). As noted earlier in this chapter, Hippocrates, Plato, and other Greek philosophers speculated on the functional relationship between the mind and body. The origination of psychology dates back to 1879, when Wilhelm Wundt established the first psychological laboratory at the University of Leipzig, Germany. He was a philosopher and physiologist who defined *psychology* as the study of immediate experience. His goal was to create a science of the mind and behavior. Thus, the discipline of psychology arose as an academic field to address questions related to the investigation of the mind and behavior by applying the methods of science. In addition, most of the persons who were significant in its formation as a discipline never considered themselves to be psychologists because they studied sensation, perception, and other intrapsychic phenomena (Resnick, 1997).

In 1892, the American Psychological Association was formed by a group of philosophers, educators, and physicians (Resnick, 1997). A defining event took place in 1898 when the organization chose not to allow a division of philosophical psychology to form. As a result, the American Philosophical Association was formed in 1901. Psychology chose a direction that moved it away from its heritage and toward psychophysics, animal behavior, and human assessment. This interest in assessment was noted as early as 1896 when the APA formed the Committee on Physical and Mental Tests. Its goal was to develop standards for the practice of human mental and behavioral assessment (Sokal, 1992). In 1906, the APA formed another committee, the Committee on the Standardization of Procedures in Experimental Tests, which was given the task of identifying standardized instruments for individuals and groups. Both of these committees had difficulty defining agendas and were disbanded by 1919.

Leightner Witmer established the first psychological clinic at the University of Pennsylvania in 1896. He wrote an article in *Pediatrics* that same year in which he defined *practical psychology* as the examination of physical and mental conditions of school children and the study of defective children (Witmer, 1896). In a published case study, Witmer (1896) described the treatment of a "feeble minded" child who experienced "mental defects as the result of severe convulsions while teething" (p. 466). His treatment consisted of 3-hour sessions each day, 5 days a week, for 4 years. He coined the term *clinical psychology*, borrowing the word *clinical* from medicine because he saw it as best describing the method he deemed necessary for this type of work.

In 1908, William Healy, a Freudian psychoanalyst, established the Juvenile Psychopathic Institute. The clinic, which was located in Chicago, is historically significant for several reasons. First, it was the first psychiatric clinic to be located in a community setting (Laughlin & Worley, 1991; Nugent, 2000). Second, it appears to be the first application of psychological skills and training to treat social problems (Laughlin & Worley, 1991). Until this time, the practical application of psychology had focused almost exclusively on mental testing. Third, the clinic utilized a multidisciplinary approach to treatment (Nugent, 2000). The psychiatrist was the professional who did therapy, a psychologist conducted the testing and assessment, and a social worker dealt with the home problems. Healy's approach to the treatment of troubled youth continued in the psychoanalytic tradition (Rogers, 1961).

Professional social work was the result of the merger of the Charity Organization Society (COS) and settlement house movements (Haynes & White, 1999). The goal of the COS movement was to help others help themselves and to encourage personal responsibility. The mechanism to accomplish this goal was termed "friendly visiting" (Haynes & White, 1999, p. 385). The settlement house movement emphasized the principle of social responsibility as well (Axinn & Levin, 1997). Settlement house workers sought to develop programs to create a just society through effective social action. These workers demonstrated a strong concern for the welfare of children, adolescents, and families who were disenfranchised and forgotten by the larger society. By the end of the 19th century, social workers had established the expertise of their profession in studying urban conditions, conducting home visits, and helping people to improve their circumstances (Fancher, 1995).

At about this same time, Frank Parsons was concerned with problems of youth. With the rapid urbanization of America that took place around the turn of the 20th century, youth unemployment quickly became a major concern in the normal developmental process of adolescents. The experience of unemployment was bewildering, especially for youth, who were accustomed to the steady work and family income afforded by the family farm (Whiteley, 1984). Parsons recognized the significance of this transition and, in 1908, founded the Boston Vocational Bureau. The goal of this organization was to match the interests and aptitudes of young persons with appropriate occupational choices (Brooks & Weikel, 1996a).

Parsons created the role of vocational counselor and, in doing so, initiated an approach of interaction and facilitation that was a forerunner of the contemporary counseling process. In *Choosing a Vocation* (Parsons, 1909), Parsons outlined a counseling process characterized by listening to and gathering information from the client regarding his or her personal interests and goals. To facilitate this process of self-exploration, Parsons developed a lengthy self-administered questionnaire that probed a wide range of variables believed to be relevant in identifying a good match between personal characteristics and vocational placement. The instrument consisted of straightforward questions but was quite lengthy. Its interpretation was complex and time consuming (Nugent, 2000).

Parsons played a key role in the development of professional counseling for several reasons. First, his approach was clearly directed to relatively normal youth who were facing a developmental transition. Second, the method of vocational counseling had prevention as a foundational goal. It may have been the first truly upstream approach (Egan & Cowan, 1979), catching a vulnerable population before more significant clinical or social problems emerged. Third, Parsons's questionnaire could be self-administered and included input from family, friends, and teachers. The ecological perspective is evident in his method. Thus, in the work of Parsons we can find many of the unique theoretical emphases and processes of mental health and community counseling in their rudimentary form.

Finally, a former patient of mental hospitals named Clifford Beers wrote a book titled *A Mind That Found Itself* (Beers, 1908). In it, he detailed the deplorable conditions of these institutions and advocated for reforms. The book was quite popular and, with the heightened awareness of the plight of the mentally ill, Beers founded the National Committee for Mental Hygiene (1909). This group was a forerunner of the National Mental Health Association (Brooks & Weikel, 1996).

MOVEMENT TOWARD THE PROFESSIONALIZATION OF COUNSELING

By the 1920s and 1930s, the primary forces supporting movement toward creation of a counseling profession were in place. This period of time was marked by a quiet expansion of approaches and the development of new applications. Among these developments were the emergence of the private practice of psychology, the child guidance clinic movement, nondirective counseling, marriage and family counseling, rapid expansion of psychological assessment, and increased sophistication of vocational counseling.

THE PRIVATE PRACTICE OF PSYCHOLOGY

Psychiatry continued to be the preeminent profession addressing the needs of the mentally ill. However, the private practice of psychology was beginning to take hold. Casselberry (1935) wrote an article in which he described the nature of services provided by these private practitioners. They included "diagnosis using tests and questionnaires; a modified psychoanalytic procedure; re-conditioning and training; suggestion; relaxation; and instruction in diet, proper breathing, posture and voice placement and control" (p. 232). These approaches addressed "warped and inferior personalities, social maladjustment, cases of nervousness, timidity, and bashfulness; fears, phobias, and complexes, marriage maladjustment, vocational maladjustment, juvenile delinquency, and child training; hysteria neurathenia and psychasthenia" (p. 58). Crane (1925) commented that the attitude of the medical profession toward practicing psychologists was "one of tolerant condescension" (p. 228).

THE CHILD GUIDANCE MOVEMENT

The 1920s and 1930s were marked by an increased interest in the mental health of children. In 1921, several child guidance demonstration clinics were established in key cities around the United States. Growth in this movement led to the establishment of many new clinics, and the team approach, first used by Healy, continued to evolve. Multidisciplinary staffs were under the leadership of psychiatrists, who were responsible for most of the treatment decisions and therapy. Psychologists were involved primarily in psychological assessment and the provision of educational and remedial therapy. Social workers conducted intake and social history interviews, did casework with parents, and acted as a liaison to enhance the social environment of the child. This basic organization continued in the years following World War II (Korchin, 1976).

CARL ROGERS AND NONDIRECTIVE COUNSELING

One young professional, Carl Rogers, became disillusioned with the predominant form of treatment conducted at the child guidance clinics. He concluded that Healy might be wrong in his attribution of juvenile delinquency to sexual conflict. Rather, he came to believe that it was the client who best knew "what hurts, what directions to go, what problems are crucial, what experiences have been deeply buried" (Rogers, 1961, p.12). He struggled, initially, with his own professional identity. And the university where he worked clearly indicated that he was not doing psychology. He began to teach courses on how to understand problem children, and the university wanted to house the courses in the Department of Education. His ideas were further refined as he taught treatment and counseling to graduate students at Ohio State.

Out of these experiences, a new approach to therapy developed known first as nondirective counseling, later as client-centered therapy, and finally as the person-centered approach (Corey, 2001). Rogers summarized the essential hypothesis of this approach in one sentence: "If I can provide a certain type of relationship, the other person will discover within himself the capacity to use that relationship for growth, and change and personal development will occur" (Rogers, 1961, p. 33). He firmly believed that the quality of the therapeutic relationship, which relied on the goodness and natural developmental tendencies toward personal growth of the client, provided a more effective orientation for therapy. These ideas, found in his early book *Counseling and Psychotherapy* (Rogers, 1942), were the start of a revolution in how clients were viewed and treated. These became important foundations for the profession and practice of counseling.

MARRIAGE AND FAMILY COUNSELING

People had discussed marital and family issues with clergy and doctors for years, but psychiatry and psychology, while recognizing the relevance and involvement of the family, focused primarily on the treatment of individuals. But in the late 1920s, marriage centers began to emerge. Abraham and Hannah Stone opened the first marriage clinic in New York City. Soon after, Paul Popenoe, a biologist, developed the American Institute of Family Relations in Los Angeles. The long running series of articles he wrote in the *Ladies' Home Journal,* Can This Marriage Be Saved?, did much to popularize marriage counseling. At about this same time, a small group of psychoanalysts broke from the Freudian tradition, which prohibited contact with the families of patients, by proposing that some couples had interlocking neuroses and required conjoint treatment.

RAPID EXPANSION OF ASSESSMENT AND INCREASED SOPHISTICATION OF VOCATIONAL COUNSELING

During this period, the study and assessment of individual differences expanded greatly. Whereas the early intelligence tests measured mental abilities and potential, the post–World War I era marked the blossoming of personality and vocational testing. The earliest personality tests were developed to screen military recruits. The Woodworth Personal Data Sheet, which attempted to present the psychiatric interview in a standardized form, was published immediately following the war. The construction of projective tests soon followed. Interest in the Rorschach inkblot test, first published in 1921, grew slowly. Its popularity increased, though, when Sam Beck wrote a doctoral dissertation in 1932 (Kaplan & Saccuzzo, 2005). In it, Beck investigated the scientific properties of the Rorschach. In 1935, Henry Murray and Christina Morgan developed the Thematic Apperception Test (TAT), a projective test that was based on Murray's personality theory of needs. Although none of these instruments had a direct or immediate impact on the profession of counseling, they did reflect distinct lines of inquiry that would prove relevant in the move toward increased specialization in the mental health professions.

Other advances in assessment, though, were linked directly to guidance and vocational counseling. In 1928, Clark L. Hull and Lewis M Terman published *Aptitude Testing.* In this book, they advocated the use of aptitude-test batteries and matching human traits with specific job requirements. Hull promoted the idea of predicting job satisfaction and success based on standardized tests. Hull's text came on the heels of the publication of *The Strong Vocational Interest Blank.* Published by Edward K. Strong, Jr., in 1927, this measure provided career counselors with a standardized tool linking the personal interests of examinees to the interests of persons in specific professional groups. This instrument gave counselors a valuable tool with which to facilitate vocational decision making.

The vocational testing movement prepared the way for E. G. Williamson, Jr., to put forth the first true theory of counseling. In 1939, Williamson published *How to Counsel Students: A Manual of Techniques for Clinical Counselors*. This text can be viewed as an extension of Parson's formulations (Zunker, 1998). However, Williamson described a straightforward approach to counseling that came to be known as directive counseling. His approach consisted of six sequential steps: analysis, synthesis, diagnosis, prognosis, counseling, and follow-up. The term *clinical counseling* reflected an empirically based, scientific method that sought to eliminate nonproductive thinking and facilitate effective decision making (Lynch & Maki, 1981).

POST–WORLD WAR II AND THE VETERANS ADMINISTRATION

Psychologists, counselors, and social workers, relatively few with doctoral degrees and many with minimal clinical experience, found themselves working in the front lines with psychiatrists in military psychiatric units during World War II. There was also a strong need for the selection and training of specialists for military and industry. Counselors and psychologists possessed the necessary knowledge and skills to fulfill this important role. In addition, thousands of soldiers were emotionally impaired as a result of their combat experiences and were entitled to professional counseling services provided by the Veterans Administration (VA) upon discharge. In 1945, the VA obtained funding to support the training of mental health professionals. Numerous internship opportunities were made available at VA hospitals.

During this time, the APA developed a training philosophy and model of clinical training (American Psychological Association, Committee on Training in Clinical Psychology, 1947). In 1949, attendees of a conference held in Boulder, Colorado, endorsed this model, which has become known as the Boulder model. It stated that the newly defined clinical psychologist should be first and foremost a scientist-practitioner, a professional trained in a Ph.D. program who would be equally adept as a clinician, researcher, and scholar. In response to this model, university programs, helped by the funding of the newly formed National Institute for Mental Health (NIMH), moved quickly to offer doctoral degrees in both counseling and clinical psychology (Cummings, 1990). Clinical psychologists were trained to diagnose and treat individuals with chronic disorders, whereas counseling psychologists dealt with issues presented by persons who displayed relatively high levels of mental health. In 1953, the APA responded to this new category of psychologists by changing the name of Division 17 from the Division of Counseling and Guidance to the Division of Counseling Psychology (Woody, Hansen, & Rossberg, 1989).

The impact of these charges on the counseling profession cannot be understated. First, a clear boundary between psychologists and counselors was created. The professional was required to earn a doctoral degree in psychology or a closely related discipline in order to be considered as a psychologist. Second, with the VA funding doctoral-level internships only, master's-level counselors were ineligible for many of the available training programs. Third, counseling psychologists began to move away from their historical link with vocational guidance and counseling. Fourth, mental health professionals with less than a doctoral-level education were now without a professional home. They were no longer eligible for full membership in the APA.

THE INFLUENCE OF PROFESSIONAL ORGANIZATIONS

By the early 1950s, the demarcation of the various counseling professions was well under way. The development of professional identity of the various mental health professions was facilitated by the formation of professional organizations that served to represent the unique interests of those professions. As noted previously, the APA and the restructuring of Division 17 played a key role in setting psychologists apart from counselors. The formation of other professional organizations helped to define and accentuate distinctions among other counseling-related professions.

The American Association of Marriage and Family Counselors (AAMFC), founded in 1945, had already set a precedent by providing members of this fledgling profession a forum in which to share ideas, establish professional standards, and foster research (Nichols & Schwartz, 1998). By the mid-1950s, the AAMFC, which was later renamed as the American Association of Marriage and Family Therapists (AAMFT), was already establishing academic and training standards for programs specializing in marriage counseling.

The restructuring of Division 17 of the APA provided doctoral-level counseling psychologists with a professional organization that represented their interests. This move was instrumental in the formation of the American Personnel and Guidance Association (APGA) (George & Cristiani, 1986). Founded in 1952, the APGA came into being through the merger of several existing professional organizations (Kaplan, 2002). The National Vocational Guidance Association (NVGA) was the oldest of the founding groups. Established in 1913, its mission was to prepare youth for the work world. It therefore had a direct tie to the pioneering work of Parsons and provided an organizational link connecting the newly formed organization with a historical root of the counseling profession. A second group, the American College Personnel Association (ACPA), was founded in 1924. Members of this group assisted college students with admissions procedures, course selection, financial aid, student employment, academic performance, and mental health. A third group, the Student Personnel Association for Teacher Education (SPATE), was established in 1931. Finally, the National Association of Guidance Supervisors and Counselor Trainers (NAGSCT) was established in 1940, making it the youngest of the founding organizations. Now known as the Association for Counselor Education and Supervision, this organization brought a tradition of training and research to the APGA.

Super (1955) notes that the APGA initially functioned more as an interest group than as a bonafide professional organization because it did not formulate standards for membership. Rather, it provided a canopy under which the original organizations were able to retain their separate identities while simultaneously facilitating cooperative efforts (Brooks & Weikel, 1996). The primary reason for the coming together of these organizations was, first, to pool their resources in order to hold a national conference and, second, to share administrative staff in order to save money. Thus, from the start, the APGA (now ACA) served as an umbrella organization for widely diverse professional groups.

The APGA provided the organizational structure necessary for the development of a true profession. With the establishment of CACREP, the profession could demonstrate that it possessed a clearly defined training model that defined core as well as specialty competencies. Second, by creating NBCC, counselors could publicly demonstrate their competency by attaining professional certification. Third, the professional association as well as specific divisions developed codes of ethics, which provided the profession with a set of standards by which it could regulate the conduct of the profession.

THE PROFESSIONALIZATION AND EXPANSION OF MENTAL HEALTH COUNSELING

Although the profession of counseling did not rapidly expand during the 1950s and early 1960s, a number of key events took place that paved the way for future expansion of the profession. These events included the crisis of overpopulated mental institutions, the increased effectiveness of pharmacological treatment of mental illness, limited community access to counseling services, and the Community Mental Health Act of 1963.

PROBLEMS IN THE MENTAL HEALTH SYSTEM

By the 1950s, public attention was again being drawn to the inhumane care received by patients in mental health hospitals. These institutions were accused of being no more than places of detainment and an inadequate solution to the social problem of mental illness. Deutsch (1948) stated that mental hospitals had become an American disgrace. Hans Eysenck (1952) wrote an important article in which he concluded that studies, up to that time, failed to demonstrate the effectiveness of psychotherapy with neurotic clients. He stated that "roughly two-thirds of a group of neurotic patients will recover or improve to a marked extent within about two years of the onset of their illness, whether they are treated by means of psychotherapy or not" (Eysenck, 1952, p. 322). His conclusions added fuel to the argument that patients were not benefiting from long-term inpatient treatment. Eysenck wrote these comments at the time when the nation's population of patients in mental hospitals was at its highest level (Cutler, 1992).

INCREASED EFFECTIVENESS OF PSYCHOPHARMACOLOGICAL INTERVENTIONS

The modern era of psychopharmacology began in 1952 with the introduction of Chlorproazine (thorazine), an antipsychotic medication that soon became the medication of choice in the treatment of schizophrenia. By the late 1950s, two classes of antidepressants, tricyclics and monoamine oxidase (MAO) inhibitors, had demonstrated clinical effectiveness and were being prescribed by psychiatrists. Clinical tests were being conducted to determine the effectiveness of lithium to treat manic depression (i.e., bipolar disorder). With the introduction of chlordiazepoxide (Librium) in 1960, a new era of pharmacological treatment for anxiety disorders began (Pirodsky & Cohn, 1992).

The significance of the introduction of psychopharmacological interventions in the treatment of mental illness and emotional distress cannot be understated. These medications were providing successful treatment for a variety of mental conditions that, up to this point, required inpatient care. The idea of community-based treatment for mental illness and emotional disorders was greatly strengthened, given the poor track record of institutionalized care and the financial burden it placed on patients and taxpayers.

INNOVATIONS IN COUNSELING THEORIES AND TECHNIQUES

The publication of *"The Effects of Psychotherapy: An Evaluation"* by Eysenck (1952) was taken by clinicians and researchers as a challenge to demonstrate that psychotherapy was, in fact, effective. A number of counselors and psychotherapists had become quite disenchanted with the traditional theories and techniques of counseling and began to experiment with alternative approaches. The new breed of theorists and clinicians included Albert Ellis (1961), Aaron Beck (1967), and Joseph Wolpe (1958). These were scientist-practitioners who combined focused treatment of specific symptoms with the precision of empirically based outcome studies. They demonstrated the effectiveness of counseling and psychotherapy in the treatment of depressive and anxiety-based disorders. Murray Bowen (1960) and Nathan Ackerman (Ackerman & Sobel, 1950) pointed the treatment of mental illness in new directions by seeing the family system as the most basic unit of treatment.

The work of these pioneers in counseling theory paved the way for counselors and psychologists to work alongside psychiatrists in the treatment of mental illness and emotional disorder. Each discipline could make unique contributions to the successful treatment of a variety of diagnosed conditions in settings that were less restrictive than mental hospitals.

LIMITED AVAILABILITY AND ACCESS TO COMMUNITY-BASED SERVICES

By the mid-1950s, flaws in the existing mental health service delivery system were being exposed. Furthermore, clinically effective and time-efficient pharmacological treatments were being developed that could be readily applied in outpatient settings. However, the number of community-based clinics was few and access to available services was limited.

It became clear that something needed to be done if adequate treatment was to be made available to meet the needs of the mentally ill living in communities. Although the VA sought to train psychologists for service delivery to the public sector, more and more professionally trained psychologists entered into private practice. Enticed by the shortage of psychiatrists and attracted to the increased autonomy and income, many psychologists left public service to hang out their shingle (Cummings, 1990). Albee (1959), in a study sponsored by the Joint Commission on Mental Illness and Health, assessed the need for mental health professionals and concluded that sufficient number of professional personnel to eliminate the glaring deficiencies in our care of mental patients would not come about without a significant increase in the recruitment and training of mental health workers.

THE COMMUNITY MENTAL HEALTH CENTERS ACT OF 1963

Given the situation just described, the United States Congress passed the Mental Health Study Act of 1958. Its purpose was to provide "an objective, thorough, and nationwide analysis and reevaluation of the human and economic problems of mental illness" (Joint Commission on Mental Illness and Health, 1961, p. 301). The final report of this commission became part of the impetus for the proposal of a new National Mental Health Program. President Kennedy believed that the implementation of this program could lead to the eventual phasing out of state mental hospitals, which would be replaced by high-quality treatment centers located in the patient's community (Cutler, 1992).

On October 31, 1963, President Kennedy signed into law the Community Mental Health Centers Act. This act set into motion the establishment of a large number of mental health centers around the country, which were mandated to provide five basic services: inpatient treatment for short-term care, outpatient treatment, partial hospitalization, crisis intervention, and consultation and education services. In addition, to be considered as comprehensive centers, diagnostic, rehabilitation, precare and aftercare, training, and research and evaluation services were required. In 1968, the act was amended to support the creation of alcohol and drug abuse services (Cutler, 1992). The act was again modified in 1970 to require mental health services for children.

Staffing needs greatly increased with the development of this national network of community mental health centers (Hershenson & Berger, 2001). A decline in the number of school counseling positions combined with an abundance of recent graduates from counselor education program created a pool of trained employees for these centers (Brooks & Weikel, 1996). Other community-based agencies were inaugurated, and by the late 1960s, many counselors were obtaining employment in youth services, drug and alcohol treatment centers, and crisis and runaway shelters. Counselors were generally trained in non–clinically oriented academic programs, so they often were hired initially as paraprofessionals. However, these counselors were soon recognized as being among the primary providers of care in community mental health and other human service organizations (Brooks & Gerstein, 1990).

EMERGENCE OF MENTAL HEALTH COUNSELING

Recognizing this trend in work settings, counselor education programs began to develop courses and training models that would equip graduates for work in community settings. A variety of community counseling programs emerged after 1970, and interest was expressed in the development of specific training standards for community counseling programs. In 1981, CACREP was established and began to accredit master's programs in community and other agency settings (CCOAS) (Hershenson & Berger, 2001). Standards for the accreditation of programs in mental health counseling were established in 1988 (Smith & Robinson, 1996).

However, the APGA did not have a division with the specific mission of serving the interests and needs of community and agency counselors. Although many of the counselors working in community and private practice settings were members of APGA, a large number of them believed that they possessed unique professional concerns that the organization was not addressing. They were not working in school settings or dealing with vocational and guidance issues. As Seiler (1990) notes, mental health counselors "did not work exclusively with mental illness; we did not work solely through the social service system; nor was our clinical work mainly with marriages or families in trouble" (p. 7). Yet the foundations of normal human development, prevention, and mental health education served counselors well in community settings.

Calls for the formation of a division within the APGA began around 1975 (Brooks & Weikel, 1996). James Messina and Mancy Spisso, in discussing their concern over the lack of a professional organization for community counselors, prompted a letter written by Edward Anderson and others to the *APGA Guidepost,* which called for greater representation and recognition of nonschool counselors within the organization. Messina contacted APGA President Thelma Daley, who sent to them information regarding the establishment of new divisions. In May 1976, the American Mental Health Counselors Association was born (Weikel, 1996).

The first AMHCA conference took place in March 1977 and was scheduled concurrently with the annual APGA convention. AMHCA grew rapidly from 50 original members to almost 500 by the end of the first conference. One year later, the membership of AMHCA had increased to around 1,500. In July 1978, the APGA approved the AMHCA proposal for affiliation, allowing it to become the 13th division. Within a few years, the membership of AMHCA had ballooned to 12,000 (Weikel, 1996).

The new division quickly went about the work of establishing a solid foundation for the profession (Weikel, 1996). A special ad hoc committee created a "Blueprint for the Mental Health Counseling Profession," which proposed the founding of the National Academy of Certified Clinical Mental Health Counselors (NACCMHC). The academy, which eventually affiliated with the NBCC and the Association for Counselor Education and Supervision (ACES), established criteria for professional certification of MHCs (i.e., the CCHMC). Publications were developed by early 1979 to communicate professional news (i.e., *AMHCA News*) and support the accumulation of scholarly literature for the profession (i.e., *The American Mental Health Counselors Association Journal*).

LICENSURE OF MENTAL HEALTH AND PROFESSIONAL COUNSELORS

With increased numbers of mental health professionals working in private practice and agency settings, it became apparent among these practitioners that their legitimacy in the eyes of the public would only occur through regulation of their professions via state licensure. In 1950, professional psychology was the first mental health discipline to legislate state licensure laws (Cummings, 1990). Clinical social work followed the path blazed by psychology but stayed behind the pace of psychologists by about 10 years.

In 1974, the APGA adopted a position paper titled "Licensure in the Helping Professions" and appointed a special committee on counselor licensure (Bloom et al., 1990). These helped to secure passage of the first counselor licensure law through the Virginia legislature in 1976.

THE CONSOLIDATION OF THE MENTAL HEALTH COUNSELING PROFESSION

As mental health counseling moved into the 1980s, it had clearly established itself as a distinct profession. VanZandt (1990) identifies distinct professions as characterized by "role statements, codes of ethics, accreditation guidelines, competency standards, licensure, certification and other standards of excellence" (p. 243). APGA and AMHCA, along with affiliated organizations such as CACREP and NBCC, had secured a place for mental health counselors among other allied mental health professions.

However, recognition of the "new kid on the block" did not come easy. In 1982, the American Psychiatric Association, National Association of Social Workers, American Nursing Association, and American Psychological Association initiated the Joint Commission on Interprofessional Affairs in an attempt to unite their efforts to raise funding for mental health (Cummings, 1990). This group saw their respective professions as the major mental health professions and acted to keep other emerging mental health professions from entering into the dialogue. Thus, although they possessed all of the properties of a profession, licensed mental health and professional counselors were not permitted to sit at the same table with the "elite four." This state of affairs blocked the young profession from procuring their "piece of the pie," such as federal funding for programming, state licensure status, recognition as a service provider for government employees and members of the armed forces, and reimbursement for professional services from Medicare or Medicaid.

Furthermore, the nation, under the influence of Reaganomics, saw significant cutbacks in federal funding of mental health programs, research, and initiatives. This shift in federal policy coincided with the rise in managed mental health care. Marked shrinkage occurred in the number of private practices as cost containment measures cut deeply into profits. Community mental health centers no longer could support extensive outpatient programs because the practice of managed care placed limits on the number of sessions.

The counseling profession evolved with these changing times. First, it became clear that the name of the professional association did not reflect the type of work done by its members. It responded by changing its name, in 1983 to the American Association of Counseling and Development, and in 1993 to the American Counseling Association (its current name). Second, to support mental health counselors' efforts at achieving consistent reimbursement of services from third parties, a comprehensive set of national standards for mental health counselors was adopted. Third, to meet the needs of a changing American society, the professional association moved to promote multicultural competencies among its practitioners. Fourth, the AMHCA moved out from under the ACA umbrella. While remaining as a division within the organization, AMHCA took steps that enabled it to function in a more collaborative and less affiliative relationship with the ACA.

CONCLUSION

This chapter has provided a brief overview of the predominant historical views of mental health and mental illness. In addition, the roots and development of the allied mental health professions have been identified. The development of these professions is summarized in Figure 2.1. I hope that reviewing Fig. 2.1 will give you a better understanding of who mental health and community counselors are by seeing their historical position relative to the other professions. Clearly, the mental health

FIGURE 2.1 Development of the Mental Health Professions

	Psychiatry	Psychology	Social Work	Mental Health Counseling	Marriage and Family Therapy
Mid—1800s	AMSMII (1844)	Wundt(1879)	Dorothea Dix		
1890s	American Medico—Psychological Association (1892) Kraepelin	Witmer (1896)	Charity Organization Society Settlement house		
1900—1920	Cure for paresis (1917)	Healy (1908) Testing (1905+) APA (1903)		Frank Parsons (1908) & the Vocational Bureau in Boston	
1920—1940	APsychiA (1927) American—Psychiatric Association	Child guidance clinics		Child guidance clinics College counseling centers	Paul Popeno Marriage and family counseling
1940—1960	WW II	WW II VA APA, Div. 17	WW II NASW (1955)	WW II Client-centered therapy APGA (now ACA) 1952	WW II AAMFC (1945) (now AAMFT)
1960—1980		Proliferation of theories and techniques Licensure movement (late 1960s)	Certification and licensure	Community Mental Health Centers Act (1963) Licensure movement (1976—present)	
1980—2000s		Reaganomics Managed care			

counseling profession has distinct historical roots that give rise to a unique philosophical perspective on the nature of the human condition and how best to facilitate mental health among those individuals, families, and communities.

It is a profession well positioned to meet the needs and demands of our contemporary society, yet concurrently struggling to emerge as a primary mental health care provider. As we have noted, psychology and social work have been recognized as service providers for over a century. As a result, they possess greater political power and, therefore, are known entities among the public and potential consumers. In contrast, mental health counselors are the new kids on the block and sometimes find themselves expending much energy justifying their reason to be among the various power holders (i.e., legislators, policymakers, third-party reimbursers, and allied professions).

The chapters that follow will provide you with additional understanding of the mental health counseling profession by exploring its underlying theoretical foundations as well as selected approaches used in working with individuals, groups, families, and communities. This information can enhance the development of your personal professional identity, and it provides the platform from which the profession may advance.

DISCUSSION QUESTIONS

1. Compare and contrast the views of early Greek philosophers with current views of mental health and wellness.
2. To what extent does our current understanding reflect advances resulting from the scientific study of behavior? Can one be justified in holding the view that "what goes around comes around"?
3. Is it appropriate to view the early treatments of abnormal behavior (e.g., the Greek era and Middle Ages) as primitive and inferior? Or is it reasonable to view such treatments through a cross-cultural lens and see degrees of relevance and validity in their approaches?
4. In what ways did the material discussed in this chapter help you to understand better the nature of mental health counseling?

SUGGESTED ACTIVITIES

1. Do further research on the historical roots of the mental health professions. Then draw a genogram of the mental health counseling profession that communicates its connections to a philosophical heritage and the allied professions.
2. Explore in more detail the life of one of the founders of the mental health professions. Consider the extent to which that person's heritage and life experiences were reflected in his or her professional legacy.
3. Identify a specific category of mental illness and investigate the way in which the understanding of it has evolved over time. For example, you might explore the historical development of conditions such as autism, attention deficit hyperactivity disorder, dissociative identity disorder, or personality disorder.
4. Investigate in more depth the interaction between sociocultural trends and the development of the counseling profession. To what extent have these forces shaped the contours of the mental health counseling profession over the past century?

3

Theoretical Foundations for Mental Health and Community Counselors

OUTLINE

Joe has a history of skipping work to go to the bar. He works third shift (12:00 to 8:00 a.m.) at a local factory. On most evenings, he wakes up at around 9:30 p.m. and begins to think about going to work on the assembly line. He does not find much personal satisfaction in the work. Furthermore, Joe complains about the ongoing conflict he has with his supervisor and not getting along with others on the job. As he reflects on his work situation, he begins to think about his favorite bar, which he passes on his way to work. Several friends are there throughout the evening hours.

Joe has become stuck in a pattern in which he tells his wife that he is going in to work early but instead goes to the bar. Joe tells himself that he will only have a beer or two in order to help him cope with his work problems. As he continues to contemplate the tension at work, he concludes that he really needs a few drinks in order to survive. And, the more he thinks about it, the stronger his urge is to get over to the bar. Joe can hardly wait! He can almost taste the beer by just thinking about it!

However, increasingly (two or three nights a week), Joe never makes it to work. His wife learns about his absences at work when she looks at the automatic bank deposit reports. His take-home pay has decreased significantly and is now a major source of marital conflict and economic hardship. But Joe feels very angry when his wife confronts him. He concludes that she doesn't understand how bad it is for him at work and that he is trying to cope the best he can.

Place yourself in the role of counselor. What is going on with Joe? What do you see as the basic problem, and what factors have contributed to its development? At its root, is Joe struggling with a conflict within himself? Is this problem an indicator of moral weakness or a spiritual problem? Is Joe dealing primarily with an intrapsychic or interpersonal conflict? Or does he have a disease that has no cure and is, perhaps, fatal unless he gets help? And, as Joe's counselor, what are you going to do about it?

Although you may have felt that a lack of detailed information placed you at a disadvantage, you probably came up with answers to the questions listed. And you may have accomplished this feat without the aid of formalized training! Each of you has personal theories that helped you to make sense out of Joe's presenting problem in specific ways. If you take the time to discuss the vignette with classmates, you will find that Joe's presenting problem could be conceptualized in a number of ways.

In a sense, everyone is a theorist of sorts. The term *implicit personality theory,* coined by Bruner and Tagiuri (1954), refers to how people develop ideas regarding the way other people's personal traits and behavioral tendencies fit together. Years of experience of living in close proximity to other people have allowed all of us to develop theories regarding partners, relatives, friends, and specific situations. Understanding the characteristics of a person based on past observations, we make predictions regarding how that person will act in a specific situation. We then apply our theory to guide our behaviors in relation to that person in situations.

For example, the telephone rings and I pick up the receiver. I am not familiar with the pleasant-sounding voice who casually but confidently says, "Good afternoon, Mr. Gerj." I do a quick assessment and make some conclusions: I do not recognize the sound of this person's voice; he used *Mr.* instead of my first name or *Dr.* and mispronounced my last name; therefore, he must be a telemarketer. My conclusion, then, guides how I listen and respond to what this person has to say. A set of concepts and assumptions that I hold to be valid enabled me to make sense out of this situation and respond accordingly.

Returning to Joe, how do your conceptualization and recommendations for Joe differ from those of a mental health or community counselor? In this chapter and the next, you will learn about the types of theories used by mental health practitioners. This chapter explores theories that provide a foundation for mental health and community counseling. In chapter 4, theories used in counseling and psychotherapy are examined. As you will discover, theory provides lenses through which counselors assign meaning to the client's story and construct cognitive maps that guide every therapeutic move they make.

THEORY AND PERSONAL CHARACTERISTICS OF THE COUNSELOR

None of you entered into your graduate training program with an empty head. Ongoing experience interacts with inherited characteristics to make you the unique person you are—a whole physical, cognitive, social, and spiritual being. This interaction takes place within a specific ecological context and contributes to the development of self-schema, worldview, and interpersonal style. These play critical roles in the formation of your motives for entering into the mental health counseling profession. They also influence your functioning in the professional role—your conceptualization of cases, generation of clinical hypotheses, and selection and application of specific theories and techniques.

SELF-SCHEMA

Persons are not passive recipients and processors of information. Rather, as incoming stimuli are sensed, it is necessary to screen, organize, and integrate new information with preexisting knowledge. As we move through early life experiences, internal cognitive structures about self develop that are referred to as self-schemas (or self-schemata). These are defined as "cognitive generalizations about the self, derived from past experience, that organize and guide the processing of self-related information contained in the individual's social experiences" (Markus, 1977, p. 64). They may also become generalizations constructed from repeated categorizations and evaluations of others with whom the person interacts with in some way (Phares, 1991).

The processing of information gleaned from ongoing experience is affected by the operation of self-schemata. Markus and Wurf (1987) note several important consequences: (a) heightened sensitivity to self-relevant stimuli; (b) more efficient information processing of stimuli that is self-congruent; (c) enhanced recall and recognition of information that is self-congruent; (d) more confident behavioral predictions, attributions, and inferences in areas relevant to one's self-schema; and (e) resistance to information that is incongruent with one's self-schema.

These consequences have important implications for counselors, especially since the operation of self-schema is outside one's conscious awareness. Information provided by the client is screened, sorted, and categorized through the operations of the counselor's self-schema. Counselors may experience delays in processing and categorizing data that are beyond their experience and do not readily fit with preexisting schemes. Furthermore, in more extreme cases, they may simply fail to pick up on data critical to understanding the perspective of the client. This can be especially problematic when working with clients from different cultural backgrounds. Picking up on aspects of the presenting problem that they, too, have personally experienced, counselors might inadvertently assume sameness and then make assumptions and inferences leading to counselor responses that are insensitive or disrespectful to the culturally diverse client.

Competent counselors are aware of what they bring to the counseling table. Specifically, they recognize how self-schema can interact with their implicit theories to bias their assessments and interventions. Developing a working knowledge of counseling theory helps counselors to understand and respond to the presenting situations of clients in ways that are not overly tainted by effects of past experience or personal bias.

WORLDVIEW

Worldview can be defined as the sum total of our beliefs about the world. It is the big picture, a vision of life that we hold of our universe that shapes the way we make decisions and act in situations. Sue and Sue (2003) define *worldview* as the way persons perceive their relationship to the world of nature, institutions, and other people. Through the socialization process, people develop a set of presuppositions and assumptions about the makeup of the world as well as their place and future in it (Sarason, 1984).

All persons entering into counselor training programs have personal worldviews. These preconceived notions about the "way things really are" develop within the context of a sociocultural setting, are deeply ingrained, operate out of personal awareness, and are often accepted without question. The contents of one's worldview includes basic assumptions about human nature, social relationships, how people relate to nature, time, human activity, the universe, ultimate reality, and the meaning of life (Mahalik, Worthington, & Crump, 1999).

Williams (2003) notes that various psychological processes, such as well-being, attributional style, and relationality, can be reliably predicted by one's worldview. For example, Oyserman, Coon, and Kemmelmeier (2002) found that persons who possess worldviews emphasizing individualism tend to display conflict resolution styles characterized by goal orientation, direct communication, confrontation, and arbitration. In contrast, persons holding worldviews that emphasize collectivism prefer indirect, high-context communication, accommodation, and negotiation (Oyserman et al., 2002).

Counseling is an interpersonal process where there is potential for the collision of conflicting worldviews. Indeed, worldview is embedded in the predominant theories of counseling. Furthermore, the worldviews of many counselors are heavily flavored by Western culture and values, which place high value on individuality, personal autonomy, freedom, timeliness, and productivity. Lyddon and Adamson (1992) found that counselors' worldviews influence their preference for counseling approaches. It is vital, therefore, that community and mental health counselors develop a self-awareness of their own worldviews (Mahalik et al., 1999). In addition, they must enter into and understand their clients' worldviews if counseling is to be effective.

INTERPERSONAL STYLE

Persons seeking admission into counseling programs often note the many experiences they have had in which friends and relatives have sought them out for informal counsel when faced with difficult life situations. They see such experiences as affirming their "natural disposition" toward the counseling professions.

Personality characteristics do play roles in our selection and application of counseling theories. For example, extroverts often choose an active role in counseling, gravitate to theories that are action oriented, and set a therapeutic tone of energy and expressiveness (Day, 2004). In contrast, introverts can make good use of time in session and not be overly alarmed by occurrences of silence. In addition, they can be very effective when making use of low-key, Columbo-type confrontations (Day, 2004). However, timing and sensitivity are critical to successful interventions, and the application of the counselor's natural inclinations might, at times, override good clinical judgment and lead to less than positive outcomes. Thus, counselors do well to identify how interpersonal styles can be used to the benefit of their clients.

So what are the implications of one's personal characteristics for his or her application of counseling theory? I concur with Corsini (1995), who states that

> I believe that if one is to go into the fields of counseling and psychotherapy, then the best theory and methodology to use have to be one's own. The reader will not be either successful or happy using a method not suited to his or her own personality. The really successful therapist adopts or develops a theory and methodology congruent with his or her own personality. (p. 14)

The initial step for counselors in training is to develop accurate self-awareness to guide themselves in the process of choosing approaches that are a good personal fit. A theory is effective to the extent that counselors are capable and comfortable to enact its principles and procedures in situations.

Kazdin (1986) noted that the "buffet table" of counseling theories contains around 400 items from which to choose! Thus, difficulty in finding an adequate approach is not due to a lack of alternatives. Rather, the mind-boggling task is to find counseling theories that are good matches to the attributes and personal style of the counselor, fit with the specific client and his or her story, and, at the same time, provide useful conceptualizations and direction in specific cases.

PROCESS OF CHANGE: THE TRANSTHEORETICAL MODEL

Prochaska and DiClemente (1984) provide an integrative framework for understanding, assessing, and facilitating behavioral change. Referred to as the transtheoretical model of behavioral change, it posits that clients move through a progression of five stages in making successful changes in their lives. The five stages of change—precontemplation, contemplation, preparation, action, and maintenance—describe the processes of client change that occur through the application of most counseling theories.

Clients in the precontemplation stage are either unaware of the behavioral problem or unwilling to or discouraged in making helpful changes in their lives (Velasquez, Maurer, Crouch, & DiClemente, 2001). By not seeing the personal costs or negative aspects of the problem, such clients are not highly motivated to change anytime soon. To move along in the change process, these clients benefit from conducting a *cost/benefit* analysis of their current behavior or situation and become more aware of its negative consequences.

The contemplation stage occurs as clients acknowledge the existence of a problem and begin to consider making changes to resolve it (Prochaska & DiClemente, 1984). However, they may not fully understand the nature of the problem, its causes, or its implications. In addition, contemplative clients may experience the ambivilence that comes with desiring a better personal situation yet not wanting to give up old and familiar patterns of behavior. Thus, clients at this stage require encouragement, support, and gentle prodding so that the balance is tipped toward making behavioral change.

In the preparation stage, clients have made an initial commitment to making changes and are on the verge of acting on that commitment (Velasquez et al., 2001). As many of us have discovered, the best of intentions do not necessarily translate into effective action. So it is with clients in the preparation stage. They are now motivated to change, but they need a systematic plan and firm commitment for its implementation. Counselors play a critical role in this stage by supporting the client through the construction of an action or treatment plan. This is accomplished through collaborative effort in the context of a strong therapeutic relationship.

The action stage is where clients implement the plan to modify their behavior (Prochaska & DiClemente, 1984). Two potential pitfalls must be avoided if clients are to move successfully through this stage. First, initial positive change may be confused with goal attainment. Clients may underestimate the energy and sustained motivation necessary to maintain the desired behavioral pattern over the long haul. Second, after making early strides toward the desired goal, clients may stumble, experience a relapse, or return to a preaction stage. Counselors become "voices of reality" by pointing out such potential traps, consistently encouraging clients, and facilitating relapse prevention planning.

The final stage, maintenance, consists of consolidation of gains made during the action stage and continued efforts in preventing relapse. In traditional counseling, termination issues are addressed as the intensity and frequency of ongoing treatment decreases. In contrast, the transtheoretical model views maintenance as an ongoing stage that may last up to a lifetime (Velasquez et al., 2001). Follow-up and booster sessions are often scheduled to give clients "check-in" points. The option of scheduling additional appointments as desired is encouraged. Finally, a maintenance plan may be developed that encourages clients to use naturally occurring support systems in their specific ecological setting.

The transtheoretical model is applicable in promoting mental health as well as in treating mental illness. Mental health and community counselors can assess the client's readiness to change as well as calibrate interventions to the specific stage of the client.

THE ROLE OF THEORY IN COUNSELING

Earlier in this chapter, I distinguished between implicit theories and formal theories of counseling. Although understanding the difference is critical, they do operate in much the same way. Counseling theory can be defined as a set of interrelated principles that are applied to describe, explain, predict, and guide the counselor's actions in relevant situations. Without such a set of interrelated principles, counselors would be "vulnerable, directionless creatures bombarded with literally hundreds of impressions and pieces of information in a single session" (Prochaska & Norcross, 1999, p. 5.)

Can you imagine describing the situation of a client without an agreed-on set of constructs and related terminology? Adequate theory provides tools with which counselors systematically select which bits of information presented by the client are relevant to the description of his or her story. By viewing the information through a theoretical lens, the client's story takes on a clear, coherent appearance as the "figure," against the "ground" of the developmental and ecological context. As Millon (2003) notes, "Theory, when properly fashioned, ultimately provides more simplicity and clarity than unintegrated and scattered information" (p. 952).

A good theory also enables counselors to posit reasonable responses to the "why" questions regarding the client's current situation and level of functioning. Although no counseling theory is capable of making truth statements regarding underlying causes, counseling theories do help counselors identify and organize the available data in ways that provide an etiological explanation. For example, psychodynamic theories call attention to the contribution of early childhood development whereas behavioral theory points to environmental stimuli and consequences. From either perspective, plausible explanations of the current condition can be derived.

With a clear description of the nature of the client's condition and an explanation of how it developed, counselors are in a better position to make predictions of the developmental course or prognosis. Being able to identify the present location of the client (description) as well as where he or she has been (explanation), the counselor can generate reasonable hypotheses regarding where the client is likely to go in the near future.

Finally, good theory guides counselors as they work to facilitate change in clients' lives. Specific techniques are suggested by theories to influence clients' thoughts, emotions, and behaviors in directions predicted by the theory. For example, if I view a person's depression through the lens of cognitive theory, I may conclude that the client's condition is at least partly maintained by the subtle operation of cognitive distortions. Based on such a theoretical analysis, I will look for cognitive restructuring techniques to lessen the influence of factors maintaining the depression.

For every person you counsel, you develop a case conceptualization—the theory counselors develop "that draws together information you have and organizes it in a way that helps explain current, past, and future behavior" (Day, 2004, p. 24). Counseling theory provides the organizational rubric to accomplish this task. Millon (2003) concludes, "What is elaborated and refined in theory is understanding—an ability to see relations more plainly, to conceptualize more accurately, and to create greater overall coherence in a subject, that is to integrate its elements in a more logical, consistent, and intelligible fashion" (p. 952). Thus, theoretically based case conceptualizations possess a natural flow that closely links observations to a coherent rationale for specific forms of intervention. Day (2004) encourages counselors to apply theory on two levels: first, to understand what makes people tick in general (the counseling theory), and, second, to understand what makes this particular client tick (the theory of this client or case conceptualization). Thus, theories are integrated systems that drive the counseling process from start to finish.

However, not all theories are created equal. Of the more than 400 counseling theories, some are better than others. On what basis are they evaluated? The following criteria are suggested by Sharf (2000, pp. 1–3) and Millon (2003):

1. *Precision and clarity.* Good theories are based on rules that are clear and use terms that are specific. In addition, they are parsimonious. They use only as many concepts and principles as are necessary to provide adequate descriptions and explanations.

2. *Comprehensiveness.* Good theories explain and predict wide ranges of human behaviors. For example, a comprehensive theory will apply to persons of different cultures or in a variety of contexts. A theory that applies only to the single males reared by ultraconservative parents is limited in its comprehensiveness.

3. *Testability.* There must be an empirical basis for the theory. If the ideas of a given theory cannot be tested, its validity or reliability cannot be determined. Anecdotal reports or reasoning are inadequate supports for the accuracy (i.e.,validity) and consistency (i.e., reliability) of a theory.

4. *Utility.* A good theory proves to be useful to practitioners. It assists counselors in developing helpful descriptions, explanations, and predictions. In addition, a good theory suggests workable plans of interventions to facilitate behavioral change.

5. *Heuristic value.* Good theories promote novel conclusions that, in turn, lead to new experimentation and discoveries.

Although none of the counseling theories fully meet all of the criteria listed, evidence acquired through empirical investigations lends increased support for some theories more than others.

FOUNDATIONAL THEORIES FOR MENTAL HEALTH AND COMMUNITY COUNSELORS

In this section, several sets of theories are described that are the bedrock on which mental health and community counselors stand. Taken together, these theories provide an orientation for the profession that sets mental health and community counselors apart from the allied mental health professions.

THEORIES OF HUMAN DEVELOPMENT

The emergence of developmental psychology served as an important antecedent in the development of mental health and community counseling (Brooks & Weikel, 1996) and is central to the professional identity of the profession (Palmo, 1996). Indeed, the preamble to the code of ethics for the ACA states that association members are "dedicated to the enhancement of human development throughout the lifespan" (American Counseling Association, 2005, p. 3). Beyond providing a theoretical platform for the profession, these theories are applied in the daily work of mental health and community counselors as they seek to facilitate growth in those with whom they treat.

Theories of lifespan development help us understand the unfolding story of persons from conception to death—from the beginning of life to its end as we know it. Several important principles underlie the lifespan perspective (Lefrancois, 1999; Santrock, 2006):

- *Development is a continuous, lifelong process.* No specific age-related stage dominates the life cycle, and change is a dynamic process occurring throughout one's life.
- *Development is relative and plastic.* The course of healthy development can follow a variety of paths and should not be viewed as a simple, straightforward linear process. In most cases, human development has an "ebb and flow" much like the rising of the tide. For most people, the general direction is increased growth, although the movement is akin to taking "two steps forward and one step backward." Human development is, therefore, viewed as a dynamic process rather than an attained state of being.
- *Human development takes place in a context.* It is common to talk about the ecology of human development. This principle is so foundational to the profession that the topic will be discussed later in this section. For now, we will simply note that lifting persons from their specific environmental context—social, historical, cultural—leads to a distorted understanding of who they are and what they are

experiencing. Individuals are changing beings whose development is influenced by multiple dimensions of a changing universe.

- *Human development is an interactional and bidirectional process.* The interaction between developing persons and their environment is ongoing and lifelong. The person influences his or her environment, which concurrently influences the person. For example, in the ongoing interactions of parent-child relationships, parents exert an important influence on the behavior of their children while their children are, at the same instance, influencing the behavior of their parents.

Broderick and Blewitt (2003) identify three classes of developmental theories: stage models, incremental models, and multidimensional models. I will briefly examine stage and incremental models in this section. Multidimensional models relate, generally, to the ecological perspective and will be considered in a later section of this chapter.

Stage Models. Stage models describe persons as passing through a sequence of stages over the course of one's lifespan. Each stage represents a level of functioning that is qualitatively different from those of preceding stages. Thus, human development is conceptualized as consisting of a series of steps and plateaus. Several of these theories are based on the epigenetic principle, which states that various characteristics of organisms have specific times of ascendancy until all parts integrate to form a functioning whole (Erikson, 1968). Several prominent theories of development constructed according to the stage model include Freud's psychosexual theory, Erikson's psychosocial theory, Piaget's cognitive theory of development, Kohlberg's theory of moral development, and Atkinson, Morten, and Sue's racial/cultural identity development theory. Stage models also serve as frameworks for understanding processes such as language development and social referencing.

Incremental Models. These models view human development as a gradual, cumulative process of change that takes place from conception to death. Whereas stage models emphasize developmental milestones, incremental models focus on smaller, often unnoticed changes that converge so that new skills can emerge. For example, when little Beth takes her first step, it is a monumental event that enables her to get around with greater efficiency. However, for Beth to move from the crawling to walking stage, a number of foundational physiological, neurological, cognitive, and social factors converged in order for the walking skill to be displayed at a particular time. Prominent theories of development whose tenets are configured according to the incremental model include Pavlov's theory of classical conditioning, Skinner's theory of operant conditioning, Bandura's theory of social learning, Vygotsky's sociocultural theory, Bowlby's attachment theory, and information processing theory.

Implications for Mental Health and Community Counselors. It is beyond the scope of this text to engage in a detailed discussion of the various theories identified in this section. With so many relevant theories from which to choose, my selection of several specific theories may seem somewhat arbitrary and influenced by personal bias. The significance of possessing a working knowledge of human development theories is made clear by the decision of CACREP to include human growth and development as one of the eight common core areas determined to be foundational for all professional counselors. Ginter (1996, p. 100) identifies the "developmental perspective" as one of the three pillars of mental health counseling.

The foundation of human development across the lifespan has numerous implications for mental health and community counselors. First, mental health counseling professionals use the perspective of human normalcy as the baseline for understanding the human condition. This stands in stark contrast to other mental health professions, whose foundational theories were derived from the study of emotionally distressed and psychologically disordered persons. Rather than generalizing from the abnormal to the normal, Van Hesteren and Ivey (1990, pp. 524–528) point out that mental health and community counselors can conceptualize remedial, crisis, and psychopathological issues from a positive developmental orientation. Achieving wellness as opposed to the mere absence of symptoms, therefore, is a goal worth pursuing.

Second, individuals are viewed in a holistic manner. Our clients are physical, cognitive, psychological, social, and spiritual beings whose component parts form a well-integrated whole. It is a therapeutic error to ignore the complex interrelationship of the component parts. In addition, an intervention focusing on one dimension necessarily influences the other dimensions.

Third, while the study of human development identifies characteristics shared in common by all persons, each individual is also viewed as a unique being—unlike any other person in the world. From this vantage point, mental health and community counselors can truly appreciate the unfathomable worth of each client with whom they interact.

Finally, developmental theories help mental health and community counselors understand the nature of normal and atypical life transitions. Clients struggling with transitions carry with them unique combinations of strengths and deficits acquired over the course of development that greatly influence the quality of their adaptation (Schlossberg, 1981). It becomes critical that mental health and community counselors assess clients and their environments in such a way that they are able to capitalize on existing strengths. In addition, clients benefit from skill-building approaches through which new strengths can develop.

ECOLOGICAL PERSPECTIVE

As noted in the previous section, persons are best understood when viewed from within their unique developmental context. In addition to the foundation of human development, mental health and community counselors are trained to view the human condition from an ecological perspective.

The ecological theory of Urie Bronfenbrenner (1979, 1989) is a multidimensional model that provides mental health and community counselors with a framework for viewing human functioning within a developmental and environmental context. Bronfenbrenner sees human development as consisting of a series of ongoing changes involving interactions between individuals and their immediate contexts. In addition,

FIGURE 3.1 The Ecological Context of Human Development

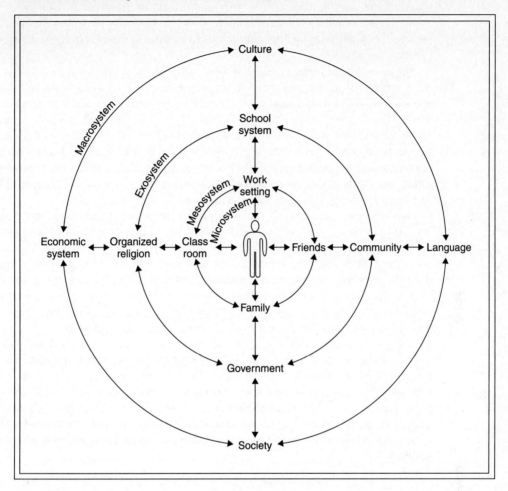

the levels of immediate contexts also interact with each other as characteristics of individuals interplay with the environment.

Bronfenbrenner (1979, 1989) identifies four different levels of environmental context in which development occurs. From most proximal to most distal, these are the microsystem, mesosystem, exosystem, and macrosystem. Figure 3.1 illustrates how each level relates to one another.

The microsystem is defined as "a pattern of activities, roles, and interpersonal relationships experienced by developing persons in a given face-to-face setting with particular physical and material features, and containing other persons with distinctive characteristics of temperament, personality, and systems of belief" (Bronfenbrenner, 1989, p. 227). At this level, persons develop within the context of primary, face-to-face relationships at home, school, playground, workplace, and so on. The person enacts specific behaviors in context that instigate a response from persons in the environment. These responses, in turn, influence and shape the behavior of the developing person. Thus, the relationships within the microsystem are best described as reciprocal and interactive.

The mesosystem refers to "the linkages and processes taking place between two or more settings containing the developing person (e.g., the relations between home and school, school and work place, etc.)" (Bronfenbrenner, 1989, p. 227). The mesosystem, then, is the system of microsystems. The peer group, school, and parents interact with each other while simultaneously interacting with the developing person. For example, Sarah's parents recently had an argument with her school teacher. A week later, they are informed that Sarah misbehaved in class and is receiving an in-school suspension. Their parental response to the misbehavior of their daughter may be tempered by the negative experience they had with the teacher.

Bronfenbrenner defines the exosystem as encompassing the linkages and processes occurring between two or more settings, at least one of which does not contain the developing person. Occurring events influence the processes of the immediate settings containing the developing person (Bronfenbrenner, 1989). Building on the illustration from the previous paragraph, the reaction of Sarah's parents to her in-school suspension might be flavored by their own negative experiences as students while in school in addition to the experience of their daughter. They may discount the personal responsibility of Sarah and see school administrators as being unfair.

The fourth level identified by Bronfenbrenner is referred to as the macrosystem. It is defined by all micro-, meso-, and exosystems that characterize a given culture or subculture (Bronfenbrenner, 1989). All of the interactive systems are embedded within a given milieu that can be described according to predominant roles, values, expectations, lifestyles, or belief systems (Lefrancois, 1996). For example, my adolescent child and his relationship to school is quite different from that which I experienced in the late 1960s. His relationships with peers and teachers are greatly influenced by the times in which he lives.

Implications for Mental Health and Community Counselors.   The implications of ecological theory on the functioning of mental health and community counselors are profound. Viewing personal development from the ecological perspective sheds additional light on how specific developmental principles and concepts play out in real-world contexts. Assessment necessarily takes into consideration a broader array of variables that function as separate but related levels of the client's environment. As a result, the case conceptualizations of mental health and community counselors increase in complexity. In addition, the treatment of the presenting conditions of clients includes direct and indirect strategies of change.

For example, the benefits of being raised by authoritative parents (Baumrind, 1967, 1991) are tempered by systemic factors. In a longitudinal study, Steinberg, Lamborn, Darling, Mounts, and Dornbusch (1994) found that adolescents whose parents use an authoritative approach display increased academic competence even after controlling for ethnicity, socioeconomic status, and household composition. However, further analysis (Steinberg, Darling, & Fletcher, in collaboration with Brown & Dornbusch, 1995) of the data revealed that African- and Asian American high school students whose parents were authoritative did not perform better in school than those adolescents whose parents were not. The hypothesized relationship did appear, though, when the parents of peers were authoritative.

This led to a focus on what is termed the *functional community* (Steinberg et al., 1995). In such neighborhoods and communities, nonrelated adults know one another (i.e., network closure) and a dominant set of values is accepted within that community (value consensus). Children raised in functional communities receive consistent messages about their behavior and obligations and are encouraged to behave according to those norms by family and nonfamily adults. Steinberg and colleagues (1995) concluded that the key to understanding the influence of parenting during adolescence must go beyond the boundaries of the home and consider the broader context in which the family lives.

The community counseling model (Lewis, Lewis, Daniels, & D'Andrea, 2003) provides an ecologically based framework through which community and mental health counselors can conceptualize assessment, treatment, program development, and research. These authors distinguish between services that are directed to clients and those directed toward the community. In addition, these services may be delivered through direct and indirect approaches. When combined, the model identifies four distinct categories of service: direct client services, direct community services, indirect client services, and indirect community services.

As Lewis and colleagues (2003) note, a truly comprehensive program requires that mental health and community counselors provide services related to each category. Effective implementation of such a multifaceted array of services rests on counselors' ability to develop conceptualizations that take into consideration the "big picture" of direct and indirect influences that impinge on their clients. In addition, techniques for intervention go beyond traditional individual, group, and family therapies to include consultation, advocacy, and various forms of psychoeducation directed toward client and community populations.

THEORIES OF MENTAL HEALTH AND THE PREVENTION OF MENTAL ILLNESS

We noted in chapter 1 that the emphasis on mental health was primary to setting apart the identity of community and mental health counselors from allied mental health professions. Unfortunately, this philosophy, which is so foundational to the profession, does not find consistent expression in practice. Frequently, licenced mental health and professional counselors working in private practice and agency settings rely on and are, therefore, accountable to the policies of third-party reimbursers. The guidelines for most managed care organizations and insurance companies can be stated succinctly: If it is not broken, it doesn't need fixing! Thus, mental health promotion is not a billable service. Practitioners engaged in such efforts obtain funding for their services through grants, independent contracting with organizations, and direct billing to clients.

Although the mental health emphasis seems straightforward, several critical issues loom beneath the surface. First, what is the relationship of mental health to mental illness? Is mental health defined, basically, as the absence of mental illness? Thus, if the professional engages in prevention work, has he or she promoted mental health? If mental health is more than mere absence of mental illness, then what is involved in the professional practice of mental health promotion? Indeed, is it possible to promote the mental health of persons diagnosed with chronic mental illness (e.g., schizophrenia or bipolar disorder)? You will search the professional literature in vain to find the definitive answers to these questions. Theories and opinion abound as scholarly debate continues.

The traditional medical model maintains that mental illness and mental health are polarities of one continuum. This model is illustrated in Figure 3.2. According to this perspective, mental health is normally distributed among the general population, and most of us are within a standard deviation of the mean. However, in times of stress, any one of us is vulnerable to a breakdown in our "line of defenses," which can lead us to experience emotional distress or diagnosable mental illness. The remediation of mental illness has the effect of promoting mental health. Hansen (2003) sees the one-dimensional model as closely linked to the medical model and a primary source of professional identity confusion for mental health counselors.

But as Tudor (1996) notes, to define something by the absence of its opposite is simply a semantic sleight of hand that only further confuses our understanding of either. Perry (1999) states that health is more than the prevention of premature death or the absence of disease. When I review the concepts and principles contained in the various definitions of mental health, I see a number of characteristics that seem to go well beyond what might be considered the mere absence of symptoms. In fact, some of these characteristics can be possessed by persons with mental illness. Viewed

FIGURE 3.2 Traditional Model of Mental Illness/Mental Health

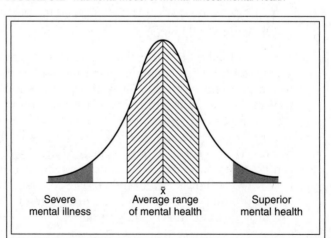

holistically, mental health is a dynamic state of physical, psychological, social, and spiritual well-being (Nutbeam, 1997; Perry & Jessor, 1985).

A mental health and community counseling orientation suggests the validity of applying mental health and wellness-promoting interventions for all persons, whether or not clients are diagnosed with mental illness. Thus, a two-dimensional model presents a theoretical foundation from which mental health and community counselors can assess, conceptualize, and treat both the mentally healthy and mentally ill. Such a conceptualization was suggested by the Canadian Minister of National Health and Welfare (MNHW), which placed mental disorder and mental health on separate continua. Downie, Fyfe, and Tannahill (1990) linked well-being and ill health and represented their relationship by crossing the two axes. The model suggested here is an adaptation of these previously mentioned models. Figure 3.3 illustrates the two-dimensional model of mental health/wellness and mental illness.

The two-dimensional model fits well with the underlying philosophy of mental health and community counselors. First, mental health and community counselors recognize

FIGURE 3.3 A Two-Dimensional Model of Mental Health/Wellness and Mental Illness

		Level of mental health/wellness	
		Low	**High**
Mental illness/ pathology	**Low**	Low degree of mental health and wellness; little or no diagnosable mental illness	High degree of mental health and wellness; little or no diagnosable mental illness
	High	Low degree of mental health and wellness; severe mental illness	High degree of mental health and wellness; severe mental illness

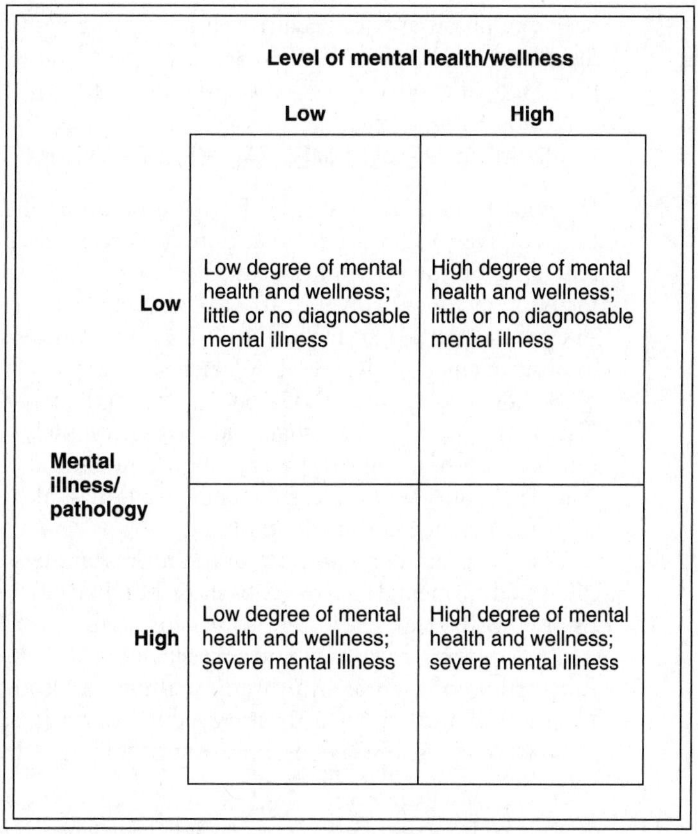

and are trained to diagnose and treat mental illness. Yet they conceptualize presenting problems from a mental health/wellness perspective. Second, mental health and community counselors believe all individuals, families, and groups can benefit from services that promote mental health in addition to those that remediate mental illness. Mental health and community counselors work from a model that integrates these services, as opposed to the one-dimensional model, which creates a fuzzy boundary between interventions related to mental health enhancement, prevention, and mental illness remediation.

The two-dimensional model of mental health has several implications for the practice of mental health and community counselors. First, it demonstrates the possibility for persons diagnosed with mental illness to have a good level of mental health/wellness (Tudor, 1996). For example, a client diagnosed with bipolar disorder may experience relatively high levels of mental health/well-being. Second, it is possible and desirable for mental health and community counselors to intervene in ways that enhance the well-being/mental health of persons diagnosed with mental disorder (Tudor, 1996). Third, a model of professional practice for mental health and community counselors is provided that integrates and synthesizes the roles of remediation, prevention, and mental health enhancement. It becomes truly possible, according to this model, for the mental health emphasis to inform the interventions of mental health and community counselors, regardless of the specific nature of the presenting problem. The mental health emphasis applies equally well in working with the mentally well and mentally disordered. As Remley (1991) notes, both populations "can benefit from a counseling philosophy that offers hope for a better tomorrow" (p. 2).

APPROACHES TO MENTAL HEALTH PROMOTION

In general, the field of mental health promotion and positive psychology is in its infancy. Myers (2000) notes that during most of psychology's first century, questions regarding personal happiness and wellness tended to be unasked as the discipline focused on illness. Myers (2000) conducted electronic searches of *Psychological Abstracts* since 1887 and found that the ratio of articles reporting on negative emotions to positive emotions was 14:1. Whereas his search turned up 8,072 articles on anger, 57,800 on anxiety, and 70,857 on depression, merely 851 articles focused on joy and 2,958 on happiness. Seligman and Csikszentmihalyi (2000) observe that we know much about surviving adverse conditions, but little about how to flourish in more normal life circumstances. Clearly, mental health has taken a backseat to mental illness in scholarly research and theory building.

The times are changing, though, and researchers and scholars are increasingly interested in mental health (Gibson & Mitchell, 2003). However, the terminology used tends to lack clarity and precision. Often, the terms *mental health, wellness, well-being, personal growth,* and *prevention* are used synonymously. In addition, the dimensions of mental health and wellness lack empirical validation. Donnelly, Eburne, and Kittleson (2001) surveyed the vast array of definitions and created a list of 10 characteristics that characterize mentally healthy individuals:

1. a positive outlook on life
2. a realistic set of expectations and approaches to life

3. effective management of emotions
4. the ability to function well with others
5. the ability to draw strength from others without being overly dependent upon them
6. reasonable appetites
7. a spiritual nature
8. effective coping skills
9. an honest self-regard and self-esteem
10. the ability to view the world honestly, accurately, and realistically (p. 24)

It is unreasonable to expect mentally healthy persons to display these characteristics at all times. However, such a pattern of behavior should be evident over given periods of time (Donnelly et al., 2001).

Several models of wellness and mental health have been put forth. Zimpfer (1992) developed a model of wellness based on his treatment of cancer patients. Areas of treatment vital for the wellness of patients, according to his theory, include medical health, immune function, lifestyle management, spiritual beliefs and attitudes, psychodynamics, energy forces, and interpersonal relationships. Hettler (1986) identified six dimensions of wellness in his model: intellectual, emotional, physical, social, occupational, and spiritual wellness. Based on theory and research from a variety of disciplines, the Wheel of Wellness (Witmer & Sweeney, 1992) is a model of treatment comprised of five life tasks vital for optimal health: spirituality, self-direction, work and leisure, friendship, and love. Hartwig and Myers (2003) found the Wheel of Wellness to be a strength-based paradigm useful in the prevention and treatment of delinquency and concomitant mental illness.

A number of other techniques and principles are used to enhance mental health. These include self-management; stress management; learned optimism and resourcefulness; resiliency and psychological hardiness; self-efficacy; diet, exercise and leisure; interpersonal competence; and spiritual practices and religious faith. By integrating such methods, counselors assist individuals, families, and communities not to get by, but to flourish.

PREVENTION IN THE CONTEXT OF PROMOTING MENTAL HEALTH

Efforts toward the prevention of mental illness are central to the mental health emphasis of mental health and community counselors. Normal living provides numerous events that serve as opportunities for either growth or hazard. Although stress is a common denominator in every person's life, discouraging circumstances, timely and untimely transitions, conflicts, and emergencies can precipitate crises in which the demands placed on individuals overwhelm their coping responses. Prevention programs and interventions seek to limit the likelihood that vulnerable persons will experience undesirable consequences when facing difficult situations. Such programs target at-risk, disorder-prone, and infected members of our society.

Mental health and community counselors have adopted a model of prevention from the health professions. A number of approaches, referred to as primary, secondary, and tertiary prevention, have been developed to enhance growth, promote crisis resistance, and limit crisis reactions.

Primary prevention often comes in the form of education, consultation, and crisis intervention. Its goal is to reduce the likelihood of persons contracting the disorder. Programs and interventions are directed toward persons identified as being at risk for experiencing adverse situations or negative reactions. Approaches to primary prevention include modifying the hazardous situation, reducing exposure to hazardous situations, and increasing coping abilities (Hoff, 1995). Examples include:

- the elimination of substandard housing for older populations and persons of lower socioeconomic status
- teen pregnancy prevention programs
- Drug Abuse Resistance Education (DARE) programs
- midnight basketball programs in urban areas
- 24-hour crisis hotlines

To be successful, adequate and accurate needs and risk assessment must be conducted. Furthermore, awareness and sensitivity to cultural values and existing support systems are essential. Organizational support for proposed programs must be strong. Finally, effective primary prevention programs integrate helpful resources already existing in the community.

Secondary prevention refers to programs and interventions that seek to limit the negative impact of disorders in persons already affected. The goal is to shorten the duration of the condition. For example, many colleges and universities have implemented early detection programs known as "screening days." Students have the opportunity to receive information on specific emotional disorders, such as eating disorders, depression, and anxiety; complete self-administered questionnaires; and receive referral information if professional counseling is recommended. Other secondary prevention measures include accessible crisis intervention services, walk-in clinics, critical incident stress management interventions, and programs for the homeless mentally ill.

Tertiary prevention aims to reduce the long-term consequences for persons recovering from mental disorders. For example, relapse prevention programs for recovering alcoholics provide skills that decrease the likelihood of falling back into the former dysfunctional pattern of thinking and drinking. Other tertiary prevention services include aftercare, assertive community treatment, and day treatment.

Mental health and community counselor training provides an excellent foundation for doing prevention work. Knowledge of human development enables the mental health and community counselor to anticipate normal, age-related transitions and initiate primary prevention measures. In addition, it provides a knowledge base that assists counselors in differentiating normal from abnormal coping responses, which is critical in the timely implementation of secondary prevention interventions. In addition, by calling attention to the environmental context, the ecological perspective increases the sensitivity of mental health and community counselors to additional stressors and resources that may either help or hinder coping responses. Finally, the mental health emphasis encourages strength-based, problem-solving approaches to prevention that are essential for the creation of workable intervention plans.

CONCLUSION: THE COMPREHENSIVE MENTAL HEALTH COUNSELING MODEL

We have surveyed a number of theories that are foundational to the profession of mental health counseling. These foundational areas are human development across the lifespan, ecological theory, mental health, and mental health promotion. Taken together, they form a unique base from which mental health and community counselors practice.

It is possible to integrate each of these emphases and construct a comprehensive model for the foundations of the profession. This is illustrated in Figure 3.4, which provides a rubric for understanding what mental health and community counselors do. The model of Figure 3.4 places the dimensions of mental illness and mental health/wellness within an ecological context.

The comprehensive mental health counseling model has numerous implications for practitioners. First, assessment necessarily involves consideration of multiple

FIGURE 3.4 Foundations for Mental Health Counseling Model: A Comprehensive Model

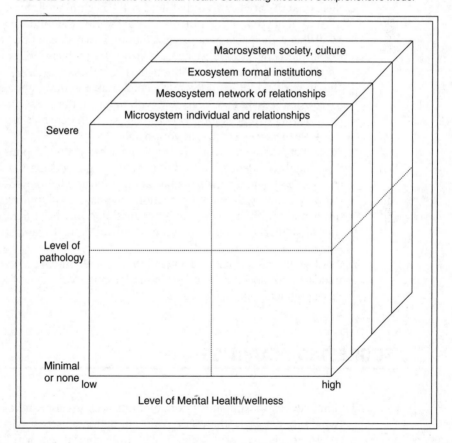

levels of the environment. Mental health and community counselors assess for personal and ecological strengths and assets in addition to symptoms and deficits. Thus, our concepts of mental health and wellness relate not only to individuals, but to groups, families, organizations, communities, and subcultures. Personal mental illness and wellness must be conceptualized within this broader context. Second, factors that directly and indirectly influence the client system must be examined. These factors must not be assessed as though they operate in isolation. Rather, mental health and community counselors must keep in mind the complex, reciprocal interactions that characterize personal behavior in situations. Third, treatment and mental health enhancing interventions can be directed to all ecological levels. It is from the perspective of this model that the integration of primary, secondary, and tertiary prevention can be conceptualized.

DISCUSSION QUESTIONS

1. Return to the brief case study found at the beginning of this chapter. Explore the operation of your implicit theories by answering the following questions:
   a. What is the etiology of Joe's condition? To what extent do you see his situation as reflecting a substance abuse/dependence problem, employee-supervisor conflict, or marital conflict? Although each of these is present, which is primary?
   b. To what extent would you feel comfortable in developing a clinical diagnosis for Joe? Discuss your position with others in the class.
   c. To what extent is Joe ready to engage in the change process? Consider the transtheoretical model in your response.
   d. What type of interventions do you see as being most helpful? What specific goals would you identify? Which of the following modalities would be your primary approach—individual, marital, family, ecological (employee-spouse-supervisor)?
2. How, specifically, does the foundation of human development influence the work of mental health and community counselors? To what extent do you see such a foundation as being incompatible with traditional diagnosis and treatment of clients who are mentally ill?
3. Analyze the case of Joe by applying the comprehensive mental health counseling model. How specifically can this model guide your assessment and treatment planning in this particular case?

SUGGESTED ACTIVITIES

1. Interview two mental health or community counselors and explore the extent to which they hold to the theoretical foundations discussed in this chapter. Seek professionals who work in clinical and nonclinical settings. To what extent does

their particular work setting influence the extent to which they apply these specific theoretical foundations in practice? Do they see the application of the comprehensive mental health counseling model as setting their professional practice apart from professionals of other disciplines (e.g., social workers, marriage and family counselors, or psychologists)?

2. Interview an LMHC or LPC working in a community mental health setting. Examine the ways in which his or her organization has programs and/or goals related to the prevention of emotional and psychological distress. What are some of these programs and what specific roles can be filled by mental health and community counselors?

3. Do a computer-assisted search of several community mental health centers in your area. Identify the extent to which the concepts of wellness, healthy human development, and human ecology are reflected in the centers' mission statements, programs, and specific goals/objectives.

4. To what extent do you see your personal characteristics and interpersonal style as being a good fit for the mental health counseling profession? Seek out the views of several persons who know you well. To what extent do they see your personal characteristics and interpersonal style as being a good fit?

4

Traditional and Contemporary Theories of Counseling

OUTLINE

Traditional Theories of Counseling and Psychotherapy

Contemporary Trends in Counseling Theories

Conclusion

I am a mental health counselor. Providing individual, group, and family counseling is primary and central to my professional identity. In contrast to other mental health–related professions that provide counseling services, we call ourselves counselors, as Gibson and Mitchell (2003) state, "not because we give tests, offer career planning information, or provide consultation, but because we counsel" (p. 135).

In this chapter, we will review a number of theories of counseling. These frameworks provide structures that help counselors organize data, make inferences, and develop intervention strategies from the numerous bits of information observed and gathered from clients. If we are lucky, our clients might provide a straightforward description of the following:

- who they are
- the nature of their presenting problem(s)
- background history that links past events to current issue(s)
- environmental context of development and current issue(s)
- their motivations (why they think they do what they do)

With the client's information in mind, mental health and community counselors use the theories described in this chapter as tools to conceptualize the client's current condition, explain its development and maintenance, predict what is likely to take place (i.e., prognosis), and exert influence so that problems can be resolved and mental health enhanced.

Although counseling theories can guide the creation of valid conceptualizations of clients' situations, they are not foolproof means to develop clinical inferences. Stevens and Morris (1995) identify several inferential errors that can distort our assessment and subsequent selection/implementation of treatment strategies:

1. *Single-cause etiologies.* We might make the mistake of selectively abstracting one fact as being the cause of the client's problem while dismissing all other potential alternatives.
2. *Availability heuristic.* Sometimes a particular theory or a recent article stays in the forefront of our consciousness and becomes the lens through which we interpret all newly gathered client information. For example, I may have a tendency to interpret my clients' stories through the lens of the particular theory of counseling that I am teaching at that time in my Theories and Techniques class. Somehow, all clients seem to benefit from Gestalt therapy one week and cognitive-behavioral therapy the next. In actuality, I may risk using the model that is most available in my consciousness rather than that which is most applicable or relevant.

3. *Fundamental attribution errors.* Generally, we have a tendency to explain our behavior in terms of situational characteristics. In contrast, we tend to explain the behaviors of others in terms of their personal characteristics. I might attribute my client's inappropriate interpersonal behaviors to her deep-seated insecurity while I attribute my similar behavior to uncertainty residing in the situation itself.

4. *Illusory correlations.* We frequently perceive two independent events occurring together in time as being somehow related. Thus, I may attribute my client's anxiety to an anniversary reaction because her panic appears to have begun 2 years after the death of a loved one. Although plausible, numerous other alternatives might provide explanations that are equally valid.

With these cautions in mind, we will now turn to a discussion of some of the traditional theories of counseling. Our focus will be on those theories that are well known and accepted. Later in this chapter, we will look at some recent trends and their influence on contemporary theory development.

TRADITIONAL THEORIES OF COUNSELING AND PSYCHOTHERAPY

PSYCHOANALYSIS

Key Theorist. Psychoanalysis is an approach to counseling derived from the discoveries of Sigmund Freud (1856–1939). Trained as a neurologist, Freud developed a private practice in Vienna, where he specialized in the treatment of "nervous disorders." Many of the patients sought treatment for hysteria, a condition in which various physical complaints were experienced with no apparent physical cause.

Freud's theory building was influenced by several cutting-edge treatment approaches of his day (Thorne & Henley, 2001). Around 1880, Heinrich Erb was exploring the therapeutic value of administering electrical shock to neurotic clients. At about the same time, Charcot was applying hypnotism to treat nervous conditions. He had discovered that symptoms of hysteria could be induced through hypnotic suggestion. It was inferred that such symptoms could be removed by similar process. In collaboration with Josef Breuer, Freud began to utilize a "talking out" approach, in which patients were encouraged to talk freely about any thoughts and feelings regardless of their relationship to the presenting symptoms. Many patients experienced a reduction or removal of symptoms through this process. Conclusions derived from Freud's keen observations of patients led to the development of psychoanalysis.

Essential Principles and Concepts. Freud saw no reason to believe that the energy that ran the human organism was any different from the energy that ran the universe. Furthermore, energy could take several forms—mechanical, thermal, or nuclear. Freud posited a psychic energy, *libido,* to "power" psychological work such as thinking, perceiving, and remembering. This energy was used by the *life instincts* to satisfy needs for survival and reproduction. These instincts were mostly sexual and aggressive in nature and were expressed not only in overt actions, but also through dreams, feelings, fantasies, wishes, and thoughts.

The fulfillment of basic needs is essential for survival of the person. Thus, individuals continuously seek immediate gratification of basic needs. But the demand for immediate gratification inevitably runs into conflict with social rules that require control over these urges. Furthermore, conditions in the specific situation limit the extent to which a basic need can be fulfilled at any given time. The core of Freud's theory is this conflict among impulses, societal rules, and the realities of the situation.

Two Basic Assumptions.   Freud made two basic assumptions about human beings. First, he assumed that everything we do, think, or feel has meaning and purpose. Nothing is left to chance, but everything relates in some way to our quest for need fulfillment. This assumption is termed *psychic determinism.* Second, most human behavior stems from urges that lie beyond our general awareness. This is referred to as *unconscious motivation.* Of course, people will present explanations as to why they do what they do, but such explanations lack insight. The actual source for all behavior lies in the attempt to resolve the conflict among urges, realities, and rules that resides in our unconscious. The nature of this unconscious conflict can be determined through the careful interpretation of the content of thoughts, feelings, self-defeating behaviors, and Freudian slips (e.g., saying "mom" when in actuality intending to say the name of my wife).

Levels of Awareness.   Freud saw persons as having varied levels of self-awareness. The *conscious* was limited to those sensations, thoughts, feelings, and behaviors that the person was aware of at any given moment. The *preconscious* contained memories of past events, related facts, as well as associated thoughts and feelings that were not in the person's awareness at the given moment but could be easily accessed. Finally, the *unconscious* was that area of the psyche that was the reservoir of urges, wishes, and conflicts that could threaten to overwhelm the person's conscious mind and that were, therefore, pushed out of awareness.

Structure of Personality.   Freud identified three basic structures of personality. The *id* is the deep, inaccessible component of personality that holds all instinctual urges. Its reason for existence is to obtain immediate fulfillment of basic needs. It operates according to the *pleasure principle,* which seeks to experience pleasure and avoid pain. Nothing else matters! The personality of the neonate and infant are almost entirely id.

However, as noted earlier, developing children soon learn that they cannot always get what they want. So, soon after the first year, a second personality structure arises, the *ego.* It mediates between the environment that surrounds the child and his or her urges and instincts. The ego is the rational problem-solver component of the mind that finds realistic means to fulfill the needs demanded by the id.

The *superego* forms around the time the child reaches the age of 4 to 6. This structure is a reflection of the values of society and culture as represented to the child through the words and actions of the parents. The primary task of the superego is to block unacceptable impulses of the id and guide the ego in the direction of moral action rather than merely to do what works.

As noted earlier, personality is driven by psychic energy. This flow of energy occurs within a closed system. There is only so much energy available, and when the libido energizes one structure of personality, less energy is available for the other structures. Thus, a highly charged id results in diminished energy for the ego or superego. Such persons would tend to be rather impulsive and "act without thinking." Persons with highly energized superegos might be immobilized in decision-making situations, unable to determine the "right" decision or vacilitating between personal desires and meeting the expectations of others. Mentally healthy persons, in contrast, are characterized by a relative balance of energy among the three structures, which leads to their cooperative and harmonious operation.

Anxiety. The concept of anxiety is central to psychoanalytic theory. Anxiety is used by the ego as a signal of impending danger and, thus, becomes a call for action. *Reality anxiety* is experienced when an external threat is accurately perceived. The intensity of the anxiety is proportionate to the degree of threat. In contrast, *moral anxiety* is experienced as guilt or shame resulting from a perceived threat of disapproval or punishment. Finally, *neurotic anxiety* is the emotional response to the threatened eruption of an unconscious impulse emerging into one's awareness.

Internal conflicts among the structures of personality are not easily controlled. The ego's job is to satisfy the demands of reality, the moral demands of the superego, and the id's demands for immediate gratification. Through the use of *ego defense mechanisms,* impulses emanating from the id are blocked from reaching consciousness or distorted in such a way that the superego is fooled. All ego defense mechanisms have several things in common. First, the person does not consciously choose to use them. Second, they always involve a denial or distortion of reality to at least some degree. Third, we all use them. Their use becomes pathological only when they are used in excess or to the extreme. Table 4.1 lists and defines specific types of ego defense mechanisms.

Nature of Psychological Disturbance. Emotional distress and behavioral problems are displayed in many ways. Yet, according to the psychoanalytic perspective, all are rooted in intrapsychic conflicts occurring at the unconscious level. Such a notion may seem far fetched and speculative. In my early days in as counselor-trainee, although intrigued by Freud's ideas, I wanted to believe that the clients I saw in my practice had more insight into the nature of their presenting problems. However, I soon learned this was not always the case.

One of my first clients was a female, in her early 30s, married and a parent of three children. Her childhood was marked by a strict upbringing and she remained in a very close relationship with her parents. Her father was quite dominant and it was very important that she please him. She described her presenting problem by saying, "I will be talking and suddenly, without warning, I lose my voice. I become mute." A complete medical exam failed to reveal an underlying physical cause.

As treatment proceeded, my client began to identify a pattern in which she would often become mute when needing to assert herself, particularly with her father. For example, she might have plans to go out for an evening with her husband but would then receive an invitation to dine with her parents. In such situations, she would "lose her voice."

TABLE 4.1	Defense Mechanism	Example
Examples of Ego Defense Mechanisms	**Repression**—the involuntary removal of material from one's conscious awareness.	A child who was sexually abused at age 7, but has no conscious recollection of the abuse.
	Regression—reverting to forms of behavior characteristic of an earlier age when the person was more secure.	A 6-year-old child who, upon experiencing the divorce of parents, begins nocturnal bedwetting after 4 years of appropriate bladder control.
	Projection—attributing one's unacceptable desires, motives, or characteristics to others.	The husband accuses his spouse of not loving him when, in fact, it is he who does not love his spouse.
	Displacement—discharging pent-up feelings or behaviors onto less threatening targets.	A father in unresolved conflict at work comes home and yells at his children for not cleaning their bedrooms.
	Rationalization—contrived "reasons" that explain away or mask personal failures or questionable motives.	A person who is not hired for a position that she truly wanted states that she probably would have become bored with the job if it had been offered to her.
	Reaction Formation—defending against unacceptable impulses or desires by expressing a seemingly opposite behavior.	A college student who wants to drop out of his program signs up for an "overload" of classes for the upcoming semester.
	Denial—refusal to believe, accept, or face an unpleasant reality.	A parent whose child tragically dies in an automobile accident expresses disbelief at the funeral that the tragedy has actually happened.
	Sublimation—redirecting sexual or aggressive energies into a more socially acceptable alternative activity.	A recently divorced person diverts anger and sexual energy by enrolling in college and immersing herself in studies.

From the psychoanalytic perspective, my client was experiencing a conflict that was entirely out of her conscious awareness. She desired to have a night in town with her spouse yet felt guilty if not abiding by the wishes of her parents. Trapped in a conflict between mutually exclusive alternatives, her "loss of voice" provided her with a convenient way to not assert herself while not offending either her spouse or father. This solution did not resolve the actual problem at hand, but did protect her from the pain that would come with acting autonomously in relation to her parents.

Goals of Treatment. If symptoms arise from deep, hidden unconscious conflicts, only a treatment that penetrates the deepest recesses of the psyche is capable of facilitating lasting change. According to Freud, the goal of counseling is to modify the structure of personality. This is accomplished through a process that makes the unconscious material conscious, thereby increasing clients' awareness. This enables clients to recognize unproductive, self-defeating patterns of behavior and develop more effective alternatives.

Process and Techniques.   Classical psychoanalysts attempt to be "blank slates" that facilitate the development of *transference* in the relationship. In transference, the patient experiences thoughts and feelings toward the counselor that do not fit the reality of his or her relationship with the counselor. The thoughts and feelings actually apply to significant others from the client's past, but are "transferred" to the counselor. Within the immediacy of the counseling sessions, these thoughts, feelings, and actions emerge as reflections of underlying conflicts between impulses and defenses that are at the core of the person's pathology. These patterns recur in the context of transference and become a major source of content in sessions for analysis.

To facilitate the production of unconscious material, clients engage in *free association.* Clients are encouraged to say whatever comes into their minds. They report anything and everything—dreams, memories, fantasies, wishes, thoughts—all are important.

Confrontation, clarification, and interpretation are primary tools for the analysis of unconscious contents. In confrontation, the counselor might reflect, "You seem to be feeling angry at me." This helps the client to be aware of what material is being analyzed. Counselors make accurate interpretations determined in large measure by psychoanalytic theory that allow clients to gain insight into the nature of their behavior. These insights are *worked through* again and again as clients slowly move to a higher, more effective level of functioning. The end result is increased self-awareness that permits clients to base behavior on present realities. Freudians see this as representing structural changes in personality.

Object Relations.   Although around 12% of practicing psychologists embrace classical psychoanalytic theory (Prochaska & Norcross, 1999), a larger proportion practice modified versions such as *object relations* or *self-psychology.* Object relations go beyond Freud's analysis of personality structures by focusing on the relationship between self and objects, which are mental representations of others. We tend to represent others mentally in ways that resemble our earliest relationships, typically how we related to our primary caregivers. Infants learn that primary caregivers have elements of "good" and "bad," and healthy development occurs as these elements "gel" to form a cohesive object. A failure in object relations takes place when the good and bad do not synthesize, which can lead to the "splitting off" of the bad parts. Splitting is expressed when a person cannot keep both the good and bad representations in mind simultaneously when frustrated by another. In such situations, the person moves rapidly from perceiving the person as all good to seeing the person as all bad.

These objects stay with us, and much of our adult life involves a repetition of our early object relations in one form or another. Persons with poor object relations tend to be emotionally unstable and insecure, quickly moving from adulation to anger when a loved person leaves them feeling disappointed or abandoned.

The goal of object relations therapy is to revise impaired object representations. This, too, involves a reconstruction of the personality as in classical psychoanalysis.

However, the focus is on the nature of the person's interactions with others and the extent to which these actions are based on unconscious images (object relations) from the past. Techniques used in object relations therapy are similar in nature to classical psychoanalysis. However, free association, transference, interpretation, and working through are used to increase the client's awareness of the operation of distorted objects. Clients can then work toward the development of a more autonomous functioning, characterized by increased self-trust, acceptance of others, and less emotional reactivity.

INDIVIDUAL PSYCHOLOGY (ADLERIAN THERAPY)

Key Theorist.   The system of counseling known as individual psychology was developed by Alfred Adler (1870–1937). Adler earned his M.D. in psychiatry from the University of Vienna and was initially a strong defender of the Freudian perspective. However, Adler began to criticize Freud's theory for its overemphasis on sexuality and discounting of conscious processes. A sharp break in Adler and Freud's relationship resulted and Adler quickly established individual psychology as an important alternative perspective.

Essential Principles and Concepts.   Six assumptions are foundational to the Adlerian perspective. First, behavior is goal oriented, purposeful, and socially motivated. Rather than being determined by unconscious conflicts or past determinants, Adler believed behavior was determined by one's outlook toward the future. In addition, behavior resulted from conscious choice and was motivated by stimuli present in the social situation.

Second, behavior is best understood from the vantage point of the client's subjective reality. Personal behavior is influenced by the person's thoughts, beliefs, perceptions, and conclusions. To make sense of the client's behavior, the counselor is advised to see the world through the eyes of the client.

Third, personality is an organized whole that interacts within a specific and unique social system. Clearly, Adlerian theory focuses on interpersonal dynamics rather than intrapsychic structures. Each person is best understood as the central piece in a "social jig-saw puzzle."

Fourth, the core motive for behavior is to *strive for superiority.* In other words, persons seek to rise above what they currently are. Each of us has self-identified deficits or *inferiorities* that we desire to overcome. This becomes the powerful force that drives behavior. Adler believed each person has some idealistic notion of who he or she would like to be, referred to as *fictional finalism,* which provides direction to each person's personal strivings.

Fifth, each person develops a type of cognitive map, referred to as a *lifestyle,* that lends consistency to behaviors as he or she strives for chosen goals. It is a private logic that provides the rationale for acting in specific ways. Thus, although one's behavior may not make sense to others, it might make perfect sense once the personal reasoning is revealed and understood. For example, a child might feel academically inferior to other children in his classroom. To compensate for the inferiority and accompanying rejection from peers, he may choose to gain acceptance from others through athletic achievements or being the class clown.

Finally, personal fulfillment and well-being are found by acting for the general *social interest*. In choosing behaviors that will move us toward our fictional finalisms, personal well-being is enhanced to the extent that our behavior does not conflict significantly with the goals of those who surround us. We must recognize that we are not self-sufficient and that merely to look out for number one brings us into inevitable conflict with others. Thus, being socially connected is critical to our emotional well-being.

Nature of Psychological Disturbance.   Adlerians see psychological disturbance as rooted in discouragement and inadequacy. In families where competition, distrust, domination, neglect, or pampering predominate, children become discouraged from attaining superiority in socially accepted ways. In addition, being raised in such environments results in a diminished social interest. Such persons try to do the best they can to get to the place in life they think they should be (fictional finalisms). Their lifestyles, then, are characterized by *basic mistakes* of overgeneralizing about the nature of life from the small but very influential sample of experiences they have experienced in their families.

Such lifestyle patterns can be set early in one's development. For example, a child who is overly pampered and shielded from the normal challenges of life may find attention-getting behaviors as a primary means of enlisting others to take care of her personal needs. Other children may have been raised by very dominant parents. Feeling impotent and unable to accomplish anything of worth, these children may resort to bullying and rebelliousness to rise above others. Such power-seeking behaviors are viewed as compensations for underlying feelings of inadequacy. Or parents who consistently nag, cajole, scold, deride, and blame raise children who fear, yet expect, failure. Forever trying, but never judging personal efforts as good enough, these persons often move through life in hesitant, indecisive manners.

Goal of Treatment.   The fundamental goal in Adlerian counseling and psychotherapy is to help clients live a more complete and perfect life in ways that contribute not only to personal well-being but also to the general well-being of others (Sharf, 2000). In other words, clients develop more effective lifestyles and healthy social interests that facilitate positive strivings for superiority. Clients come to see how current lifestyles are really self-defeating patterns of behavior that are leading to destructive goals. As personal insights increase, clients are more capable of choosing new and more creative ways of attaining goals that are socially useful and self-enhancing (Prochaska & Norcross, 1999).

Process and Techniques.   The process of counseling involves an analysis of the client's lifestyle to help clients become more aware of how they are directing their lives toward destructive goals. Clients are then encouraged to put these insights into action. Typically, Adlerian therapy involves four phases: establish the relationship, explore the individual's dynamics, encourage insight, and promote reorientation.

Initially, a collaborative relationship is established on a foundation of mutual trust and respect. In this phase, counselors utilize active listening and responding with genuineness and understanding, demonstrating their faith in the client's ability to make desired changes.

The goal of the second phase, exploring the individual's dynamics, is to gain an understanding of the client's lifestyle and how it is affecting the client's functioning in life's tasks. Frequently, a *lifestyle assessment questionnaire* is administered, which poses questions to the client that explore family constellation (e.g., psychological position in the family of origin, birth order, and family interactional patterns), earliest recollections, dreams, and priorities. The counselor then presents a summary of each area and identifies false or impossible goals of security, misperceptions of life's demands, and faulty values that support the self-defeating lifestyle. The summary also identifies the client's assets and strengths that can be harnessed to make beneficial changes.

In the *encouraging insight* phase, counselors use a combination of supportive and confrontive approaches to help clients gain insight into mistaken beliefs, goals, and self-defeating behaviors. While self-understanding is an important step toward change, these insights must be translated into productive action. Interpretation, as practiced by Adlerians, involves relating specific thoughts, attitudes, and behaviors to their undesirable consequences. Counselors move back and forth from "here-and-now" situations to the basic mistakes and lifestyle patterns identified through the lifestyle analysis. This enables clients to grasp how they contribute to their current problems and how they might contribute to their solution. Interpretations are always presented tentatively as hypotheses, rather than factual statements of cause and effect. The collaborative efforts of clients are welcomed.

The final phase of *reorientating* is an action-oriented stage in which clients put insight into action and make new decisions, goals, and action plans. A wide range of techniques is used to motivate clients toward effective lifestyles (Dinkmeyer & Sperry, 2000):

1. Acting as if — suggesting a limited task where clients act in the manner they desire or wish, but feel incapable of doing.
2. Spitting in the client's soup — reframing the client's behavior in a manner that makes it less appealing or desirable.
3. Paradoxical intention — increasing the client's awareness of their ineffective behavior by prescribing an increase in the display of the symptom.
4. The question — Asking the client, "What would be different if your were well?"
5. Catching oneself — Once aware of their goals, clients are asked to consciously call to their attention behavioral displays that they are desiring to change.

The influence of Adlerian theory extends well beyond the counseling room. The emphasis on personal growth and its teleological focus lends itself to applications in a variety of educational programs. Furthermore, a number of important parent skill training programs are based on Adlerian principles. Finally, the concepts apply readily to communications training, problem solving, and rehabilitation programs.

BEHAVIOR THERAPY

Key Theorists.   Behavior therapy is an application of the behavioral learning theories of Ivan Pavlov and B. F. Skinner. Ivan Pavlov was a Russian physiologist who initially was actively investigating the role of the salivatory response of dogs in the digestion process. Specifically, he was trying to determine exactly how the stimulus of food in the mouth elicited saliva. However, he encountered a fundamental problem. The dogs would salivate before the food reached their mouths. He soon reasoned that he had stumbled on a basic principle of learning, which is referred to as *classical conditioning.* His focus was on the type of learning that took place when specific stimuli elicit particular behavior.

B. F. Skinner earned an undergraduate degree in English and aspired to be an author. However, he gave up his dream and was awarded a Ph.D. in psychology from Harvard University in 1931. He did not see behaviorism as a theory of personality or psychotherapy. Rather, he saw it as the underlying philosophy of psychology, which was defined as the scientific study of behavior. He rejected general theories of personality and therapy because they fell short of the ideals of science, which entailed the ability to truly predict and control behavior. He believed psychology could only be a science as it established lawful relationships between individual histories of behavior and the consequences of that behavior. Cognitive factors lacked precise measurement and their relationship to overt behavior could be assessed by mere speculation only. Thus, the focus of Skinner's theory building was on environmental stimuli and overt behavior, the relationship of which could be empirically verified. His theory is known as *operant conditioning.* He was concerned with how a person's behavior *operates* on the environment to elicit specific consequences.

Essential Concepts and Principles.   This section first reviews the essential concepts and principles related to classical conditioning and then those related to operant conditioning.

In Pavlov's classic studies, Pavlov noted, first, that an unlearned stimulus (i.e., food—the unconditioned stimulus) elicited an unlearned response (i.e., saliva—the unconditioned response) from the organism. This response was viewed as reflexive and not the result of prior learning. Then a neutral stimulus (i.e., sound of a bell) was presented just prior to the presentation of the unconditioned stimulus. Finally, after several presentations, the bell was capable of eliciting the saliva without any presentation of food. Once this learned stimulus-response was displayed, the bell and saliva were referred to as the conditioned (i.e., learned) stimulus and conditioned (i.e., learned) response, respectively.

Figure 4.1 illustrates the basic principles and concepts of classical conditioning.

Several related concepts are associated with classical conditioning. *Acquisition* occurs when the new conditioned response is elicited on presentation of a conditioned stimulus. *Extinction* can be considered as the "unlearning" of the conditioned response. It takes place when the conditioned response is no longer elicited after repeated presentations of the conditioned stimulus without any occasional presentation of the unconditioned stimulus. In *stimulus generalization,* a neutral stimulus that approximates the conditioned stimulus is able to elicit the conditioned response. For example, a young child bitten by a dog may develop a strong fear not only of the specific dog but of other dogs and four-legged household pets. Stimulus generalization occurs when the unconditioned response of fear to the specific dog is elicited when presented with the stimuli of other similar creatures. Finally, one approach to preventing child sexual abuse involves teaching the difference between "good touch" and "bad touch." The ability to distinguish between the two types of touch illustrates *stimulus discrimination.*

Whereas classical conditioning is concerned with behavior that is elicited in response to the antecedent conditions (i.e., environmental stimuli), operant conditioning focuses on the consequences of behavior (i.e., what happens after a behavior is

FIGURE 4.1 Basic Paradigm of Classical Conditioning

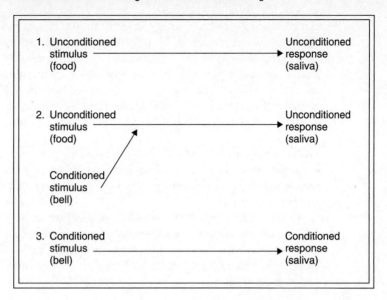

emitted). Generally, behavior is followed by two types of consequences: reinforcers and punishers. A *reinforcer* is defined as any event following a behavior that increases the likelihood that the specific behavior will recur. In contrast, a *punisher* refers to any event following a behavior that decreases the likelihood that the specific behavior will recur.

In addition, we can identify two types of reinforcers and punishers. When a behavior is positively reinforced, an event is introduced into the situation that has the effect of increasing the likelihood of recurrence of the behavior. In contrast, negative reinforcement occurs when something is taken away or removed from the situation and has the effect of increasing the likelihood that the behavior will recur. Similarly, punishment can involve either the introduction or removal of an event from the situation, which has the effect of decreasing the likelihood that the behavior will recur. Figure 4.2 illustrates the basic concepts of operant conditioning.

FIGURE 4.2 Basic Concepts of Operant Conditioning

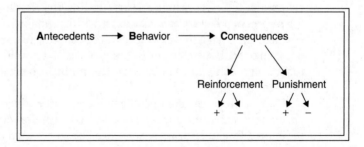

Note that the determination of reinforcers and punishers does not lie with the qualities of the event per se. Whether or not an event serves as a reinforcer or punisher depends solely on the effect of the event on the behavior. If the frequency of behavior increases, it is a reinforcer, by definition. Thus, giving children candy bars to reward good behavior may or may not serve as a reinforcer. It all depends on the effect on the desired behavior. Similarly, parents who yell at their children do well to consider what effect their yelling is having on the child's specific behavior. It may bring an immediate cessation to the problem behavior, but does it decrease the likelihood of that behavior recurring? Sometimes such yelling has been found to serve as a reinforcer.

Goals of Behavior Therapy.   Behavior therapists view pathological behavior as being acquired through the processes of learning. It logically follows, that the goals of counseling involve a relearning process. If a behavior can be learned, it can also be unlearned and relearned!

Behavioral therapists see maladaptive behavior in itself as being the problem. Counseling is directed toward correcting problem behavior rather than focusing on underlying conflicts, personality structures, self-esteem, or faulty life decisions. The goals of counseling are typically formulated as belonging to one or several of the following categories:

1. Behavioral deficits
2. Behavioral excesses
3. Inappropriate environmental stimulus control
4. Inappropriate reinforcement contingencies

Thus, the principles of classical and operant conditioning are applied to facilitate the extinction of identified problem behaviors and the learning of more effective and functional alternatives.

Process and Techniques.   Behavior therapy is pragmatic. The validity of techniques cannot be assumed simply because they sound good or make logical sense. Rather, techniques are accepted and applied to the extent that they have demonstrated efficacy in relation to the specific problem. This empirical orientation applies to the therapeutic process itself. Scientific methods are used to identify problem behaviors, identify goals, and monitor therapeutic progress.

The process of behavior therapy begins with *functional behavioral analysis*. The counselor gathers detailed and specific information from the client or through direct observation of the client in problem-relevant situations. Specifically, counselors identify circumstances surrounding the development of the problem, what environmental factors are associated with the maintenance of the problem, how the problem has changed over time, and the consequences related to displays of the problem behavior. The statement of the problem is typically framed in terms of the ABCs (e.g., **a**ntecedents to the behavior, the problem **b**ehavior, and the **c**onsequences of the behavior).

A target behavior (e.g., goal statement) is identified and stated in terms that are specific, concise, and measurable. Initially, the frequency of the target behavior is monitored by gathering *baseline* data. Approaches used to gather baseline data include client self-monitoring, behavioral rating scales, interviews, and direct observation. Specific intervention strategies are then selected and implemented based on empirical evidence of their efficacy. The client's response to treatment is monitored by gathering data on the occurrence of the target behavior after the intervention strategies have been implemented. Treatment goals are added or deleted as needed and the overall treatment plan is revised according to the progress noted.

For our purposes, several specific techniques will be noted that illustrate the nature of behavioral therapy. Counterconditioning approaches are based on the classical conditioning paradigm and seek to alter clients' behavior by altering antecedent conditions. *Systematic desensitization* is the treatment of choice for phobias involving nonhuman objects, animals, and anxieties. *Assertiveness training* is used to treat a variety of social anxieties. Clients learn to assert themselves in social situations that were previously anxiety provoking. In addition to counterconditioning, the assertive behavior is reinforced by the reduction of fear and increased success in social interactions.

Contingency management approaches are based on operant principles and seek to alter behavior by changing the link between the behavior and its consequences. For example, *self-management* techniques train clients to monitor and manipulate situational antecedents and consequences to change behavior. Making reinforcements contingent on desired behavior through use of *token economies* is applied in settings such as classroom for troubled students, hospitals for chronic psychiatric clients, and skill training for developmentally disabled training skills (Ayllon & Azrin, 1968). *Behavioral exchange* is applied in marriage and family counseling to increase satisfaction with the relationship (Jacobson & Margolin, 1979).

COGNITIVE APPROACHES

A number of counseling approaches arose, beginning in the mid-1960s, that had a common emphasis on cognitive factors. Some arose out of a response to criticisms of the traditional psychoanalytic approaches. Others represented revisions or extensions of behavior therapy. However, all had in common the idea that behavioral and emotional change was best accomplished through interventions that seek to alter the client's cognitive style.

Generally, cognitive therapies accept behavioral principles but take into account the covert behaviors such as thoughts, beliefs, and underlying attitudes that occur within the person and that are not readily observable. The most widely practiced cognitive approaches are Albert Ellis' rational emotive behavior therapy, Aaron Beck's cognitive therapy, and Donald Meichenbaum's cognitive-behavioral modification.

Key Theorists. Two pioneers of the cognitive approaches, Albert Ellis and Aaron Beck, practiced psychoanalytic therapy in the 1950s but became disillusioned by the approach. In addition, each was impressed by the role faulty cognitive processes played in the psychological distress of their clients. Ellis was especially impressed with the irrational thoughts contained in the internal dialogue of his clients. In rational emotive behavior therapy (REBT), clients are made aware of what they are saying to themselves and how such self-statements relate to the emotional pain they experience.

Clients become aware of the occurrence of such thoughts and learn to replace them with more rational alternatives. Beck was also impressed with how a person's *automatic thoughts* stemmed from the operation of cognitive distortions. Cognitive therapy (CT) seeks to alter these distortions, which leads to the construction of thoughts that more accurately reflect the reality of situations.

In contrast to Ellis and Beck, Donald Meichenbaum came out of the behavioral camp. He was impressed by the research and theories of Bandura and Vygotsky, both of whom demonstrated the roles of social process and observational learning in the acquisition of new behavior. Meichenbaum's cognitive-behavioral modification (CBM) incorporates modeling, learning through observation, and verbal mediation to facilitate behavioral change.

Essential Principles and Concepts.   For each of the approaches mentioned previously, cognition is the target for many of the interventions. However, we must note that the human thought process takes place at several different levels. By understanding the distinction among these levels, the differences among REBT, CT, and CBM are seen more clearly.

At the deepest level, cognition takes the form of *cognitive structures.* Also referred to as *self-schemata,* these cognitive structures consist of the basic underlying assumptions individuals make about self and the world. These deeply engrained and relatively enduring characteristics are established through one's past experiences. Schemata play a critical role in the cognitive therapies because they can introduce bias and distortion into the processing of ongoing experience and influence the recall of past events. For example, Beck (1967) identifies a "*cognitive triad*" that consists of the following underlying assumptions: I am worthless and inadequate; the world (or the specific event) is an awful place; and the future is bleak. The cognitive triad provides the structure that supports the cognitive processing and products characteristic of emotional disorders.

The second level, cognitive processes, refers to the underlying reasoning styles that are used in the actual processing of the ongoing events in our lives. Emotionally healthy persons process in such a way that an accurate, realistic meaning is assigned to the event experienced. The consequent self-talk and emotional experience is appropriate, both in quality and intensity, for the nature of that event. In contrast, the processing of specific events by emotionally distressed persons is often characterized by the use of cognitive distortions. These distortions, when in operation, lead to the misinterpretation of events by assigning meanings to events that contain degrees of inaccuracy (Beck, Rush, Shaw, & Emery, 1979). Examples of cognitive distortions identified by Beck include:

1. *Arbitrary inference.* Drawing conclusions without accurate supporting evidence or even despite contradictory evidence. For example, after receiving a C− on a research proposal, I conclude, "I might as well drop out of my doctoral program now, since I will never be able to write a doctoral dissertation."
2. *Selective abstraction.* Focusing on one aspect while ignoring or discounting other relevant features of the situation. As David Burns (1999) notes, it is like placing a drop of black ink in a beaker of clear water. The whole container of water is

darkened by the small amount of ink. I engage in selective abstraction if I allow one negative comment made by a colleague to color my entire day.

3. *Overgeneralization.* Developing a general rule on the basis of only a few isolated events or facts. For example, my son comes in late one evening and leads me to conclude, "He never comes home on time!"

4. *Magnification or minimization.* Either severely exaggerating or underestimating the significance of an event. As a result, the meaning assigned to such events is grossly distorted. For example, I might stutter over a word in giving a lecture and conclude, "Those students think I'm a bumbling idiot because of my speech deficit."

5. *Personalization.* Relating external events to yourself when there is no objective reason for doing so. The dean passes me in the hall and fails to say, "Hi." I say to myself, "The dean intentionally snubbed me."

6. *Dichotomous thinking.* Events are placed in one of two opposing, mutually exclusive categories. Thus, if one's performance is not perfect, it was totally awful.

The third level of cognition, *cognitive products,* is most apparent to us. These are the statements we say to ourselves. This internal dialogue can be likened to the radio sports "play-by-play" announcer, who sees, interprets, and verbally communicates what is happening on the playing field. These statements become the subjective reality on which our emotional and behavioral responses rest. In his book *Reason and Emotion in Psychotherapy* (1962), Ellis put forth a list of 11 irrational beliefs that lead to emotional distress and psychological disorder. For example, "It is essential that a person be loved or approved by virtually everyone in the community" is an irrational statement because it is very possible to live a productive life without being loved by almost everyone.

Goals of Cognitive Therapies. The primary goal of all cognitive therapies is the removal of or relief from presenting symptoms. But ultimately cognitive therapies seek to correct the flawed cognitive structures, processes, and products that give rise to emotional distress. Thus, progress in counseling is noted as clients are able to "catch" styles of thinking that are associated with their presenting condition and substitute more reasonable and accurate alternative thoughts. For example, one of my previous clients displayed a very strong fear of flying and would report self-statements such as, "I don't think I will make it through this flight." After eight sessions the client stepped on to an airplane for the first time in 2 years and reported the following self-statement: "I may experience some turbulence during the flight which will cause discomfort. But I can handle it. The presence of turbulence does not signal impending doom."

Process and Techniques. In general, treatment progresses through several phases. First, a congenial, collaborative relationship with the client is established. Then clients become aware of what they are thinking and doing and how these relate to the presenting problems. Third, clients learn to identify which specific thoughts represent distortions and are in need of revision or replacement. In addition, they identify behaviors that might interrupt the dysfunctional pattern. Finally, clients substitute the more productive style of thinking and behaving and gather evidence to determine the extent to which the alternative thoughts and behaviors are facilitating more effective functioning.

In REBT, clients are taught that emotional disturbances are explained by a simple ABC formula, where A = activating events; B = irrational beliefs; and C = the emotional and behavioral consequences. The counselor actively works with the client to modify the faulty beliefs to more rational alternatives. By learning to *dispute* (D) the irrational thoughts and replace them with rational alternatives, clients experience the positive *effect* (E).

Beck's CT makes extensive use of Socratic questioning and personal experiments to assist clients in changing thoughts and behaviors. This process is referred to as *guided discovery*. Clients are taught to monitor the relationship of thoughts to emotional and behavioral consequences by keeping journals. A variety of cognitive and behavioral techniques are used to alter cognitive processes and promote more effective behaviors. Cognitive techniques include cognitive appraisal, cognitive restructuring, covert rehearsal, and imagery. Behavioral techniques include abdominal breathing, progressive muscle relaxation, systematic desensitization, activity scheduling, and assertiveness training.

Cognitive-behavioral modification (Meichenbaum, 1977) also makes use of the cognitive and behavioral techniques listed previously. In addition, CBM makes extensive use of self-instruction, self-reinforcement, graduated in vivo exposure, and personal narrative repair.

HUMANISTIC THERAPIES AND EXISTENTIAL THEORY

Key Theorist.   Carl Rogers (1902–1987) is the founder of person-centered therapy and has been recognized as one of the preeminent leaders in the humanistic movement. Raised in rural Wisconsin, Rogers initally went to college to prepare for a career in Christian ministry. After a period of searching and questioning, he left the seminary and received a Ph.D. in psychology from Columbia University in 1931. He rejected his psychoanalytic training and developed an approach to counseling based on the "goodness of humanity." He believed in the inherent worth and growth potential of individuals. His approach downplays the importance of techniques while highlighting the vital significance of the therapeutic relationship and atmosphere.

Essential Concepts and Principles.   Rogers' approach advocates understanding clients as *persons* and developing case formulations from that vantage point rather that invoking a theory to understand *clients*. Thus, his approach is truly person centered and not theory centered (Day, 2004).

Elements of existential theory run through Rogers' approach. The concept of *self* is central and includes an awareness of one's total being, how one relates to or is in touch with the immediate environment, and one's existence in the *here-and-now*. Person-centered therapy has a phenomenological orientation and underscores the significance of personal meaning and subjective reality. Other important themes include personal autonomy, freedom, responsibility, connectedness, and isolation.

Rogers believed all people have an inherent tendency to develop all of their capacities in ways that serve to maintain and enhance the person (*the actualizing tendency*). In addition, we possess a *valuing system* that places positive value on those experiences that are growth enhancing and negative value on those experiences that limit personal growth. Thus, we possess inherent tendencies that motivate us toward growth and direct us toward growth-enhancing experiences. Finally, as our awareness of self emerges, we develop a strong need for positive self-regard. This is a universal need to be valued and loved.

However, significant others tend to make their love contingent on *what we do* and not *who we are*. Thus, developing persons learn to regard themselves as they are regarded by others. In doing so, they begin to seek the acceptance of others, forsaking personal sets of values to receive acceptance from others contingent on meeting the requisite conditions of worth.

According to Rogers, a positive correlation exists between the conditional love of our parents and the level of pathology that develops. A state of *incongruency* develops in which persons feel and act in ways that do not truly represent who they really are. Incongruent persons do not have the *talk* together with the *walk*. They are alienated from self and their surroundings. Overt behaviors are inconsistent with what that person feels. Incongruence, then, is at the core of all emotional disorders.

Goals of Person-Centered Therapy. People enter counseling for a variety of reasons. Whether the person is seeking relief from severe stress, emotional breakdown, lack of meaningfulness, or social alienation, the goal of treatment is to increase the degree of congruence between self and experience. In other words, the mentally healthy person is more in touch with immediate experience, more trusting and accepting of self, and more capable of self-validation.

Process and Techniques. As noted earlier, Rogers did not emphasize a specific set of therapeutic strategies. He believed the necessary and sufficient ingredients for successful treatment were contained in the counseling relationship (Rogers, 1961). Six specific characteristics of the relationship are required for constructive change:

1. Psychological closeness develops within the context of a meaningful relationship.
2. The client experiences vulnerability and is in a state of incongruency. This motivates the client to stay in the relationship.
3. The counselor is congruent and genuine within the relationship.
4. The counselor experiences unconditional positive regard for the client.
5. The counselor experiences accurate empathic understanding of the client.
6. The client perceives the unconditional positive regard and empathic understanding of the counselor.

In such a counseling relationship, the client is more able and willing to be who he or she really is. The counselor actively attends to the client through listening, posture, and eye contact. He or she seeks clarification through skillful use of questions. Often, such questions help clients clarify in their minds what they are truly thinking and feeling. Finally, the counselor uses words to reflect accurately the client's subjective experience. This becomes a mirror in which clients see more clearly who they really are. As counseling proceeds, the self-experience discrepancy and tension that accompany incongruency decrease, leading to more autonomous, fulfilling lives.

FAMILY THERAPY

Key Theorists. There are numerous approaches to conducting family therapy. Although many persons have made important contributions to the field of family therapy, this discussion focuses three important family systems theories. Noteworthy theorists of family therapy include Murray Bowen, Virginia Satir, Salvador Minuchin, and Jay Haley.

Essential Concepts and Principles. Just as there are a number of individual approaches to counseling, family therapy also consists of a wide array of theories and techniques. Many of these approaches have unique theoretical foundations. Generally, though, family systems approaches focus on the interactions that occur among individuals in a three-generational family system. The entire system becomes the unit for analysis in assessment and therapeutic intervention.

Several general assumptions and related concepts guide family systems theory:

1. The family functions as a system (i.e., a complex unit consisting of interacting elements and relationships that organize them).
2. Circular causality provides more accurate explanations of personal behavior and emotional responses.
3. An accurate understanding of individuals can only be attained when persons are viewed within the context of their family system.
4. Understanding the nature of families involves more than simply summing its components. In other words, the whole is more than the sum of its parts.
5. Individual disorders are viewed as family disorders.
6. Pathology serves a family function.
7. *Boundaries* are largely emotional barriers that protect the integrity of individuals, subsystems, and nuclear families within the larger system. *Enmeshment* occurs when individuals and subsystems lose autonomy due to a blurring of boundaries within the system. In contrast, overly rigid boundaries around individuals and subsystems lead to *disengagement.*
8. *Triangles* are three-person subsystems that are the smallest stable emotional unit within a system. When under stress, dyads become unstable and seek the support of a third person.

Generally speaking, assessment, diagnosis, and treatment in family therapy focus on the interpersonal rather than the intrapsychic. In addition, family therapists zero in on the nature of transactions and interactions taking place within the system rather than the specific contents of the presenting problem. Finally, whereas individual-oriented counselors tend to narrow their focus when stuck (reductionism), family therapists often enlarge the focus of treatment by inviting extended family into the sessions.

Goals, Processes, and Techniques. As noted previously, family therapy is a diverse field that encompasses a wide variety of orientations and techniques. Therefore, instead of attempting to impose an artificial set of conclusions regarding general goals, processes, and techniques, three prominent approaches are discussed: Bowenian family therapy, Minuchin's structural family therapy, and Haley's strategic family therapy.

Boweninan Family Therapy. Bowenian family therapy sees personal, emotional and behavioral problems as being due to difficulties the individual experiences in differentiating self from his or her family of origin. In some cases, *fusion* blurs the psychological boundaries between the individual and other family members. This contaminates the emotional and behavioral functioning of persons within the system and leads to the formation of an *undifferentiated ego mass.* Individuals in other family systems may be extremely *disengaged,* wherein the boundaries between individuals are so rigid that little or no emotional transactions can take place within the family. Sometimes *emotional cutoff* occurs in which the person flees (physically) from an unresolved emotional attachment.

The goal of Bowenian family therapy is to develop a healthy differentiation of self from one's family of origin. This involves being able psychologically to separate one's intellectual from emotional functions so the individual is more capable of responding in a reasonable and autonomous manner rather than emotionally reacting in stressful situations. Primary techniques used by Bowenian counselors include teaching clients basic family system concepts to promote self-awareness, and conceptualization of the presenting problem in a systemic perspective. Counselors, work with clients to strengthen the intellectual functioning while decreasing emotional reactivity. When clients become more capable of acting in a reasonable, autonomous manner, the counselor coaches them as they return to their families of origin. The counselor supports clients' efforts to maintain an appropriate balance between personal autonomy and connectedness while in the midst of the highly enmeshed or disengaged system.

Minuchin's Structural Family Therapy. Minuchin sees families as governed by their *structure,* a set of covert rules that regulate family transactions. These rules are revealed as the counselor picks up on the consistent, repetitive, and predictable patterns of family behavior. Emotional boundaries, coalitions, and alliances are revealed by these patterns. As a result, subsystems emerge that influence how individuals and subsystems relate to one another within the family. Furthermore, the distribution of power and authority within the family reveals a power *hierarchy* that greatly influences the existing structure.

The goal of structural family therapy is to establish an effective hierarchical structure within the family. The parents must function as an executive coalition capable of providing mutual support and accommodation while providing a loving but firm united front to their children. If the family is disengaged, the goal includes increasing interactions and easing boundaries between its members. The goal for enmeshed families is to facilitate differentiation and autonomy within the family.

Initially, counselors join with and accommodate to the interactional style of the family. They then work with the interactions and develop a systemic diagnosis. Techniques are used to accentuate and modify interactional patterns and boundaries.

Haley's Strategic Family Therapy. This approach is sometimes referred to as brief, problem-solving therapy because it is method oriented and problem focused. It takes a very cognitive approach to the assessment of presenting problems but often makes little or no attempt to promote family insight into the nature of family problems. Rather, strategic family therapists direct family members to act in specific ways to disrupt patterns of behavior that maintain the presenting problems.

The goal of strategic family therapy is to solve the presenting problem. The counselor analyzes the behavioral sequences among family members in situations where the presenting problem occurs. Common-sense solutions have been attempted and have not succeeded in reducing symptoms, so strategic family therapists often resort to the use of indirect and paradoxical techniques. Counselors may assign symptoms to bring about symptom control by the client. Or clients may be directed *not* to attempt to resolve the problem (i.e., restraining the client), whereby client reactivity leads (paradoxically) to increased client effort. In addition, predicting relapses might be used paradoxically to prevent relapse. Finally, a variety of metaphorical tasks may be used that present clients with analogs that, when resolved, facilitate resolution of presenting problems.

CONTEMPORARY TRENDS IN COUNSELING THEORIES

The application of counseling theories does not occur in a vacuum but in a specific, dynamic, and ever-changing context. Thus, effective mental health and community counseling is responsive to current characteristics and trends present in the contemporary treatment environment. These trends influence the application of traditional theories and the development of new approaches. In this section, the following trends will be discussed briefly: pluralism (D'Andrea, 2000; Prochaska & Norcross, 1999), postmodernism (D'Andrea, 2000; Jankowski, 2002), spirituality (Young, Cashwell, Wiggins-Frame, & Belaire, 2002), the biologicalization of psychopathology and human behavior (Williams, 2001), the contemporary economic context (Staton, 2000), and technological advances (Locke, 2001; Riemer-Reiss, 2000).

PLURALISM

Originally, counseling and psychotherapy were envisioned as universal and transcultural processes (Prochaska & Norcross,1999). However, we now recognize the human diversity that surrounds us. Clients seen by mental health and community counselors differ by age and cohort, race, ethnicity, gender, national origin, religion, sexual orientation, physical and intellectual capabilities (D'Andrea, 2000). Our ability to help others benefits when we possess increased awareness of the cultural background that clients bring with them into the counseling encounter (Day, 2004). In addition, whereas the developers of the classic theories of counseling were almost exclusively Western white males, today's counselors are much more diverse. The demographic characteristics of counselors are becoming more representative of the clientele they serve. Finally, pluralism extends to the manner in which services are delivered. No longer is the delivery of counseling and psychotherapeutic services limited to 50-minute sessions, taking place in an office setting, and using individual treatment. Counseling services are provided in schools, the workplace, home, shopping centers, or over the Internet using a variety of timeframes and modalities.

Contemporary theory building demonstrates increased sensitivity to multicultural principles and values that influence the ways in which assessments and interventions are conducted. *Culture-sensitive therapy* transforms traditional approaches by replacing or adapting culture-specific approaches to the values and characteristics of the particular cultural group. Counseling with cultural sensitivity is so central to the training of counselors that CACREP identifies social and cultural diversity as part of its core curriculum (CACREP, 2001). Cultural sensitivity is also central to the practice of mental health and community counseling. Thus, chapter eight of this text is devoted to the topic.

Feminist therapy is rooted in pluralism and the women's movement philosophy of the 1960s. It recognizes the social, political, and cultural forces that influence a person's identity and behavior. Sexism, racism, classism, and monoculturalism are harmful to personal well-being (Brown, 1994). Feminist therapists work to validate and empower clients while also advocating societal change. Women learn to value their female characteristics and female-centered values such as empathy, cooperation, intuition, interdependence, and connectedness (Sturdivant, 1980).

The goals of feminist therapy, include not only personal change, but also institutional change (Enns, 1997). After reviewing various theorists, Sharf (2000) identified the following goals as central to the feminist perspective: symptom removal, enhancement of self-esteem, increased quality of personal relationships, internal locus of acceptance of body and sexuality, increased valuing of diversity, and increased political awareness and social action. *Feminist therapy* assumes that the female point of view should be accepted, equality should characterize personal relationships, and the potential for social processes in diverse societies is discriminatory.

In counseling, clients learn the repressive influences of gender roles and their negative impact on self-concept. Feminist therapy assists clients in developing a cognitive framework that supports skills necessary for developing and maintaining positive self-evaluations (Russell, 1984). In addition, counselors using feminist therapy use assertiveness training to empower clients. Sands (1998) found feminist therapy to be an effective approach to treating adolescent depression. Feminist therapy is frequently applied in consciousness-raising groups and has been integrated with other approaches in the treatment of men and children (Sharf, 2000).

POSTMODERNISM

Postmodernism is a new paradigm that is having a profound influence on a variety of disciplines such as philosophy, literary science, anthropology, and psychology (Wieling et al., 2001). Its impact on the counseling profession is indicated by the number of recent publications examining the influence of postmodernism on classic theories of counseling and the practice of mental health counseling (e.g., D'Andrea, 2000; Ellis, 1996; Guterman, 1994; Hansen, 2002; Jankowski, 2002). It is shaping the way many practitioners are thinking about the practice and content of their professon (D'Andrea, 2000).

To understand the influence of postmodernism, it is important to review the philosophical presuppositions of modernism that undergird the thinking of traditional theorists and practitioners. Modernism assumes that objective truth exists and can be ascertained by objective observers. The scientific method rests on these assumptions. The method presumes that carefully designed experiments that control for threats to validity and researcher bias yield findings that help us approach an understanding of "the way things really are." When applied to the practice of counseling, the presuppositions of modernism provide support for the implicit assumption that truth about clients and their situations can be ascertained by counselors, who are capable of maintaining objective stances within the relationship.

In contrast, postmodernism assumes that reality is constructed by the observer or social group (D'Andrea, 2000). The notion that humans can ascertain truth or objective reality is either deemphasized or rejected (Hansen, 2002). Although not rejecting outright the methods of science, postmodernism is viewed as only one of many ways of knowing. Other, more subjective ways of knowing are seen as equally valid (Jankowski, 2002). Reality, then, resides in the mind of the observer. For example, you and I may observe the same event and yet come out of the experience with very different personal meanings and emotional responses. Rather than engaging in a futile attempt to determine what really happened, postmodernism recognizes that each of our subjective experiences is a valid portrayal of the reality of that specific situation.

Postmodernist assumptions fit well with the multicultural context discussed earlier. Postmodernism encourages us to accept the validity of multiple perspectives while rejecting traditional views of progress and universal organizing categories (D'Andrea, 2000). It calls our attention to the way in which traditional theories of mental health are social constructions of Western thinkers. Such ways of thinking are so deeply embedded in our cultural landscape that we fail to recognize their sociopolitical-historical context (Cushman, 1990).

Given its multidisciplinary nature, many of the recent theoretical developments in mental health and community counseling are being shaped by the postmodern paradigm. This is perhaps most clearly seen in the rise of *narrative therapy* (White & Epston, 1990). Counselors who practice narrative therapy note that clients come into sessions with personal stories they tell in the present but that also shape their past. In other words, the nature of the events experienced is not nearly so important to the client's current level of functioning as is the subjective rendition of those events. The client's story is the client's reality. In assessment, narrative therapists identify subjective meanings, themes, and metaphorical objects and processes running through clients' stories.

The goal of counseling, then, becomes personal narrative repair or reconstruction. The target is the story itself, not the client or family system. For example, one of my female clients reported the following history: Her mother died on the client's twelfth birthday; as the oldest child, she was given excessive parental responsibility for younger siblings by her father, who was a heavy drinker; she was verbally and physically abused by her father; and she married a workaholic who was distanced yet controlling. She concluded that she was a victim and characterized her life as a personal tragedy. The goal for this client was to see herself not as a victim of a sad and repressive past but as a responsible person who was strong, competent, persistent, and resilient. The process of counseling was directed toward disconnecting old, hurtful themes from her story and weaving alternative meanings of empowerment into the fabric of the narrative.

The primary techniques used by narrative therapists involve telling the story and examining it to identify alternative ways of reconceptualizing and telling it. Essentially, the major tasks of treatment are the *deconstruction* and *reconstruction* or *reauthoring* of the client's story (Sharf, 2000). In doing so, counselors help their clients beat the problem rather than hold onto their stories of the problem (Becvar & Becvar, 1999).

SPIRITUALITY IN COUNSELING

I was serving as cotherapist in an internship setting. My supervisors were sitting behind the one-way mirror doing live supervision. I was gathering information in an intake session with a family who was presenting with an adolescent boy described as being "out of control." The mother had just finished commenting on how God and her church have been important sources of support for her when the telephone rang. At the other end was the familiar voice of my supervisor saying, "Get your client off of the God-thing . . . he is much too big for our counseling room." Religion, counseling, and psychology had been at odds for many years.

Recently, though, spirituality and religion in counseling have made a significant comeback. Take a glance through the local bookstore and you will discover numerous titles relating spiritual concepts and practices to the enhancement of personal well-being. This is expressed in several ways in the professional literature. First, the counseling profession recognizes spirituality as an integral aspect of the whole person. In fact, spirituality has been viewed as "the core characteristic of healthy people" and "the source for all other dimensions of wellness" (Myers, Sweeney, & Witmer, 2000, p. 253). Thus, it is central to our understanding of the mentally healthy person. Furthermore, the spiritual and religious dimensions can have either beneficial or negative repercussions in one's life (Kelly, 1995). Thus, mental health and community counselors must be sensitive to the developmental issues that spiritual and religious content/processes carry in the lives of clients.

Second, counselors' increased appreciation for social and cultural diversity includes being sensitive to the religious and spiritual practices of their clients. It is critical that counselors understand the great diversity that exists within specific religious groups. For example, persons practicing Christian, Jewish, and Islam religions vary greatly in matters of faith and practice. Consider Christianity. Distinctions can be made on the basis of the following dimensions: Catholic versus Protestant; denominational affiliation; frequency of attendance; or religious orientation. In applying theory and techniques, mental health and community counselors must be careful not to err by taking a "one size fits all" approach toward their treatment. Recently, numerous approaches have been developed to assist counselors in assessing the manner in which dimensions of spirituality and religiousness are expressed in their clients (Sherman & Simonton, 2001).

Third, many counselors are integrating spiritual and religious concepts and techniques into their counseling interventions. For example, a review of the counseling literature reveals numerous efforts of integrating religious beliefs with traditional counseling theory. For example, Polanski (2002) has found that Christian and Buddist spiritual beliefs can be readily integrated into an Adlerian stance. Applicable Adlerian concepts include inferiority, striving for superiority, social interest, and lifestyle. Nielsen (1994) discusses how religious doctrine and biblical scripture can actually enhance and accelerate the impact of rational emotive behavior therapy when working with Christian clients. Gendlin's *focusing* procedure (Gendlin, 1981) can be used to help clients integrate their spiritual experiences into counseling (Hinterkopf, 1994). In addition, counselors are integrating religious beliefs in the treatment of substance abuse (Hanna, 1992) and helping clients cope with chronic illness (Gordon et al., 2002).

BIOLOGICALIZATION OF PSYCHOPATHOLOGY AND HUMAN BEHAVIOR

With recent advances in research technologies, we are gaining greater insight into the physical and neurological foundations of normal and abnormal behavior. All aspects of human behavior, including motives, preferences, emotions, cognitions, and spirituality, are now being explained in biological terms (Newberg, D'Aquili, & Rause, 2001; Williams, 2001). While supporting the mind-body connection, this trend at times seems to trivialize the potency of counseling interventions as it overemphasizes medical interventions to treat emotional and psychological problems. The fast action of psychopharmacological interventions has increasingly become the benchmark in the selection of treatment alternatives. Somehow, taking a pill to find relief from emotional distress can appear more attractive than committing oneself to the difficult tasks that can accompany working through issues in counseling.

The mental health counseling profession has been influenced by the biologicalization of mental health in a number of ways. For example, many formal structures and processes that affect professional practice have increased their implicit support of the medical model and clinical diagnosis of presenting conditions. Thus, mental health and community counselors must have good handles on diagnostic and treatment planning processes, including the ability to write adequate goals and objectives that meet the standards of agency and managed care policies. In addition, mental health and community counselors frequently consult with psychiatrists regarding the appropriateness of psychopharmacological interventions. A working knowledge of psychopharmacological agents, indications/contraindications, and potential side effects is necessary to provide useful information to the psychiatrist as well as to monitor client response. Finally, mental health counselors are integrating their increased awareness of the mind-body connection into their professional practices. Mental health interventions may assist clients in coping with physical conditions. Or physically based interventions can be implemented as part of comprehensive treatment plans to treat emotional disorders or enhance mental health. For example, Degges-White, Myers, Adelman, and Pastoor (2003) describe the application of cognitive-behavioral interventions in the management of migraine headaches. Other counselors, working from a wellness framework, have used physical exercise as a counseling intervention in working with self-esteem and locus of control issues (Okonski, 2003).

THE CONTEMPORARY ECONOMIC CONTEXT

One of the most significant trends influencing the development and application of theory concerns the economic context in which counseling services are delivered (Polkinghorne, 2001). Into the second half of the 1900s, the delivery of counseling services was primarily one to one, office based, with no restrictions on the number of sessions. The severely disordered were treated in publicly funded institutions.

Over the last four decades, though, the costs for health care (and mental health care in particular) have increased dramatically. Staton (2000) notes that the aggregate cost of treating mental illness and substance abuse in the United States ranks third among disease categories, behind heart disease and injury/trauma. Costs for mental health care are higher than many payers are able, or willing, to pay. Federal and state budget cutbacks have resulted in limited funding for mental health programs. At a time when mental health and community counselors are asserting their legitimate right to be service providers, they are experiencing increased competition for limited mental health funding with members of the allied mental health professions (Kelly, 1996).

To remain viable as a profession, all mental health practitioners and the agencies they serve are asked questions such as, What theory and set of techniques works best and for whom? How many sessions are required to treat this specific condition? Can you demonstrate the necessity of each session? Are you using a form of treatment that has demonstrated efficacy for the specific presenting problem? Thus, the contemporary economic environment demands increased validation and accountability from counseling theories and their application.

These pressures have led to efforts to bring greater definition and control to the application of counseling theories through the creation of practice guidelines and treatment manuals (Erskine, 1998). Generally, such guidelines and protocols identify conditions in which a specific approach is the treatment of choice and then go on to specify frequency, duration, objectives, and method of determining outcome. Hershenson (1992) recommends that the theory base for mental health counseling must include empirically validated interventions, with an emphasis on existing theories that have established efficacy in helping clients cope with specifically defined problems of living.

Unfortunately, the use of treatment manuals places restrictions on the extent to which treatment plans can be derived through interactions taking place in a collaborative counseling relationship. This is especially problematic for mental health and community counselors because the reviews of the counseling literature consistently reveal that the counselor-counselee relationship is one of the most important factors in determining successful outcomes (Walborn, 1996). Thus, an important counseling skill in the current treatment environment is the ability to negotiate a workable treatment regimen in limited timeframes, within the context of a warm, supportive, and collaborative counseling relationship.

TECHNOLOGICAL ADVANCES

In the early 1980s, I typed my master's thesis on an electronic typewriter and calculated many of the statistical tests using a hand-held calculator. Page by page, I leafed through psychological abstracts in search of articles for my review of the literature. Soon afterward, I found employment as a licensed professional counselor in Ohio, where I communicated my progress notes to the secretary via a dictaphone. She would then listen to my mutterings contained on the cassette tape and type each entry onto the appropriate form. By 1991, I was able to write my doctoral dissertation on my desktop computer, and I used SPSS on the university-based computer for the statistical analysis. I kept the U.S. Postal Service in business by regularly using overnight delivery to relay the most recent drafts to my committee chairperson. Today, I have access to SPSS on my desktop computer, carry around a laptop when I am "writing on the run," search for the pertinent professional literature by conducting detailed searches of databases in mere minutes without leaving the confines of my office, and distribute drafts of this text to readers and editors as attachments to e-mail messages.

In recent years, computers and the capability to transfer information electronically have revolutionized our profession. The applications of such technology are too numerous to mention. But clearly, the mental health counseling profession has fully entered the era of electronic information transmission. For example, Riemer-Reiss (2000) notes the usefulness of e-mail systems for the delivery of mental health counseling services. Telecounseling can assist in connecting underserved clients with needed or desired services. Distance individual and group counseling can take place in Internet-based chat rooms and are potentially conducive to openness and honesty in a less threatening environment than traditional service settings (Ancis, 1998). Consumers have increased access to a wide array of online mental health–related resources (Kreutzer, West, Sherron, Wehman, & Fry, 1992) and counselors play a critical role in directing clients to credible sources of information. Employee assistance and psychoeducational programming on topics such as stress management, eating disorders, depression, or parenting skill training can be delivered to persons who might not otherwise take advantage of traditional services (Onstad, & Banks, 1997). Video conferencing is being used to conduct supervision of practicum and internship students across international borders (Panos, Panos, Cox, Roby, & Matheson, 2002).

A recent online survey revealed the ways in which practicing psychologists aged 40 years and younger use technology in their professional practice (American Psychological Association, 2002). The respondents reported using technology in the following ways:

- 92% search for relevant information
- 89% use e-mail
- 79% subscribe to news/updates
- 78% purchase materials online

In addition, 77% of respondents reported that they go online at least once a day.

In light of the utility of technological resources for counselors, the American Counselor Education and Supervisor's Technology Interest Network developed a set of competencies that counselor education students should have upon graduation (Myers & Gibson, 1999):

- Help clients search for various types of counseling-related information.
- Use computerized testing, diagnostic, and career decision-making programs with clients.
- Possess knowledge of the strengths and weaknesses of counseling services provided via the Internet.
- Understand the legal and ethical issues that relate to Internet-based counseling services.
- Use the Internet to locate and participate in continuing education opportunities.

Recognizing the trend of using electronic communications, the ACA put forth *Ethical Standards for Internet On-Line Counseling* (American Counseling Association, 1999). In addition, these concerns and related ethical principles are addressed in the ACA *Code of Ethics* (American Counseling Association, 2005). These standards lay out principles to ensure that counselors protect the privacy of those they serve and secure privacy in the storage and transfer of client information. In addition, special precautions are identified to address informed consent, assessment, treatment planning, implementation, and counselor competency concerns. Mental health and community counselors must also have a working knowledge of new federal regulations, such as the Health Insurance Portability and Accountability Act (HIPAA), that require standard formatting of electronic transmissions to ensure the privacy and security of client-related information. HIPAA has set mandatory standards that mental health practitioners must adhere to.

CONCLUSION

As mental health and community counselors, we have the privilege of helping our clients through difficult times and attain improved mental health and interpersonal relationships. Typically, they turn to us after having found self-effort and the advice of others unhelpful. We look to our theories of counseling for guidelines on how to proceed as we attempt to facilitate positive change in the lives of our clients.

You may now feel inundated and overwhelmed by the vast array of counseling theories presented in chapters 3 and 4. On the one hand, you have so many theoretical options from which to choose. On the other hand, clients present with such diverse problems and backgrounds. How do counselors select a theoretical perspective that they call their own? How do counselors manage to relate theory to practice?

Prochaska and Norcross (1999) note that the majority of counselors do not hold to a single theoretical position but are eclectic in practice. The term *eclecticism* refers to the use of a wide variety of theories and techniques, sometimes in combination, so that treatment is tailored to best fit the specific needs of the client (Slife & Reber, 2001). Beginning counselors, though, need to proceed with caution before they jump onto this bandwagon. First, it is too easy for professionals to use the term *eclecticism* to mask what is more accurately described as being "jacks of all trades, masters of none." The worst-case scenario is the misapplication of theory where clients are actually harmed. Second, without a firm grasp of specific theories, a quasi-eclectic may blend a variety of concepts and principles in such a way that results in fuzzy conceptualizations and incoherent treatment plans.

Your selection of a theoretical stance must consider not only the needs of the client but also your personality style and values. As noted in the previous chapter, you will impede your therapeutic effectiveness if you choose a stance that does not fit who you are as a person. Avoid yielding to the pressure of identifying a theoretical perspective prematurely. Give yourself time to try several on for size as you engage in your practicum and internship. You will initially gravitate toward those that fit well with your implicit theories. But also be aware of the goodness of fit between the theory and the ecological context (e.g., mission, policies, and culture of your agency; needs and cultural background of your client/system). Seek out the best supervision available. Finally, be open to new information and be willing to experiment.

It is likely that a particular theoretical orientation will rise to the surface. I suggest that you select that approach as a theoretical base of operations. Become very good at its application. Then begin to integrate one or two other approaches at those times when their application is clinically justified. This will help to enlarge and enhance your theoretical foundation. Developing your personal theory takes time. Be patient with the process.

DISCUSSION QUESTIONS

1. In chapter 3, the characteristics of good theories were listed. Discuss the extent to which the theories discussed in chapter 4 actually meet these standards. For example, do the major traditional theories, such as psychoanalytic, Adlerian, or cognitive-behavioral theory, enable counselors to adequately describe, explain, predict, and facilitate change?

2. The theories described in this chapter vary in the extent to which they are precise, comprehensive, testable, and useful (see chapter 3 for discussion of these criteria). To what extent do the theories described in this chapter meet the criteria?

3. Identify several theories described in this chapter that fit best with your implicit theory of counseling. Discuss why you might gravitate to certain theories rather than others. Consider your personal values and worldviews.

4. Do you believe it is important to consider and utilize issues of spirituality in mental health and community counseling? Cite several examples of how clients might benefit from such a focus. What cautions should the counselor be mindful of when integrating spirituality into the process of doing counseling?

SUGGESTED ACTIVITIES

1. Read the biographies or autobiographies of several theorists. Identify the ways in which their personal life experiences and values might have influenced the theories they developed.

2. Identify and explore several specific applications of computer technology in counseling. What are the potential strengths and weaknesses in such applications? To what extent do you possess the necessary knowledge and skills to use computer applications in your counseling practice? How might you upgrade your skills if necessary?

3. Ask several mental health professionals to discuss the ways in which their practice has been influenced by the increased biologicalization of mental illness and its treatment. For example, has increased reliance on medication altered the role of traditional counseling interventions in treatment plans? Or has a shift in the roles of case managers, master's-level counselors, and psychologists changed?

4. Survey a sample of mental health and community counselors, social workers, and psychologists working in counseling settings. Determine which of the traditional and contemporary theories they find most useful in their professional practice. Are there significant differences in theory preference based on professional group or work setting? Do the practitioners see specific strengths and limitations in their application of traditional theories in contemporary treatment environments?

Part 2

The Credentialing and Practice of Mental Health and Community Counseling

5

Education, Licensure, and Certification

So you want to be a licensed professional or mental health counselor. What a great vocational choice. You can already envision the setting of your practice and the clientele you will serve.

For most of you, two important hurdles lay between your present status and the ability to practice independently—training and licensure. These are not inconsequential. Academic training entails earning a graduate degree in counseling. With diploma in hand, you then engage in professional practice under the supervision of a qualified mental health professional. Upon working the appropriate number of hours under qualified supervision, you have only one major hurdle to cross—passing the licensure exam. After passing the exam, you enter the "promised land".

This chapter discusses the important topics of academic preparation, licensure, and certification. First, the chapter explores the training model for mental health and community counselors set forth by CACREP. The model's components provide a solid foundation of knowledge and skills for entry-level practitioners. The chapter then discusses the licensure and certification processes. Through these processes, CACREP and the individual states are able to regulate the mental health counseling profession.

Ideally, licensure and certification rest on an interactive dynamic among professional practice, the training model, and professional identity. Figure 5.1 presents this complex relationship.

FIGURE 5.1 Interaction of Practice, Training Model, and Professional Identity

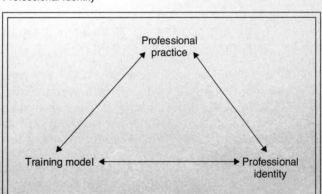

Mental health and community counselors perform specific tasks in a variety of occupational settings. In these settings, they work alongside other mental health and human service professionals. Mental health and community counselors exist as a professional group because they bring to the table a unique perspective and contribution to the treatment process. Their training model provides students with working knowledge and skills that set them apart from those trained in social work, psychology, or marriage and family therapy programs. In addition, the training model stays within the boundaries of the definition of the profession while being responsive to client and community needs in the ever-changing ecological context of service provision. The viability and vitality of the mental health counseling profession are ensured to the extent that licensure reflects the unique training and contributions of licensees relative to members of the allied mental health professions.

Licensure and certification, then, reflect the professional identity, training, and practice of mental health and community counselors.

ACADEMIC PREPARATION OF MENTAL HEALTH AND COMMUNITY COUNSELORS

Numerous paths are available for persons seeking to pursue training and licensure in counseling-related professions. In fact, Hollis and Dodson (2000) note that 542 departments of higher education presently offer one or more programs in counselor preparation. These represent a vast array of counseling-related professions and specializations. The primary professional organizations, such as ACA, APA, AAMFT, or NASW, have established accrediting bodies that set national standards of academic preparation by which the relative merits of specific training programs can be evaluated. Specialized accreditation is a voluntary process in which academic programs demonstrate that their curriculum, department, faculty and staff, and institution meet high professional standards. The national standards for the training of mental health and community counselors are established by CACREP, which is the largest specialized accreditation body for graduate programs in counseling.

THE CACREP MODEL OF TRAINING FOR MENTAL HEALTH AND COMMUNITY COUNSELORS

A brief history and description of CACREP was given in chapter 1 of this text. As you may recall, CACREP is the accrediting arm of the ACA. Its mission is to develop, implement, and maintain national standards of preparation for graduate programs in counseling (CACREP, 2001). The standards are established to ensure that "students develop a professional counselor identity and also master the knowledge and skills to practice effectively" (p. 55).

CACREP sets standards for and renders accreditation decisions on the following counseling programs: career; college; community; gerontological; marital, couple, and family; mental health; school; student affairs; and counselor education and supervision (doctoral level only). The standards assess the overall quality of the academic institution, its administrative structure and organization; program objectives and curriculum; clinical instruction; faculty and staff; program organization and administration; and evaluation procedures.

The general curricular model established by CACREP consists of three general components: a common core curriculum, standards for the specializations, and clinical experiences. Figure 5.2 illustrates the general design of graduate training programs for mental health and community counselors that follow the CACREP model.

The categorization of curriculum leaves the false impression that the content areas are encased in specific courses. This is not necessarily the case. Instead, the CACREP model takes an infusion approach that integrates contents of core areas throughout the curriculum rather than compartmentalizing it in unique courses. Thus, for example, instruction in the core area of assessment occurs not only in the assessment course but in other courses, such as human development, research and program evaluation, psychopathology, and practicum/internship. As a result, students gain exposure to core contents in a variety of courses throughout their academic program.

FIGURE 5.2 The General Curricular Model of CACREP

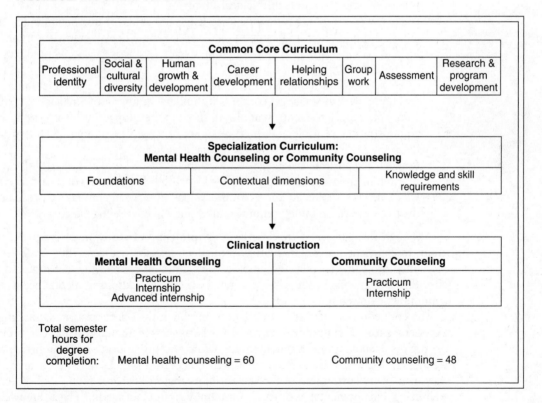

Common Core Curriculum

Professional identity	Social & cultural diversity	Human growth & development	Career development	Helping relationships	Group work	Assessment	Research & program development

Specialization Curriculum: Mental Health Counseling or Community Counseling

Foundations	Contextual dimensions	Knowledge and skill requirements

Clinical Instruction

Mental Health Counseling	Community Counseling
Practicum Internship Advanced internship	Practicum Internship

Total semester hours for degree completion: Mental health counseling = 60   Community counseling = 48

Common Core Curriculum.   It is vital that all counselors possess specific knowledge and skills regardless of specialization. Thus, CACREP has identified eight common core areas of study that are required of all students in counseling programs (CACREP, 2001).

- *Professional identity*—Studies that provide an understanding of the history and philosophy of the counseling profession, professional roles and functions, organizations and credentialing, advocacy process, and ethical standards.
- *Social and cultural diversity*—Curricular experiences in which students gain an understanding of multicultural contexts and trends; issues, strategies, and theories for working with culturally diverse individuals, groups, and families; ethical and legal issues; and social justice and advocacy skills.
- *Human growth and development*—Studies focusing on the nature and processes of physical, cognitive, socioemotional, and family development across the lifespan; normal and abnormal human behavior; exceptionality; and strategies for enhancing optimal development.
- *Career development*—Studies that explore career selection, decision making, and development; and career assessment guidance and counseling (including technology-based approaches).
- *Helping relationships*—Studies that provide knowledge and skills of counseling and consultation processes such as predominant models of counseling; counselor/counselee characteristics and relationships; interviewing and counseling skill development; and technological strategies.
- *Group work*—Studies that provide knowledge and skills for understanding, facilitating, and providing leadership in the development and evaluation of various forms of group work; principles of group dynamics, theories, and techniques; and ethical and legal issues.
- *Assessment*—Studies that provide knowledge of the theories, principles, and psychometric and statistical concepts for understanding individual and group approaches to assessment. In addition, skills are developed in the selection, administration, scoring, and interpretation of a variety of standardized, nonstandardized, and computer-assisted assessment devices.
- *Research and program evaluation*—Studies that provide knowledge and skills in research methodology, statistical analysis (including application of statistical software), needs assessment, and program evaluation. Special emphasis is placed on the role of research in determining and improving counseling effectiveness.

Although the categories are described as core areas of study, most graduate programs in counseling organize them as content for specific courses. Thus, a survey of accredited programs reveals a common set of eight core courses that are required for all students in graduate counseling programs with specializations in mental health and community counseling.

The core courses provide a foundation on which the specializations and clinical experiences rest. Through these curricular experiences, mental health and community counselors become knowledgeable in the nature and promotion of mental health and wellness and as well as the assessment and treatment of emotional disorder. In addition, they gain an understanding of the social factors that influence personal and systemic well-being. Finally, mental health and community counselors acquire a basic knowledge of what it means to be a licensed mental health or professional counselor by becoming familiar with their professional associations, codes of ethics, and standards of preparation, licensure, and certification.

STANDARDS FOR MENTAL HEALTH AND COMMUNITY COUNSELING PROGRAMS

In addition to taking coursework covering the eight core curricular areas, mental health and community counseling students are required to have additional academic experiences that cover critical areas of their respective specializations. The standards for mental health counseling programs are listed in Figure 5.3. Overall, students in mental health counseling programs are required to complete a minimum of 60 semester credit hours of study. This includes coursework in the core, specialization, and clinical areas.

FIGURE 5.3

Standards for Mental Health Counseling Programs

FOUNDATIONS OF MENTAL HEATLH COUNSELING

1. Historical, philosophical, societal, cultural, economic, and political dimensions of and current trends in mental health counseling;
2. Roles, functions, and professional identity of mental health counselors;
3. Structures and operations of professional organizations, preparation standards, credentialing bodies, and public policy issues relevant to the practice of mental health counseling;
4. Implications of professional issues that are unique to mental health counseling, including recognition, reimbursement, right to practice, core provider status, access to and practice privileges within managed care systems, and expert witness status;
5. Ethical and legal considerations related to the practice of mental health counseling (e.g., the *ACA Code of Ethics* and *AMHCA Code of Ethics*); and
6. The role of racial, ethnic, and cultural heritage, nationality, socioeconomic status, family structure, age, gender, sexual orientation, religious and spiritual beliefs, occupation, and physical and mental status, and equity issues in mental health counseling.

CONTEXTUAL DIMENSIONS OF MENTAL HEALTH COUNSELING

1. Assumptions and roles of mental health counseling within the context of the community and its health and human services systems, including functions and relationships among interdisciplinary treatment teams, and the historical, organizational, legal, and fiscal dimensions of public and private mental health care systems;
2. Strategies for community needs assessment to design, implement, and evaluate mental health care programs and systems;
3. Principles, theories, and practices of community intervention, including programs and facilities for inpatient, outpatient, partial treatment, and aftercare, and the human services network in local communities; and

FIGURE 5.3

(Continued)

4. Management of mental health services and programs, including administration, finance, and budgeting, in the public and private sectors; principles and practices for establishing and maintaining both independent and group private practice; and concepts and procedures for determining outcomes, accountability, and cost containment.

KNOWLEDGE AND SKILL REQUIREMENTS FOR MENTAL HEALTH COUNSELORS

1. General principles and practices of etiology, diagnosis, treatment, referral, and prevention of mental and emotional disorders and dysfunctional behavior, including addictive behaviors;
2. General principles and practices for the promotion of optimal human development and mental health;
3. Specific principles and models of biopsychosocial assessment, case conceptualization, and theories of human development and concepts psychopathology leading to diagnoses and appropriate treatment plans;
4. Knowledge of the principles of diagnosis and the use of current diagnostic tools, including the current *Diagnostic and Statistical Manual*;
5. Application of modalities for initiating, maintaining, and terminating counseling and psychotherapy with mentally and emotionally impaired clients, including the use of crisis intervention and brief, intermediate, and long-term approaches;
6. Basic classifications, indications, and contraindications of commonly prescribed psychopharmacological medications so that appropriate referrals can be made for medication evaluations and identifying effects and side effects of such medications;
7. Principles and guidelines of conducting an intake interview, a mental status evaluation, a biopsychosocial history, a mental health history, and a psychological assessment for treatment planning and caseload management;
8. Knowledge and provision of clinical supervision, including counselor development;
9. The application of concepts of mental health education, consultation, collaboration, outreach and prevention strategies, and community mental health advocacy; and
10. Effective strategies for influencing public policy and government relations on local, state, and national levels to enhance funding and programs that affect mental health services in general and the practice of mental health counseling in particular.

CLINICAL INSTRUCTION

For the mental health counseling program, the 600-clock-hour internship occurs in a mental health setting. The requirement includes a minimum of 240 direct service clock hours. Beyond these 600 clock hours, the mental health counseling program requires an additional 300 clock hours of internship in a mental health setting under the appropriate clinical supervision of a site supervisor as defined above. This requirement includes a minimum of 120 direct service clock hours. Therefore, the total requirement for mental health counseling internship is a minimum of 900 clock hours of supervised experience in an appropriate setting, which includes a minimum of 360 direct service hours.

Note: From "CACREP Accreditation Manual of the Council for Accreditation of Counseling and Related Educational Programs" (pp. 89–91) by CACREP, 2001, Alexandria, VA: CACREP. Copyright 2001 by CACREP. Reprinted by permission.

Standards for community counseling programs are listed in Figure 5.4. Overall, students in community counseling specializations complete a minimum of 48 semester credit hours of study, which also includes the core, specialization, and clinical areas.

FIGURE 5.4 Standards for Community Counseling Programs	**FOUNDATIONS OF COMMUNITY COUNSELING** 1. Historical, philosophical, societal, cultural, economic, and political dimensions of and current trends in the community human service/mental health movement; 2. Roles, functions, preparation standards, credentialing, licensure and professional identity of community counselors; 3. Policies, laws, legislation, recognition, reimbursement, right to practice, and other issues relevant to counseling; 4. Ethical and legal considerations specifically related to the practice of community counseling (e.g., the *ACA Code of Ethics*); and 5. The role of racial, ethnic, and cultural heritage, nationality, socioeconomic status, family structure, age, gender, sexual orientation, religious and spiritual beliefs, occupation, and physical and mental status, and equity issues in community counseling. **CONTEXTUAL DIMENSIONS OF COMMUNITY COUNSELING** 1. The roles of community counselors in various practice settings and the relationships between counselors and other professional in these settings; 2. Organizational, fiscal, and legal dimensions of the institutions and settings in which community counselors practice; 3. Strategies for community needs assessment to design, implement, and evaluate community counseling interventions, programs and systems; and 4. General principles of community intervention, consultation, education, and outreach; and characteristics of human services programs and networks (public, private, and volunteer) in local communities. **KNOWLEDGE AND SKILL REQUIREMENTS FOR COMMUNITY COUNSELORS** 1. Typical characteristics of individuals and communities served by a variety of institutions and agencies that offer community counseling services; 2. Models, methods, and principles of program development and service delivery for a clientele based on assumptions of human and organizational development, including prevention, implementation of support groups, peer facilitation training, parent education, career/occupational information and counseling, and encouragement of self-help; 3. Effective strategies for promoting client understanding of and access to community resources; 4. Principles and models of biopsychosocial assessment, case conceptualization, theories of human development and concepts of normalcy and psychopathology leading to diagnoses and appropriate counseling plans;

FIGURE 5.4

(Continued)

5. Knowledge of the principles of diagnosis and the use of current diagnostic tools, including the current edition of the *Diagnostic* and *Statistical Manual;*
6. Effective strategies for client advocacy in public policy and other matters of equity and accessibility; and
7. Application of appropriate individual, couple, family, group, and systems modalities for initiating, maintaining, and terminating counseling, including the use of crisis intervention and brief, intermediate, and long-term approaches.

CLINICAL INSTRUCTION

For the community counseling program, the 600-clock-hour internship occurs in a community setting, under the clinical supervision of a site supervisor. The requirement includes a minimum of 240 direct service clock hours.

Note: From "CACREP Accreditation Manual of the Council for Accreditation of Counseling and Related Educational Programs" (pp. 82–83) by CACREP, 2001, Alexandria, VA: CACREP. Copyright 2001 by CACREP. Reprinted by permission.

As you can see, each set of standards consists of four general components: foundations, contextual dimensions, knowledge and skill requirements, and clinical instruction. Significant areas of overlap in these respective sets of standards are apparent. Although important differences in the foundations can be identified, particularly in the development and history of mental health and community counseling, the foundations share common elements:

- roles and functions
- preparation standards for licensure
- ethical and legal concerns

Historically, mental health counselors have shown greater interest in issues pertaining to third-party reimbursement, right to practice, and core provider status. However, with the increased emphasis on licensure, community counselors share these concerns as they, too, advocate for increased privilege for licensed mental health and professional counselors.

Similar differences can be noted between the specialization standards related to *contextual dimensions* of mental health and community counseling programs. The contextual dimensions of mental health counseling build on the standards set for community counseling programs by adding increased emphasis on the human service continuum of care network in communities. In addition, mental health counseling programs offer increased attention to the management of services and programs. Although such differences are apparent in a reading of the CACREP standards, such differences are much less visible in practice. Again, as mental health and community counseling programs prepare students for state licensure, the boundary between specializations blurs. Students trained in either specialization may pursue direct service or administrative roles in a variety of settings across the continuum of care.

The list of standards for *knowledge and skill requirements* for mental health counselors is more extensive and clinical in orientation. A more in-depth focus on assessment, diagnosis, and treatment of mental illness, including psychopharmacological interventions, is required. In addition, mental health counselors receive instruction and skills training in clinical supervision and counselor development. In contrast, the knowledge and skill requirements for community counselors emphasize detailed understanding of community-based resources and programs, program development, and service delivery. Both specializations require training in the principles of assessment and diagnosis, using standard criteria contained in the current edition of the *Diagnostic and Statistical Manual* (i.e., *Diagnostic and Statistical Manual*, 4th-edition-Text Revision [*DSM-IV-TR*]).

The clinical training of mental health and community counselors is the most important component of academic preparation. It is in the applied, practical setting that classroom learning takes on a face of reality. Increasingly, counselor education programs are integrating hands-on counseling experience throughout their curriculum. By trying on the counseling role, students can better assess their "goodness of fit" with the profession.

Two types of clinical experience are required—practicum and internship. For both mental health and community counseling programs, the requirements for practicum include

- a minimum of 100 clock hours in an appropriate setting;
- at least 40 hours of direct service to clients, including experience in individual and group counseling;
- an average of one hour weekly individual or triadic supervision, typically provided by a program faculty member or a person supervised by a program faculty person;
- an average of one and one-half hours of group supervision, again, typically provided by faculty members or supervisors under the supervision of the faculty; and
- site supervisors must have a minimum of a master's degree in counseling or a related profession, have at least 2 years of experience, and hold appropriate licenses or certifications.

Both programs require a supervised internship of 600 hours that can begin following the successful completion of the student's practicum. Frequently, the internship serves as a capstone for the student's graduate program. It is here where students have the opportunity to pull together all components of their previous graduate training experiences and experience the joys and frustrations of professional life firsthand. To have an optimal training experience, students should take the time and energy necessary to identify internship settings and supervisors that will promote their personal and professional development. Many students find internships to be the most critical and exhilarating learning experience of their programs.

The requirements for the internship include

- 240 hours of direct service with appropriate clientele;
- weekly 1-hour sessions of individual or triadic supervision, typically conducted by the site supervisor;
- weekly 1.5-hour supervisory sessions, typically conducted by program faculty; and
- site supervisors must have master's degrees in counseling or a related discipline, have at least 2 years of experience, and hold appropriate licenses or certifications.

Students in the mental health counseling specialization take an advanced internship, which requires an additional 300 clock hours. Within these, a minimum of 120 hours involves direct service to clients. Thus, for mental health counselors, a total of 900 hours is required for successful completion of the internship requirements.

Few studies have investigated the impact or benefits of receiving counselor education from a CACREP-approved program (Schmidt, 1999). Vacc and Loesch (2000), though, note several positive consequences that result from graduating from such programs. First, the inherent strength of a program is communicated by its accreditation relative to programs that have not attained or attempted to achieve accreditation. Second, graduates from CACREP-approved programs are increasingly provided advantages when seeking counselor-related credentials. For example, the processing of state licensure applications may be expedited when the academic program is CACREP accredited. In addition, graduates from CACREP-approved programs can sit for the National Certification Exam (NCE) prior to completion of their postgraduate supervised experience. Thus, with passing scores on the NCE, students are eligible for certification pending completion of the other requirements.

THE CREDENTIALING OF MENTAL HEALTH AND COMMUNITY COUNSELORS

Credentialing is a process that takes place following successful completion of the appropriate academic program. Since holding proper credentials is critical to being able to practice in the profession, it is important that students entering in mental health and community counseling programs determine that the curriculum offered by the program fulfills the academic requirements of the relevant credentialing bodies.

Sweeney (1995) defines *credentialing* as an approach that identifies individuals by professional group. Three basic methods are used: registry, certification, and licensure. Of these, *registry* is the simplest and least restrictive method. Being listed on a registry is often accomplished by simply providing the necessary information and paying a small fee. Although it is least useful in regulating the profession, being listed on a registry can provide useful information for consumers and professionals seeking to make referrals.

Certification, generally speaking, is a credentialing process by which a specific group or profession seeks to set standards to ensure quality within itself. Sweeney (1995) defines certification as a process of verifying the truth of individuals' assertion of qualification as professional counselors. Thus, counselors who are certified have gone through a voluntary process to confirm that they meet or exceed the minimum standards for practice as set by the profession. Certification restricts use of the professional title to those who have met the established standards but does not regulate, govern, or ensure the quality of professional practice.

Various types of certification are available to mental health and community counselors. The most visible and highly recognized counselor certifications are issued by the

National Board of Certified Counselors (NBCC) (Hollis, 2000). Established in 1982, the NBCC offers both general practice and specialty certifications. The National Certified Counselor (NCC) credential is the general practice credential that signifies that practitioners have met specified requirements in training, experience, and performance (Gladding & Newsome, 2004). These include possession of a graduate degree in counseling of at least 48 semester hours, completion of coursework that reflects the CACREP core content, and postgraduate clinical experience of at least 3,000 hours and/or 100 hours of face-to-face supervision over at least two years since graduation (National Board of Certified Counselors, n.d.). In addition, applicants are required to attain a passing score on the NCE, a comprehensive exam consisting of 200 multiple choice questions covering the eight CACREP core content areas and an additional five work behavior areas: fundamentals of counseling, assessment and career counseling, group counseling, programmatic and clinical intervention, and professional practice issues.

Qualified mental health and community counselors who have attained the NCC may seek specialty certification as CCMHCs or MACs. The CCMHC was established by the AMHCA and was merged with NBCC in 1992 (Sweeney, 1995). In addition to holding the NCC, professionals seeking the CCMHC must demonstrate the following:

- Sixty hours of graduate coursework including theories of counseling, psychotherapy, and personality; abnormal psychology and psychopathology; human growth and development; professional orientation and ethics for counselors; research; appraisal; and social/cultural foundations;
- An academic program of study that included 9 to 15 semester hours of clinical training in supervised practica/internships in settings relevant to the practice of mental health counseling;
- A passing score on the Examination of Clinical Counseling Practice (ECCP). This exam presents examinees with 10 clinical vignettes typically encountered by mental health counselors and assesses the counselor's ability to apply knowledge and skills in diagnosis, treatment, evaluation, and other pertinent professional areas;
- Submission of an audio- or videotape of a clinical counseling session for review following the successful passing of the ECCP.

The MAC is a certification for counselors specializing in the treatment of substance abuse and dependence. In addition to the NCC certification, counselors seeking the MAC credential must be able to document a minimum of 12 semester hours of graduate credit in the area of addictions *or* 500 hours of continuing education units, 3 years of supervised experience as an addiction counselor (with no fewer than 20 hours per week and 2 of the 3 years completed after the master's degree was conferred), and a passing score on the Examination for Master Addiction Counselors (EMAC). Many mental health and community counselors work in addiction settings and find the MAC to be a relevant certification option.

In contrast, *licensure* is a statutory process whereby the state regulates the counseling profession. Thus, licensure is a legal process and may regulate the use of the professional title (e.g., licensed mental health counselor, licensed professional counselor, etc.) and/or the practice of the profession (i.e., an identified scope of practice that is limited to those professionals holding the counselor license). A mental health or community counselor who is licensed can legally use the specific professional title used in that state and engage in the activities of the profession as defined by the law. Licensure is viewed as the most desirable form of state regulation of a profession because it demarcates the uniqueness of the profession and regulates both the use of the title and the practice of the profession (Corey, Corey, & Callanan, 2003).

Counselor licensure laws typically share several general components. First, the law contains several legal definitions relevant to the licensed profession. For example, basic concepts of the profession, such as *appraisal, counseling, professional counseling, counselor, mental health counselor,* and *the practice of mental health counseling* may be defined in very specific terms in state statutes. It is important that licensed mental health and professional counselors understand and practice within legal definitions of *appraisal* and not go beyond their scope of practice.

Second, state licensure laws establish a licensure board and set rules regarding its structure and responsibilities. The responsibilities of a licensure board include the development of administrative rules regarding professional practice, application for and renewal of licenses, approval of continuing education providers, administration of licensure exams, and enforcement of the ethics code. A list of the state licensure boards for mental health and licensed professional counselors is found in Appendix B.

Third, the law specifies the precise requirements of licensure within the particular state. This includes requirements for education, clinical experience and supervision, examination of applicants, continuing education, and licensure fees. Although many requirements for licensure are shared among states, a variety of specific requirements vary from state to state. For example, the official professional titles used vary among states. Although the majority of states use the title of licensed professional counselor (LPC), others have chosen variants of the mental health counseling designation (e.g., LMHC, LPC-MH, CCH, or LCMHC). In addition, certain states require graduate programs of 48 semester hours whereas other states require 60 semester hours of graduate training in counseling. Furthermore, the number of required hours of practicum/internship clinical experience and postgraduate supervised experience differs. Even the criteria for determining acceptable supervision and the number of supervision hours varies.

Thus, it is highly recommended that students closely study the licensure laws of the state in which they desire to practice. It is vital that students enroll in or construct for themselves programs of study containing academic and clinical experiences that meet the specific state licensure requirements. Too often, I have been approached by persons who have graduated from well-respected programs in counselor education who discovered after graduation that the state in which they desired to practice had set requirements that their academic program did not fulfill. These are often the very fine points that are easily overlooked by the counselor trainee. Faculty advisors and specialization coordinators can assist students in traveling the maze of licensure requirements. But, it is ultimately the responsibility of the student to be aware of the specific requirements of the state in which they desire to practice.

Corey and colleagues (2003) have identified arguments for and against the licensure and certification of counselors. It is generally held that the welfare of consumers is safeguarded more with licensure laws than without them. Professionals are required to demonstrate their ability to work at a specific level of competence and held accountable if they do not. Furthermore, licensure helps to demarcate the various mental health professions, which helps consumers choose the most appropriate practitioner for their specific needs. Also, licensure makes counseling services more accessible because third-party reimbursers tend to cover the fees for services rendered by licensed professionals. Finally, licensure laws enable professions to regulate themselves.

Some, however, question the altruistic motives supporting professional licensure (Corey et al., 2003). They argue that professional licensure is more about protecting the "turf" of a profession and is, therefore, self-serving in nature. Too often, the allied mental health professions are pitted against each other in efforts to protect scope of practice with little or no regard for the needs of consumers. Goldin (1997) conducted a survey of AMHCA branch presidents to assess the level of interprofessional cooperation concerning licensure and found the greatest support for the efforts of the mental health counseling profession came from AAMFT, followed by NASW, American Psychological Association, and the American Psychiatric Association. Interprofessional cooperation is most likely to take place when the respective professional organizations see it as beneficial to their own interests. Furthermore, once legal definitions and scope of practice are in place, the profession becomes less responsive to changes in the socioeconomic-political environment. Thus, the profession becomes less capable of adapting to the changing needs of the clientele and communities it serves.

CONTEMPORARY ISSUES

As noted at the beginning of this chapter, a complex relationship exists among counselors' academic training model, credentialing, and professional practice. This dynamic relationship is seen clearly in several contemporary issues facing the profession, as discussed in this section.

LICENSURE FOR ALL 50 STATES

The journey toward establishing counselor licensure in the United States began in 1976 in Virginia. In little more than a quarter century, the profession has made amazing strides in pushing for and achieving licensure laws in 47 states, Washington, D.C., and Puerto Rico. This is a remarkable feat, especially when contrasted with the longer period of time required to accomplish similar results by social workers and psychologists (Bemak & Espina, 1999).

Obtaining licensure in the remaining states remains a priority for the ACA and AMHCA (Pennington, 2003). Increased recognition occurs as the profession establishes licensure laws, and licensure laws in the remaining two states will further enhance the credibility of the mental health counseling profession. The viability of mental health and professional counselors is increased among mental health colleagues, managed care organizations, and the general public when title and scope of practice receive legal recognition (Bemak & Espina, 1999). Thus, the ACA and AMHCA continue to rally available resources to secure the passage of licensure laws in the remaining states.

CACREP SPECIALIZATIONS AND STATE LICENSURE

The boundary between the CACREP specializations of mental health and community counseling has become increasingly blurred with the current emphasis on state licensure. The history of community and mental health counseling was noted in chapter 2. Given their somewhat unique historical roots, specific sets of specialization standards for each were put forth by CACREP.

However, as noted earlier in this chapter, recent revisions of the CACREP standards for mental health and community counseling specializations show substantial similarity. Over the past several decades, mental health and community counselors have competed for similar job positions in private and public agency settings. Furthermore, upon licensure, graduates from each specialization are capable of working independently in private or small group practices. Licensure laws reflect the generic, rather than specialized nature of the profession. The educational requirements for licensure do not differentiate between the specializations but only cite requirements in terms of required degrees, credit hours, course content, and clinical experiences. Persons trained as either mental health or community counselors can be licensed in any of the 48 states as long as they meet the required educational requirements built into the laws.

The utility of the CACREP distinction between mental health and community counseling specializations is controversial. Are the distinctions so significant that separate areas of specialization are necessary or even useful? Is it truly a difference in specialty or does it have to do with differences in emphasis and orientation? Is the distinction more of a historical artifact reflecting the bureaucratic structures of higher education that hinder programmatic change processes? Or does the distinction reflect the ongoing political sticking points in the relationship between the ACA and AMHCA? Perhaps loyalty to existing training models reflects the training and professional allegiance of counselor educators. Hershenson and Berger (2001) found a split of opinion on whether or not community counseling was a distinct identity and called for active discussion within the area regarding its future direction.

I do not have the answers to these questions. However, I believe that the professional identity and advocacy efforts of the counseling profession suffer to the extent that these issues are allowed to linger.

LICENSURE AND THE LACK OF PROFESSIONAL UNITY

The impact of licensure on the profession has been paradoxical. On the one hand, as noted previously, it has brought mental health and community counselors together as they both seek and qualify for state licensure. On the other hand, licensure is regulated by the state and, as noted earlier, each state has the right to regulate the profession as it chooses. A survey of the various licensure laws reveals numerous state-specific paths by which licensure is obtained. The number of required credit hours of the academic program, as well as clock, direct service, supervision, and postgraduate hours all vary among states. Although passing scores on the NCE or ECCP exams are required in most states, several states have devised their own licensure exams. Furthermore, the professional titles (e.g., licensed professional counselor, licensed mental health counselor, licensed professional counselor of mental health) used vary from state to state. This incoherence contributes to professional identity confusion among students, consumers, the general public, and members of allied mental health professions.

PORTABILITY OF LICENSES

Portability of licenses refers to the ability of professionals to move their licensed status from state to state. The ability of licensed mental health and professional counselors to do so is hindered by the variance in state regulation of the profession. The profession of clinical psychology has moved to implement a system of reciprocity, whereby certain states have negotiated agreements with other states so that the license in one state would be automatically accepted in the other, as long as appropriate fees are paid. In contrast, processes for the portability of mental health and professional counselor licenses and state reciprocity have lagged far behind. However, realization of licensure portability has recently moved closer to reality through the implementation of the American Association of State Counseling Board's (AASCB) National Credential Registry (Williams, 2005).

The right of states to regulate professions reflects the general protection of a state's autonomy relative to the national government and is fundamental to our system of government. Thus, it is unlikely that states will give up this right by passing this responsibility to the federal government. The present situation, though, makes it difficult for licensed practitioners to move from one state to another. As Robert Nielson notes (as cited in Bemak & Espina, 1999), "It is important to honor every state's unique aspect as far as licensure [is concerned], yet still help professionals move from one state to another without having undue [difficulties]."

CONCLUSION

Licensure of mental health and professional counselors has become a reality in most states. Through the hard work of many individuals in cooperation with local, state, and national professional organizations, the profession has, finally, reached professional maturity and attained the recognition that it so deserves. Or has it?

Many LMHCs and LPCs still find themselves picking up the crumbs of the more privileged therapists and clinicians who sit at the table of the allied mental health professions. The high expectation of increased professional recognition that was to come with licensure has been only partially realized. Social workers continue to have an advantage in the job market and in reimbursement from third parties. Furthermore, too often the mental health counseling profession is simply overlooked when consultations regarding state mental health policy take place.

A similar picture emerges when one reviews the existent literature on the impact of counselor licensure. In a survey of 203 directors of mental health agencies in Ohio, it was found that three times as many social workers as counselors were employed (Ritchie, Partin, & Trivette, 1998). Furthermore, the authors found that LPCs were rated highly in their ability to provide counseling services but rated lower in their ability to diagnose or file for third-party reimbursement. The researchers (Ritchie et al., 1998) noted that most of the directors were, themselves, licensed as social workers. Geisler (1995) concluded that licensure was but one step toward gaining professional credibility, and 10 to 15 years beyond the passage of the Michigan licensure law were required for LPCs in that state to achieve a more complete professional recognition. In another study, the public perception of mental health professions was compared (Fall, Levitov, Jennings, & Eberts, 2000). The sample of 190 participants selected social workers most frequently as their choice for provider of mental health services. However, the participants in this study had the least confidence in social workers' ability to successfully treat adjustment disorder, marital problems, psychotic depression, posttraumatic stress disorder, and borderline personality disorder relative to psychologists, psychiatrists, and master's- and doctoral-level professional counselors. In addition, master's-level professional counselors were ranked above psychiatrists and psychologists in perceived ability to treat adjustment disorders and marital problems.

Given the restricted samples used in these studies, caution must be used in attempting to generalize the results. We may conclude, though, that licensure has helped to place the mental health counseling profession as a key player in the field of mental health professions. But the profession has not achieved equal status in the eyes of other professionals or the general public. The strengths of our training model and product (i.e., services provided by mental health and community counselors) continue to be well-kept secrets. Professional excellence and advocacy are the primary tools we must use if we are to receive consistent invitations to sit at the table with, gain a hearing with, and receive respect from the other mental health professions.

DISCUSSION QUESTIONS

1. What do you see as the major distinctions between training as a mental health and community counselor? In your opinion, do the identified differences have important implications when it comes to seeking licensure or employment? Or are the differences in training models historical artifacts that have less relevance in today's era of professional licensure and managed care?

2. As you reflect on the training models for the profession, to what extent do you believe counselors-in-training are able to gain the knowledge and skills necessary to be effective in the contemporary treatment environment?

3. How, specifically, could you use your knowledge of the CACREP model in marketing yourself for professional positions in counseling when competing against social workers, marriage and family therapists, or psychologists?

4. In your opinion, who does professional licensure protect more—consumers of counseling services or the professional rights of the professional relative to the allied professional groups?

SUGGESTED ACTIVITIES

1. Obtain a copy of the counselor licensure law in the state in which you reside or desire to practice. What is the professional title that may be used by licensees in that state? What are the educational, clinical, supervision, and exam requirements that must be fulfilled to become licensed?

2. Compare and contrast the licensure laws between states using the term *licensed professional counselor* and those using *licensed mental health counselor.* What noteworthy similarities and differences can be identified?

3. Compare and contrast the scopes of practice in the licensure laws of licensed professional counselors and licensed clinical social workers in the state in which you reside or desire to practice. What noteworthy similarities and differences can be identified?

4. Find the Web sites for the ACA, AMHCA, and your state professional associations. Toward what specific professional issues related to licensure, professional recognition, and scope of practice are they directing their advocacy efforts? How specifically might you get involved?

Employment Settings: Where Mental Health and Community Counselors Work and What They Do

OUTLINE

As part of the admission process to master of arts in counseling program, prospective students are often required to interview with faculty who teach in their chosen area of specialization. Among other things, it is vital that persons entering into the program know what, specifically, they are getting into because their expectations regarding the nature of the profession often guide their decision to enter one specialization (e.g., mental health counseling) instead of the another (e.g., marriage and family counseling/therapy). So, early in the interview, applicants are posed the question, "What do mental health counselors do?"

The responses I have received to this question reveal certain myths and stereotyped beliefs regarding the profession. Frequently, the applicant responds, "Mental health counselors work with individuals and, primarily, diagnose and treat mental illness. They usually work in an office setting for sessions that are around 50 minutes in length."

Although such responses may be accurate up to a point, they fail to capture the breadth and depth of the mental health and community counselors' scopes of practice. In many ways, the nature of the profession continues to be one of mental health care's best-kept secrets. This chapter considers the dimensions of professional practice by exploring where mental health and community counselors work and what they do. Certainly, no text can provide an exhaustive review of the contemporary work environment. The creativity with which my professional colleagues engage in their professional endeavors knows few boundaries or limitations. I will, therefore, limit the focus to several exemplary roles that will help you grasp the breadth, depth, and significance of the mental health counseling profession. The foundations model presented in chapter 3 will serve as an organizing template to guide this discussion. In this chapter you will catch a glimpse of the exciting possibilities that await as you anticipate professional practice.

APPLICATION OF COMPREHENSIVE MENTAL HEALTH COUNSELING MODEL

In chapter 3, a comprehensive model for mental health and community counseling was presented. The professional practice of mental health and community counseling was described as occurring along three dimensions—mental health/wellness, mental illness/dysfunction, and ecological context. Specifically, all client systems and services provided can be plotted along these interacting dimensions. The model and its application in the mental health service environment reflect the operation of four contemporary trends in the counseling profession (McAuliffe & Eriksen, 1999).

- The move of the primary locus of client issues from the individual to an understanding of the ecological contexts in which all persons are embedded;
- Increased emphasis on strength and development rather than deficits and pathology;
- Increased acceptance of multiple and subjective realities than empirically based objectively defined truth;
- Increased reliance on education and prevention with a decreased emphasis on remediation.

Mental health and community counselors must resist the pressures of the traditional medical model and third-party reimbursers to take a narrow view of professional practice. For example, it is an error to assume that the definition of *client system* is necessarily limited to individuals, groups, and families. Although these are certainly legitimate foci for assessment and intervention, we must be alert to the needs and possibilities of intervention that exist in larger networks such as the extended family, peer group, formal and informal organizational structures and processes, neighborhood, community, subculture, or society. In addition, the model alerts mental health and community counselors to the variety of interactions that suggest involvement of multiple ecological levels actively operating simultaneously in the presenting concerns of clients.

In the context of the comprehensive model, we can see how the vast array of direct and indirect services identified in the community counseling model (Lewis et al., 2003) are fundamental contributions that mental health and community counselors make in their respective service delivery settings. These services seek to promote wellness and treat dysfunction using assessment and intervention strategies that cut across the interacting levels of ecological context.

STAGES OF HELPING

Several primary modalities of intervention used by mental health and community counselors will be discussed in a later section. But regardless of modality used, the people-helping process consists of four primary stages (Cormier & Nurius, 2003):

1. establishing the relationship
2. problem identification, assessment, and goal setting
3. planning of strategy and its implementation
4. evaluation and termination

ESTABLISHING THE RELATIONSHIP

As I noted in chapter 3, many counselors see the therapeutic relationship as being the primary curative factor in the treatment process. Although numerous definitions have been put forth, two fundamental characteristics of effective counseling relationships stand out (Martin, 2000). First, a positive relational bond is developed, characterized by personal warmth, empathy, and acceptance. The effective counselor communicates a focused interest in and acceptance of the client as worthwhile and significant. These elements are communicated from the start by the counselor and become the foundation on which trust and genuine self-disclosure can take place. By using the term *client* in this context, we do not intend to limit our focus to single persons who come in with the presenting problem. Depending on the modality in use, the term *client* may also refer to a family, group, organization, or community. Thus, the term client refers to the specific unit to which the focus of assessment and intervention is directed.

Second, a counseling relationship establishes a mutual commitment to the colaborative process and goals of counseling (Martin, 2000). The occurrence of productive change is unlikely if clients do not understand what to expect in the counseling process. Furthermore, clients need to know "who does what" in order to make change happen. They are more likely to commit to the "work" of counseling when they know what to expect and what is expected of them. For this reason, mental health and community counselors seek to obtain the client's informed consent to treatment early in the process of developing the counseling relationship. For consent to be truly informed, clients should be provided information regarding the following issues (Moline, Williams, & Austin, 1998):

- *Treatment modalities and theoretical perspective*—Explain the general forms of treatment that may be used and, in layperson's terms, the theoretical strategies used.
- *Treatment timeframes*—Inform clients about the length and frequency of sessions. In addition, clients should have a general idea of the overall timeframes for treatment (i.e., how many sessions should be expected before significant goal attainment).
- *Method of payment*—Clients must have a clear understanding regarding fees for services provided and billing procedures for sessions and collateral contacts, letter writing, consultations, and court appearances. In addition, the policy regarding third-party reimbursement should be communicated.
- *The nature of confidentiality*—The relational safety that comes with the confidential nature of the counseling should be clearly communicated. However, clients must understand the statutory (e.g., duty to warn or mandatory reporting laws) and logistic limits to confidentiality (e.g., inability to guarantee maintenance of privacy in group counseling where other participants might divulge sensitive information to persons outside of the group).
- *Risks and side effects of treatment*—Although clients expect benefits through counseling, they must be made aware of potential side effects (e.g., a spouse's increased assertiveness may lead to increased frequency of conflicts within the marital relationship).
- *Qualifications of the counselor*—Inform clients on the training, experience, and credentials that qualify you to treat their presenting problems. This information is often presented in a separate counselor self-disclosure statement.

- *Additional issues*—Other concerns that may be included are use of video or auditory recording devices, parental/guardian permission to treat minors, use and nature of supervision and consultation, and intended uses of specialized assessment procedures (i.e., psychological testing).

Thus, the counseling relationship is established when clients perceive that they are viewed as significant and valued; understand the nature, process, and mutual responsibilities of counseling; and consent and commit to that process. Motivational interviewing skills (Miller & Rollnick, 2002) are helpful in establishing a productive counseling relationship. Once established, the potential of successful outcome is increased and counseling can proceed to the next stage.

PROBLEM IDENTIFICATION, ASSESSMENT, AND GOAL SETTING

Often when working with couples in conflict, I note that they come into the initial session feeling very stuck. They want to tell me about the various futile attempts they have made to solve their problem. However, as they discuss the nature of the problem, it soon becomes apparent that each person has a different perspective. The couple has failed to develop a coherent, mutually held view of their problem. How can they solve the problem if they have not clearly determined what it is they need to resolve?

Entry-level counselors often make the same mistake. After hearing the client's brief description of the situation that brought the client in for counseling, they move too quickly to the resolution phase. Strategies of change are much less likely to succeed when the client and counselor lack a clear view of the precise nature of the actual problem. Thus, for any intervention to succeed, mental health and community counselors must carefully assess the nature of the presenting problem and then, in collaboration with the client, develop a set of worthwhile and realistic goals.

Two tasks are primary to doing assessment: information gathering and decision making. These tasks are woven throughout the entire process of counseling. In the initial phases, information is gathered to help the counselor and client gain a better, more accurate view of the presenting problem that led the client to seek services at the particular time. The information obtained in assessment provides raw material for conceptualization of the problem and, in some settings, formal diagnosis of the client's condition, using criteria and codes of the *Diagnostic and Statistical Manual of Mental Disorders, Fourth Edition, Text Revision (DSM-IV-TR)* (American Psychiatric Association, 2000). Furthermore, information gathered assists the counselor and client plot a course of action or formalized treatment plan. Finally, assessment provides important data for determining whether or not the implemented strategies are having their desired effects.

The Initial Interview and Assessment. The transition to the problem identification, assessment, and goal-setting stage is marked frequently by an unstructured invitation extended by the counselor to the client, such as "How can I help you?" However, counselors must be flexible in their approach to problem identification and assessment to ensure that they are responsive to and respectful of the cultural diversity of clients. The culturally sensitive counselor, therefore, moves with caution by regulating the amount of structure within the session, depth of personal exploration requested, and degree of directives made. Within the warmth and safety of the setting, clients soon discover that counseling provides them with an opportunity for exploration and sharing unlike most interpersonal relationships they have encountered.

Counselors use a variety of responses to solicit information and encourage clients' expression of feelings (Cormier & Hackney, 1999). These include open- or closed-ended questions, requests for clarification, paraphrasing, acknowledgment of nonverbal behaviors, reflection and summarization of feeling, statements of summary, and "Columbo-type" incomplete statements. These latter statements reflect a style of information gathering used by the main character of an old television detective show. Columbo came across as a rather bumbling and confused investigator but whose questions and incomplete sentences drew out critical information and metaphors that would lead to the solving of the case. In a similar way, counselors can use this style of communication to gain critical information for constructing case conceptualizations.

Although counselors often set the tone of the session by opening with an unstructured question, they must assume responsibility and control over the direction and pace of the interaction. It is, after all, conversation with purpose. In most settings, counselors seek to gather the following types of information in the initial setting:

1. *Identifying and demographic information:* It is vital that counselors have accurate identifying information such as clients' names, addresses, and phone numbers for business operations of the agency and in the event that the counselor must contact the client between sessions. Counselors also gather information regarding demographic variables such as age, gender, ethnicity, race, marital status, vocation, and educational status.

2. *Presenting problems:* It is critical to obtain a description of the problems experienced by the client and to record them in the client's own words. Often, clients present with complex situations with several problems occurring at various levels. Thus, counselors want to determine who is involved in the expression and context of the problem; its specific, objective description, including related antecedents and consequences of the problem; and related thoughts and feelings. In addition, information is gathered that enables counselors to conceptualize clients and their presenting problems in the ecological context. This includes gaining an understanding of how the client and problem(s) interact with family and social relationships and academic and vocational performance. The strengths and deficits of subgroups, community, formal and informal institutions and supports, and the larger social and cultural context (including economic and political) are also assessed.

3. *Current life setting and functioning level:* Answers to the following questions help the counselor better understand the client's overall quality of life: How adaptive is the client in daily functioning? What is a typical day and week for the client? To what extent are wellness practices a part of this client's routine and repertoire?

4. *Client's biopsychosocial history:* The history of clients sheds light on the nature of their current circumstances. Counselors gather information regarding the following: medical history (e.g., unusual illness, injuries, or hospitalization), educational

history (academic achievement and extracurricular interests), past vocational experience, past social and sexual relationships, partnerships and marriages, divorces, traumatic experiences (e.g., physical, sexual, or emotional abuse and neglect, or natural disasters) and substance use/abuse patterns.

5. *Family history and constellation:* The family plays an important role in the development of the client. Patterns of behavior and relating often cross generational boundaries. McGoldrick (1999) notes that persons can be compared to music, in which the individual notes are only understood as we perceive them in conjunction with each other note played, the memories of the combination of notes played in the past, and the anticipation of what is to played next. Useful family information includes strengths of relationships between family subsystems (including relative level of differentiation, disengagement, or enmeshment), histories of emotional disturbance, substance abuse, significant physical illness, losses, vocational patterns, residential locations and moves, and so on. Genograms are useful tools for gathering and organizing such family information and provide a means of visually presenting the data so that significant patterns of behavior and relating within the family can be discovered and explored (Nichols & Schwartz, 1998).

6. *Behavioral observations:* Counselors pay careful attention to the behavioral and nonverbal presentations of clients to assess current level of functioning. This includes physical appearance, dress, posture, communication skill and style, gestures, facial expressions, degree of self-awareness, level of cognitive and sensoriperceptual functioning, and general level of vocabulary and comprehension.

In clinical settings, counselors may systematically gather this information by conducting a *mental status exam.* These global assessments of a client's mental functioning are to mental health practitioners as general physical examinations are to a medical practitioner. Figure 6.1 lists the types of information gathered in a thorough mental status exam. Whereas a psychosocial history encompasses the entire life of the client, the mental status exam provides a picture of the mental functioning of the client at a particular point in time.

What do counselors do with this mass of information? First, the data are organized in a manner that describes the client's *story.* Counselors document the assessment stage by writing an intake report, which becomes a part of the client's clinical file. In writing this document, counselors present the information in a concise, coherent manner and stick to the factual data as presented by the client. Professional jargon, elaborate inferences, and biases are avoided.

Client Diagnosis.   For many mental health and community counselors, making a diagnosis is a primary objective in conducting the initial assessment interview. As the client's presenting problem, current situation, and background information are explored, counselors are trained to pick up on behavioral indicators of significant emotional or behavioral patterns associated with the client's present distress. The counselor then considers these patterns in relation to criteria that define recognized categories of emotional and mental disorders. When a good fit between the displayed patterns of the client and recognized categories occurs, the counselor makes a tentative

FIGURE 6.1

Major
Components
of a Mental
Status Exam

Whereas a psychosocial history is a record of the client over the course of his or her life, a mental status exam is an evaluation of the client at one point in time. During the clinical interview, the counselor should make note of the following:

1. *Appearance*—a general description of overall appearance, dress, grooming, unusual features or gestures, posture (rigid, slumped, etc.);

2. *Motor activity*—gait position, bizarre postures, overall level of activity, any twitches, mannerisms, tics, agitation, clumsiness, rigidity, combativeness;

3. *Attitude*—level of cooperation, boredom, seductiveness, hostility, openness, defensiveness, guardedness, playfulness, and so on;

4. *Speech*—rapid or slow, pitch, pressured, hesitant, emotional, monotonous, volume, slurred, mumbled, relevance, spontaneity;

5. *State of consciousness*—alertness, responsiveness to environment, ability to carry out tasks (simple, then complex—e.g., touching nose with finger, then touching another body part simultaneously);

6. *Affect*—mood is client's internal emotional state, whereas affect is the outward expression of the internal state; congruity between client's description of mood and counselor's observation of affect; appropriateness to situation, anxiety level, stability of affect;

7. *Perception*—hallucinations (false perceptions of a sensory stimulus in the absence of a sensory stimulus); illusions (the misinterpretation of a true sensory stimulus); depersonalization and derealization;

8. *Thinking process*—abstract reasoning, loose associations, tangential thinking, circumstantiality, blocking, perservation, echolalia, flight of ideas;

9. *Content of thought*—delusions, obsessions, suicidal, homicidal, paranoid ideation;

10. *Judgment*—extent to which the client understands the consequences of his or her actions;

11. *Memory*—ability to recall and/or recognize remote and recent past;

12. *Intelligence*—assessment of general level or intellectual functioning (average, above or below average);

13. *Concentration and attention span*—client's ability to attend and focus;

14. *Orientation* $\times$ 3—assessment of client's orientation to time (time, date, year), place (where client is), and person (who client is and who clinician is).

diagnosis. Technically, the diagnosis of a client is always a conceptualization-in-progress and subject to revision upon the receipt of additional information.

The professional literature bears evidence to the widespread acceptance among counselors and counselor educators of client diagnosis (Mead, Hohenshil, & Singh, 1997; Ritchie, Piazza, & Lewton, 1991; Seligman, 1999). However, the practice remains controversial within the counseling profession. Some see the profession's emphasis on normal human development and mental health promotion as incompatible with diagnosis, which is perilously similar to the traditional medical model of clinical psychology

(Vacc, Loesch, & Guilbert, 1997). In contrast, others see knowledge and skills in diagnosis as essential for community and mental health counselors. Increasingly, graduates from programs with these specializations are providing counseling services in community mental health centers, psychiatric inpatient facilities, employee assistance programs, and other community settings (Hinkle, 1999). Frequently, mental health and community counselors are required to diagnose clients as part of their role in these settings. In fact, one study found that mental health agency directors reported a need for licensed professional counselors to have more training and experience in diagnosing (Ritchie et al., 1998).

Hinkle (1999) notes that the establishment of a valid diagnosis is at the foundation of problem conceptualization and treatment planning. Thus, coursework in abnormal psychology and diagnosis are increasingly emphasized in graduate community and mental health counseling programs. This emphasis reflects the 2001 CACREP standards, which require the knowledge of principles of diagnosis and use of current diagnostic tools for all students in community and mental health counseling programs (CACREP, 2001).

By far, the most widely used diagnostic system for classifying mental disorders is the *Diagnostic and Statistical Manual of Mental Conditions, Fourth Edition, Text Revision* (*DSM-IV-TR*) (American Psychiatric Association, 2000). It defines mental disorder as

> a clinically significant behavioral or psychological syndrome or pattern that occurs in an individual and that is associated with present distress (e.g., painful symptom) or disability (i.e., impairment in one or more important areas of functioning) or with a significantly increased risk of suffering death, pain, disability, or an important loss of freedom. In addition, this syndrome or pattern must not be merely an expectable and culturally sanctioned response to a particular event, for example, the death of a loved one. Whatever its original cause, it must currently be considered a manifestation of a behavioral, psychological, or biological dysfunction in the individual. Neither deviant behavior (e.g., political, religious, or sexual) nor conflicts that are primarily between the individual and society are mental disorders unless the deviance or conflict is a symptom of a dysfunction in the individual, as described above. (p. xxxi)

DSM-IV-TR attempts to use objectively based criteria for defining the various disorders included in its classification system. Typically, a specified number of symptoms must be present before a diagnosis can be made. As a result, diagnostic reliability is enhanced.

In addition, the *DSM-IV-TR* assesses the presenting condition according to five dimensions. Its authors note that

> the use of the multiaxial system facilitates comprehensive and systematic evaluation with attention to the various mental disorders and general medical conditions, psychosocial and environmental problems and level of functioning that might be overlooked if the focus were on assessing a single presenting problem. (American Psychiatric Association, 2000, p. 27)

These dimensions, or axes, are components of any diagnosis of mental illness and are described as follows:

Axis I: *The Clinical Disorders and Other Conditions That May Be a Focus of Clinical Attention.* This axis includes the major categories of mental illness, such as Early

Childhood Disorders, Substance Abuse Disorders, Schizophrenia and other Psychotic Disorders, Mood Disorders, Anxiety Disorders, Eating Disorders, Sexual and Gender Identity Disorders, Impulse-Control Disorders, and Adjustment Disorders.

Axis II: Personality Disorders or Mental Retardation. The category of personality disorders includes a variety of pervasive and long-standing patterns of inflexible and maladaptive behaviors that interfere with the client's social and/or occupational functioning. Specific diagnostic classifications include borderline, antisocial, narcissistic, dependent, paranoid, and schizoid personality disorders.

Axis III: Current Medical or Physical Condition. On this axis, counselors list current medical conditions relevant to the understanding or managing of the client's mental disorder.

Axis IV: Severity of Psychosocial Stressors. Counselors report any psychosocial or environmental factors that might influence the course of the mental disorder, its treatment, and its prognosis. Both negative and positive stressors require clients to adjust accordingly to the demands placed on them and are, thus, considered on this axis.

Axis V: Global Assessment of Functioning. On this axis, counselors report the client's general level of psychological, social, and occupational functioning, using the Global Assessment of Functioning (GAF) Scale. This scale provides a system for rating the level of general functioning on a hypothetical continuum of mental illness–mental health that ranges from 0 to 100. (American Psychiatric Association, 2000).

It is important that licensed mental health and professional counselors be aware of the specific scope of professional practice as defined in the state in which they practice. Although all mental health and community counseling programs abiding by CACREP standards require a working knowledge of the diagnostic process and systems, individual state licensure laws vary in what is legally permissible professional behavior. Many states include *diagnosis* within the scope of practice of licensed mental health and professional counselors. However, other states limit the practice of *diagnosis* to several of the mental health professions, typically psychiatry, psychology, and social work. A few states, such as Indiana, have chosen to use the word *evaluation* rather than *diagnosis* in the wording of their licensure law. Although licensed counselors in these latter states are successful in submitting diagnostic impressions or evaluations to third-party reimbursers, they must be careful to utilize appropriate terminology and not overstate their areas of competence.

Goal Setting. With an accurate grasp of the problem, the counselor and client are in a good position to specify desired outcomes. Some clients come into counseling knowing what they want to receive from the service. Others, though, are primed to tell their story, elaborate on the nature of their problems, and identify what they don't want. Thus, mental health and community counselors assist clients in developing a future vision of what life might look like in the absence of the concerns and problems that brought them into counseling. Bertolino and O'Hanlon (2002, p. 91) have found the following questions useful in moving clients to think in more positive, goal-oriented ways:

- How will you know when things are better?
- How will you know when the problem is no longer a problem?
- What will indicate to you that therapy has been successful?

- How will you know when you no longer need to come to therapy?
- What will be happening that indicates to you that you can manage things on your own?

Frequently, the goals of clients are worded in contrast to their problem statements. For example, a client might complain of feeling overly anxious in a variety of settings. In identifying a goal, the client might simply state that he desires to feel calm and relaxed. Through a collaborative process, the counselor and client arrive at a concise and precise statement of what it would look and feel like to be calm and relaxed in specific settings. This helps both the client and counselor understand their purpose for meeting and better recognize when they no longer need to meet.

Thus, goal statements are products of the assessment data. They specify the focus of ongoing assessments throughout treatment to determine the extent to which desired outcomes are being attained. Goal statements should include the following five components:

1. *Who:* Who specifically will be performing the behavior?
2. *Direction:* Does the goal involve an increase, decrease, or maintenance of a specific behavior?
3. *Behavior, thought, or affect:* What is the observable activity that the identified person is to do? As noted previously, a goal statement specifies what the client should rather than should not do.
4. *Conditions:* What is the specific setting(s) in which the observable activity is to be performed? In other words, what are the trigger events or antecedent conditions that provide the context for the new behavior, thought, or emotion?
5. *Degree:* What is the level of performance desired? Because realistic goals rarely entail perfect performance at all times, the counselor and client determine the quality (level of proficiency), quantity (frequency), and level of stability that is to be present for the client to conclude that counseling is no longer necessary.

For example, for clients seeking to lose weight, merely setting a goal in terms of pounds to be lost is not particularly helpful because the specific antecedents, thoughts, and behaviors necessary to accomplish the weight loss are not specified. Consider the following goal statement:

- Judy will lose 20 points over the next 3 months.

Although losing 20 pounds might be a very good thing, Judy has not identified exactly what she must do in order to lose those 20 pounds and maintain that weight. In contrast, consider this alternative: Judy will

- eat three meals each day until the goal of 20 pounds lost is attained and maintained for 3 weeks
- limit caloric intake to 1,800–2,000/day for the first week and 1,400–1,700/day for succeeding weeks until weight loss of 20 pounds is attained
- jog or exercise walk at least five times per week for 20 minutes per session
- eat snacks only when physically hungry

Goals specified in this manner are defined in terms of specific behaviors that can be integrated into Judy's daily routine. As these specific behaviors are developed and strengthened, Judy's lifestyle becomes more supportive of the long-term maintenance of her goals. In counseling, such goal statements enable the counselor and client to identify the specific therapeutic activities that will be most helpful and efficient in attainment of the client's goals.

PLANNING OF STRATEGY AND ITS IMPLEMENTATION

The process of counseling can be likened to going on a journey. Once the counselor and client have determined their current location (i.e., problem identification and/or diagnosis) and destination (i.e., treatment goals), it is much easier to decide which specific path to take in order to get from here to there. As Seligman (1999) notes, using an accurate view of the presenting problem and diagnosis to determine treatments likely to succeed is essential to the work of mental health and community counselors.

Seligman (1998) developed an acronym, *DO A CLIENT MAP*, to guide the steps of developing treatment plans for particular clients. The 12 steps are as follows:

- *Diagnosis*—accurate problem identification and *DSM-IV-TR* diagnosis;
- *Objectives of treatment*—treatment goals;
- *Assessments*—integration the results of scales, inventories, and tests used to assess the nature of the person and problem;
- *Clinician characteristics*—warmth, genuineness, empathic understanding, age, gender, race, ethnicity, and so on;
- *Location of treatment*—inpatient, outpatients, office- versus home-based interventions, and so on;
- *Interventions to be used*—particular counseling theories and techniques;
- *Emphasis of treatment*—level of directiveness; cognitive, behavioral, experientially focused;
- *Numbers*—how many clients targeted for intervention (e.g., individual, group, or family);
- *Timing*—how many sessions, at what frequency, length of session;
- *Medications*—psychopharmacological interventions;
- *Adjunct services*—involvement of other services or agencies;
- *Prognosis*—the direction that treatment will take and its expected outcome.

Taken together, the concise statement of presenting problem and diagnosis, identified goals, and selected strategies form the components of a therapeutic contract. The general form of therapeutic contracts is shown in Figure 6.2. Such contracts become roadmaps allowing clients and counselors to see where they started, their current location, and where they are going. The information contained on therapeutic contracts is also fundamental to establishing the client's *informed consent* for the proposed treatment, an essential ethical element for the counseling process.

Modalities of Intervention. Various modalities of intervention are used by mental health and community counselors. Mental health and community counselors select from among the many specific techniques derived from traditional and contemporary counseling theories (see chapters 3 and 4) as strategies of change. As noted previously, strategies are selected after consideration of the presenting problem, goals, unique client

FIGURE 6.2

Treatment Plan
and Contract

Treatment Plan

Client Name:

Case #:

Date:

Summary of Presenting Problem(s):

Provisional Diagnosis:

       Axis I:

       Axis II:

       Axis III:

       Axis IV:

       Axis V:

Justification for Diagnosis:

Date of Review:

Signatures

       Counselor: Date:

       Supervisor: Date:

       Consultant: Date:

Service Plan

Problem Statement	Goals/Objectives
1.	1.
2.	2.
3.	3.
4.	4.
5.	5.
6.	6.
7.	7.

FIGURE 6.2	Treatment Recommendations and Rationale:
(Continued)	

Signatures:
      Client(s):   Date:

      Counselor(s):   Date:

      Supervisor: Date:

and counselor characteristics, number of persons participating, and the appropriate emphasis of treatment. Often, more than one modality is implemented to facilitate desired outcomes. The primary modalities used by mental health and community counselors are individual, group, and family counseling; consultation; and advocacy.

Individual Counseling. In the minds of most laypersons and some counselors, the process of counseling is viewed as involving an interaction between the counselor and client. Indeed, a number of traditional theories were designed to fit this one-to-one model. The individual format is familiar to counselors and most incoming clients and ensures the relative privacy that is so critical to the establishment of trust. It provides an intimate yet flexible structure for establishing an effective counseling relationship that meets varying demands and characteristics of the particular client. For these reasons, individual counseling remains the most prevalent modality for psychiatric treatment (Perry, Francis, & Clarkin, 1985).

Group Work. Group work refers to a broad array of strategies that have in common the application of procedures to a collection of two or more individuals that meet in face-to-face interaction for the purpose of achieving mutually agreed upon goals. The Association for Specialists in Group Work (ASGW), a division of the ACA, defines *group work* as

> a broad professional practice involving the application of knowledge and skill in group facilitation to assist an interdependent collection of people to reach their mutual goals, which may be intrapersonal, interpersonal or work related. The goals of the group may include the accomplishment of tasks related to work, education, personal development, personal and interpersonal problem solving, or remediation of mental and emotional disorders. (ASGW, 2000, p. 330)

Specific forms of group work include task and work groups, psychoeducational groups, group counseling, and group psychotherapy (Corey et al., 2003).

Frequently, mental health and community counselors working in agency settings are assigned specific responsibilities that include *task- or work-related groups*. For example, a community mental health agency may have a standing committee whose purpose is to ensure that the policies and procedures of its various programs are compliant with the standards of specific federal programs, such as Medicaid. The task of the group's members is first to understand the specific requirements of Medicaid, which are subject to continual revision. The members then are charged with developing appropriate intraagency standards, forms, and instructions to enable agency staff to provide a standard of care and documentation that fulfills Medicaid's requirements. The work of such groups is critical to the financial well-being of the mental health center because fulfillment of these standards enables the center to bill and collect funds for services provided to Medicaid-eligible clients.

Sometimes communities set up task forces in which a variety of representatives from community agencies meet to identify problems, set goals, and develop programs to meet the needs of specific target populations. For example, Sault Ste. Marie, Michigan, a community located on the American-Canadian border, had a well-recognized problem with transients who would hitchhike up the interstate highway only to find that they could not cross over into Canada. Some of these persons were homeless and without funds and placed a burden on the limited resources of community human service organizations. To address these concerns, a Homelessness Task Force was set up to assess needs and community resources and make specific recommendations on ways agencies and organizations could assist these persons. After conducting a community needs assessment, it was recommended that a homeless shelter be created. Staffed by volunteers, financial resources from a variety of sources were pooled to support the shelter. In addition, community agencies and organizations developed an interagency support network that organized existing systems to assist transient, homeless persons in finding needed mental health, substance abuse, and crisis intervention services. The training and experiences of mental health and community counselors, along with members of other helping professions, played key roles throughout the program development process.

Psychoeducational groups are group experiences intentionally structured to teach knowledge and skills for the wellness and prevention of relational, psychological, and educational problems. These groups provide the audience with relevant information and skills in a context that encourages discussion and sharing; the goal is to enhance important skills for living. Specific themes for psychoeducational groups include parent skill training, stress management, anger control, relationship enhancement, and social skill development. Group participants learn specific types of knowledge and skills and are better prepared to cope with future stressors. As the participants' resources are bolstered, vulnerability and risk decrease.

Group counseling involves the application of group processes and techniques to help participants resolve difficult but normal problems of living. The focus is on prevention, personal growth, and the remediation of nonclinical problems. Typical topics include management of chronic pain, adaptation to divorce, maintenance of sobriety, development of coping skills for adults who were abused as children, and personal wellness/growth issues. These groups may be offered in community mental health settings but may also be located at schools, college dorms, women's shelters, churches, group homes, and juvenile detention centers. Although some counseling groups may have open-ended structures that have no specific time limits, many counseling groups utilize brief, time-limited formats, with the number of sessions ranging from 6 to 16 sessions (Gladding, 2003). Ideally, groups are composed of five to eight participants who commit to consistent, voluntary attendance for the duration of the group.

Psychotherapy groups are defined as the application of group processes and techniques for the treatment of psychological disturbance. Research has demonstrated the advantages of group psychotherapy over individual therapy for specific diagnostic categories, on the basis of both time efficiency and outcome effectiveness (McKay & Paleg, 1992). In addition, group psychotherapy can be used as an adjunct to individual counseling for mild to moderate depression, social phobia, panic, substance abuse/dependence, and adjustment disorders. Typically, participants in such groups have been diagnosed as having mental or emotional disorders. Thus, leaders of these groups must have specialized skills in assessment, diagnosis, treatment planning/evaluation, and specific models of group intervention. Group leaders must be able to take sessions deep enough to involve each participant in therapeutically meaningful experiences. Commonly applied approaches in group psychotherapy include cognitive-behavioral, gestalt, interpersonal, and transactional analysis. In addition, crisis management skills are required to help clients manage acute stressors and in-session or between-session episodes of decompensation. (i.e., gradual or sudden breakdowns in a client's defenses marked by increased levels of depression, anxiety, or psychotic symptoms).

Thus, possession of knowledge and skills in conducting group work is foundational to the counseling profession and is identified as a core area of study by CACREP. Training and experience in group work are critical for the counselor's professional survival in the contemporary mental health climate, where cost containment and treatment efficiency are demanded by employers, clients, and managed care organizations.

Family Counseling. Clients often describe the nature of their presenting problems in individualistic terms and anticipate treatment to follow a stereotyped one-to-one format. It is recognized, though, that persons and the problems they experience do not occur in a vacuum. Family counseling assumes that the family is the most basic emotional unit and is, therefore, the most appropriate target for intervention. Thus, using a jigsaw puzzle as a metaphor, if one of the pieces to the puzzle seeks to reconfigure itself, the adjacent pieces must adapt. From the family counseling perspective, human change is accomplished most efficiently when all of the puzzle pieces are on the table.

Numerous presenting concerns lend themselves to family systems interventions. In fact, it can be argued that all presenting problems have family dimensions. For example, families who have children with attention deficit disorder (ADD) are confronted with numerous behavioral, academic, social, and developmental challenges (Erk, 1997). Mental health and community counselors must not err by believing that ADD is an individual entity requiring individual treatment. Family stress, relational and communication patterns, family rules and roles influence and are influenced by the ADD child. In general, family counseling is recommended for the following conditions: families with a member who has a chronic mental illness; families with acting-out adolescents; families with multiple presenting issues; clients presenting with problems in family structure or family relational process; and families with marital problems. The general effectiveness of family counseling has been demonstrated through numerous empirical studies, although it has not been clearly determined which specific disorders or clients are most likely to benefit (Seligman, 1998).

As noted in chapter 3, numerous theories and techniques guide the process of family assessment and treatment. Family counseling differs from individual counseling on both conceptual and pragmatic levels (Beamish & Navin, 1994). Unfortunately, many mental health and community counselors lack in-depth training in family counseling and may be called on to make difficult treatment and ethical decisions for which they have been poorly prepared. For example, who exactly is the client—the symptom bearer or the family unit itself? How does the systemic assessment and diagnosis relate to *DSM-IV-TR* diagnostic categories? How does one accomplish *informed consent* when all family members are involved in treatment, some of whom (e.g., children or adolescents) may not be especially interested in participating? To what extent can confidentiality be maintained? How does the counselor manage information differentially shared among family members (e.g., knowledge of an extramarital affair)? It is, therefore, critical that mental health and community counselors receive adequate training and supervised experience before working with family systems.

Consultation. In contrast to the modalities discussed up to this point, consultation is an indirect form of problem solving. It may be defined as a helping process in which a specialized professional (the consultant), such as a mental health or community counselor, assists another party (the consultee) in carrying out work- or role-related activities within the client system. Mental health and community counselors can work with individuals, organizations, or entire communities in consultant-consultee relationships (Lewis et al., 2003).

Several important characteristics of consultation are identified in this definition. First, the goal of consultation is *problem solving*. The interactions between the consultant and consultee have a specific problem- and solution focus. Obviously, a very wide range of concerns can be the focus of the consultant-consultee relationship. For example, an elementary school teacher may consult with a mental health counselor to explore alternative ways of managing the behavior of a particular student or class. Or the director of a small, private human service organization desires to conduct an evaluation of specific programs offered to determine their effectiveness. A community counselor is hired as a consultant to assist in designing an evaluation process that enables the director to learn the extent to which program goals are being attained.

Second, consultation typically involves three parties (a *tripartite relationship*)—the consultant, consultee, and the client system. The services of the consultants are contracted by consultees to assist in management of specific problems in the client system.

Third, consultation is an *indirect helping relationship*. As noted previously, the consultant does not provide direct interventions to the client system but provides assistance to the consultee, who then implements the plan in collaboration with the client system. For example, a local church is experiencing rapid growth. With this growth, a number of new families are bringing with them specific issues, such as past abuse, family dysfunction, parenting concerns, and life adjustment issues. The pastor and staff are overwhelmed and limited in their abilities to meet these congregational needs. The services of a consultant are sought to explore ways in which the church may be empowered to minister more effectively to its attendees. The goal of consultation, as illustrated in this example, is not for the consultant to intervene in the lives of the church attendees. Rather, the consultant works toward the goal of empowering the church, which will, in turn, implement a plan for developing a functional support system to facilitate personal growth among its members.

A number of specific models of consultation are practiced (Dougherty, 2000). These include organizational, mental health, behavioral, and school-based consultation. It is beyond the scope of this text to discuss these models. There is, however, a generic model of consultation that provides a framework for performing these specific services (Kurpius & Fuqua, 1993). It consists of six phases: preentry; entry, problem exploration, and contracting; information gathering, problem confirmation, and goal setting; solution searching and intervention selection; evaluation; and termination. Often, it is necessary to recycle through these stages, especially as information gathered at a later stage provides insights necessitating the revision of the identified goal. In this model, the consultant-consultee relationship is egalitarian, democratic, and collaborative. The consultant has faith in the consultee's ability to identify the problem and generate potential solutions. The primary goal of the consultant is to provide an environment that facilitates the problem-solving process.

As consultants, mental health and community counselors engage in a broad range of roles: advocate, expert, trainer/educator, collaborator, fact finder, and process specialist (Dougherty, 2000). As *advocates*, consultants may persuade the consultee to do something that the consultant deems desirable, such as suggesting specific approaches that might facilitate intraagency relationships. Another example of appropriate advocacy by consultants occurs when discrepancies are noted between how an organization purports to treat clients and how it is actually treating them. However, counsultants serving as advocates must avoid *forming* unhealthy triangles and alliances that may be a part of the organization's dysfunctional dynamics. Self-awareness, possession of skills in organizational assessment, and retaining an objective problem-solving foci help the counselor-consultant stay within appropriate role boundaries.

Second, consultants also serve as *experts* or technical advisors. For example, a small, private mental health agency seeking accreditation may desire the expertise of a mental health counselor to conduct an independent audit of services and programs and, in so doing determine the agency's readiness to proceed with the accreditation process.

Third, consultants may act as *educators* to provide in-service training to the professionals of an organization. A mental health agency may seek the assistance of a consultant to train its staff in the use of the *DSM-IV-TR*. To serve in this role, consultants must possess the prerequisite knowledge and skills to fulfill the specific educational needs of the organization.

Fourth, consultants often work as *collaborators* who work alongside the consultee to accomplish a specific task within a given timeframe (Dougherty, 2000). Here the consultant and consultee might gather data independently, share observations, brainstorm alternative solutions to the problem, select and implement a specific alternative, and monitor the result. In this role, the consultant provides a level of objectivity that the consultee is less able to attain.

Fifth, consultants serve in *fact-finder* roles. Consultants gather information, analyze it, and provide accurate feedback to the consultee (Lippitt & Lippitt, 1986). Finally, a consultant may function as a *process specialist*. In this role, consultants serve as outside observers and facilitators to assess how a particular process is proceeding. Consultants then provide consultees with feedback that can be used to increase the efficiency of the process or remediate glitches in the service delivery system.

Advocacy. Grounded in ecological theory, mental health and community counselors recognize that the problems clients face are embedded within an ecological context. Unfortunately, too many persons in our society are subjected to forms of injustice, inequity, and stigmatization. Although counselors encourage clients to take appropriate responsibility for their wellness, counselors recognize that barriers inhibiting wellness are sometimes institutionalized. Thus, it is necessary for counselors to work for change not only in the behavior of clients but also in the attitudes and actions of the larger systems.

Advocacy is an indirect approach to helping clients in which mental health or community counselors engage in the process of "arguing or pleading for a cause or proposal" (Lee, 1998, p. 8). Generally, there are three types of advocacy—case advocacy, class advocacy, and professional advocacy. *Case advocacy* occurs when counselors represent the interests of the clients they serve. For example, a counselor may confer with school administrators in support of the client's right to have access to specific services available to persons with special needs. Or counselors may advocate on behalf of a young client who, because of her family's practice of religion, is forced to celebrate specific holiday rituals at school that go against the teachings of her faith. Mental health professionals sometimes work indirectly by intervening at the larger systems level to assist in bringing about client change and empowerment. In *class advocacy*, counselors represent the interests and rights of an entire group. March (1999), for example, documents the inaccurate images of mental illness that are depicted across mass media and suggests how counselors as advocates can act as agents of social action by calling attention to the ways in which such distorted depictions are sources of oppression. In this way, counselors intervene on behalf of clients by being agents of change at the ecological levels of the mesosystem, exosystem, and macrosystem.

The legitimacy of such advocacy efforts by mental health and community counselors rests on ethical principles that guide professional behavior. The primary ethical principle obligates counselors to respect the worth and dignity of all clients (AMHCA, 2001). This is accomplished when counselors

- ensure that clients possess the right to choose freely and can act autonomously;
- avoid doing harm;
- promote clients' welfare;
- seek fair treatment of clients regardless of gender, race, religion, and so on.

In addition to being directly involved in advocacy efforts, mental health and community counselors can help consumers of mental health services become advocates for change. The trend of mental health consumers helping themselves as advocates has been termed the *quiet revolution* (Carling, 1995). A number of consumer mental health advocacy groups exist at the national, state, and local levels. Among these are the National Alliance for the Mentally Ill, where the family members of mentally ill become sophisticated advocates for change to improve the lives of mentally ill family members (Citron, Solomon, & Draine, 1999). The National Mental Health Consumers Association is a network of over 500 self-help groups that focuses on the protection of human rights, promotion of consumer-run alternatives, elimination of stigma and discrimination, and improvement of responsiveness and accountability of mental health services (Carling, 1995).

In order to be effective as advocates on behalf of those served, the profession of mental health counseling must be understood, well received, and respected by both the general public and other mental health professions. Thus, *professional advocacy,* or advocacy on behalf of the profession itself, is imperative (Myers, Sweeney, & White, 2002). Myers and Colleagues (2002, p. 398) propose seven actions necessary for a strong professional advocacy effort:

1. Agreement on a common professional identity;
2. Development and implementation of a national initiative to increase public awareness of the unique role of counselors as mental health providers;
3. Intraprofessional collaboration on issues of concern regarding clients and the profession;
4. Inclusion of advocacy in counselor training;
5. Outcome studies on counseling work of mental health and community counselors that demonstrate strengths of counselor training model and credentials;
6. Development of curricular materials and resources for both professional and client advocacy;
7. Development and implementation of a comprehensive advocacy plan for the profession.

Advocacy, then, is best viewed as an indirect, multidimensional effort in which mental health and community counselors seek to promote the well-being of others. The effectiveness of this approach requires a strong, highly respected profession whose voice draws the attention of relevant power holders embedded in the ecological system to the needs and concerns of the mentally ill and consumers of mental health services. The benefits to the client and profession are interactive and reciprocal when case, class, and professional advocacy efforts are interconnected and well integrated into professional practice.

THE TRADITIONAL CONTINUUM OF MENTAL HEALTH CARE AND EXPANDED SETTINGS OF PROFESSIONAL PRACTICE

Mental health counselors serve the needs of clients in a variety of settings. The Community Mental Health Centers Act of 1963 mandated the development of a nationwide network of community-based mental health clinics in every community around the country. These clinics were required to provide five essential services: inpatient counseling (short term), outpatient counseling, emergency services, crisis

FIGURE 6.3 Continuum of Mental Health Care

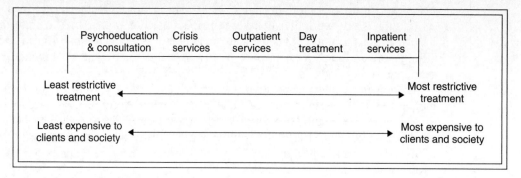

stabilization, and consultation/education (Lourie, 2003). These essential services gave rise to what is referred to as the continuum of mental health care (Hoff, 1995), illustrated in Figure 6.3.

One of the factors in determining appropriateness of treatment concerns the extent to which effective interventions are delivered in ways that place minimum restrictions on the client's freedom. Services identified on the continuum of mental health care are arranged from the least to most restrictive. In general, services that provide clients with the greatest amounts of independence are least costly to both the client and society (Hoff, 1995). In recent decades, the clear trend has been toward the provision of least restrictive treatment in community-based settings. Hospitalization is reserved primarily for persons experiencing acute, severe episodes of mental illness, or who are extremely lethal and in need of stabilization.

Mental health and community counselors are employed in the full range of settings along the mental health care continuum. Hollis (2000) reported that 58% of community counselors and 52% of mental health counselors take jobs in agency settings the first year after graduation. Furthermore, 21% of mental health counselors and 13% of community counselors were found to have taken positions in private practice/agencies. More mental health counselors (12%) were found to be working in managed care than community counselors (9%).

Several comments regarding the findings of Hollis (2000) are in order. First, it is apparent that mental health and community counselors work in similar settings. This similarity is not surprising, given the common emphases in underlying philosophy and training. In addition, as we noted in chapter 5, common scopes of practice contained in state licensure laws encourage similar work settings. Second, the categories of private practice/agency and public agency mask the variety of work that mental health and community counselors do. It is a mistake to equate agency settings with clinical counseling taking place in traditional office settings. As we shall see in the next section and in chapter 11, mental health and community counselors employed in agency settings actually apply their trade in a wide range of settings. In the contemporary world of mental health, interventions and treatment are truly community based.

MENTAL HEALTH AND COMMUNITY COUNSELORS ON THE JOB

This section briefly describes the work of mental health and community counselors performed in several specific settings. You will gain some idea of the range of potential roles available to mental health and community counselors through the small sample of settings described. In doing so, you will discover how the training model and experiences of mental health and community counselors enable them to make unique professional contributions that facilitate mental health and wellness to the clients they serve.

AGENCY/COMMUNITY MENTAL HEALTH CENTERS

Several times throughout my career, I have been employed at community mental health centers (CMHCs). Earlier in my career, I served as the Outpatient Program Director for a small community CMHC in the upper peninsula of Michigan. Located in Sault Ste. Marie, a city with a population of around 17,000, the CMHC served two large but sparsely populated counties. The agency offered a wide range of services, including outpatient individual, group, and family counseling; 24-hour crisis intervention; testing; assertive community treatment; and day treatment for the chronically mentally ill and developmentally disabled. A diverse population was served, and a large population of native Americans resided in the catchment area.

This position provided me with a wide array of professional opportunities and experiences. Indeed, no two days were ever the same. My primary responsibilities revolved around overseeing the operations of the outpatient program, supervising the master's-level counselors, and providing direct services to individuals and families. Extensive supervision was offered at the agency. I provided individual and group supervision to eight counselors. Although some supervisory time was spent reviewing ever-changing policies and procedures, our primary focus was on monitoring the process of problem identification/diagnosis, development and implementation of treatment plans, and addressing specific questions regarding treatment and professional development. Personally, I carried a case load of around 20 to 25 clients. I worked with a wide range of diagnostic categories using primarily cognitive-behavioral and Bowenian theoretical frameworks. The majority of clients presented with depression, anxiety, substance abuse, and domestic violence/abuse–related issues. The agency's clinical director supervised my counseling and supervision. Sometimes the services I rendered were part of a more comprehensive treatment plan involving staff from other programs within the agency. For example, I provided family counseling as part of a multidisciplinary team with one family whose 8-year-old was being treated for autism. My treatment goals with this family included strengthening relational communication and support within the family unit, increasing conflict management skills in the marital dyad, and reinforcing of the home-based interventions directed toward the child.

Currently, I am the Manager of Crisis Services for Hiawatha Behavioral Health, of Sault Ste. Marie, Michigan. I supervise a small staff of full-time professionals who provide crisis intervention services around the clock in a three-county region. A typical work rotation consists of a 72-hour shift followed by 7 days off. When on duty, workers carry a pager. After-hours calls are received by an independent hot-line service and are forwarded to the crisis worker. On some nights, the frequency and intensity of calls is light. Other nights, however, are quite busy, with the crisis worker receiving pages to respond to the crisis needs of current clients of agency programs and persons from the public, city lock-up, or hospital emergency room. Although no two calls are alike, a rather standard process is followed to determine quickly the immediate needs of the client and assess whether emergency responses are required. For example, calls are received from the jail or emergency room requesting the crisis worker to do a pre-screening to determine level of lethality and need for hospitalization. If the person is presenting a clear and imminent risk to self or others, arrangements are made for the immediate transport to a psychiatric hospital for brief, intense treatment. If the risk is not clear and imminent, a crisis management plan is devised in collaboration with the client to ensure his or her safety and management of the current crisis. Often, referrals are made to counseling agencies to link the client to the support of individual, group, or family counseling. In addition, psychiatric consultation are sometimes required when severe symptoms are part of the clinical picture.

In addition to managing the crisis intervention program, I also oversee the agency's crisis stabilization and jail diversion programs. The crisis stabilization program provides an intense service to clients experiencing severe crises but not requiring inpatient hospitalization. In this way, such clients are able to receive intense 24-hour services in the community setting. Our jail diversion program works with persons who are in contact with the corrections system but who are not likely to benefit from incarceration because they have severe mental illness. For such persons, arrangements are made for the receipt of intense mental health services in lieu of incarceration. In addition, our jail diversion specialist provides brief focused counseling services to persons incarcerated in the city and county jail. This program gives inmates an opportunity to express thoughts and feelings and develop coping strategies that are not typically available in a corrections setting.

In addition to clinical, supervisory, and crisis work, I participate in several agency and community committees. These include the agency's quality management committee and recovery committee. I have been given the opportunity to develop a comprehensive three-county suicide prevention program. Finally, I am involved in several community committees—community housing, the interagency collaborative committee, and the community crisis response team committee. In these various areas of responsibility, I have found that my training as a mental health counselor has provided me with a unique combination of knowledge and skill for addressing issues of wellness and pathology from an ecological perspective.

PRIVATE PRACTICE

After working in agency settings for 10 years, Jim chose to develop a private practice. He is now self-employed as an independent, full-time counselor. His counseling practice is housed in a suite of offices, where a central reception and business operation is shared by other practitioners—a psychologist, a financial advisor, and a chiropractor. The expenses for the services of a receptionist and office manager are shared. Beyond that, Jim functions with almost total autonomy. Services offered include individual, group, marriage, and family counseling; consultation; and psychoeducational programming for church groups, parent-teacher organizations, and local/regional professional organizations.

In a typical week, Jim works in the office approximately 50 to 55 hours. He schedules four to five individual, marital, or family sessions Monday through Friday and an additional three on Saturday. To be successful as a private practitioner, he must be responsive to the scheduling needs of his potential clientele. Thus, most sessions are conducted in the late afternoons and evenings to accommodate family schedules. In addition, he runs a brief, structured group on Tuesday nights. His special areas of expertise include parent skill training, anxiety, depression, self-management, and self-esteem. He has built a professional reputation that has enabled him to establish a strong referral network. In addition, Jim offers an ongoing group on Thursday evenings for adults who were abused as children. His morning hours are spent doing necessary administrative tasks involved with maintaining a business operation, service-related paperwork such as intakes, treatment plans, 30-day case reviews, and case closing reports.

Although he enjoys the autonomy and variety in his current work setting, Jim readily identifies a number of drawbacks to being a full-time private practitioner. First, he experiences difficulty finding relevant and required continuing education hours offered at nonpeak office hour times. In addition, fees, rooms, and transportation for attending national conferences offered by his professional association are prohibitive. For him, time is money and taking time off can cause a significant cash flow problem. Second, although someone might naively think that having your own private practice is the way to riches, the operating costs are extensive. Consider the costs for reasonable auto, health, life, and professional liability insurance, vacation and sick days, holidays, professional dues, continuing education, office rental, equipment maintenance, and salaries and benefits for support staff. Add to this amount a desired salary and you quickly discover the type of pressure experienced by Jim to generate enough income to simply break even or make a small profit.

Although Jim clearly enjoys and finds fulfillment in his work, he recognizes that building and maintaining a private practice is hard work. Self-care skills are essential if the mental health practitioner is to survive and thrive. He advises those considering going this route to keep their heads up and eyes open. If one's professional path can be likened to a journey, one must be aware that traffic is moving at fast rates of speed and is subject to slowdowns and detours. But the scenery can be grand, and in many ways the trip itself often brings as much pleasure as does arrival at the destination.

SUBSTANCE ABUSE TREATMENT PROGRAM

Linda serves as primary counselor in an intensive outpatient program for substance abuse. She earned her master's of arts in counseling with a specialization in mental health counseling. In addition, she is a licensed professional counselor and holds the master addiction counselor certification. In this setting, she provides assessments, individual and group counseling for substance-dependent and dually diagnosed (i.e., co-occurring substance abuse disorder and mental illness) populations. She has worked in personal recovery for over 15 years, and she is passionate about her vocation. The work is demanding and she carries a very large caseload.

Initial assessments are conducted by a multidisciplinary team. Linda conducts mental status examinations in the context of structured clinical interviews. She writes up intake reports that summarize clients' presenting problem, psychosocial history, and readiness for change. In collaboration with other team members, Linda develops provisional diagnostic impressions and treatment plans. Clients are provided with information regarding the nature of the presenting problem, treatment options, and potential benefits/side effects. The input of clients is given significant consideration in the development of the individualized treatment plans.

Linda provides individual counseling to persons admitted to the intensive outpatient program. Although her clients may be in a great deal of emotional pain at the onset of treatment, many resist or deny their need for treatment. Linda finds it necessary to provide a balance of warmth and unconditional acceptance with varying amounts of confrontation. She has found advantages-disadvantages analysis (Beck, Wright, Newman, & Liese, 1993) and "spitting in the client's soup" (Dinkmeyer & Sperry, 2000, p. 107) to be helpful in moving clients to a psychological place where they are more aware of the problems brought on by their substance abuse. Psychoeducational techniques are also used to enhance clients' understanding of chemical addiction and its clinical picture if left untreated. Linda relies heavily on cognitive-behavioral strategies in helping clients identify triggering events, emotions, and memories that elicit the craving of substances. She then works with her clients to develop and implement strategies to deal effectively with the identified situations and specific triggers.

Linda also works as a cotherapist for several groups that are key components of the program. In the anger management group, clients develop an awareness of anger issues, interpersonal boundaries, and triggering events and cognitions. The participants then work on strategies and develop skills in assertiveness and effective problem solving. Linda also cofacilitates relapse prevention groups. Clients learn the role of situational factors and "hot" cognitions in precipitating relapse. They develop strategies to prevent relapses and limit the damage when they revert to old patterns of thinking and using.

Professionals working in substance abuse treatment centers are especially at risk for burn-out. Clients are often resistant to treatment. High attrition and relapse rates can lead to feelings of discouragement. Linda has found it vital to take care of herself in order to survive and thrive in this professional niche. She attends to her personal wellness through consistent, healthy dietary practices; physical exercise; and focused practice in spiritual disciplines. These, along with her strong desire to make differences in the lives of others, help her maintain a faith in the human capacity to make positive changes toward greater levels of functioning.

SMALL COLLEGE COUNSELING CENTER

Cynthia was trained as a community counselor and is presently employed at a small, private liberal arts college in the Midwest. In this position, she serves in four different capacities: counselor at the college counseling center, adjunct professor, advisor for the Department of Community Service, and an academic support professional for the student retention program.

As counselor, Cynthia meets with traditional and adult students who encounter a variety of problems in the process of pursuing academic degrees. The counseling center provides brief counseling services and refers those experiencing severe mental disorders. Cynthia works with a wide range of emotional and behavioral problems, such as depression, anxiety, self-mutilation, eating disorders, posttraumatic disorders, and self-esteem issues. In addition, she provides premarital counseling and works with female students who have unplanned pregnancies. Cynthia enjoys working with the variety of presenting issues seen at the college counseling center and finds them to be similar to those seen in other clinical settings.

Cynthia also teaches a course for the Department of Education titled "Diversity in the Classroom." In this course, her training and experiences enable her to help future K–12 educators learn about the needs of the diverse students they will serve. She sees it as vital that they become aware of their own biases and helps them work toward breaking down any stereotypes and prejudices they hold that may prevent them from being effective teachers.

The college encourages its students to engage in volunteer work around the community, doing such diverse tasks as painting houses or cleaning parks, alleys, and riverways. As advisor for the community service program, Cynthia organizes these opportunities and monitors and oversees the volunteer work of students, staff, and faculty.

Finally, Cynthia provides services in the retention program, for students at risk of dropping out of college, by linking them to available campus resources. She receives a list of the names of students who are failing three or more courses at midterm, meets with them, and assesses the problems related to poor academic performance. These problems include interpersonal problems with roommates, financial problems, health-related issues, adult attention deficit hyperactivity disorder (ADHD), and learning disorders. She collaborates with students in developing an individualized plan that integrates available services such as mentoring, coaching, tutoring, counseling, and financial assistance.

Through her position at the college, Cynthia has been able to pursue a variety of personal and professional interests with community agencies and programs. For example, she serves on the board of a local home for teenage mothers. In addition, she has become involved with Community United Religious Efforts, a task force that assists persons of diverse backgrounds in getting to know, understand, and embrace one another. Finally, Cynthia works closely with the House of Higher Learning, an on-campus house where students work through issues of racial reconciliation.

Cynthia believes her broad-based training in counseling has uniquely prepared her to serve in these various roles. The pace is fast, and each day brings a new set of challenges and opportunities. She finds great fulfillment as she assists students in enhancing their lives while pursuing their academic goals.

UNIVERSITY HEALTH SERVICE

Suzanne works at the Sexual Assault Crisis Service (SACS), a unit within the Department of Counseling and Psychological Services (CaPS) at the health center of a large state university. The health center has approximately 180 employees, including eleven full time and three part-time counselors, one full-time psychiatrist, two part-time psychiatrists, and seven support staff workers who work exclusively for CaPS.

The SACS was created in 1988 to meet the unique counseling needs of individuals with sexual assault issues. It offers individual and group counseling, advocacy, a 24-hour crisis line, referral resources, and educational programming. The service is open to all students, faculty, and staff of the university.

All clients seen by Suzanne have some presenting issue involving sexual assault. It may be a recent incident or stemming from past childhood or adolescent experiences. Clients may identify sexual assault as the reason for seeking counseling, or they may present with psychological symptoms that may be attributable to sexual assault. Frequently, clients present with depression, anxiety, eating disorders, academic issues, interpersonal conflict, or somatic symptoms and, upon intake, reveal a history of sexual assault. Therefore, patients enter either by scheduling an appointment at SACS, a crisis response, or as a referral from other counseling staff or health center personnel.

Suzanne takes a thorough psychosocial history at intake that includes a description of the presenting problem, symptoms, family history, medical /psychological history, social/developmental history, and a mental status exam. This information provides the foundation for creating a diagnostic impression. She then develops a treatment plan with the patient. This can include individual counseling, a group for individuals who have been sexually assaulted, referral to other counseling groups, and/or referral to needed medical or legal resources.

Suzanne's position is full time, although she is normally in the office for only 25 hours a week. She is compensated additional hours for serving on call, which requires her to carry a pager 2 weeks per month and respond to crisis calls. During the day, Suzanne sees persons in her office who have requested crisis intervention. After hours, most responses are by returning phone calls to individuals who have been victimized or to other concerned parties. The remainder of her time is divided among clinical work, outreach, consultation, and administrative duties. Overall, she sees an average of 10 clients a week for individual counseling during the academic year and occasionally facilitates a group. In addition, she is a member of a multidisciplinary peer review team, the county domestic violence task force, the network of campus service providers, and the university's commission on personal safety, where she chairs a subcommittee.

Suzanne is engaged in professional activities beyond her job. She is active in state professional organizations. In addition, she develops educational programs and workshops, designs fliers and pamphlets, presents visiting lectures in a variety of academic units, and has moderated a live call-in television program that broadcasts on the campus cable system.

Suzanne has worked in this setting since 1988. Her academic preparation includes a bachelor's degree in sociology and a master's of science degree in counseling, with a specialization in community counseling. Prior to being employed at SACS, she worked in agencies that dealt primarily with abused and neglected children. In addition to her academic preparation, she has gained much knowledge about the treatment of sexual assault victims through research, workshops, and experience. Overall, she believes the current position works well for her. The variety and flexibility it offers offset the stress of the position.

SECONDARY SCHOOL SETTING

Madeline was trained and is certified as a school counselor but has chosen to obtain additional graduate credits to become license eligible as a mental health counselor. In addition to deepening her skills in working with the clinical needs of the students with whom she works, she would like to develop a small, part-time private practice in the future. In the state where she is choosing to practice, a total of 60 hours of graduate credit is required for licensure. However, this requirement can be fulfilled by taking 12 credit hours in addition to the 48-hour school counseling she previously earned. Thus, Madeline has taken additional coursework in mental health counseling to fulfill the educational requirements.

Madeline is employed in a large high school where over three thousand students attend. She shares her work with seven other school counselors and a mental health counselor, who is contracted to work at the school through the local community mental health center. Unlike some school counselors, Madeline does quite a bit of mental health counseling in her particular setting. Although it is not within the role of the school system to provide extended counseling, Madeline conducts brief counseling with many students on a weekly or biweekly basis for the duration of a month or so depending on the students' situation. She also does the traditional work of a guidance counselor, which includes advising, scheduling classes, and consulting with teachers, administrators, and parents.

Students present with a wide range of presenting problems. The more common issues include adjustment disorders and temporary situational problems revolving around relationships with friends or significant others. These students need help seeing their situations more objectively and find it helpful to have counseling services accessible that are provided within a nonjudgmental, accepting atmosphere. Even well-adjusted teens experience frustration as they proceed through the developmental process. Madeline provides these students an opportunity to vent their thoughts and feelings, reframes their situations, and assists them as they move in new, more positive directions. Typically, she works with students using the individual counseling modality, but on occasion, and always with the student's consent, invites parents to participate in the sessions.

A number of students are seen who have been diagnosed with learning disabilities or ADD. Students with learning disabilities are supported well academically through special education services. Madeline helps these students and their families learn and implement problem-solving skills to enhance their academic success. In addition, she participates in case conferences and provides input to the development of individualized education plans. Often, students with ADDs are already receiving treatment from mental health professionals and taking medications for their condition. Many, however, still benefit from the support of counseling to help them deal with the distractions and demands of high school.

Madeline does become involved with students who present more serious mental health issues, such as bipolar disorder, borderline personality disorders, eating disorders, chemical abuse, and schizophrenia. Without the involvement of mental health professionals, many of these students would not graduate due, in large measure, to the interaction of the emotional condition with academic performance. Thus, Madeline collaborates with the students' primary care providers to, for example, intervene with students who cut themselves or perform other self-destructive behaviors while at school.

By far, the most common mental health issue seen is depression. School counselors are on the front lines and make referrals for treatment of depression. For those students who do not seek help themselves, often a friend brings them into Madeline's office, where the level of depression is appraised. Some of these students display suicidal thoughts or have actually made attempts to take their lives. Decisions regarding future treatment depend on the outcome of the assessment. Several times, parents have been notified due to Madeline's "duty to warn" and inpatient hospitalization was required. Less serious cases result in referrals to community providers who follow up with outpatient services.

Her training in mental health counseling has assisted Madeline in working more effectively with the array of issues presented by students. She enjoys working in the school setting and desires to continue in her current vocation until retirement. But she is also excited about the prospect of providing services as a private practitioner to young female clients struggling in destructive relationships. Her goal is to provide affordable services that will enhance the physical and emotional well-being of this vulnerable population.

CONCLUSION

Over the past several years, I have enjoyed reading "Finding Your Way," a column that has been a regular feature of *Counseling Today*, a monthly publication of the American Counseling Association. It is refreshing to hear the experiences of rookie and seasoned counseling professionals as they traverse the terrain of counseling work. Numerous metaphors arise from the pages that communicate what it is like to be a counselor.

The title of the column itself conjures visions of taking a journey and the adventure entailed in that process. Some set out with a very clear view of the destination in mind and can hardly wait until they reach that specific locale. Others, in contrast, get the most pleasure out of the trip itself. Arriving at the final destination is almost anticlimactic. Although some travel directly from point A to point B, others meander, get lost along the way, get stuck in the traffic, or are redirected by a detour. Occasionally, a tire goes flat or the vehicle breaks down.

Kottler (2003) has learned some important lessons from surfing that apply to the work of counselors, supervisors, and teachers. First, he notes that "no matter how ready I am to ride a wave, or help a client, there's little that can be accomplished until the timing is right. It doesn't have to be perfect, because you can take a wave a little early or late and compensate accordingly, but you must wait patiently for the opportunities as they arise" (p. 27). Second, he has discovered that catching a wave is much like counseling. You may have some idea where things will end up, but frequently you may go someplace totally unexpected but not necessarily less desirable.

Thus, be patient. You may be starting out on the journey or taking a trip down a side road. Enjoy the scenery! Take the time to know your surroundings. Don't be so overly focused on your destination that you miss the pleasures and lessons found along your way. Take on passengers—mentors, colearners, and colleagues. Growing into the profession is a developmental process. Make use of the numerous resources that surround you.

Finally, take care of yourself. Graduate study and professional life can become black holes that consume all that surround them. Maintain a balanced lifestyle that facilitates physical, emotional, social, and spiritual development. Build health-promoting behaviors into your daily routine. Above all, find the time to enjoy the journey and those persons who you are fortunate enough to encounter on your path.

DISCUSSION QUESTIONS

1. The text states that motivational interviewing skills can be useful in the process of establishing the counseling relationship. Identify three components of motivational interviewing and discuss how you would use them to increase your effectiveness in professional practice.
2. In this chapter, it was noted that one common error of the novice counselor was to jump into the problem resolution stage prematurely. Why do you think this occurs so frequently? What personal and situational factors could lead you to such behavior? What steps might you take to prevent premature jumps into problem resolution?
3. To what extent are you comfortable diagnosing clients? To what extent do you see diagnostics as a necessary skill for the contemporary mental health and community counselor? How would you avoid using diagnostic labels in ways that could be personally demeaning or harmful to the clients you serve?
4. To what extent do you see the role of consultant as part of your future job description? Give several examples of counseling situations and settings where consultation might be a useful or important tool in your professional practice.

SUGGESTED ACTIVITIES

1. Imagine you are a licensed professional counselor in private practice. Design an informed consent form to be used with the clients you serve. Your instructor might provide you with useful models to guide you in developing of this form.
2. Survival in the counseling professions requires the utilization of wellness practices in the daily routine of the professional. To what extent are you practicing wellness presently? Can you identify specific wellness practices from which you could benefit? Develop a self-management plan to assist you in implementing the identified practices in your personal routine.
3. The class separates into triads. Practice conducting intake sessions. Assign the roles of counselor, client, and observer. Learn to gather the pertinent information, conduct mental status exams, and develop a complete diagnosis. Use the questions identified by Bertolino and O'Hanlon (2002, p. 91) to develop client-identified goals. The observer is to provide objective feedback to the counselor and assess the extent to which the client felt comfortable throughout the process. As time permits, rotate roles. (Several class sessions may be required to complete this activity.)
4. Interview several professional counselors and gain a better understanding of their professional roles and the issues they face in professional practice.

7

Appraisal and Research in the Practice of Mental Health and Community Counseling

OUTLINE

Appraisal

Ethical Practice in Appraisal

Research and Program Evaluation

Ethical Practice in Research

Conclusion

In chapter 3, I began with a statement, "I am a mental health counselor," and then went on to quote Gibson and Mitchell (2003), who noted that we call ourselves counselors because that is what we do. Although career development, advocacy, or consultation may be roles we fill, counseling is central to our professional identity. This close identification to the process of counseling leads students to wonder sometimes why they must have a working knowledge of appraisal and research. As Hadley and Mitchell (1995) observe, those entering the counseling profession tend to be socially oriented and motivated to help others. They are not pursuing a counseling degree due to a strong desire to gather data, test hypotheses, or crunch numbers.

Traditionally, mental health professionals have been viewed as scientist-practitioners. In other words, counselors are expected to possess competencies that enable them to conduct and publish research as they provide direct services to clients. They *make* as well as *apply* knowledge. Indeed, CACREP identifies *assessment* and *research and program evaluation* as two of the eight core areas required of all students in graduate-level counseling programs. In addition, appraisal and research content appears on the certification exams of the NBCC and licensure exams of most states.

However, the "why" question lingers. Many practicing counselors do not find the scientific research found in professional journals to be particularly relevant to their work. Why might this be so? Much of the problem has to do with the extent to which research conditions in the laboratory are artificial and sterile. In the world of professional practice, the lack of control over extraneous variables is the rule, not the exception. For example, an empirical study investigating the response of depressed clients to cognitive-behavioral therapy (CBT) will attempt to control for all extraneous variables in order to isolate the effect of the independent variable (CBT) on the dependent variable (level of depression). However, clients do not live in vacuums and are influenced by numerous factors in addition to the treatment administered by their counselors. Thus, counselors rarely have the opportunity to treat a case of "pure depression." In addition, basic research tends to compare the differences between the means of groups, whereas counselors treat individuals. To what extent, then, do the results and conclusions from empirical research generalize to the counseling context? Do such results and conclusions really apply to what counselors do?

To conclude that appraisal and research methods are irrelevant to mental health and community counselors, though, is akin to throwing the baby out with the bath water. Knowledge and skills in appraisal and research are vital for several reasons. First, mental health professionals must be able to determine the extent to which their interventions are truly effective. For example, a mental health counselor might receive a grant from a federal agency to provide parent skill education within the catchment area of the community mental health center. Typically, in writing a grant to receive funding, the author must develop a plan that specifies the manner in which the effectiveness of the program will be measured. Providers of the program are held accountable and are expected to be good stewards of the monies received. This entails conducting a formative and summative evaluation that communicates how the funds were used in the development, implementation, and outcomes of the program. Thus, skills in appraisal and research are critical skills in the development and provision of psychoeducational programs. In addition, third-party reimbursers often require evidence that demonstrates the mental health professional's ability to achieve successful and efficient clinical outcomes if the practitioner is to remain in good standing as a member of a provider list.

Second, new therapeutic techniques and preventive psychoeducational programs are discussed in the professional literature. This is one of the ways mental health professionals are introduced to innovative ideas that might be readily applied to their clients. The understanding of psychometric and research concepts and principles enables mental health and community counselors to discern the extent to which the reported approaches are appropriate for their purposes. It is important that counselors not rely on anecdotes or testimonials but apply their knowledge of sampling procedures to determine the extent to which the described program or techniques generalize to other populations. Furthermore, a firm grasp of psychometric and research concepts and principles enables counselors to be more confident in expecting that the implementation of procedures as described will lead to outcomes similar to those described in the professional literature.

Finally, counselors are bombarded with numerous reports of the latest and greatest therapeutic breakthroughs. Some of these statements are more valid than others. Mental health and community counselors sometimes must apply their knowledge of appraisal and research methods as if donning hip waders to move through the mucky wetlands to find solid ground.

APPRAISAL

THE USES OF TESTS

Tests can be defined as measurement devices used to quantify a sample of an individual's behavior. Basically, tests assign numbers to individuals in a systematic way that becomes a means of concisely representing a characteristic of that person. In order to be useful, tests must follow prescribed procedures regarding their construction, administration, scoring, and interpretation to ensure that the obtained results accurately reflect the characteristic being measured (i.e., validity) and are replicable (i.e., reliability).

Many situations are encountered in professional settings where we must find answers to very specific questions or make decisions based on our understanding of the particular nature of the person. Clinical interviews typically serve the purpose for the development of diagnoses and treatment plans. However, what if you are called on to determine if a person could benefit from specialized rehabilitative services? Furthermore, the outcome of your assessment would have a major bearing on whether or not the client could procure financial assistance to pay for the needed services. Or your input is requested by the court to determine arrangements for custody, child placement, or probation. Although data gained through a clinical interview would serve important purposes in the decision-making process, the results of specific tests can provide focused, objectively based information on which conclusions can be based.

At other times, counselors may request the release of information for clients who have received services from other institutions or agencies. Frequently, the client's file may contain the results and conclusions from psychological testing. It is critical that mental health and community counselors are able to assess independently the meaning, validity, and reliability of the test results so that the information be used appropriately in the construction of the treatment plan. Thus, it is essential to understand key concepts and principles.

KEY CONCEPTS AND PRINCIPLES IN APPRAISAL

Classical True-Score Theory. Classical test score theory assumes that any observed score (X) on a given test consists of two components: (a) the true score (T), and (b) the error score (E). Stated as a formula, $X = T + E$. On any given psychological variable, classical test score theory assumes that there is an actual true score or level that is stable for the particular individual. However, random and unsystematic error influences obtained scores so that they vary from the individual's true score on any given day. Factors that can contribute error to an obtained score include changes in mood, level of fatigue, conditions in the testing environment, or subtle changes in the procedures of test administration. When the error is truly random, it is assumed that with repeated administrations of the test, the mean of the summed Xs would approach T. The *standard error of measurement* communicates how much an observed score varies from the true score. It can be used to estimate the reasonable limits of a person's true score, given an obtained score.

Reliability. In testing, *reliability* refers to the degree to which scores obtained on tests are consistent, dependable, and repeatable (Drummond, 2004). It is a function of the amount of error influencing given test scores. The reliability of a test increases as the sources of random error are controlled.

There are three basic types of reliability with which you should be familiar. *Test-retest reliability* concerns the extent to which there is consistency of scores when examinees take a test at two different times. For example, there should be an appropriate degree of consistency when a person takes an intelligence test on two different occasions. If each person obtained the same score each time the test was administered, the reliability coefficient would be 1.0. In contrast, if test scores and scores obtained on the test's readministration are completely unrelated, the reliability coefficent equals 0.0.

Internal reliability concerns the extent to which the test items are measuring the same thing (i.e., the internal consistency of the test itself). Again, internal reliability is reported by the calculation of a coefficient. For example, a test can be divided into two parts—even/odd items or first half/second half. The correlation between the obtained responses on the two halves indicates the extent to which they were consistently measuring the particular variable. Thus, if a test purports to measure level of depression, a strong positive correlation should be found between the even and odd items.

Sometimes appraisal involves the direct observation of behavior. For example, when two or more counselors are rating the on-task versus off-task behaviors of children in classroom settings, there should be a significant agreement between raters. This is referred to as *interrater reliability*.

Validity. If I am developing an appraisal instrument to measure psychological construct, it is vital that my instrument accurately measures the construct that it purports to measure. There must be a high degree of agreement between the test score or measurement and the quality being measured. Confidence can be placed in the results of a test only to the extent that the test is actually measuring what it says it does. Generally speaking, *validity* refers to the extent to which an instrument accurately measures what it is supposed to measure.

Several methods are used to determine the validity of tests. *Content validity* refers to the extent to which a test measures the skills or subject matter that it is supposed to measure. In its simplest form, content validity is assessed by expert opinion. For example, in developing a licensure exam for mental health counselors, a group of experts would review the items to determine the extent to which the instrument covers the specific areas of knowledge and skills deemed foundational for the practice of mental health counseling. Although it is essential, content validity must be supplemented by other forms of validity because of its reliance on subjective judgment.

Criterion-related validity is the correlation between a test score and some performance measure. Relatively high correlation coefficients are indicative of increased predictive power of the test. For example, the Graduate Record Exam (GRE) is often used to predict students' success in graduate-level programs. The criterion-related validity of the GRE rests on the correlation between attained GRE scores and measures of academic success (e.g., grade point average [GPA]).

Construct validity refers to the extent to which a test is an accurate measure of a specific theoretical concept. The construct validity of an instrument is established when the results obtained from the administering of a test are in the direction of what are predicted by an underlying theory. For example, the cognitive theory states that the thought process of depressed persons is characterized by the operation of cognitive distortions and negative self-statements. The construct validity of specific tests measuring cognitive distortions or irrational thoughts is established when scores on these instruments correlate highly with measures of depression (e.g., Beck Depression Inventory—II).

Standardization. Suppose you completed a life adjustment scale and the counselor reported that you obtained a score of 35. I suspect you would immediately ask, "What does that mean?" An individual score on a test is meaningless unless accompanied by additional interpretative information. An important component of test construction is to have available data on the performance of a sample of persons who are representative of those with whom the test will eventually be used. This process is referred to as *test standardization*. Its primary purpose is to establish the distribution of raw scores in the standardization group (or norm group). It also establishes a set of standard procedures for the administration of the test. The obtained scores are then converted into percentile ranks, grade equivalents, or standard scores (*norms*). Most test manuals contain tables of raw and converted scores established through the standardization process. The scores of examinees take on meaning when evaluated according to the table of norms for their appropriate group. Thus, norms become a frame of reference for interpreting the raw scores by indicating how that person's performance compares to the scores of persons of similar age, gender, or grade (Aiken, 2003).

CATEGORIES OF APPRAISAL TECHNIQUES

Intelligence Tests. The area of intelligence testing represents somewhat of a paradox for the counseling professions. On the one hand, the measurement of intelligence has a long history and played a foundational role in the development of psychology as a profession with practical applications beyond teaching and research (Aiken, 2003). On the other hand, the conceptualization and definition of intelligence testing has proven to be among the most elusive in the area of appraisal (Kaplan & Saccuzzo, 2001). Generally, *intelligence* refers to one's capacity to learn and one's ability to reason, judge, and effectively adapt to the environment. Intelligence tests measure the examinee's ability to think abstractly and use verbal, numerical, and abstract symbols (Drummond, 2004).

Intelligence testing originated in 1905, when Simon Binet, a French psychologist, was asked develop a process by which children not likely to benefit from public school education could be identified. Originally, Binet developed a scale that was age related and used *mental age* (MA) as an index to indicate level of intellectual functioning possessed by an average child at a given chronological age. Terman (1916) further developed the concept by introducing the *intelligence quotient* (IQ), computed by dividing one's mental age by his or her chronological age and then multiplying the quotient by 100 (to remove decimals). The IQ has become the standard index of intelligence, although it is now determined based on the *deviation IQ,* which assumes the normal distribution of IQ among the general population.

Intelligence tests have been developed for administration to individuals and groups. For example, the Wechsler scales are individually administered inventories with age-related versions for preschoolers (the Wechsler Preschool and Primary Scale of Intelligence—Revised), primary and secondary schoolers (the Wechler Intelligence Scale for Children—IV [WISC-IV]), and adults (the Wechsler Adult Intelligence Scale—III). On the Wechsler tests, specific subtests are administered to the examinee. Some of these subtests require verbal responses, whereas other subtests require performance responses. The raw scores obtained on these subtests are converted to scaled scores and summed to yield verbal and performance IQ indices. The full-scale IQ is calculated by summing the verbal and performance

FIGURE 7.1 Relationship of Full-Scale IQ to Verbal IQ, Performance IQ, and Subtests

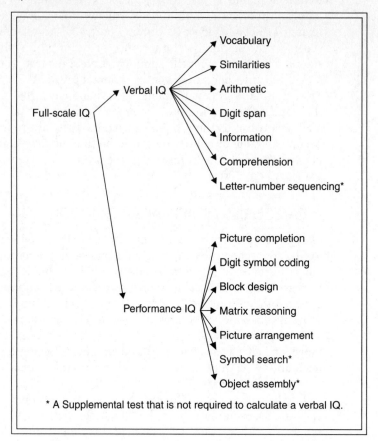

* A Supplemental test that is not required to calculate a verbal IQ.

scores. Figure 7.1 shows the relationship of the various subtests to the calculation of verbal, performance, and full-scale IQ.

Intelligence tests are used to make decisions regarding the placement of children in school programs, diagnosis of mental retardation, and learning disability. In addition, performance on intelligence tests can provide valuable information on individuals' information processing skills. However, the use of intelligence tests continues to be controversial. With widespread disagreement regarding the nature of the concept, opinions differ on the weight that should be placed on obtained scores when making basic decisions that greatly affect examinees' lives.

Achievement Tests. Of the varieties of appraisal instruments, achievement tests are by far the most numerous. Included in this category are teacher-made tests encountered in primary and secondary school settings, standardized tests administered at various grade levels across school systems, comprehensive exams administered to graduate students as they near completion of their academic programs, and minimum competency exams used by states as part of licensure requirements. Generally, achievement tests are appraisal instruments that measure a person's degree of learning in a specific subject or task.

Until the 20th century, the primary method of measuring achievement was by administration of oral exams. It was not until 1864 that George Fisher, of England, developed an objective test for measuring achievement in spelling, and by the early 1900s, objective formats became the norm (Aiken, 2003). Recently, though, there has been a marked increase in the construction of standardized achievement tests using an essay format.

Achievement tests serve a number of purposes. Traditionally, they have been the primary tools used in determining the level of students' academic achievement. Second, the results and conclusions derived from these tests provide instructors with useful feedback concerning the extent to which classroom instructional activities are meeting the individual learning needs of students. Third, the public is increasingly demanding that school systems be held accountable for the services they provide. The outcome measures derived from the results of achievement testing are used in determining the extent to which a given teacher, school, or system is living up to its stated objectives.

You might ask, "What relevance do achievement tests have for mental health and community counselors?" Frequently, achievement tests provide counselors with useful information in determining the young client's current level of functioning and what can reasonably be expected. Such information is useful in establishing what Vygotsky (1962) referred to the person's *zone of proximal development*. This concept refers to the range of tasks currently beyond the child's capabilities but that can be mastered through the verbal guidance and modeling of a more skilled child or adult. The information attained from achievement tests can be used by counselors to assist the child, teachers, and parents adapt to each other's requirements within the context of reciprocal relationships (Santrock, 2006).

Furthermore, scores on achievement tests may be included in a school's response to a request made by the mental health counselor for the release of confidential information, which might be critical for case conceptualization, diagnosis, and treatment planning. For example, diagnosis of learning disorders requires evidence of a significant discrepancy between obtained scores on intelligence and achievement tests. Thus, a child who attains an IQ of 100 on the WISC-III but a 70 on the Wide Range Achievement Test—2nd Edition (WRAT-II) might receive the diagnosis of learning disability because the differential between scores is two standard deviation units. Other tests measure not only the general level of achievement but also the degree of strength or weakness in specific subskills. Thus, further testing may reveal the precise nature of the learning disorder and suggest useful approaches for therapeutic intervention.

Aptitude Tests and Interest Inventories. Aptitude tests are used in a variety of settings to predict what people can learn (Drummond, 2004). A number of specialized aptitude tests are used as sources of information in the selection of candidates for academic programs. The Scholastic Aptitude Test (SAT) and the American College Testing

Program (ACT) are used by many colleges and universities to assist in making undergraduate admissions decisions. The SAT consists of two major sections: The first assesses verbal and mathematical reasoning; the second includes an English essay. The ACT contains a series of subtests that cover the following subjects: mathematics, social studies, and natural sciences. Other exams are used to guide decision making for graduate school admissions. Examples of these include the Graduate Record Exam (GRE), Medical College Admissions Test (MCAT), Graduate Management Admissions Test (GMAT), Law School Admissions Test (LSAT), and the Millers Analogies Test (MAT).

Other aptitude tests are designed to measure skills necessary for successful on-the-job performance. Some are measures of general skills such as mechanical ability, manual dexterity, or spatial relations. For example, the Purdue Pegboard test consists of five tasks that measure fine hand and finger movement. On one part of the test, examinees put small pins into holes, placing a small washer and collar over the pin. This task is repeated and the entire task takes from 5 to 10 minutes. Times scores are compared to those of machine operators, production workers, and general factory applicants. In contrast, some aptitude tests measure skills for specific professional groups such as clerical, artistic, musical, or computer aptitude. The Clerical Aptitude Test is a pencil-and-paper test and measures the ability to check numbers, names, dates, and addresses.

Interest inventories are self-report tests where the examinee expresses his or her likes and dislikes for a variety of activities and attitudes. These are compared to the interest patterns of the members of different occupational groups and used by professional counselors to assist persons in finding jobs that match their interests. As we learned in chapter 2, the vocational counseling movement and the development of interest inventories were central in the establishment of counseling as a unique profession. Today, interest inventories are administered for a variety of purposes and in high schools, colleges, and rehabilitation contexts. They are also used to assist persons in making midlife career changes and pre/postretirement decisions. Although school counselors and career counselors are among the most frequent users, consumers of interest inventories also include industrial consultants and human resources practitioners (Aiken, 2003).

The Strong Interest Inventory (SII) Fourth Edition is a widely used interest inventory that integrates the personality theory of John Holland. It is designed to assist persons in making educational and vocational decisions and retirement plans and understanding employees' job satisfaction or dissatisfaction. All occupations are viewed as falling into one of six types: realistic, investigative, artistic, social, enterprising, and conventional. These form the basis for the General Occupational Theme Scale. In addition to identifying the predominant occupational types of the examinee, the SII includes 23 basic interest scales, 207 occupational scales, 12 professional scales, and an academic comfort scale. Comprehensive computer-generated reports synthesize the wealth of data to provide counselors and examinees with relevant information to facilitate career decision making.

Personality Tests. *Personality* can be defined as the relatively stable and distinctive characteristics of behavior that reflects the person's reactions to the environment and unique adjustment to life. Personality tests attempt to assess the following characteristics of individuals:

- *Personality traits*—relatively enduring tendencies to act, think, and feel in a certain manner in any given situation;
- *Personality states*—emotional reactions that vary from situation to situation;
- *Personality types*—general descriptions of personal styles, such as high social interest, high activity levels, and subjective styles of personal decision making;
- *Self-concept*—the person's view of self.

Frequently, personality tests are used in clinical settings to provide useful data for diagnosing or gaining insight into the nature of the client's problems. However, numerous personality tests tap into the personal strengths and generally healthy characteristics of examinees. These can provide insight into client's behaviors and style of relating for the purpose of growth enhancement. In addition, personality tests are used in numerous research studies.

Several strategies are used in personality assessment. Often, a structured, objective format consisting of true/false or multiple-choice items is used. These present structured, unambiguous stimuli, and the interpretation of responses is fairly evident and specific. For example, the Myers-Briggs Type Indicator uses an objective item format and is based on the personality theory of Carl Jung. Its purpose is to determine where examinees fall on the introversion-extroversion continuum and, in addition, identify the primary way in which the examinee experiences or comes to know the world: sensing, intuiting, feeling, or thinking. In contrast, the Minnesota Multiphasic Personality Inventory—2 and California Personality Inventory also use objective formats but are constructed by the criterion-group strategy. Items were selected for inclusion on these tests on the basis of how the standardization group responded and not on the basis of mere item content.

Other personality tests use a projective format. These tests present examinees with relatively unstructured stimuli such as inkblots, ambiguous pictures, or play materials. The underlying assumption is that examinees will project personal thoughts, feelings, and interpretations on the stimulus that is seen. Examples of projective personality tests are the Rorschach Inkblot Test, Thematic Apperception Test, and a House-Tree-Person "drawing".

Self-Report Clinical Scales. Hundreds of self-report scales have been developed over the past 2 decades that are routinely used in clinical settings. Often, mental health and community counselors must assess clients along specific cognitive, emotional, or behavioral dimensions to determine the frequency or intensity of the symptoms being treated. Such assessment may be required to measure pretreatment levels of presenting symptoms, monitor progress during the process of counseling, or measure outcomes.

Clinical scales focus on specific dimensions of the client's experience, such as depression, anxiety, anger, assertiveness, or hopelessness. Because most have been developed for efficient administration, scoring, and interpretation, self-report clinical scales are usually brief and written in objective formats. The intent of the items is apparent to the examinee, which creates the potential for faking good or bad.

The Beck Depression Inventory—II (BDI-II) is a widely used self-report clinical scale. It consists of 21 items, each of which contains four statements relating to the symptoms of depression. The following provides an illustration of an item on the BDI-II:

A. 0 I have not experienced recent difficulty falling asleep.
   1 I have recently experienced some difficulty in falling asleep.
   2 Frequently, I am unable to fall asleep.
   3 I am never able to fall asleep.

The examinee selects the response that most closely reflects his or her recent experience. Upon completion, the responses are summed. The scores can range from 0 to 63. Normal mood fluctuations are indicated by scores ranging form 1 to 10; mild mood disturbance 11 to 16; borderline clinical depression 17 to 20; moderate depression 21 to 30; severe depression 31 to 40; over 40, extreme depression (Beck, Steer, & Brown, 1996).

Although such appraisal instruments share the weaknesses of other self-report measures, they do provide an efficient means of monitoring client progress and outcome. In addition, these tools are useful for gathering data when conducting program evaluations. Thus, mental health and community counselors should have a working knowledge of the vast array of self-report clinical scales so that they can establish the effectiveness of their professional practice.

ETHICAL PRACTICE IN APPRAISAL

The ethical practice of appraisal encompasses five specific tasks: test selection, administration, interpretation, reporting, and storage of test-related materials (AMHCA, 2000). In addition, mental health and community must attain and maintain professional competence in appraisal skills to protect the client's welfare. Only professionals who have adequate education, training, and experience can select, administer, score, and interpret test responses. Those who fail to recognize and practice within professional boundaries can cause great harm to clients. Such unethical practice can result in legal action or restrictive sanctions against the counseling professional.

Test Selection. In selecting specific appraisal instruments, professional counselors take into consideration the specific question(s) to be answered and the unique characteristics of the examinee. To find the appropriate instruments, they must have a working knowledge of the vast array of instruments and be able to access information that can validate the usage of the particular test in the specific situation. Test manuals provide useful information on the purpose, construction, and psychometric properties of the test. In addition, reference tools such as *Tests in Print VI* (Murphy, Plake, Impara, & Spies, 2002) or *The Fifteenth Mental Measurements Yearbook* (Plake, Impara, & Spies, 2003) contain publisher information, concise overviews, and reviews of specific tests. Finally, articles found in the professional literature frequently discuss specific test applications. A firm grasp of psychometric theory and techniques is required if professional counselors are to develop sound rationales to justify their test selection.

In addition, the selection process must be sensitive to the specific needs and characteristics of the client. Factors such as age, gender, cultural background, and cognitive developmental level must be considered. The mental health and community counselor needs to be sure the specific test has been standardized and has norms that allow test results to be valid, reliable, and generalized.

Test Administration. Great care is taken when administering tests. Instructions must be carefully followed to ensure standardization. A comfortable yet professional setting for test taking includes adequate lighting, seating, noise control, privacy, and temperature. It is vital that all extraneous environmental factors that might contribute unexplained variance be controlled. Test administration should be postponed if client illness or extraordinary events might influence obtained results. Information regarding the presence of physical disabilities, such as limitations of visual or auditory senses or eye/hand coordination, should be gathered in advance so that adequate accommodations can be made. Finally, adequate time must be allowed for completion of the test.

Test Interpretation. Procedures for scoring tests are usually clearly explained in the test manual. The professional is responsible for accurate scoring and interpretation of test responses, even when based on computerized services. Conclusions must be solidly based on and justified by empirical evidence. Because the data obtained through testing are considered a sample of the examinees' repertoire of behaviors, conclusions are never based solely on test results. Rather, the results are always considered within the context of client's specific situation and take into account test-taking circumstances and cultural factors. If the test used lacks sufficient degrees of validity and reliability, conclusions can only be tentatively made. In addition, great care must be taken to prevent preconceived judgments or examiner biases from influencing interpretations.

Test Reporting. It is essential that the results and conclusions of testing be communicated in an ethical and professional manner. Although tests are administered by counselors seeking to inform diagnositic and treatment decision making, results and conclusions are frequently directed to other professionals who are working with the client. In addition, clients have a right to be fully informed regarding the rationale for testing as well as results obtained.

Thus, test reports are written to meet the demands of various audiences. The bottom line, of course, is that test reports be written in such a way that the rationale for and conclusions derived from testing be communicated clearly and directly. In general, unnecessary use of professional jargon should be avoided. And as with other forms of professional writing, conciseness and precision are virtues. The writer's professional reputation is reflected in the style, readability, and grammatical correctness of the document. Reports should be written in a straightforward, positive, and nonjudgmental manner so its contents will respond to the specific questions that originally necessitated the testing.

Clients have a right to receive feedback regarding their test performance, how the test results will be used, and who will have access to the information (ACA, 2005). Again, counselors must be sensitive to language and cultural differences that might influence the client's ability to construct accurate meanings for and implications of the results.

In addition, all documents related to the client's testing are confidential and the release of such information requires the client's informed consent. Electronic transfer of test results can occur only upon guarantee that information transferring devices are capable of delivering the data to the intended receivers only. Staff involved in typing, filing, and mailing test reports must be trained in the importance of maintaining confidentiality.

Finally, mental health and community counselors are responsible for the security of test materials, data, and reports. Test materials should be stored in a secure file cabinet and room. Adequate office management requires that the location of test-related files and documents be known at all times. Counselors should avoid leaving files containing test results open on desktops where others can determine the examinee's identity. In general, ethical practice in appraisal maintains and supports the integrity and well-being of those served.

RESEARCH AND PROGRAM EVALUATION

Basically, research is a systematic process of obtaining data for the purpose of answering questions, resolving problems, and gaining greater understanding into the nature of specific phenomena and processes. The systematic process used is often referred to as the *scientific method*. It consists of the following stages:

1. A statement of the problem or research question is constructed. This is a concise statement of what it is you are proposing to investigate and why it is significant. The specific variables to be explored are identified and may include dependent, independent, intervening, and potentially confounding variables.
2. Based on existing information, a hypothesis is constructed. This is the researcher's hunch on which direction the gathered data will point.
3. A specific plan or procedure to gather information to answer the research question is developed. This plan includes determining who will participate in the study, what specifically is to be measured, and the procedures to be used in gathering the information.
4. The plan is implemented resulting in the collection of data. In other words, the researcher carries out his or her plan according to its stated intention.
5. The data are analyzed and interpreted. This is where the data are transformed into numbers for statistical analysis. Meaning is then attached to the results obtained. The results are conveyed, initially, by stating if the hypothesis was supported.
6. Conclusions are made that respond to the original research questions. In addition, limitations of the study are noted and future directions for research are identified.

Relatively few practicing mental health and community counselors spend significant time and energy conducting research to develop theories or investigate related theoretical issues. Rather, they find themselves working in the trenches of direct service delivery. They are more likely to apply research methods to determine the extent of clinical progress, measure outcomes, determine the effectiveness of psychoeducational programs, or conduct needs assessments as part of a program development process. The results of such studies have immediate relevance to practitioners. But because such studies take place in the real world, they lack the sterile conditions that are typical of laboratory research.

KEY CONCEPTS AND PRINCIPLES IN RESEARCH

Sampling. Counselors are rarely able to have access to all the members of a population or the entire range of potential behaviors. *Sampling* refers to the techniques used to gather data from a subset of the entire population or set of behaviors in such a way that the data gathered are representative of the population. If I conduct an empirical study to determine the extent to which interpersonal therapy decreases symptoms of depression, I will limit my study to a selected sample of persons who are representative of the entire population of depressed persons. This is accomplished by taking a *random sample* of participants, where each person in the population has an equal opportunity of being selected for the study. When more than one variable has the potential to confound the outcome of the study, researchers sometimes use *stratified random sampling*. For example, the outcome might be influenced by differences in the age or gender of the participant and there is a risk that the experimental and placebo groups might be imbalanced according to these variables. Using stratified random sampling, the researcher subdivides the sample according to the identified variables and then randomly samples each variable separately. This allows the characteristics of the sample to resemble more closely the characteristics of the population.

Sometimes extraneous variables operate within the selected group that are beyond the direct control or the awareness of the researcher. The operation of these variables may go undetected and influence the outcome of the study. The easiest way for researchers to overcome this problem is through the *random assignment* of participants to the groups. For example, we might take the group of depressed persons and randomly assign them to either interpersonal treatment or placebo groups in such a way that each person has an equal opportunity to be placed in either group and the placement of any particular participant does not affect the probability of another from being assigned to a group.

Validity. *Validity* refers to the *accuracy* of definitions and research methods. Actually, two types of validity must be considered simultaneously—*internal* and *external validity*. Internal validity refers to the extent to which the results of a study can be interpreted accurately. Suppose we are interested in comparing the effectiveness of cognitive and interpersonal therapies in treating depression. To do so, student volunteers are assigned to either the cognitive or interpersonal groups. Each group receives 10 sessions of treatment, delivered using a group modality, in which counselors, self-identified as either cognitive or interpersonal therapists, follow protocols developed by the researchers. Data are gathered and the researchers conclude that cognitive therapy is more effective than interpersonal therapy in decreasing levels of depression. To what extent can or should we have confidence in the accuracy of the conclusions? Due to the lack of control over extraneous variables or initial levels of depression in participants, we have no way of knowing whether the results obtained are, in fact, due to the interventions. The impact of delivering counseling through group modalities introduces dynamics into the design that might add to or detract from the power of the identified independent variables. The results of such a study cannot be interpreted accurately due to a lack of internal validity.

External validity exists to the extent that the results of a study can be generalized to other populations and conditions. Why might the study in the previous example lack external validity? To what extent can the results of the study be generalized to persons who are clinically depressed? Because the participants in the study were volunteer students, we have no way of knowing whether the quality of affect in the experimental groups resembles that of clinical populations. Furthermore, administering treatment in group modalities limits the extent to which the results would generalize to the treatment of individuals.

Reliability. A concept closely related to validity is reliability. In fact, reliability is a necessary characteristic for validity (Wiersma, 2000). When we consider reliability in research, the focus is on the consistency of methods, conditions, and results. *Internal reliability* deals with the extent to which methods of data collection, analysis, and interpretation of results are consistent within a study. In contrast, *external reliability* refers to the extent to which independent researchers using the same methods can obtain the same or similar results.

Operational Definitions. Many of the variables of interest to counselors are often defined in subjective terms that defy direct, concise measurement. If interested in investigating or assessing aggressive behavior in children, an agreed-upon definition must be constructed that provides researchers an accurate description of the phenomenon under study. Furthermore, the construct must be defined in such a way that independent raters agree on the presence or absence of the aggressive behavior.

Operational definitions are used in research and appraisal to safeguard against threats to the validity and reliability by defining concepts and variables in terms of the specific operations in which they can be measured. For example, mental health or community counselors may want to determine their effectiveness in treating anxiety. Using operational definitions, anxiety can be defined in terms of a test score, observations of social withdrawal, and specific behavioral indicators of the activation of the sympathetic nervous system. Such definitions guide researchers toward more precise measurement of constructs being investigated and reduce measurement error, therefore increasing the validity and reliability of the study.

SPECIFIC MODELS OF RESEARCH DESIGN

Direct Observation. *Observational research* refers to methods in which the researcher observes and records the ongoing behavior of participants, but does not seek to exert influence on the situation or manipulate behavior in any way. For example, in classic research on attachment using the Strange Situation (Ainsworth, 1978), researchers observed the behaviors of young children in a play room alone, with a stranger, and upon unification with their primary caregivers. Their conclusions provided data for the creation of specific research questions and hypotheses that, upon further investigation, led to the discovery of secure and insecure attachment relationships.

Observational research can take two general forms. In *naturalistic observation,* data collection occurs in the existing context with no manipulation of the environment. The researcher measures the behavior of individuals in their natural environment. In contrast, *participant-observer research* takes place when the researcher joins and participates in the group under study. Researchers using observational methods must control for the *Hawthorne effect*—knowledge of being observed sometimes leads participants to behave differently than when in natural settings.

Mental health and community counselors may use observational methods as part of assessment and treatment monitoring. A school system might refer a third-grade student who is frequently unmanageable in classroom settings. To understand the nature of the presenting problem, the counselor may identify operational definitions of *unmanageable behavior* and then conduct an observation to assess the behavior in context. Or an agency may be interested in determining the effect of implementing a peer/consumer support component in an existing day treatment program. Data gathered through direct observation of clients' behavior would be important in evaluating the relative benefits of the program.

If observational research is to be valid and reliable, counselor-researchers must attend to several factors. First, the behavior or phenomenon under study must be well defined. This is the only way the researcher can know what to count and what not to count. If, for example, the variable being observed is "aggressive behavior," those rating the behavior must have an operational definition that can facilitate high interrater agreement of its relative presence or absence. Second, it is important for researchers to specify the exact conditions in which the observations are made. In other words, what are the antecedent conditions potentially supporting the behavior? Does the aggressive behavior take place during instructional time, recess, lunch, or immediately prior to dismissal? Such information places the behavior in context and assists in the construction of case conceptualizations and treatment plans. Third, researchers must decide how to "count" the behavior. For example, a simple frequency count of the displays of aggressive behavior might be used as the measure of the dependent variable. But does the report of mere quantity deliver the quality of data desired? To what extent should levels of intensity or severity be considered? Do aggressive actions against inanimate objects count? What about verbal aggressiveness? Clearly, valid and reliable observational studies require operationally defined variables that accurately reflect the characteristic being investigated.

Survey Methods. Research studies using survey methods are concerned primarily with determining *what is* and much less interested in finding explanations. In addition, survey methods are used to gather information on how people feel, think, perceive, or behave in specific contexts. Typical applications include consumer satisfaction surveys, needs assessments in program development, determination of levels of interests or preferences, and program evaluations.

A variety of methods are available when conducting survey research. Structured and unstructured interviews can be conducted in person or over the phone. But in either case, an oral exchange takes place between the interviewer and interviewee.

In contrast, questionnaires can be used to elicit numerous forms of responses. For example, checklists, Likert scales, multiple choice, or brief written responses each have unique strengths and weaknesses. The researcher weighs these strengths and weaknesses in selecting the approach that best serves his or her purposes.

Correlational Methods. Correlational research seeks to explore the relationship between two or more variables. For example, a researcher may be interested in the relationship between measures of religiosity and mental health. Although it would be extremely difficult to establish a causal relationships between religious orientation (e.g., Allport's intrinsic, extrinsic, and indiscriminately pro-religious orientations) and level of mental health, it is possible to explore the manner in which mental health covaries with religious orientation.

The strength of the relationship is communicated by calculating a correlation coefficient, which may range from −1.0 to +1.0. A positive correlation exists when levels of mental health increase as levels of intrinsic religious orientation increase. If an inverse relationship exists, a negative correlation between the two variables is present. It is beyond the purpose and scope of this text to discuss the statistical procedures. The statistical analysis of data is greatly facilitated through the application of statistical packages for computers, such as SPSS (Statistical Package for the Social Sciences).

If a relationship between two or more variables can be established, it is theoretically possible to predict how a person will perform on one variable based on his or her performance on the other variable. For example, decisions regarding the admission of students to a graduate program can be partially based on the relationship among graduate GPA and scores on the GRE, undergraduate GPA, and ratings of performance in the admissions interview. Or scores obtained on measures of negative self-statements and cognitive distortions might be used to predict one's level of depression. In both examples, multivariate methods (e.g., multiple regression analysis) are required because more than two variables are being correlated.

Experimental Methods. In simple experiments, a researcher deliberately manipulates or varies one or more variables (i.e., the independent variable) and measures the effect on one or more variables (i.e., the dependent variable). When control is exerted over potentially confounding variables, a true experiment is conducted that is capable of detecting cause-effect relationships. Ideally, clinical studies attempt to control for all critical variables other than the type of treatment. For example, a researcher may seek to answer the following research question: "Which of several prominent treatment regimens is most effective in decreasing levels of social phobia in clinical populations?" In order to test the hypothesis, members of a clinical populations diagnosed with social phobia are randomly selected and assigned to a person-centered, cognitive-behavioral, strategic family, and placebo groups. Treatment manuals are used to insure that the implementation of treatments is accurate and consistent. The outcome data for the groups are analyzed to establish if statistically significant differences occur.

Sometimes, though, researchers are unable to exert the level of control over variables necessary for true experimentation to occur. For example, the researcher may be interested in determining if significant differences in diagnosis occur between males and females or among individuals of various socioeconomic classes presenting with similar symptoms. Because it is impossible to create groups through random selection assignment, the researcher relies on random selection of participants from within existing populations. Such studies are described as using quasi-experimental methods. No experimental manipulation occurs because the differences between groups are based on preexisting characteristics of the participants. The importance in the distinction between experimental and quasi-experimental approaches lies in the ability of the former to detect causal relationships.

Within-Subject Designs. In a variety of situations, it is desirable to focus on individual participants. Frequently, mental health and community counselors are interested in determining the effect of treatment on individual clients. Within-subject designs investigate individuals under both experimental (i.e., treatment) and nonexperimental conditions and are sometimes known as $N = 1$ studies. These approaches are characterized by the single-subject rule, which means that only one variable is manipulated at a time. All other variables are held constant. This is necessary to ensure that the results of treatment can be attributed to the treatment. In a simple A-B design, the participant is observed until a stable rating of the dependent variable over a set length of time can be established. This period of "no treatment" is referred to as the baseline condition (A). After the baseline is established, the treatment (i.e., independent variable) is introduced and measured at intervals equal to those in the baseline. Interpretation of results is based on the assumption that changes noted in the dependent variable are due to the action of the independent variable.

Within-subject designs have numerous applications in the practice of mental health and community counseling. For example, Joe was referred to the college counseling center because of poor academic performance. In collaboration with his counselor, Joe developed and implemented a self-management program to enhance his studying of undergraduate coursework. To establish a baseline, he operationalized the dependent variable in terms of minutes spent studying per night. He gathered baseline data for one week. He then implemented a plan that involved removal of television while studying. The effect on minutes of study was monitored for 1 week. This was followed by the implementation of a token system in which points were earned for specific number of minutes spent in study and could be used toward the purchase of a CD. The plan was effective in significantly increasing the amount of time spent in study. As the new behavior stabilized over time, Joe weaned himself from his self-management plan while continuing to monitor the dependent variable for indicators of relapse.

Qualitative Methods. Increasingly, researchers are utilizing methods that are less reliant on quantitative measures. Qualitative methods use words rather than numbers to describe phenomena. Studies using qualitative methods are often descriptive and exploratory in nature and are less concerned about testing specific hypotheses or establishing the validity of theories or techniques. Frequently, this method uses direct observation, in which the researcher is a participant-observer, as a means of gathering data. Examples of qualitative methods include case studies, ethnography, or phenomenological investigations.

PROGRAM EVALUATION

Program evaluation is a form of applied research that systematically investigates the effectiveness of intervention programs. Frequently, mental health and community counselors must answer questions on the extent to which specific agency programs are producing the positive benefits that they purport to promote. Funding organizations, mental health boards, tax payers, and consumers need to distinguish effective from ineffective programs. Programs failing to live up to expectations must be revised, replaced with more productive alternatives, or simply eliminated. Systematic evaluation of programs serves as a basic feedback mechanism enabling program managers to devise and implement corrective measures as needed to ensure that consumers benefit from program participation.

Program evaluation involves, first, the thorough description of the entity to be evaluated and, then, the establishment of standards or criteria by which the performance of the program is judged (Rossi, Freeman, & Lipsey, 1999). Two general approaches are *formative* and *summative evaluation*. *Formative evaluation* is research activities undertaken to provide useful information that will inform decisions on how to improve the operations of a program. It focuses on all operations of the service delivery system. In contrast, *summative evaluation* is research activities designed and implemented to determine the overall effectiveness of the program. Thus, summative evaluation is concerned with outcomes.

Well-designed programs have several important characteristics. First, it is critical that an accurate assessment of the needs and wants of the intended recipients be conducted. Based on an accurate understanding of community needs, program developers can develop a mission statement that expresses the vision and purpose of the program. In addition, the identified program goals and objectives are anchored in the belief that their attainment will lead to the fulfillment of the identified needs. The program then becomes the step-by-step means by which the specific goals and objectives are attained. Furthermore, the staff possesses the working knowledge and skills necessary to carry out the program successfully. Finally, the delivery system has the necessary backup supports required for successful implementation and maintenance of the program. This includes human resources, equipment, facility, and technical supports.

Numerous research methods are used in conducting program evaluations. Their selection depends on the specific purpose of the evaluation, the needs and expectations of the stakeholders, and the specific nature of the questions being asked. For example, survey research, often using interviews or questionnaires, may be used as part of the initial needs assessment. In addition, survey research is used in measuring program delivery processes or level of consumer satisfaction. Sometimes information from the organization's existing data management systems provides an efficient means of obtaining information regarding the day-to-day operations of the program. Participant-observer methods are useful in gathering qualitative data for formative evaluation. Quasi-experimental methods can be used to assess the extent to which program recipients benefited from their participation in the program by comparing scores on outcome measures with those of a control or waiting list group.

Given the immense number of variables that run out of control in implementing and evaluating programs, researchers must choose the best possible design from a scientific perspective. But they must also consider the potential uses and importance of the results, the practicality of the various design options, and the likelihood that the selected method will produce credible results (Rossi et al., 1999). Thus, the results obtained in program evaluation may lack the validity and reliability of true experiments. But when conducted with appropriate rigor, program evaluations enable program managers to assess the quality of service provided in the context of real-world applications.

ETHICAL PRACTICE IN RESEARCH

Mental health and community counselors who conduct research must always act within the ethical standards as put forth by the ACA (2005) and AMHCA (2000). The most basic responsibility is to respect the dignity of participants and promote their welfare. Every effort is made to protect participants from potential harm, misuse, and discomfort. The principles of informed consent and confidentiality have specific applications for researchers.

Informed consent is a fundamental right of participants in a research study to make decisions regarding their participation in a study based on the accurate description of all features of the investigation. Researchers must openly communicate the purpose and procedures of the study, the potential risks of harm or discomfort, and potential benefits or changes that might be expected. Furthermore, it is communicated that participation is voluntary and participants are free to withdraw from the study at any point without repercussion. If deception is used, researchers explain the necessity of this procedure as soon as possible. Following the collection of data, participants are fully debriefed in order to dispel any potential misconceptions. Finally, the right to informed consent is extended to sponsoring or participating agencies, organizations, and institutions.

Mental health and community counselors understand that any gathered data or information pertaining to participants in the process of conducting research is confidential. The personal identity of participants must be protected. Researchers gather data in such a way that data cannot be linked to the identity of the specific participants. Any possibility that personal information might be divulged to others should be fully explained as part of the informed consent process.

Finally, counselors must report results of their investigations in an ethical manner. Care is taken to communicate the results of research accurately. The limitations of the investigation and possible alternative interpretations of results should be stated clearly so that readers will not be mislead in any way. Due recognition should be given to students/research assistants or others who made significant contributions to the design or conducting of the investigation.

CONCLUSION

Now that you have been introduced to the role of appraisal and research in the practice of mental health and community counseling, the question that may linger is, "So what?" After reading the previous pages, you may be convinced that tasks of appraisal and research are peripheral to the professional role you anticipate. Thus, you do not see such skills as having a significant impact on your professional identity.

However, our involvement in research and appraisal has much to do with the integrity of our profession. With little or no concern for the empirical validation of the procedures we use, little foundation exists for our proclamations of therapeutic efficacy. If consumers are to benefit from the availability of effective counseling, and if counselors are to survive this era of increased accountability, it is essential that the mental health counseling profession act to promote the interventions of proven effectiveness (King & Heyne, 2000).

How would you defend your practice against the accusation that the mental health profession foists on consumers a product that is suspect (Koop, 2004)? This is a question of professional integrity—the extent to which counselors actually do that which they purport. To advocate to consumers, the general public, legislators, and third-party reimbursers on behalf of the profession, several basic skills are required. First, it is vital that mental health and community counselors comprehend the current, existent literature on empirically validated therapies. This requires, at the least, a working knowledge of literature searches and the ability to critically review relevant research on their psychometric and methodological merits. Second, mental health practitioners must be capable of evaluating their own professional practice. In most cases, this entails the ability to design and carry out research using $N = 1$ and program evaluation methodologies. In addition, this research needs to be more qualitative and contextually sensitive if conclusions are to reflect accurately the realities of our clinical worlds.

Most mental health professionals agree that there is much more to determining whether a particular approach to treatment is valuable than simply demonstrating that it can produce statistically significant outcomes under controlled conditions (King & Heyne, 2000). From the consumers' point of view, services are sought with an expectation of positive outcomes in mind. In many ways, it comes down to our ability to meet clients where they are, gain an accurate understanding of their situation, identify goals, and implement a devised plan that achieves these goals. The competent mental health and community counselor will utilize appraisal and research skills to achieve these ends.

DISCUSSION QUESTIONS

1. In your own words, what is meant by the term *scientist-practitioner?* To what extent does your understanding of this term fit with what you see as being the primary function of mental health counselors?

2. What specific factors do you see as limiting mental health and community counselors' ability to be scientist-practitioners? Do these influence the quality or quantity of original research and theory emanating from the mental health counseling profession?
3. To what extent will you depend on the use of standardized appraisal instruments to understand the presenting problems of your clients? What specific clinical situations do you see appraisal instruments as being necessary components of the assessment process?
4. In what specific ways might research inform your clinical practice? At what particular times in your future practice of counseling might you engage in empirical research? Identify ways in which having a research orientation will strengthen your effectiveness as a counselor.
5. What training and clinical experiences would enable you to be considered an expert in the use of a particular psychological test (e.g., MMPI-2)?

SUGGESTED ACTIVITIES

1. Read the section of your state's licensure law that discusses scope of practice for licensed mental health or professional counselors. Does it specifically define or specify any limitations regarding the use of psychological tests or appraisal instruments?
2. Locate the most recent edition of *Tests in Print* and *The Mental Measurements Yearbook*. Select a specific test of interest and review the information that is provided by these important reference tools.
3. Look through recent issues of the *Journal of Counseling and Development* and *Journal of Mental Health Counseling*. What topics are the subjects of empirical research? To what extent would you be able to apply the findings of the articles contained in these journals to your professional practice? What topics of interest would you like to investigate empirically? Would you consider publishing your results in a professional journal? Why or why not?

8

Professional Practice in Multicultural Contexts

W̶e had invited a small group of students to our home for a fish fry. As Antowine and Anika approached the small town in which we lived, a police car pulled out from a parking lot and began to follow them. After making several turns and still being followed, Antowine decided to take a more indirect route to our home, turning several times and going into other neighborhoods. The police car stayed behind several car lengths, not missing a turn. Finally, as Antowine turned into our driveway, the police car slowly drove on.

Upon their arrival, Antowine told us about touring our town while being followed. The couple took it in stride and noted that they have come to expect such "welcomes." As young African- and Asian Americans, they had experienced similar episodes as they ventured into small-town America. Yes, we are all created equal, but, unfortunately, and in the words of George Orwell, some are created more equal than others. Much has changed since the Civil Rights Movement of the 1960s, but the "problem of race" is still with us (Jones, 1997 p.2). Simply reflect on the public reactions to the beating of Rodney King, the O. J. Simpson case, or University of Michigan's fight to maintain its right to consider race in making undergraduate admission decisions.

The multicultural perspective is foundational to the practice of contemporary mental health and community counseling. Clearly, diversity in race and culture is the rule and not the exception in our society. Multiculturalism tolerates and even supports alternative views of mental health, taking into account not only differences in race and ethnicity but also differences in nationality, education, gender orientation, religion, age, geographic location, and socioeconomic influences. To do so is a logical consequence of being ecologically minded. Thus, mental health professionals who embrace the multicultural perspective are able to work with persons of different backgrounds without assessing recognized differences between themselves and their clients in terms of being right and wrong, superior and inferior.

This chapter introduces the implications of diversity and multiculturalism on the profession of mental health counseling. First, the chapter describes the current multiracial, multicultural face of America and the necessity for skilled mental health and community counselors to demonstrate multicultural competence. Second, foundational principles for respectful counseling of diverse populations are discussed. Competent counselors must be aware of numerous barriers to effective cross-cultural counseling and be aware of the influences of their personal cultural self. In addition, a working knowledge of the implications of racial/cultural identity development theory, within- versus between-group differences, and the convergence of multiple identities helps counselors recognize and work with the diversity among various groups of people.

DIVERSITY AND MULTICULTURALISM IN AMERICA

The face of America has changed. The nation is not becoming diverse or multicultural, it *is* diverse and multicultural. This reality makes it vital that counselors develop prerequisite multicultural knowledge and skills if they are to work effectively with the vast array of people in their communities.

Although the U.S. population has always been multicultural in its composition, it has continued to diversify in recent decades as minority populations have increased at higher rates than white non-Hispanic populations (U.S. Census Bureau, 2003). At 69% of the total population in 2002, there are more white non-Hispanics in the U.S. population than ever before. White non-Hispanics comprised 75% of the total population in 1970. In contrast, the Hispanic population has grown from 4.5% in 1970 to 13.5% of the U.S. population in 2002, making it the largest minority population in the country. Black, Asian/Pacific Islanders, and American Indian/Alaska Natives make up about 13%, 4%, and 1% of the U.S. population, respectively.

These various racial and ethnic groups are not evenly distributed throughout the United States (U.S. Census Bureau, 2003). The majority of African Americans (54%) lived in the South in 2000, making up 20% of the population in that region. Similarly, half of all Hispanics live in just two states: California and Texas. The Asian American population, which grew by 72% between 1990 and 2000, is centered in California, New York, and Hawaii. Whereas more than 500,000 declare themselves to be native American/Alaskan, more than 2.2 million declare themselves to be at least partially native American/Alaskan. The majority of native American/Alaskan live in the West and South.

Other important demographic differences, such as educational attainment, labor force participation, and poverty, can be noted among these groups (U.S. Census Bureau, 2000). Eighty-eight percent of white non-Hispanics have completed high school compared to 86% of Asian Americans, 78% African Americans, and 57% of Hispanics. However, 44% of Asian Americans have earned at least a bachelor's degree, compared to 28% of white non-Hispanics, 16% of African Americans, and 11% of Hispanics. Regarding employment, 80% of Hispanic males participate in the civilian labor force, compared to 74% of white non-Hispanics and Asian Americans and 68% of African Americans. For females, though, a higher percentage of African Americans are in the labor force, as compared to 61% of white non-Hispanics, 59% of Asian Americans, and 57% of Hispanics. Generally speaking, married couples have lower poverty rates than other types of family structures. However, all minority groups are more likely to live in poverty as compared to white non-Hispanics. In addition, with 44% of African American households headed by females, race interacts with what has been termed the feminization of poverty.

Dividing the population into the aforementioned groups masks the complex multicultural fabric of contemporary society (U.S. Census Bureau, 2003). For example, considered within the category of Hispanic population are Mexicans, Puerto Ricans, Cubans, and South and Central Americans. Similarly, American Indian is a broad category encompassing persons of various tribal descent, such as Cherokee, Chippewa, Navajo, Choctaw, and Sioux. As we shall see in later sections of this chapter, conceptualizing race and ethnicity as such broad constructs obscures the extent to which within-group and individual differences operate. The well-intentioned but straightforward application of a simple knowledge of the general differences among these groups without more refined ecological reflection can result in stereotyping and counselor insensitivity. Mental health and community counselors must carefully view clients in their unique milieu. Given the interactional nature of the counseling process, it is appropriate to conclude that all counselor-client relationships are, in fact, multicultural (American Psychological Association, 2004).

MULTICULTURALISM AS THE FOURTH FORCE IN COUNSELING

It is common to speak of the counseling profession as having been influenced by specific forces, which have emerged in chronological order. Freud and the psychoanalytic perspective, behaviorism, and humanistic psychology are recognized as the first three forces, respectively (Locke, 1992).

Mental health and community counselors have become alert to the changing face of America and the extent to which basic Western assumptions about the person and helping process are deeply woven into the fabric of the theory and techniques that have historically guided counselors' work. Contemporary trends and the composition of American society have led the counseling profession to view the multicultural orientation as integral to the work of mental health and community counselors. As a result, multiculturalism is rightly recognized as the fourth force in counseling.

The multicultural emphasis grew out of several social trends of the late 1950s and 1960s. The decade of the 1960s was marked by social turmoil and incremental change. While President Kennedy announced his vision of a "New Frontier," the attention of the nation was being called to the deep inequities that existed in U.S. society along the lines of race, culture, and gender. Rosa Parks, Martin Luther King, Jr., and many others took stands against patterns of unfairness, prejudice, and subjection by acting according to higher sets of moral principles. As the industrial era gave way to a multicultural, urban society of the information age, the "melting pot" gave way to a vision of a "mosaic." The globe was shrinking and America was becoming increasingly diverse.

It is from this context that increased sensitivity to issues of race, ethnicity, and culture emerged. By the late 1960s, counselors from minority groups were expressing concern that the practice of counseling ethnically different clients without special training was unethical. In 1973, the American Psychological Association's Vail Conference Follow-Up Commission declared that the provision of counseling services to persons of culturally diverse backgrounds by persons lacking in knowledge and skill in servicing such groups was unethical. Furthermore, it was considered unethical to deny such persons service due to a lack of trained staff. Thus, it became the obligation of mental health agencies to employ culturally competent staff or provide opportunities for continuing education to prepare staff to meet the needs of the culturally diverse population it served (Korman, 1973, cited in Midgette & Meggert, 1991).

Thus, it is no longer possible (or permissible) for counseling professionals to ignore the implications of their own culture or the culture of their clients. They must increase their cultural sensitivity if they are to work effectively with and meet the needs of the diverse members of their communities. This entails becoming more knowledgeable about their own backgrounds and the specific cultural groups with whom they work. It also requires the development of counseling skills that are culturally sensitive and relevant to their clients.

The requirements of nondiscrimination and need for multicultural competence are now codified in the ethical standards of the ACA and the AMHCA. The ACA *Code of Ethics* (1995) and *Code of Ethics* of the AMHCA (2000) require that their members not engage in any form of discriminatory behavior based on the client's age, skin color, culture, disability, ethnic group, gender, race, religion, sexual orientation, marital status, or socioeconomic status. Furthermore, counselors must seek to understand the diverse cultural backgrounds of the clients with whom they work. These principles have specific applications in the ongoing counseling process. In addition, mental health and community counselors respect diversity and resist discriminatory practices when conducting research or when serving in the roles of supervisor, employer, or instructor.

Counselor educators share responsibility in developing and enhancing multicultural awareness and competence among mental health and community counselors. First, and as noted in chapter 5, the standards for the accreditation of graduate school training programs in counseling as specified by CACREP identify social and cultural diversity as one of the common core areas (CACREP, 2001). Second, it is important that practicum and internship experiences provide students with opportunities to work with populations that reflect the racial, ethnic, cultural, and demographic diversity of their communities. Third, graduate students in counseling programs gain important knowledge and skills on relating the many facets of multiculturalism to the specific practice of their specialization (i.e., mental health and community counseling). Finally, academic programs are called on to design recruitment and retention strategies for the employment of faculty members who reflect the diverse backgrounds in society.

KEY DEFINITIONS AND CONCEPTS

Before moving farther along in our discussion, it is helpful to define several foundational terms and concepts that appear repeatedly in any discussion of multiculturalism. Although these are familiar, they are often used interchangeably in a manner that masks subtle distinctions that, when recognized, can lend clarity to the subject. The misuse of these terms in certain contexts is sometimes interpreted as cultural insensitivity.

Can clear, precise distinctions be made among the terms *race, ethnicity,* and *culture?* Much confusion exists and is due to the overlap in specific dimensions that are subsumed under each concept. *Race,* for example, may be defined as a biologically based classification system of people groups based on visible physical characteristics (e.g., skin pigmentation, facial features, texture of hair). Clearly, the identification of racial differences based on differences of physical appearance is one of the most prominent boundary markers used in the construction of individual and group identities. However, given that the Human Genome Project found 99.9% of the 30,000 human genes shared by everyone (Anderson, 2003), to what extent are such biologically based distinctions truly valid or meaningful? Furthermore, Zuckerman (1990) found the major component of genetic diversity to be between persons of the same tribe or nation (84%), with race and geographic region accounting for 10% and 6%, respectively. Thus, any attempt to anchor racial categories on a biological foundation is misguided. Race may carry popular meaning as a social construction and status variable. But counselors must avoid using the term and its implications in ways that support any form of prejudiced attitude or discriminatory practice (Robinson, 2005).

Ethnicity is a related term that carries several interpretations (Atkinson, Morten, & Sue, 1998). In a broad sense, *ethnicity* refers to a group of persons who identify with one another by virtue of sharing common ancestry, religion, language, *skin* color, and/or culture. When used in this manner, the term can be interchangeable with *race*. The more narrow sense focuses on the setting apart of groups of persons on the basis of national origin and distinctive cultural patterns.

Culture can be defined as "a way of living that encompasses the customs, traditions, attitudes, and overall socialization in which a group of people engage that are unique to their cultural upbringing" (Gopaul-McMicol & Brice-Baker, 1998, p. 5). These are shared patterns of learned behavior and are transmitted across generations by members of a particular group. Culture is a dynamic force that is ever changing while simultaneously providing its members with a sense of commonality and consistency that allows for the development of common identity.

It naturally follows, then, that a multicultural orientation is inclusive and provides the opportunity for persons of differing backgrounds to celebrate similarities and differences without requiring the determination of rightness, wrongness, or rankings of superiority/inferiority. As we shall see, multiculturalism has implications not only for the training and practice of mental health and community counselors but also for the larger discipline of counselor education. Counselor education must be fundamentally committed to contributing for the betterment of the human condition for *all* people.

Mental health and community counselors must be able to understand and empathize with persons from diverse groups who have experienced devaluation, disadvantage, disregard, and unfair treatment based on their racial/ethnic identities. The terms *prejudice, racism,* and *discrimination* are frequently used when describing such treatment. *Prejudice* is "an attitude, judgment or feeling about a person that is generalized from attitudes or beliefs held about the group to which the person belongs" (Jones, 1997, p. 10). When prejudice operates, people are judged by the color of their skin and according to preconceived stereotypes. When prejudices are held by mental health professionals, the risk significantly increases for potential inaccurate assessments and mistreatment.

In contrast to prejudice, racism builds on prejudice by assuming the superiority of one's race/ethnic group over others. *Racism,* generally speaking, refers to the use of power and position, overtly or covertly/intentionally or unintentionally, to treat others differentially on the basis of perceived racial differences between or among groups of people. It comes in two forms—individual and institutional (Atkinson et al., 1998). *Individual racism* occurs when a person holds attitudes and beliefs of his or her racial superiority that often lead to discriminatory acts against others viewed as racially inferior. *Institutional racism,* in contrast, takes place when social policies and laws have the intentional or unintentional consequence of positioning one racial/ethnic group in positions of privilege, power, and advantage over other groups.

Finally, *discrimination* refers to biased treatment of a person based on the view one holds of the group to which that person belongs. For example, a white middle-class female may be given special privileges over persons of other groups in the rescheduling of missed appointments. Whereas the stated excuses of the white client may be accepted at face value, similar excuses from a young African American female might be viewed as a form of resistance (Tidwell, 2004). Self-awareness and honesty are necessary attributes if mental health and community counselors are to recognize the operation of discriminatory practices. Such behaviors are typically guided by underlying prejudices that are so much a part of the professional's worldview that they go unquestioned in a manner similar to automatic thoughts (Beck, 1976). Corrective action toward culturally sensitive practice hinges on, first and foremost, the counselor's capacity to recognize prejudices that can serve as seeds for racist and discriminatory behaviors.

Various definitions of *cross-cultural counseling* are put forth in the professional literature. Atkinson and colleagues (1998) define it as "any counseling in which two or more of the participants are *racially/ethnically* different" (p. 17). When the mental health professional assumes the ecological perspective, there is a sense in which all counseling work is multicultural in nature (Pedersen, 1991).

BARRIERS TO EFFECTIVE MULTICULTURAL COUNSELING

Specific barriers, such as the implications of the concepts discussed in the previous section, must be overcome if effective cross-cultural counseling is to be achieved. Additional barriers that deserve mention include cultural encapsulation of the counselor, systemic barriers within counseling delivery systems, misapplication of traditional theories of counseling, miscommunication, and mistrust.

CULTURAL ENCAPSULATION

Historically, the profession of counseling tended to assume the appropriateness of the universal application of its concepts, principles, and techniques. In doing so, culturally specific alternatives were excluded from serious consideration. For example, Evans, Valadez, Burns, and Rodriquez (2002) note that mental health counselors tend to choose traditional therapeutic approaches that are in accordance with their own cultural experience. In contrast, minority mental health counselors hold more favorable views of nontraditional techniques. Furthermore, traditional counseling theories and techniques have been developed primarily by persons of non-Hispanic white, Western, male, middle-class heritage.

Wrenn (1962) coined the term *cultural encapsulation* to describe the tendency of counselors to (a) define and dogmatically cling to viewing reality according to their own sets of cultural assumptions to the exclusion of alternative interpretations, (b) demonstrate insensitivity to persons of other cultural backgrounds who hold alternative perspectives, (c) resist or simply not recognize the necessity of testing the validity of one's underlying assumptions, and therefore (d) become trapped in what may be referred to as "cultural tunnel vision" (Corey et al., 2003). pp. 112–113). Too often students enter graduate training programs wearing monocultural lenses and quickly subscribe and adhere to specific theories as doctrinal truth. As Pedersen (1994) notes, good counselors can no longer ignore through their own encapsulation the fundamental role culture plays in their lives and the lives of their clients.

MISAPPLICATION OF TRADITIONAL THEORIES AND TECHNIQUES

Frequently, the theories and techniques of counseling are presented and accepted as special sets of insights, principles, and approaches that have universal application for the understanding and treatment of the human condition. These are accepted as though they carry the strength of divinely inspired truths. They are so much a part of the predominant culture's landscape that their presence and the implications of their operation are ignored. Only recently has the profession begun to unpack the cultural baggage encased in the traditional "tool kits" provided to graduates of counselor education programs. However, it remains common practice of many graduate programs to offer a single course with a multicultural emphasis rather than to integrate the insights of multiculturalism across the curriculum (Das, 1995).

A number of fundamental presuppositions undergirding traditional approaches can be identified that accept a particular view of the world that is, in fact, culturally based:

1. *Individualism*—There tends to be an unquestioned acceptance of the autonomous, self-preoccupied individual as being the primary psychological entity in the assessment, conceptualization, and treatment of the human condition. What the client thinks and feels represent the realities on which problems and therapeutic goals are based. Frequently, self-will and self-advancement are emphasized without an accompanying concern for others. When stuck in the treatment process, counselors-in-training are taught to move deeper in the psychic of the individual rather than expand the therapeutic system by actively including relevant ecological factors that takes a client-in-situation/context orientation. Although human ecology may be given lip service, the theories and techniques of intervention, as used in professional practice, remain firmly entrenched in a very narrow individualistic perspective.

2. *View of normalcy and pathology*—Most theories of counseling hold views of what constitutes normal and abnormal behavior. These views reflect a Western, Euro-American perspective and can stand in stark contrast to views held by other cultures. Indeed, the major distinction most theories make between physical and psychological/psychiatric disorders is not universally held. Mental health professions and members of the predominant Western culture commonly talk about being anxious, depressed, or stressed and may attribute these conditions to nonphysical causes. This assumption may not be

strongly held among persons of different cultures (Angel & Williams, 2000). Such clients might, therefore, question the rationale for the existence of autonomous professions that treat "emotional disorders." Rather, it might make more sense within their cultural framework to be seen by a medical doctor, religious leader, or good friend. Furthermore, "talking out" or "working through" related/underlying issues to relieve emotional distress may seem odd to the culturally different client, who might be expecting a more direct intervention such as medicine, advice, or specific directives. Finally, the cross-cultural literature is replete with descriptions of unique *culture-bound syndromes*, in which patterns of disordered or psychotic behaviors cluster in unique ways that are found only in particular cultural settings (Smart & Smart, 1997). Discussions of such syndromes are absent in the contents of traditional theories of counseling.

3. *Functional agnosticism and antireligiousness*—Spirituality, organized religion, spiritual beliefs, and the role of priests and spiritual leaders may be central to the functioning and worldview of clients from different cultures. Although spirituality is much more in vogue these days in our profession, most theories and techniques fail to acknowledge and integrate religious/spiritual dimensions into their tenets. Furthermore, mental health and community counselors receive little training in the integration of religion and spirituality in their professional practice.

4. *Personal happiness as a legitimate goal of counseling*—In our culture, people often see the possession of personal happiness as an unalienable right and, thus, seek it as a measurable outcome in counseling. Being pleased with personal physical appearance or feeling good about self are important to many persons in Western culture but may be nonissues among those living in or emigrating from third world countries. Instead, persons from other cultures might place more value in the pursuit of personal contentment with their situation. Furthermore, the acceptance of one's situation within the context of that person's understanding of the common good may be viewed as a more legitimate goal.

5. *Insight and process of change*—The traditional theories and techniques of counseling rely on self-awareness and insight as important change agents. It is assumed that personal adjustment can be enhanced by increasing knowledge and awareness about self, others, and the situation. The success of many approaches hinges on the client's willingness and ability to engage in activities that can facilitate and enhance the client's insight and awareness. However, many cultural groups do not value insight and self-exploration and, in fact, might see "thinking about it too much" as a causative factor of one's emotional distress (Sue & Sue, 2003).

SYSTEMIC BARRIERS WITHIN COUNSELING DELIVERY SYSTEMS

A number of widely accepted conventions are built into traditional delivery systems of counseling. The scheduling of a one-to-one meeting of a counselor and client, sometimes made several weeks in advance, for a 50-minute session occurring at a frequency of approximately once a week at the counselor's office to explore presenting problems and one's innermost thoughts is rarely questioned. These and other structures and processes of the traditional delivery of mental health services may act as barriers that keep the culturally different from receiving needed treatment.

The fact that children, adolescents, and families of color have been underserved by most public and private human service delivery systems in the United States is well documented (Hernandez, Isaacs, Nesman, & Burns, 1998). Many youth of color who are identified with mental health problems do not receive adequate services. Magnitude of poverty, family disintegration, community disorganization, family and community violence, chemical abuse, illiteracy, and teenage pregnancy interact with and contribute to the development and maintenance of emotional distress. Geographic location of mental health services, unavailability of affordable transportation, inconvenient office hours, and lack of minority staff converge to create systems of mental health services that discriminate against certain groups. Numerous indirect, systemic interventions are required if the problem of underserved populations is to be remedied.

LANGUAGE BARRIERS AND MISCOMMUNICATION

The effectiveness of counseling relies on the transmission of meaning through verbal, nonverbal, and written communication. The counselor's language, as well as his or her observations of the client's use of language, influences all aspects of the counseling process. The grammatical structure delineates how various pieces of reality fit together (Dell, 1980). Furthermore, words assist persons in perceiving and understanding reality. They are used as labels and become symbols representing persons, places, and objects. Indeed, it can be argued that one's vocabulary shapes one's views of reality and worldview (Sanchez, 2001).

Problems in communication between clients and counselors can prevent minorities from using appropriate services (Sherer, 2002). Adequate command of the spoken language is necessary for accurate information gathering, assessment, identification of goals, treatment planning, and treatment. Members of the predominant culture in the United States have become comfortable with psychological jargon. The Dr. Phils and Lauras of the media have captured the fascination of the country and toss out words and concepts that laypeople understand.

Unfortunately, mental health and community counselors may mistakenly assume that clients from minority racial/ethnic groups who communicate reasonably well in other social situations can accurately express and comprehend the meaning of words exchanged in counseling settings. Counselors may use slang or colloquialisms that confuse minority clients. Furthermore, clients may not understand the use and meaning of common words when used in unique contexts. For example, one client was fluent in conversational English but encountered difficulty when attempting to complete the MMPI. He encountered terms such as *constipation* and *bowel movement* in specific questions and became confused regarding their precise meaning when in the context of a psychological test. He responded to the items in an arbitrary manner, which resulted in a test protocol with questionable validity.

MISTRUST

In multicultural counseling situations, the potential presence of mistrust must be assessed and dealt with early in the counseling relationship. It can take various forms and be directed toward individuals or institutions. In addition, feelings of mistrust can be reciprocal.

Counselors may hold preconceived notions and assumptions that impede the establishment of effective therapeutic relationships. Social psychologists have noted the general tendency for people to underestimate contextual influences and overestimate dispositional influences in explaining the behavior of others. This tendency is so basic that it is referred to as the fundamental attribution error (Jones & Harris, 1967). For example, in attempting to explain why I failed to meet a deadline for writing this text, I might point to having to prepare for new courses, dealing with several clients who went into crisis, and remedying problems with my computer. However, when attempting to explain the similar behavior in another person, I commit the fundamental attribution error if I attribute his or her behavior to laziness, irresponsibility, or ethnicity.

Certain underlying assumptions supported by Western culture strengthen our propensity to commit fundamental attribution errors. As we have noted, Western culture places a high value on individualism and personal autonomy. It supports the belief that each person is self-sufficient and can be successful by taking personal responsibility and making good choices. Thus, we assume people cause events, and we pay less attention to interacting situational factors (Myers, 2002). We encourage others by saying, "You can make it if you try!" It naturally follows from this perspective that those who struggle or fail to get ahead did not try hard enough, are irresponsible, or are lazy. Too often, such faulty reasoning becomes the basis for stereotypes and prejudiced behavior.

The bottom line is that culture and the operation of fundamental attribution errors can be a foundation for the mistrust of certain minority groups. Mental health and community counselors of the predominant culture must refute flawed personal assumptions that operate without question if they are to view each client accurately for the uniqueness the client brings to the counseling situation.

In addition, many minority clients may come into counseling with varying degrees of mistrust. Mistrust may be directed primarily at the counselor, who becomes a symbol of the dominant culture or the holders of societal power. Too often, non-Hispanic whites fail to appreciate the impact of history in the lives of other ethnic groups. Several students in my social and cultural diversity classes have gotten defensive when confronted with racial and ethnic inequities and state, "It is unfair for you to perceive me or other members of my race as though we have personally committed wrongs toward you or persons of your race. I have never owned a slave and do not hold any bigoted attitudes!" Such statements reveal the extent to which members of the dominant group do not understand the historical basis for mistrust and how, unfortunately, mistrust receives reinforcement in contemporary society. Thus, the caution, hesitancy, or guardedness displayed in initial sessions may reflect the generalization of mistrust. Mental health and community counselors must be careful not to automatically conceptualize such behavior as resistance.

In addition, the roots of mistrust among many minority clients may lie in a lack of information regarding the nature of services provided or inappropriate referrals and treatment. Immigrants or members of minority groups often enter counseling as a result of being referred to an agency by school personnel or human service agencies (Gopaul-McNicol & Brice-Baker, 1998). They may not have a clear understanding of the reasons for the referral. Sometimes such clients do not have accurate information about the roles of agencies or the nature of services to be provided. For example, one female, single parent who was a recent immigrant was concerned about her fifth-grade child, who was being teased by other children on the school bus. Not knowing where to turn for assistance, she looked for resources in the yellow pages of her phone book and saw "Child and Family Assistance Agency Services." Not knowing much about this agency or its primary role, which was Child Protective Service (CPS), she naively contacted the agency, saying that she "was having difficulties with [her] child" and that the situation was "out of control." She was interviewed by a CPS worker and noted in response to a question that she did, at times, use corporal punishment to discipline her child. Alarmed at this admission, the CPS worker promptly removed the child from the home and placed her in the temporary custody of foster parents. It was mandated that the mother complete a "parent skill training" program before the mother could regain custody. Language and cultural differences were obstacles for this young mother, and she did not regain custody of her child for over a year. Such intermittent occurrences serve as powerful reinforcers of avoidant behavior. It is not surprising that no-show rates are higher among minority clients (Tidwell, 2004).

FOUNDATIONAL PRINCIPLES IN MULTICULTURAL COUNSELING

Culturally sensitive counselors are continually mindful of a number of foundational principles. These include the activation of schema and confirmatory bias; awareness; between- versus within-group differences; racial/cultural identity development; and multiple identities.

ACTIVATION OF SCHEMAS AND CONFIRMATORY BIAS

As noted in chapter 3, each person possesses schema and a set of values that are formed through developmental processes taking place within specific cultural contexts. The schema and values include sets of personal attitudes and assumptions that are activated in specific interpersonal contexts. Once activated, schema and associated values held by the counselor and client, respectively, flavor how each perceives and interacts with the other.

When the counselor and client engage in interpersonal communication, which is central to the process of counseling, the perceiver in the interaction integrates not only what is said and related cues (e.g., intonation, facial expression, and posture) but also information regarding the person's physical appearance, age, gender, and physical ability/disability (Kunda & Thagard, 1996). These incoming stimuli cue schema used to differentiate people according to observable characteristics. For example, once counselors categorize a client as black or white, male or female, the content of that particular schema influences what counselors perceive, how quickly they perceive it, and their interpretation of what is noticed (Fiske & Taylor, 1991).

These principles of social cognition have important implications for mental health and community counselors engaged in multicultural practice. First, schemas play critical roles in organizing persons we encounter into in-group and out-group categories. In-groups tend to be more highly valued, trusted, and favored. It is common to have biases and stereotyped attitudes about persons from out-groups, who in our society might be persons from minority groups. Because our schemas operate beyond conscious awareness, mental health and community counselors must be aware of and sensitive to their personal attitudes and underlying assumptions, which may be more culturally biased than they believe.

Second, mental health professionals must recognize the potential for *confirmation bias*. This refers to a human tendency to search for information that confirms one's preexisting conceptions (Myers, 2002). For example, a counselor who holds a biased view regarding the behavioral patterns of a minority group will tend to seek out data during the assessment phase that confirm his or her preexisting schemas. Mental health and community counselors must carefully stay in the present and recognize when their clinical hypothesis making moves them from observable, in-session data.

The preceding discussion highlights the necessity that mental health professionals possess accurate self-awareness and the ability to be honest with self. These skills are vital if counselors are to avoid the potential pitfalls presented by confirmatory bias and our tendency toward making in-group/out-group distinctions. Being sensitive to these tendencies helps mental health and community counselors fulfill their primary ethical responsibility of truly respecting the dignity and promoting the welfare of their clients (ACA, 1995).

BETWEEN- VERSUS WITHIN-GROUP DIFFERENCES

For years, the mental health professions have been aware of the ethnic differences among the clients they serve. Clients raised in and who have assimilated the values of non-predominant cultures often display different customs, traditions, attitudes, and behavioral styles that are expressed in situations. Evans-Pritchard (1962) characterized the differences between Christian and Muslim faiths this way: "A Christian man shows respect for his religion by taking off his hat and keeping on his shoes, while a Muslim man in an Arab country will show similar respect by keeping on his hat and removing his shoes" (p. 2). The implications for mental health and community counselors are obvious. Behaviors, similar in appearance, displayed by different clients can carry different meanings. To assume and act according to the accepted meaning of the predominant culture is a sure path leading to misunderstanding between counselor and client and, potentially, misdiagnosis and misguided interventions. Thus, mental health professionals must possess baseline knowledge of the differences in and implications of the cultural backgrounds of their clients.

Yet it is risky simply to act on differences assumed to exist between the counselor and client. On practically every socially meaningful category, there are as many within-group differences as there are between-group differences. For example, it is helpful to borrow from principles of behavioral statistics. For any characteristic of a given population, we can identify a particular range, mean, and standard deviation of scores. Often, when graphed, the obtained scores take on the appearance of a normal curve. We use inferential statistics when investigating the differences that may exist between groups. Technically, a difference between groups on a given characteristic is judged as being statistically significant when the difference (or variance) between groups is greater that the difference within each group.

As noted, important differences *do* exist among the groups we serve. However, to focus only on the between-group differences while ignoring very real within-group differences opens up the potential for misunderstanding, misdiagnosis, and mistreatment due to counselor insensitivity to the specific client system. Functioning from the ecological perspective is the best way to find a balanced way to navigate through the sometimes erratic waters created by perceived differences between and within groups.

RACIAL/CULTURAL IDENTITY DEVELOPMENT

Persons vary in the extent to which they personally identify with their particular race or culture. Thus, one factor contributing to within-group variations is individual differences in clients' racial/cultural identity development (Atkinson, Morten, & Sue, 1998; Sue, 2003). This model identifies five stages of identity development persons may experience as they attempt to come to terms with their minority culture in relation to the predominant culture. At each stage, personal identity is characterized by four corresponding attitudes regarding self, others of the same minority, others of different minorities, and persons of the dominant culture. Not all persons in a specific minority group experience each of the stages. Furthermore, moving through the earlier stages is not a prerequisite to being in the later stages. For example, a young person may be in stage 5 without having moved through stages 1 through 4 by virtue of being born into a particular family of origin.

Persons in the first stage, *conformity,* tend to show strong preference for the values of the dominant culture. Thus, the minority person emulates and seeks to assimilate the role models, value systems, and lifestyles of the dominant culture while devaluing self as a member of the minority group. Personal attributes that serve as minority group identifiers may be viewed with contempt and become sources of distress.

Minority persons, though, tend to have experiences with the dominant culture that contradict the assumptions and conclusions held in the conformity stage. Thus, the second stage is characterized by *dissonance,* which stems from an increased awareness that one's minority culture has strengths and is not as bad as previously believed. In addition, minority persons begin to see problems in the dominant culture. The dissonance stage, then, is marked by a questioning and challenging of previously held beliefs.

The third stage, *resistance and immersion,* occurs as minority persons move toward and endorse the values and lifestyles of their minority group. They may experience shame and guilt at having previously sold out to the dominant culture and, in a sharp turnaround, express anger at the racism and oppression that they have experienced at the hands of the dominant group. As a consequence, they distrust and dislike dominant group members.

The fourth stage is characterized by *introspection*. Here, minority members are more comfortable with self and their own heritage. This frees them to be less compelled to view culture in a dichotomous manner. As their energies move from such strong investment in highlighting the minority group against the negatives of the dominant culture, persons find a balance between minority group identification and establishing personal autonomy. They are more willing to draw from those characteristics of both their minority culture *and* the dominant culture in moving toward a sense of self-fulfillment.

In the final stage of *integrative awareness,* minority persons' experience greater flexibility and inner control. They can now examine the qualities of minority and dominant cultures and take positions on issues based on an objective analysis that reflects their personal values. The views of all groups can be considered with little or no need to take the position held by any particular group. Persons in this stage are motivated to work toward the elimination of racism, prejudice, and stereotyping in all expressed forms.

ACCULTURATION

Acculturation may be defined as "the gradual physical, biological, cultural, and psychological changes that take place in individuals and groups when contact between two cultural groups takes place (Cardemil & Battle, 2003, p. 280). In multicultural societies, it is common for individuals or groups from one culture to move into a region dominated by another cultural group. Pressure is exerted on those of the minority culture to conform with and accommodate the norms and mores of the dominant group while simultaneously abandoning and devaluing their own cultural roots.

People experience and navigate through these pressures differently (Cuellar, 2000). For some, both the ways and values of minority persons' own and dominant culture are valued. Such may be the case for the first-generation immigrant who experiences the economic and social benefits reaped through successful employment in U.S. urban settings. Yet the native language and practices of his or her culture are maintained in the home. For others, though, the dissonance between their own culture and the lifestyle and values of the dominant culture can be a source of individual and familial stress. Consider the eighth-grade student who masters English as a second language, establishes a strong social network of close friends who are native to the dominant culture, and actively participates in a wide range of school and extracurricular activities. However, in the home, the language and ways of the native culture are practiced. The child's parents might be alarmed at and discipline the child for the display of behaviors and attitudes that are widely accepted in the dominant culture but viewed as unacceptable within the perspective of their native culture. The accompanying revision stress can result in increased vulnerability to certain health problems and the development of psychological symptoms (Cuellar, 2000).

Mental health and community counselors must be aware of the ways in which acculturation-related issues can influence the process of counseling. For example, clients' preference for particular counselors might be influenced by the extent to which clients have assimilated the values of the dominant culture. Minority clients who devalue their original culture might actually desire to be seen by a counselor from the dominant culture. Furthermore, differing levels of cultural assimilation and accommodation among family members might be powerful dynamics underlying the presenting problem. Thus, a culturally insensitive conceptualization of the presenting problem might lead to treatment of the oppositional child with little consideration of the underlying conflict in cultural values. It is also possible that a child may be referred for counseling services when, in fact, the behaviors in question are socially appropriate when viewed through the lens of the family's native culture. In such instances, advocacy and psychoeducational interventions directed to referral sources might be indicated.

MULTIPLE IDENTITIES

Our ability to gain full and accurate understanding of the clients we serve will be incomplete if we take a narrow view of personal identity. One's racial/cultural identity, important as it may be, does not develop or express itself in a vacuum; nor does it define personal identity. As noted by Das (1995), there is simply no one-to-one correspondence between the ethnographic description of a cultural group and the psychological makeup of a particular individual belonging to that group. Differences in personal identities are best conceptualized by considering the manner in which a variety of identity constructs interact and converge to form one's unique personal identity. Thus, each person is best viewed as being composed of multiple identities (Robinson, 2005).

Arredondo (Arrendondo, 1992; Arrendondo & Toporek, 1996) has identified three dimensions of personal identity that must be considered if assessment and treatment are to be effective. The A dimensions include those characteristics into which people are born, such as gender, sexual orientation, race, culture, socioeconomic status, and physical abilities/disabilities. In contrast, B dimensions include those personal characteristics that are less visible but are influenced by the person's achievements, such as work experience, academic background and performance, religion, hobbies, and marital status. The C dimensions are specific historical events that affect the direction and quality of the person's life.

Although being mindful that the three dimensions of identity can raise the counselor's awareness to issues of diversity, a truly holistic view of the client can be achieved only as the quality of interaction and integration among these constructs is understood. To do so, mental health and community counselors rely on the ecological perspective (Bronfenbrenner, 1979, 1989) and comprehensive mental health counseling model (chapter 3) as foundational pillars. Clients incorporate into their personal identities ideas, values, attitudes, and behaviors from their multileveled environmental contexts. The process is dynamic and interactive but not necessarily reciprocal.

Thus, the old adage that "the whole is greater than the sum of its parts" holds true for counselors striving to develop a holistic understanding of and appreciation for the diverse clients they serve. Knowing that a particular client is Hispanic, male, Catholic, single, a father, and living in the south side of Chicago helps the counselor to grasp the complexity of the client's makeup. Knowledge of the generic descriptions of each descriptor and treating descriptors as though their boundaries are impenetrable creates a barrier to understanding the person. To understand and appreciate that unique person for who he or she is, the counselor must go beyond the superficial gathering of data regarding each characteristic. This is accomplished by listening to the client's story, seeking out information that clarifies the nature and quality of these interacting identities, and comprehending the personal meanings as they are perceived by the client from within his or her particular frame of reference.

THE CULTURALLY COMPETENT COUNSELOR

This chapter has discussed the changed face of American society, which is truly multicultural in its composition. In response, many counselors have become increasingly aware of numerous barriers to effective counseling that occur when traditional models and delivery systems are applied in a "one size fits all" manner to meet the needs of diverse populations. It is in this context that multicultural competencies have become necessary skills for effective professional practice.

In the early 1990s, the leadership of the Association of Multicultural Counseling and Development (AMCD) assumed responsibility for assisting "mental health professions in recognizing the assets of culture, ethnicity, race, and other social identities as indelible dimensions of every human being, and for addressing concerns about ethical practice" (p. 45). The then presidents of the AMCD directed the AMCD's Professional Standards Committee to prepare a set of Multicultural Counseling Competencies (Sue, Arrendondo, & McDavis, 1992) that were operationalized as specific beliefs, attitudes, knowledge, and skills (Arrendondo & Toparek, 1996).

Arrendondo (1999, p.103) notes several operating premises running through the list of Multicultural Counseling Competencies:

1. All counseling is cross-cultural.
2. All counseling happens in a context influenced by institutional and societal biases and norms.
3. The relationships described are primarily between a white counselor and clients of ethnic racial minority status.
4. Constituencies most often marginalized and about which counselors have been least prepared to serve are from Asian, black/African American, Latino, and Native American heritage.
5. Counseling is a culture-bound profession.

Supporting this entire effort is the underlying assumption that the effectiveness and ethical conduct of mental health and community counselors are enhanced when training programs are culturally sound.

The Multicultural Counseling Competencies (Arrendondo et al., 1996; Sue et al., 1992) set standards for the development of beliefs and attitudes, knowledge, and skills in three specific domains: the counselor's self-awareness of personal beliefs, attitudes, values, and assumptions; understanding the worldview of the client; and the development of appropriate intervention strategies (Arrendondo, 1999). These are summarized in Table 8.1.

TABLE 8.1 Summary of the Multicultural Counselor Competencies		**Cultural Awareness of One's Assumptions, Values, and Biases**	**Understanding the Worldview of the Culturally Different Client**	**Developing Appropriate Intervention Strategies and Techniques**
	Beliefs and Attitudes	• Identify own culture/cultural groups from which counselor derives significant beliefs and attitudes • Recognize impact of one's beliefs on ability to respect persons of other groups • Identify learned cultural attitudes that both demonstrate and hinder respect • Recognize limits of their multicultural competencies	• Understands how personal assumptions can be similiar to and different from members of that group, and how these influence counseling interactions • Understands how personal emotional reactions could influence counseling effectiveness • Understands how race, ethnicity, culture, and minority status influences personality development, display and recognition of normal/abnormal behaviors, and utilization of	• Respects client's religious and spiritual beliefs, values, and practices as they contribute to wellness, level of functioning, and the indigenous helping process • Value bilingualism • Recognizes operation of fundamental attribution errors (i.e., the tendency to blame others for their circumstances)

(Continued)

TABLE 8.1 (Continued)		Cultural Awareness of One's Assumptions, Values, and Biases	Understanding the Worldview of the Culturally Different Client	Developing Appropriate Intervention Strategies and Techniques
			counseling services • Recognizes the socio-political forces that influence the lives of racial and ethnic minorities	
	Knowledge	• Awareness of how their cultural heritage influences view of healthy and unhealthy mental health and behavior • Possesses understanding of oppression, racism, discrimination, and stereotyping and capability of acknowledging own racist attitudes, feelings, beliefs • Understands the social impact that personal communication style and relating has those of diverse backgrounds.	• Can articulate differences in verbal and nonverbal behavior of the 5 major cultural groups • Describe 2 models of minority identity development • Explain history of ethnic groups • Identify within group differences • Discuss viewpoints of other cultural groups regarding major issues • Become aware of how own cultural socialization shapes intolerance and disrespectful attitudes	• Can articulate context in which traditional theories have developed and inherent cultural biases contained in their underlying presuppositions and explicit goals and techniques • Aware of institutional barriers operating in the counseling service delivery system that inhibits utilization by racial/ethnic minority groups • Aware of potential cultural biases and misuses of traditional counseling appraisal and assessment tools • Possess knowledge of diverse family/community structures and

TABLE 8.1 (Continued)		Cultural Awareness of One's Assumptions, Values, and Biases	Understanding the Worldview of the Culturally Different Client	Developing Appropriate Intervention Strategies and Techniques
			• Understand how race, culture, etc. may affect personal formation	dynamics and their inherent strengths • Understands the nature of social and cultural prejudice and discrimination and its influence on personal wellbeing of clients
	Skills	• Recognize own limitations relative to culture and seeks out professional development experiences to improve understanding and skills in working with culturally different • Actively seeking to enhance understanding of diverse cultures and to develop a non-racist personal identity	• Familiar with pertinent and current research regarding mental health and illness as it relates to cultural diverse populations • Participate in multicultural activities outside of the counseling setting or vocation to promote an understanding of other ethnic groups and cultures that goes beyond mere academic training • Become involved with minority individuals outside counseling setting	• Skilled in application of various verbal and nonverbal helping responses in language of client • Able to apply counseling technique with flexibility so that specific approaches used are a good fit the needs of the culturally different client • Able to apply systemic and advocacy interventions on behalf of the oppressed and victims of discrimination • Educate clients in counseling process, legal and ethical concerns

Culturally competent counselors share certain characteristics. First, they are aware of the underlying assumptions, values, beliefs, and attitudes they bring to the counseling relationship. They are in touch with their *cultural selves* and recognize the manner in which their attitudes, thoughts, feelings, and behaviors have been shaped by cultural forces. In addition, they grasp the extent to which forces of the predominant culture have influenced the course of their personal development and how these forces operate within their particular ecological context. And if they are white, non-Hispanic counselors, they understand the advantages of their privileged position in society and its association to power and overt/covert oppression. These attitudes and sets of knowledge and skills help mental health and community counselors relate to and empathize with the culturally different. As a consequence, their ability to establish and maintain an effective therapeutic relationship is enhanced.

Second, competent multicultural counselors assume the responsibility of becoming aware, knowledgeable, and skilled about other ethnic groups (Arrrendondo, 1999). Counselors' self-awareness of their own culture forms the base for understanding the worldview of others. This is more than a mere academic exercise in which counselors-in-training learn about the worldview characteristics of specific cultural groups. Rather, all counselors learn about the ongoing, dynamic interactions among culturally different clients, their particular group, the various elements of their immediate sphere, and society. A working knowledge that expresses itself in practical skill is best developed when counselors step out of their cultural boundaries and actively participate in community events, celebrations, and meetings of other cultural groups. In other words, they benefit from seeing the culture of others in action rather than through the pages of a book. Thus, the goal is to gain knowledge of the worldview of the culturally different that is ecologically contextualized.

Third, culturally competent mental health and community counselors develop a repertoire of strategies and techniques that enable them to effectively and sensitively intervene in the lives of the culturally different clients they serve (Arrondondo, 1999). They recognize the limitations of traditional models of counseling, which has been prepared, cooked, and simmered in the kettle of the predominant culture. Such concoctions have left many ingredients out, resulting in a less flavorful and fulfilling product. Specifically, competent counselors acquire culturally sensitive interviewing skills, assessment techniques, and sets of intervention strategies that are sensitive to and effective in treating the *full* range of human behaviors expressed in its cultural context. Indigenous practices and referral resources can be important components of the comprehensive treatment plan.

The guidelines for culturally competent counseling developed by the AMCD do not stand alone in the professional literature. Other organizations have put forth alternative guidelines. These include the American Psychological Association (APA, 2003) and the Child and Adolescent Service System Program (Mason, Benjamin, & Lewis, 1996).

The cultural competency guidelines (Arrendondo & Toporek, 1996; Sue et al., 1992) have not been met with universal acceptance. Thomas and Weinrach (Thomas & Weinrach, 2004; Weinrach & Thomas, 2002), in fact, have declared that the AMCD multicultural counseling competencies are extremely flawed. Specifically, they state that to focus exclusively on issues of race and ethnicity, in itself, is racist. Furthermore, they contend that the set of competencies lacks an empirical base. It is questioned whether any set of competencies should be imposed on mental health professionals (Thomas & Weinrach, 2004). Arrendondo and Toporek (2004) counter these arguments by noting that the competencies have been endorsed by the ACA and American Psychological Association. They conclude that multicultural competency p.53 "is becoming a way of life" for mental health professionals and anticipate a widespread positive response from counselors, educators, and researchers.

CONCLUSION

In this chapter, we have moved from establishing the rationale that gave birth to the multicultural counseling movement to identifying foundational principles and specific competencies for its practice. Most multicultural counseling theorists and researchers conclude that the practice of multicultural counseling is much more than the application of intervention recipes from a techniques cookbook for application with members of specific racial or ethnic minorities. Most agree that the effectiveness of multicultural mental health interventions hinges on the application of specified skills with special sensitivity to the multiple identities of the particular client(s) being served. This is viewed as attending to the ecological context of culturally diverse clients.

It strikes me as odd, though, that given all of the rhetoric about being aware and sensitive to the operation of Western presuppositions in the practice of mental health counseling, we seem to stumble into the very trap that we warn against. Namely, our conceptualization of multicultural counseling seems too often to be laced with the individualistic bias that is so prominent in traditional theory and techniques.

What ultimate good do we accomplish if we, as counselor educators, produce mental health counselors who are multiculturally competent but who practice in settings whose structures, policies, and procedures exemplify the presuppositions, values, and worldviews of the predominant culture? This new breed of counselor could be extremely sensitive to and skilled in the treatment of clients from diverse groups. But if the cultural values and assumptions are, indeed, institutionalized, relatively few minority persons in need of our services will voluntarily seek them out. Is this fourth force in the counseling profession powerful enough to influence the many institutional barriers that prevent effective outreach to minority groups? Or has the individualized focus of our cultural lenses prevented us from developing ecologically relevant, systematic interventions to overcome these institutional barriers? Does our continuing emphasis on treating identified clients reflect the extent to which our "culturally sensitive talk" is much stronger than our "walk"?

For example, is not a cultural and institutional bias of the mental health system in operation when children of color are served in disproportionate numbers through special education and juvenile justice systems rather than through alternative community mental health options? In addition, numerous policies have institutionalized practitioner and agency behavior that predates contemporary concern over diversity issues. These policies and procedures should be revisited. It is no longer reasonable to have token representation in leadership roles of persons whose roots are in minority culture but who no longer maintain any direct tie to that culture (Mason et al., 1996). Members of the community should be allowed to make a larger contribution to the direction of agency policy and operations. The physical appearance of the agency, including its décor, locations, name, hours of operation, reading materials in the waiting room, and its furnishings can better reflect the diversity of the clients and, actually, "jump-start a positive relationship" (p. 177).

We do well to recognize the extent to which the profession of counseling is, in many ways, a unique culture. It has socialized many of us to view our worlds in particular ways. We have learned to speak a unique language with various nuances that carry specific meanings to its members. A particular set of values is held and advocated on that platform. The counseling culture also reflects a particular view of wellness and mental health and a process through which both may be attained.

From an ecological perspective, then, mental health and community counselors must recognize not only the interaction of cultures at the individualistic level as the counselor meets with a client. Although it is important that counselors bring multicultural competencies to the relationship, it is vital that they be aware of the clash among the culture of counselors, client systems, and that of the larger society. As we advocate for causes the counseling profession holds dear, we might experience frustrations that result from the unavailability of funding to update physical structures or change locations of our treatment facilities and the plodding bureaucratic process that prevents the development and implementation of policies and procedures more sensitive to the cultural variations of our constituencies. But when we have strong emotional reactions to such barriers to change, some of us for the first time in our lives might be coming face to face with and experiencing the dynamics of power, partiality, bias, prejudice, and discrimination that operate on us as members of a minority culture. We, indeed, have many lessons to learn.

DISCUSSION QUESTIONS

1. Discuss the following statement: "Given the interactional nature of the counseling process, all counselor-client relationships are multicultural." Do you agree with this statement? How, specifically, can a counseling interaction be truly multicultural when the counselor and client are members of the same culture?
2. In your future practice, to what extent will you seek to serve clients of diverse cultural backgrounds? If so, what specific steps will you take to ensure that your professional practice is culturally sensitive?

3. Identify and briefly discuss the four components of cultural encapsulation. Identify which component would be most difficult for you to overcome. Explain why.
4. Are there times in which it is appropriate and necessary to overstep the boundaries of the traditional delivery system of mental health services to meet the various needs of the culturally different client? Identify specific examples. How would you do so in ways that are ethically and professionally responsible?

SUGGESTED ACTIVITIES

1. Identify a civil rights leader or individual who is culturally different from yourself and who has influenced you personally. Name the specific characteristics of this person that you admire and which have been influential. In what ways have you attempted to live out the characteristics in your personal life?
2. Identify a person you know who is culturally different from you. Set a time to discuss with this person the ways in which you are similar and different from him or her. Consider perspectives on time, family, politics, spirituality, religions, sexuality, work and productivity, individuality, and consumerism. The goal of this activity is to increase personal awareness.
3. Conduct a class exercise in which each person brings to class an object that is symbolic of an important aspect of that person's culture. This can be a fun and informative way of learning more about the cultural diversity that surrounds you.
4. Invite the director of a community mental center or mental health association to speak to the class about the cultural barriers to receiving adequate mental health services and efforts to make such services more accessible to culturally diverse populations.

Ethical and Legal Issues

OUTLINE

Nowhere is the interaction of self, training, and practice more critical in counseling than in the promotion of ethical and legal behavior. Possession of a working knowledge of professional and legal issues is essential for establishing a professional identity and engaging in effective professional practice. This knowledge comes as counselors-in-training learn about the law, codes of ethics, and various institutions and professional organizations that regulate the practice of counseling.

However, knowledge of the law and ethics is not capable of guiding the conduct of practitioners. Counselors face many situations in sessions where they must determine which course of action best supports the interests and well-being of their clients. The schema of counselors, which includes their worldviews, values, and biases, are activated, along with their working knowledge of ethics and the law, *in situations*. These schema interact with the processing of data gathered throughout the counseling interview, which, ideally, leads to effective therapeutic responses that are both legal and ethical.

Ethical and legal practice is really about professionalism and excellence—possessing the right combination of attributes and skills to facilitate beneficial change and growth to clients as claimed. Welfel (1998, pp. 3–4) identifies four dimensions that ethics encompass:

1. Possessing adequate knowledge, skills, and judgment to produce effective interventions;
2. Respecting the dignity, freedom, and rights of the client;
3. Using power inherent in the counselor's role judiciously and responsibly;
4. Conducting oneself in such a way that promotes the public's confidence in the profession.

Both the ACA (2005) and AMHCA (2000) have put forth codes of ethics to inform and regulate the behavior of their members. CACREP (2001) includes the study of the ethical standards of the ACA and AMHCA and the application of ethical and legal principles in professional practice as key criteria for fulfilling the core requirement of professional identity. Although central to the development of one's professional identity as a counselor (CACREP, 2001), the implications of the topic are pervasive and extend into all other core areas of study and specializations in counselor education. In addition, local, state, and federal law specifies the profession's scope of practice. Furthermore, such laws specify minimal standards for professional behavior that society will tolerate. Indeed, ethical and legal considerations are a part of practically every task performed by professional counselors.

Understanding and acting in accordance with the ethical code and the law are important for several reasons. First, acting ethically and within the law promotes professionalism and excellence. Ethical behavior refers to conduct judged as good or right for counselors who practice as members of a professional group (Remley & Herlihy, 2005). The ethical code expresses the profession's intent to regulate the behavior of its members. In contrast, legal codes express standards of behavior that are enforced by governmental agencies. Ideally, ethics and the law provide guidelines that mental health and community counselors use to self-regulate their professional behavior in ways that promote the well-being of others and prevent harm. Counselors striving for professional excellence rise above merely fulfilling the demands of codes and continually strive to be the best counselor they can possibly be.

Second, mental health and professional counselors encounter many situations and dilemmas that defy easy resolution. Often, the break-even point that determines whether a specific course of action will benefit the client is unclear. For example, reporting suspected child abuse may protect the child. Yet doing so jeopardizes the positive counseling relationship that has been established between the counselor and family. How is the counselor to proceed if the goal is to promote the client's welfare? What happens if the family reacts to the allegation by withdrawing from treatment? Or how should the counselor respond when offered an expensive gift by a client? Is it always appropriate to follow social convention and be a gracious receiver? Or is it sometimes ethically or clinically expedient to explore the action's potential meanings and, when indicated, choose not to accept the gift, even when doing so might hurt the client's feelings (Gerig, 2004)? Although codes of ethics do not prescribe courses of action for many specific therapeutic events, they do provide principles on which appropriate courses of action can be identified.

Third, consumers of counseling services are protected from those mental health and community counselors who are impaired, make poor decisions, misapply power and influence, and engage in overt misconduct. Unfortunately, the history of the mental health professions is littered with numerous incidents in which consumers have been victimized by bad judgment or inappropriate behavior by professionals to whom their care had been entrusted. An early study (Kardener, Fuller, & Mensh, 1973) surveyed 114 psychiatrists in Los Angeles and found that 10% admitted to sexual contact with patients. In a later study, Holroyd and Brodsky (1977) explored the occurrence of sexual misconduct among psychologists and found that 5.5% of the male psychologists and 0.6% of the female psychologists had engaged in sexual intercourse with a client. Of these, 80% admitted to intercourse with more than one client. Less extreme illustrations of poor judgment and inappropriate behavior include release of confidential information about counseling contacts, failure to contact potential victims of a client who is dangerous to others, and improper billing practices. Again, ethical and legal codes cannot prevent such actions. However, they set parameters so that proper action by professional organizations or legal authorities can take place when allegations are made. When allegations against practitioners are substantiated, specific sanctions may be implemented by the professional organization to habilitate the impaired practitioner or, in extreme cases, suspend or revoke the practitioner's license. In this way, counselors who represent a danger to consumers may be removed from the profession.

Finally, we live in a highly litigious society. Mental health and community counselors find some protection from litigation by adhering to ethical and legal codes. As the mental health professions experienced significant professional growth and public recognition in the mid-1970s, the number of malpractice claims more than doubled (Montgomery, Cupit, & Wimberly, 1999). Montgomery and colleagues (1999) noted the following activities in which consequent malpractice litigation might be both initiated and successful: sexual misconduct, incorrect treatment, financial loss from diagnosis and evaluation, breach of confidentiality, failure to warn, client suicide, and child custody decisions.

Researchers find it difficult to quantify accurately the number of ethical and legal violations taking place. For obvious reasons, studies using self-report survey methods are likely to provide low estimates. Furthermore, reports of ethical violations investigated by professional associations (e.g., American Counseling Association Governing Council, 2003) offer only a limited picture of the ethical practices of counselors because they do not review cases involving nonmembers. However, when considered alongside data reported from other sources, certain trends might be identified (Neukrug, Milliken, & Walden, 2001). General conclusions drawn from these sources have led counselor educators to include risk management strategies in courses covering legal and ethical issues and thus to help counselors practice legally and ethically and avoid or lessen the impact of malpractice litigation.

THE RELATIONSHIP BETWEEN THE LAW AND CODES OF ETHICS

Various processes have been established by society and professions to protect consumers from incompetent, unlawful, or unethical counselors. These include criminal law, civil litigation of malpractice complaints, federal regulations, and peer control mechanisms (Hess, 1980).

Criminal law sets forth the legal rules for what the federal and state governments consider to be illegal behavior. They also specify the manner in which violations are to be punished. Most violations of criminal law involve social crimes such as murder, larceny, theft, assault, or rape and are prosecuted by local, state, or federal officials (i.e., county prosecutors, attorney generals). Typically, an act is judged criminal when the person committing the act intended to do something wrong. The state seeks to punish only those persons who are morally blameworthy. For example, a licensed professional counselor who practices outside of the scope of practice as specified by the licensure law in the state in which she practices has engaged in illegal behavior and may be prosecuted by the state for a misdemeanor offense. Fines, jail terms, and probation can be consequences for professionals convicted of illegal activity.

In contrast, *civil law proceedings* are the responses of courts to controversies between two or more people. The focus is not whether a statute has been violated but whether one person has been harmed by another. When this is judged to have occurred, an amount of money is paid by the hurt or offended party. No criminal sentence is imposed because the focus was not on the breaking of the law. For example, a counselor might be held liable for emotional harm caused due to an improper, though legal, dual relationship with a client. In such a case, no sentence is served because no law was broken. However, the counselor is sued and must financially pay for emotional damages incurred.

Federal regulations are sometimes put into place to which licensed mental health professionals must adhere. For example, HIPAA has had an enormous effect on how mental health and medical professionals gain informed consent and transfer information electronically. This federal law and its regulations, implemented on April 15, 2003, require that practitioners who electronically transfer client records comply with procedures regulating the informed consent process. Furthermore, the regulations define what is considered to be therapy notes and how they are to be secured (Gillman, 2004). Penalties for failing to comply with the regulations are $100 for each violation and up to $25,000 per year for each requirement. Furthermore, penalties for the wrongful disclosure of information can include prison time (HIPAA: Here's what to do, 2004).

Finally, *peer control mechanisms* are implemented by professional groups who seek to monitor and exert control over members of their group. The most relevant peer group mechanisms for mental health and community counselors are the ethics committee of the professional organization and its development and application of that profession's code of ethics. The Ethical Practice Committee of the ACA (then the American Personnel and Guidance Association) was established in 1953, one year after the establishment of the organization (Walden, Herlihy, & Ashton, 2003). The first draft of the association's code of ethics was reviewed by members in 1950 and adopted in 1961 (Allen, 1986). The code has been revised on the average of every 7 years to reflect changes in professional practice, the needs and issues of clients, and American society (Walden et al., 2003). Hubert and Freeman (2004) noted that the recently appointed ACA Code Revision Task Force was reviewing the previous code (ACA, 1995) and was looking at the integration of existing standards for Internet online counseling (ACA, 1999). In addition, it was given the charge to develop revisions with a special focus on multiculturalism, diversity, and social justice (Hubert & Freeman, 2004). These mandates have been realized with the publication of the 2005 Code of Ethics (ACA, 2005).

Obviously, there is a significant amount of overlap between ethics and the law. Their underlying purpose is to encourage harmonious relating of persons within a society. Ideally, boundaries are set that encourage autonomous behaviors of professionals while simultaneously protecting the rights of others.

There are times, though, when ethics and law are found to be in conflict. For example, specific laws, such as existing racial segregation laws, were overturned when it was determined that they did not protect human rights or promote personal well-being. Counselors might experience such conflicts between the purposes of the law and ethical code when submitting copies of a clinical record to the court in response to a subpoena when doing so may risk the personal well-being of the client. Thus, the counselor who fails to release confidential information to the court in order to protect the best interests of the client can be found in contempt of court.

Finally, ethical codes often address issues that are not concerns of the law. For example, the professor who lectures from notes yellowed through years of use may be acting in an unethical manner by not presenting current information to students. But such actions are not considered illegal. Generally speaking, the ethical code upholds professional standards of conduct that are higher than legal standards.

FOUNDATIONAL PRINCIPLES OF ETHICAL CODES

Various authors have identified moral principles that provide the foundation on which professional codes of ethics rest (Beauchamp & Childress, 1989; Kitchener, 1984; Meara, Schmidt, & Day, 1996). These include autonomy, nonmaleficence, beneficience, justice, fidelity, and veracity.

Autonomy has to do with facilitating increased independence and self-direction in clients. We respect the inherent freedom and dignity of each person and, in doing so, recognize his or her freedom to choose. This requires that clients are always informed about matters related to the counseling process that they may want or need to know. Counselors avoid paternalistic behaviors or creating inappropriate dependence that needlessly prolongs the therapeutic process. Rather, clients are encouraged to think, feel, decide, and act for themselves and take responsibility for doing so. Sometimes it is necessary for counselors to help clients develop important skills, such as accurate cognitive appraisal of situations, self-awareness, and assertiveness, that serve as a foundation for increased autonomy.

Nonmaleficence refers to the avoidance of doing intentional or unintentional harm. In order to do so, mental health and community counselors must be sensitive to and evaluate the potential risks presented by the process and outcome of counseling. The application of this principle applies not only to doing therapy but also to teaching and conducting research. Thus, counselors are required to act when clients are presenting a threat to themselves and others or when the physical abuse of children is suspected. In addition, counselors avoid potential harm by not utilizing therapeutic approaches or directives that run counter to the foundational values of the culturally different client.

Beneficience involves promoting good for others. Mental health and community counselors provide services that promote personal well-being, growth, and relief from inappropriate unhappiness and distress. In general, the identified goals of counseling guide clients toward more effective and productive lives. For example, counselors recognize and work within the boundaries of their expertise, selecting interventions wisely and based on professional outcome literature. This principle applies not only to direct services with clients but also to larger networks, institutions, and processes of the ecological setting. It supports the use of indirect services, such as consultation and advocacy, as means to promote the well-being of immediate groups, organizations, cultures, and societies.

Justice has to do with fairness and equality of treatment (Corey et al., 2003). Persons are entitled to equal access and quality of treatment regardless of race, ethnicity, gender, sexual orientation, or religion. The application of this principle extends beyond the counselor-counselee relationship to the development and implementation of agency policy and procedures. For example, counseling agencies engage in hiring practices that do not discriminate and provide services that are sensitive to persons whose "difference" is relevant (e.g., culturally diverse or physically disabled clients).

Fidelity relates to the practice of honoring commitments and keeping promises. Doing so is foundational to the development and maintenance of trust and trustworthiness. Contracts are honored. This includes fee arrangements, the keeping of appointments as scheduled, and conducting the counseling process as expressed on the mutually agreed upon therapeutic plan. In addition, commitments made to clients are honored even when assigned counselors become unavailable due to prolonged illness or relocation.

Finally, *veracity* has to do with honesty and genuineness. Counselors act with integrity and avoid the use of deception and covert manipulation of clients. They represent their training, credentials, and qualifications accurately and do not make reports to accrediting bodies, third-party reimbursers, peers, or clients that are untrue, biased, or distortions of actual fact.

CODES OF ETHICS

As noted previously, the primary way a professional organization monitors and regulates the behavior of its members is through the development and enforcement of a code of ethics. A number of professional organizations and codes are relevant to the practice of counseling. Most relevant for mental health and community counselors are the codes developed by the ACA (2005) and AMHCA (2000). In addition, the NBCC has put forth a code applicable for mental health professionals who have been awarded the NCC, MAC, and CCMHC. Other codes of ethics have been developed by the American Psychological Association (2003), NASW (1999), and AAMFT (2001). Finally, state licensure laws frequently include a section within the legal statute identifying standards for ethical practice.

According to Herlihy and Corey (1996), the codes of ethics fulfill three primary objectives. First, codes of ethics are developed to educate members about the components of sound professional conduct. By reading and reflecting on the codes, mental health and community counselors increase sensitivity regarding the presence and nature of ethical issues embedded within the content and process of their ongoing work with clients. Knowledge of the codes becomes a guide that assists counselors in dealing with the challenges and dilemmas faced in professional practice. Second, the codes identify a set of standards to which professional counselors are accountable. By virtue of their professional membership, mental health counselors are obliged to monitor their own professional behavior as well as that of their peers. Third, the codes of ethics can act as catalysts for improving counseling services. Once sensitive to the contents of the ethical codes, mental health and community counselors analyze and direct their professional conduct in the direction of *best practice.*

The ACA Code of Ethics (2005) consists of a preamble, a purpose statement, and by eight sections, each of which covers a specific area of ethical behavior:

1. *The counseling relationship*—specifies the ethical dimensions of the counselor-counselee relationship. The primary responsibility of respecting the dignity and promoting the welfare of clients is emphasized. Specific areas discussed include respecting diversity, client rights, dual relationships, fees and bartering, and termination issues.
2. *Confidentiality, privileged communication, and privacy*—focuses on the need for professional counselors to respect the privacy of clients and clinical records. Special

applications of this standard include working with groups, families, minors, or incompetent clients in therapy, research and training, and consultation.

3. *Professional responsibility*—discusses standards of training, credentialing, and professional competence. Responsibilities toward the general public and other professionals are explored, including ethical practices of advertising and the solicitation of prospective clients.

4. *Relationships with other professionals*—notes standards of ethics relating to employers, employees, and consultees.

5. *Evaluation, assessment, and interpretation*—specifies principles for ethical use of assessment techniques. This includes the selection, administration, scoring, interpretation, and storage of tests.

6. *Supervision, training, and teaching*—provides specific guidelines for counselor educators, students, supervisors, supervisees, and other trainers.

7. *Research and publication*—discusses specific ethical issues for research involving human participants and the reporting and publication of results. This section emphasizes the importance of gaining informed consent and protecting participants from any potential harm or side effects through their involvement in projects.

8. *Resolving ethical issues*—communicates that it is the responsibility of counselors to possess knowledge of the ethical code. In addition, this section outlines the manner in which suspected violations of the code should be handled.

The code concludes with a glossary of terms.

THE ROLE OF THE ACA ETHICS COMMITTEE AND INVESTIGATION OF ALLEGED VIOLATIONS

The ACA Ethics Committee promotes sound ethical behavior within the counseling profession by monitoring the professional conduct of ACA members. The responsibilities of this committee include educating the membership of the ACA *Code of Ethics*; periodically reviewing and recommending revisions to the code; receiving and processing complaints of alleged ethical violations of ACA members; providing interpretations of the ethical standards of the code; and recommending reasonable disciplinary actions to be taken against members where violation of ethical standards is substantiated (ACA Governing Council, 2003).

The ACA Ethics Committee receives complaints from persons who believe an ACA member has violated the ACA *Code of Ethics* (ACA Governing Council, 2003). When a complaint is accepted, evidence and documents supporting the complaint are provided to the charged member, who is then asked to respond to the complaint. Once the responses of the charged member to the allegations have been received, the committee members receive copies of the complaint, supporting evidence, and related documents sent to the charged member and responses received from the charged member. The committee then determines if any standard of the code has been violated. If it is determined that violations have occurred, the committee will impose one or a combination of the following possible sanctions (ACA Governing Council, 2003), listed by according to increasing levels of severity.

1. The ethics committee may choose to mandate specific *remedial requirements* to be completed with given time limits.
2. The member might be placed on *probation* for a specified length of time. Often, remediatory requirements must be completed within the probationary period.
3. The professional might be *suspended* for a specified length of time. In addition, completion of remediatory requirements within the specified time period is often imposed.
4. The professional might be *permanently expelled* from the ACA. For this sanction to be implemented, a unanimous vote among voting committee members is required.

The ethics committee monitors a suspended member's compliance with the sanctions and may expel the member when failure to fulfill remediatory requirements is demonstrated. The committee seeks to act in an educative and remedial, and not punitive, manner. Other corrective actions in addition to the preceding sanctions can include further education and training, supervision, or personal evaluation and treatment.

SPECIFIC ETHICAL AND LEGAL ISSUES

COMPETENCE AND SCOPE OF PRACTICE

The establishment of trust is the cornerstone to developing and maintaining an effective therapeutic relationship. And establishing competence is central to any discussion of trust and trustworthiness, because most clients would not enter into a counseling relationship if the counselor cannot demonstrate evidences of competence. It is this expectation of the counselor's competence that enables clients to place trust in the counselor quite early in the counseling process.

It is essential that mental health and community counselors practice within their boundaries of competence. However, defining competence and assessing its presence is difficult. The ACA *Code of Ethics* (2005) clearly communicates the centrality of competent practice in section C.2.a.:

> Counselors practice only within the boundaries of their competence, based on their education, training, supervised experience, state and national professional credentials, and appropriate professional experience. Counselors gain knowledge, personal awareness, sensitivity, and skills pertinent to working with a diverse client population. (p. 9)

The question arises, though, regarding what specific criteria are used to determine competence. What are valid evidences of professional competence that can and should be communicated to prospective clients? How can we determine that a professional possesses a level of competence in a specialized area? For example, at what point may a professional legitimately refer to himself or herself as a cognitive or play therapist?

Clearly, one's academic transcript and diploma, state license and professional certification, continuing education, and supervised experience indicate competence. It is important to note the distinction between minimal competence and demonstration of mastery. Education, licensure, and supervised experience demonstrate that the person has met or exceeded the minimal standards for practice of the profession. But advanced degrees or licenses do not necessarily guarantee that the professional engages in best practice, consults with more experienced practitioners, or stays current in his or her area of specialization. At a minimum, practicing within one's boundaries of competence requires that the counselor be sensitive to his or her strengths and weaknesses and in humility seeks additional training, supervision, and consultation throughout his or her career.

State licensure laws identify the *scope of practice* for a professional group. The scope of practice outlines those professional roles and tasks that the person licensed under the law can legally perform. Generally speaking, the legally defined scope of practice reflects the knowledge and skills of the profession's training model. Thus, from a legal perspective, a licensed professional is bound to practice within the areas of competency as identified by the state law. For example, some states have not included diagnosis within the scope of practice of professional counselors. In such states, mental health and community counselors must practice within the parameters established by the law. Mental health professionals who diagnose in these states violate a legal statute and can be taken to court by consumers or relevant professional organizations.

INFORMED CONSENT: CLIENT'S RIGHTS AND RESPONSIBILITIES

Informed consent refers to the right of clients to be clearly informed regarding the nature of their counseling and make autonomous decisions regarding it (Corey et al., 2003). Its practice demonstrates counselors' respect for the dignity, autonomy, and human rights of their clients and is foundational for the development of the counseling contract (Hall & Lin, 1995). Although it is a critical component in the initial stages of counseling, the principle of informed consent is applicable to all stages of the counseling process.

Consideration of the principle of informed consent raises several concerns. First, the word *informed* implies that specific types of information should be provided to clients. The ACA *Code of Ethics* is clear:

> A.2.a. Informed Consent. Clients have the freedom to choose whether to enter into or remain in a counseling relationship and need adequate information about the counseling process and the counselor. Counselors have an obligation to review in writing and verbally with clients the rights and responsibilities of both the counselor and the client. Informed consent is an ongoing part of the counseling process, and counselors appropriately document discussions of informed consent throughout the counseling relationship. (ACA, 2005) p. 4

It is good counseling practice to have written informed consent forms that are presented to clients prior to the beginning of treatment (Moline et al., 1998). The following information should be included:

- nature of treatment, including the counselor's preferred theoretical perspective
- time parameters for sessions
- methods of payment
- no-show/cancellation policy
- nature of and limitations to confidentiality
- potential risks and/or side effects of treatment
- qualifications of the counselor (often presented as a separate *professional self-disclosure form*)

For consent to be truly informed, it is vital that clients understand the concepts, procedures, and implications conveyed. Thus, it is not sufficient merely to provide clients with a sheet of information and have them sign on the dotted line indicating that they have read the material. Ethical counselors seek evidence to confirm that the client fully comprehends prior to giving consent. This principle also applies to participants in research projects.

Second, the client gives consent for treatment. It is legitimate to raise the question, "Who is the client?" Consider, for example, the complexities of conducting marriage or family counseling. When working with multiple participants in session, who specifically gives consent? The ACA *Code of Ethics* (A.7. Multiple Clients) provides the following guidance:

> When a counselor agrees to provide counseling services to two of more persons who have a relationship, the counselor clarifies at the outset which person or persons are clients and the nature of the relationships the counselor will have with each involved person. If it becomes apparent that the counselor may be called upon to perform potentially conflicting roles, the counselor will clarify, adjust, or withdraw from roles appropriately. (ACA, 2005) p. 5

At the outset, participants in family therapy should understand what is meant when told that the system or family unit is the focus of treatment, rather than its individual members. Furthermore, the counselor must be clear regarding who should attend. The family should know if all members are required to attend all sessions. Finally, family members should know the limits of confidentiality, a topic discussed later in this chapter. For example, the counselor must explain how individual secrets will be dealt with in the context of family therapy.

Third, informed consent occurs when the client makes a voluntary, autonomous decision. However, not all identified clients are capable of giving informed consent. A minor can enter into a therapeutic contract (a) by parental or guardian consent; (b) involuntarily at a parent's insistence; or (c) by order of juvenile court (Lawrence & Kurpius, 2000). The primary exceptions occur if the child is considered emancipated (i.e., under the age of 18 and living separately from parents and managing personal financial affairs) or, in some states, if waiting to gain parental consent would create a life- or health-endangering condition (Lawrence & Kurpius, 2000). In cases of parental divorce, the custodial parent must grant consent for the treatment of his or her children (Stein, 1990) p. 367.

Furthermore, the ability to give autonomous, informed consent assumes the client has the psychological capacity to do so. For example, certain clients may be so impaired that they are unaware of their need for treatment. In such extreme cases, guardians, significant others, or the state may petition the involuntary commitment of the client for inpatient treatment. Or the consent of parents or guardians is required when mental retardation limits the client's capacity to make an informed, autonomous decision.

CONFIDENTIALITY AND PRIVILEGED COMMUNICATION

Confidentiality and privileged communication relate to the fundamental right of the client to privacy; that is, the right of persons to determine what information about them will be shared or withheld from others (Remley & Herlihy, 2005). *Confidentiality* refers to the ethical responsibility to safeguard client-related information gained through the professional relationship and disclose it only when fully informed clients freely give consent to do so. Privileged communication, a related concept, refers to the legal obligation to protect clients against forced disclosure in legal proceedings of information conveyed in the context of the professional relationship (Corey et al., 2003).

The assurance of confidentiality is central to the counseling process (Hackney, 2000). The U.S. Supreme Court recognized its centrality in the 1996 *Jaffee v. Redmond* decision:

> Effective psychotherapy, by contrast, depends upon an atmosphere of confidence and trust in which the patient is willing to make a frank and complete disclosure of facts, emotions, memories, and fears. Because of the sensitive nature of the problems for which individuals consult psychotherapists, disclosure of confidential communications made during counseling sessions may cause embarrassment or disgrace. For this reason, the mere possibility of disclosure may impede development of the confidential relationship necessary for successful treatment. (p. 10)

Information protected by confidentiality includes all information related to the counseling contacts, words spoken in sessions, business records, the clinical record, test results, and client-related information received from other parties.

However, the right to confidentiality is not absolute. Certain modalities of treatment make the guarantee of confidentiality impossible. The potential for unauthorized disclosure occurs when multiple clients are seen in treatment. For example, Corey and colleagues (2003) note that privileged communication does not typically apply for group counseling, unless there is a statutory exception (p. 432). Furthermore, although group counselors should clearly define and express the importance of confidentiality, they cannot prevent group members from revealing information outside the group setting. This risk of unauthorized disclosure should be communicated when seeking to obtain informed consent from prospective group clients.

Decisions must be made by the counselor on the extent to which confidentiality can be honored or broken when counseling minors. Children and adolescents are most often seen at the request of parents, teachers, or someone else (Slovenko, 1998). Particularly problematic situations involve unwanted pregnancies, substance abuse, crimes against property, sexual behavior, and dangerousness to self or others (Isaacs & Stone, 2001). Generally speaking, four possible options are available (Hendrix, 1991). These include (a) complete confidentiality with no disclosure to parents, (b) limited confidentiality for which minors waive the right to know what may be disclosed in advance, (c) informed forced consent when a child is provided advance notice that information will be revealed to parents, and (d) no guarantees made about confidentiality at all. Each option presents potential ethical and legal dilemmas. Isaacs and Stone (2001) found that mental health counselors tended to grant greater autonomy to minor clients as the age of the child clients increased. Furthermore, decisions to breach confidentiality related to degree of seriousness of the activity. Finally, the personal values of the counselor (e.g., liberal versus conservative, pro-choice versus pro-life) interact with the previously mentioned factors when the mental health counselor is deciding whether to breach confidentiality with a minor client.

PROTECTION OF CLIENTS OR OTHERS FROM HARM

Confidentiality must be breached when a risk of harm to clients or others exists. This includes suspected abuse or neglect of children, clients who pose a danger to themselves, clients who pose a danger to others, and a clients who have a communicable disease and whose behavior puts others at risk. The specific responsibilities of the mental health or community counselor in such situations include the duties to warn, to protect, and/or to report (Remley & Herlihy, 2005). Because the counselor makes a deliberate choice to break confidentiality, the decision to do so requires compelling evidence. These are among the most stressful situations faced by professional counselors (Deutsch, 1984; Farber, 1983).

Taking Action When Child or Older Adult Abuse or Neglect Is Suspected. The AMHCA *Code of Ethics* (2000) states, "The protection of a child, an elderly person, or a person not competent to care for themselves from physical or sexual abuse or neglect requires that a report be made to a legally constituted authority" (Principle 3.C). Indeed, all 50 states have legal statutes requiring that suspected abuse be reported to law enforcement. The specific time frame in which a report must be made varies according to jurisdiction. The role of mental health and community counselors is to report suspicions rather than hypotheses or hunches. Furthermore, this does not entail conducting an investigation to substantiate the suspicion. When uncertain as to whether to report, mental health professionals consult with supervisors and colleagues.

Protecting Clients Who Pose a Danger to Themselves. Clients can pose a danger to themselves when presenting evidence that a suicide attempt is clear and imminent. Thus, mental health and community counselors are ethically and legally required to break confidentiality when they determine that their clients represent a clear and imminent threat to themselves. To determine risk of self-destructiveness, a *lethality assessment* is conducted. The following signs are considered (Hoff, 1995):

- presence of a suicide plan*
- past history of suicide attempts*
- absence of preventive psychological and social resources*
- communication (i.e., relative isolation of client)*
- experience of recent loss
- physical illness
- chemical abuse
- unexplained change in behavior
- depression
- social factors or problems
- mental illness
- statistical predictors—age, gender, race, marital status, sexual identity

The level of risk increases with increased number of signs present. However, the risk is very high if the four signs followed by asterisks exist in the particular client (Hoff, 1995). When it is determined that the client is dangerous either to self or others, appropriate interventions can range from having the client sign a no-suicide contract to having the client involuntarily committed to a psychiatric facility. In addition, mental health professionals should always seek consultation with supevisors and colleagues to determine a path of action that is both ethically and legally sound.

Clients Who Pose a Danger to Others.   Mental health professionals are required to contact law enforcement agencies when they determine that their client poses a high risk of assault or homicide. In addition, and based on principles of the Tarasoff case (*Tarasoff v. Board of Regents of the University of California,* 1976), potential victims of homicide must be warned. The following guidelines are useful in assessing the risk of assault or homicide (Hoff, 1995):

- history of homicidal threats
- history of assaults
- current homicidal threats and plan
- possession of lethal weapons
- use or abuse of alcohol or other drugs
- conflict in significant social relationship (e.g., infidelity, threat of divorce, work-related problem)
- threats of suicide following homicide

The mental health professional responds in measure to the degree of risk presented. Interventions can range from the development of a contract to involuntary commitment to psychiatric institutions. Furthermore, it is incumbent that the mental health professional take appropriate measures to protect self from danger. These are not situations where "playing the Lone Ranger" is recommended.

Clients With Communicable Diseases Whose Behavior Poses a Danger to Others.   One of the most controversial applications of the *Tarasoff* decision has emerged as mental health and community counselors determine how to respond in AIDS-related cases. The duty to warn may apply in situations where HIV-positive clients engage in unprotected sex or share needles with unsuspecting third parties (Cohen, 1997). The ACA *Code of Ethics* (ACA, 2005) states as follows:

> When clients disclose that they have a disease commonly known to be both communicable and life threatening, counselors may be justified in disclosing information to identifiable third parties, if they are known to be at demonstrable and high risk of contracting the disease. Prior to making a disclosure, counselors confirm that there is such a diagnosis and assess the intent of clients to inform the third parties about their disease or to engage in any behaviors that may be harmful to an identifiable third party. (Section B.2.b.) p. 7

The code states that counselors *may be justified in disclosing information,* which falls short of requiring the warning of vulnerable third parties. The dilemma for mental health practitioners involves deciding the extent to which the duty to warn outweighs the need to protect confidentiality. In addition, states differ not only in requiring disclosure of confidential information to the vulnerable third party, but also in who is required to disclose.

Cohen (1997) identifies the following conditions for justifiable disclosure:

- The presence of conclusive medical evidence indicating that the client is HIV seropositive;
- The third party is placed at a high risk for contracting HIV, according to current medical standards, due to unprotected, ongoing sexual intercourse with the client;
- No other person is likely to disclose to the third party;
- The third party may be identified and contacted by the counselor with no intervention of law enforcement or other investigative agencies.

Counselors must be cautious and seek legal and professional consultation in determining the appropriate ethical and legal path to follow. Although justified to disclose, mental health and community counselors must be mindful of the ethical, legal, and professional principle of maintaining confidentiality.

PROFESSIONAL BOUNDARIES AND DUAL RELATIONSHIPS

Most persons, when asked to identify the most significant ethical problem related to professional boundaries, will typically place sexual contact or intercourse between counselors and clients at the top of the list. However, a wide range of boundary issues exists when a theoretical line marking the boundary between counselor and client is crossed. The nature of the specific boundary is defined by the context of its occurrence, the specific human dimension(s) involved, and the nature of the rules in operation. Thus, the specific boundaries crossed may be physical, psychological, emotional, or social. For example, physical boundaries are crossed when touch occurs in treatment. Or counselors who become incapacitated by inappropriately taking on the emotional pain of their clients have crossed an emotional boundary.

Dual relationships are a specific type of boundary issue that occurs when a counselor assumes two or more roles concurrently or sequentially with a person seeking help (Pearson & Piazza, 1997). For example, a dual relationship exists when the counselor dates a current client or when the exchange of gifts between counselors and clients blurs personal and professional roles (Gerig, 2004). Often, it is the least extreme boundary issues that are most difficult to handle. I have much more problem determining how to respond to a current client who approaches me while shopping at the mall with my family than in deciding whether it is ethical to accept an expensive gift from a client.

Pearson and Piazza (1997) identify several categories of multiple relationships:

- circumstantial multiple relationships
- structured multiple professional relationships
- shifts in professional roles
- personal and professional role conflicts
- predatory professionals

Although professionals uniformly agree that sexual contact between counselors is unethical, they differ regarding the positions they take regarding nonsexual multiple roles and boundary issues. In general, counselors are advised to avoid dual relationships when possible, especially when there is potential for exploitation or impaired clinical judgment (ACA, 2005, Section A.5.a.). Certain multiple relationships represent significant conflict of interests and roles and must, therefore, be avoided if the well-being of the client is to be promoted. However, it is awkward and perhaps harmful to avoid less extreme multiple relationships. For example, it is probably unnecessary to change the church I attend because one of my clients attends the same church. Or if the only teller window available is staffed by my current client, it is better for me to do my banking business at that window (assuming, of course, that the transaction does not involve cashing checks that reveal the names of other clients). Indeed, the ACA *Code of Ethics* (2005) notes the possibility that certain counselor-client nonprofessional interactions might be beneficial (Section A.5.d.). The counselor is encouraged to document in case records the rationale for engaging in such a relationship in advance, when feasible.

To minimize risk to clients, mental health and community counselors are advised to set healthy boundaries early in the therapeutic relationship. Informed consent and open, ongoing communication regarding the nature of the treatment process provide added protection for clients. Consult with supervisors to maintain an objective perspective on the therapeutic relationship. And when a dual relationship becomes problematic, work under close supervision, and document the nature of this supervision in your records along with a detailed account of your interactions with the client.

CONCLUSION

A number of models for making ethical decisions are found in the professional literature (Corey et al., 2003; Cottone & Claus, 2000; Garcia, Cartwright, Winston, & Borzuchowska, 2003). The following steps are identified by Corey and Colleagues (2003):

1. Recognize the problem or dilemma.
2. Identify the potential issues involved.
3. Review the relevant ethical codes.
4. Determine what laws and regulations, if any, are applicable to the situation.
5. Obtain consultation.
6. Consider possible and probable courses of action.
7. Identify potential positive and negative consequences possible courses of action.
8. Decide on the best course of action, implement, and monitor the process and outcome in relation to desired goal.

It is prudent to be mindful of the difference between ethical decision making and ethical or moral behavior. Rest (1983) identifies four components of moral behavior that must be present if moral action is to occur. First, the counselor must exhibit *moral sensitivity*. This refers to the process of recognizing the situation as one that has implication for the welfare of the client. Second, the counselor must possess the ability to engage in *moral reasoning*. It is necessary for counselors to recognize and think through the moral dimensions involved in the specific ethical problem or dilemma. Third, counselors must *decide to carry out the moral alternative*. Alternatives must be evaluated and the counselor then resolves to implement the most moral of the options available. Fourth, the counselor *implements the moral action*. This involves the capacity to enact the desired behaviors *in context*.

DISCUSSION QUESTIONS

1. You are employed at a local community mental health center and lead a group of adolescent males who have been mandated into the conduct disorder group that you facilitate. A lack of participation by any member of the group is viewed as a violation of probation criteria and is to be reported to the probation officer. What are the implications of informed consent when working with involuntary clients? Suppose you have four group members who choose to remain silent. They attend, but they do not participate in group activities. What are the ethical dilemmas for you, and how would you respond?

2. In what ways do counselors' personal sets of values interact with their ability to behave in professional and ethical manners? To what extent can a counselor's personal set of values be incongruent with the set of ethics he or she is required to hold?

3. Counselors frequently work with clients who express suicidal ideation. How would you assess the level of risk presented by a client? At what point would it be necessary for counselors to break confidentiality to protect the client? What specific steps would you take in such situations?

4. What type of boundary issues or dual relationships will tend to be most difficult for you to manage? Discuss what these are and how you would choose to manage them.

SUGGESTED ACTIVITIES

1. How specifically would you discuss the ethical concerns of confidentiality and informed consent with your clients? Practice your skills with one or two peers. Then, discuss the significance and limitations of confidentiality and informed consent with your client by doing a roleplay. Assign the roles of counselor and counselee. How would your discussion differ if you were conducting family or group counseling?

2. Suppose you choose to work in a private practice upon licensure. Develop a self-disclosure statement that you might provide to new clients as a way of introducing them to who you are, areas of specialization, and the services offered.

3. Suppose you operate a small, privately owned counseling practice. Develop a Web page to advertise your services. What ethical issues require special consideration when promoting a counseling service in this manner?

4. Develop several ethical dilemmas that you are likely to face as a professional counselor. Then apply the steps of ethical decision-making (e.g., Corey, Corey, & Cullanan, 2003- discussed on pp. 359–360) to assist you in resolving the dilemmas.

Part 3

Contemporary Issues and Trends

10

Managed Care and Third-Party Reimbursement

OUTLINE

Managed Care in Context

What Is Managed Care?

Impact on the Practice of Mental Health Counseling

Surviving in the Era of Managed Health Counseling

I entered the counseling profession as an individual and family counselor in 1983. The small, not-for-profit, mental health agency that I worked for specialized in what was viewed as brief therapy. Clients were scheduled for sessions at varying intervals and might be seen over the course of a year or so. However, the average number of sessions scheduled for typical clients being seen for outpatient counseling ranged from 12 to 20. The agency set fees according to a sliding fee scale and billed insurance companies for services rendered. A copayment of 20% was the norm for most clients' insurance plans that provided mental health benefits. In addition, these plans set limits on the maximum benefit for outpatient treatment. Sometimes the number of sessions per year was limited to 50. Other policies set a maximum annual payout for outpatient treatment at $2000.

Although insurance companies occasionally audited the agency's business and clinical recordkeeping practices, counselors at the agency were able to assess, diagnose, and treat clients with a great deal of autonomy. After conducting the initial interview and assessment, a treatment plan was devised. Goals, objectives, and estimated timeframes for accomplishing goals and objectives were developed in collaboration with clients and were stated explicitly. In addition, the specific treatment approaches used to assist clients in attaining their goals were listed. This document served as a therapeutic contract between the client and counselor and was reviewed by our clinical supervisor. It became the basis for guiding treatment and monitoring outcome. Insurance companies were billed and reimbursement occurred at regular intervals. The treatment process was within the control of the counselor.

The process just described seems like a distant memory for most veteran mental health care providers. Few would have predicted the shift in professional practice that has occurred due, in large measure, to the advent of managed care. Most practitioners have been required to alter the manner in which counseling is conducted and managed. A number of private practitioners have been forced out of business. The change in the profession has been so great that some refer to it as the "mental health care revolution" (Zimet, 1989).

This chapter addresses a number of issues concerning the contemporary practice of mental health counseling in the managed care environment. Responses to the following questions are explored: Was managed care a mental health care revolution and a radical shift that came "out of the blue"? Or was it a logical response to the rising costs in health care, which had reached crisis proportions? What is managed care? How does it, in fact, manage care? What procedures are implemented to control costs of service? How have mental health practitioners reacted and responded to managed care?

FINANCIAL RISK AND THE RISE OF INSURANCE COMPANIES

It is typically stated or inferred that the manner in which mental health care is managed and delivered in the United States represents a radical shift from how business was conducted previously. The mechanisms that have been put into place by managed care organizations are new. Several decades ago, procedures such as pretreatment authorization, utilization reviews, capitation, and other incentives for "efficient treatment providers" were not part of the mental health care environment. However, it is important to recognize the extent to which the history of third-party reimbursement for physical and mental disorders has contributed to the current situation.

Through the mid-1800s, society was much less fragmented. It was more rural and agrarian, and less mobile. The population was less dense, and resources to meet the needs of society were virtually inaccessible for many. When unexpected needs arose, resources were pooled from within small social groups. In this way, families and other small social units, such as churches or loosely woven community associations, were able to "take care of their own."

The Amish culture provides us with a contemporary model of social support that was much more common in the past. The practice of Amish religion prohibits participation in insurance plans. Thus, when tragedy strikes, Amish people are on their own. Amish families support each other with money, goods, and services in times of crisis. For example, when a barn is ignited by lightning and burns to the ground, families from the surrounding area organize and assist in the clean-up and rebuilding of the structure. They have a "barn-raising" get-together and, in a matter of days, have the burned-out structure cleared away and a new barn constructed in its place. When a young child suffers from a heart condition and requires open heart surgery, Amish families band together and provide financial support so that required medical services can be obtained. Their social group operates according to the priniciples of modified communalism. Thus, financial risk is spread to all members of the group when a hardship besets any of its members.

By the mid- to late 1800s, Western society was being influenced by increased industrialization and urbanization. Among the consequences were loosened kinship ties and a decreased sense of community and shared meaning (Cushman, 1995). People were much more vulnerable to the increased risk of injury and occupational hazard. Various sorts of insurance programs began to spring up by the mid-1800s to protect families by the pooling of financial risk. In this way, insurance plans began to fill the void created by loosened social and familial ties (Faulkner, 1960). Initially, accident insurance programs arose in England to cover medical expenses for injuries that did not lead to death (Throckmorton, 1998). In 1864, the Travelers Insurance Company of Hartford was established, and by 1866, 60 different insurers existed in the United States to provide coverage for injury as well as for health and sickness (Faulkner, 1960; Throckmorton, 1998).

In 1883, Germany became the first nation to legislate national health insurance. Other European countries soon followed suit (Throckmorton, 1998). In the United States, national health insurance was promoted by the Socialist party as early as 1904. President Woodrow Wilson proposed a national health care plan in the 1920s in an attempt to improve labor-management relations (Numbers, 1984). However, his proposal failed. Although the American Medical Association supported such proposals initially, support weakened considerably when limits on the reimbursement of medical care were included in the package (Numbers, 1984).

Citizens of the United States were hard hit by the devastating impact of the Great Depression, and calls for national health insurance were renewed (Numbers, 1984). In this context, Congress experienced increased pressure to develop a national program that would provide at least minimal coverage for all citizens. The forerunner to Blue Cross/Blue Shield developed in 1929 when a group of school teachers arranged for Baylor University Hospital to provide health care in exchange for a monthly prepayment (Throckmorton, 1998).

This model took hold and, in 1937, the Health Service Plan Commission was established to oversee the Blue Cross plans, which were becoming more numerous across the country (Throckmorton, 1998). Blue Cross covered expenses for physician services occurring within the hospital. Blue Shield was developed in 1939 and provided coverage for medical expenses for physician services outside the hospital setting. The success of Blue Cross/Blue Shield, the emergence of the United States from the Great Depression, and the nation's involvement in World War II led to a rapid increase in the number of health care insurers (Faulkner, 1960). During the 1950s and 1960s, insurance policies rapidly expanded the range of benefits. Policies could now be written that not only covered health issues, but also vision, dental, and prescriptions for medicine.

With the passage of the Community Mental Health Centers Act of 1963, increased acceptance of counseling and decreased stigma of the recipients of such services led to the coverage of mental health services in insurance plans. Mental health benefits often have taken center stage in the national discussion over rising health care costs (Wiggins, 1988).

THE PUSH TOWARD MANAGED CARE

Chambliss (2000, p. 26) notes that until the late 1970s, the delivery of health care in the United States was guided by two underlying assumptions: "The doctor knows best" and "We must spend whatever is necessary." By the 1980s, though, treatment guided by these principles was beginning to be viewed as "deluxe" and excessively expensive. This change in perspective, precipitated by rapidly accelerating health care costs, was responsible for the push toward managed care.

The costs for health care had become excessive. Mirin and Sederer (1994) note that, in 1965, payments for health care in the United States totaled approximately $42 billion. By 1985, these costs multiplied 10-fold to $442.3 billion. In the next 7 years, health care costs doubled to over $800 billion. By the early 1990s, health care costs were rising at a rate three times greater than the rate of inflation and were consuming more than 14% of the gross national product (Polkinghorne, 2001). The typical American family spent 16.4% of its income on health care (Smith, 1999). In addition, mental health care had increased at a rate that exceeded the increased cost of health care in general (Smith, 1999). From 1987 to 1992, the annual benefit cost per employee for substance abuse and mental health coverage jumped from $163 to $400 (Mirer & Sederer, 1994). Of this amount, outpatient mental health care accounted for about 3 to 4%.

Employers bore the burden of this financial expense. In 1963, employers were spending on the average of between 4 and 8 cents per dollar of profit for employees' health care benefits. By 1990, that amount had increased to around 50 cents per profit dollar. These costs were projected to continue their upward spiral.

A second factor contributing to the move toward managed care was findings suggesting that unnecessary services were being provided and consequently billed to third-party reimbursers. Insurance companies had long suspected that diagnostic categories were being applied loosely, the claims for which were submitted for reimbursement. The findings of Vessey and Howard (1993) provided some support for the validity of such suspicions. Their study, in which data were pooled from a number of epidemiological surveys, reported that as many as 50% of persons being seen in psychotherapy did not meet the *DSM* diagnostic criteria of the disorder for which they were being treated (Vessey & Howard, 1993).

From the aforementioned trends the managed health care movement emerged. This movement has been driven by the need to control spiraling health care costs. To control costs, managed care has replaced the traditional fee-for-service system and has placed limits on the amount and types of services rendered by providers (Foos, Ottens, & Hill, 1991). In doing so, managed care has made a significant impact on the way mental health services are delivered, regardless of discipline (Smith, 1999).

WHAT IS MANAGED CARE?

The bottom line of all managed care efforts is the containment of costs for health services. Total health care costs may be calculated by applying the following formula (Broskowski & Marks, 1992):

$$\text{total costs} = \text{utilization} \times \text{cost per unit}.$$

Thus, attempts at containing the costs of mental health care are directed toward managing the frequency with which specific services are used and the fees associated with those services.

Related to the goal of cost containment is the focus on accountability to ensure efficiency and value (Chambliss, 2000). From the viewpoint of a third-party reimburser, value of a service is achieved when there is a significant and positive outcome from the investment of time and resources. The true value of a specific mental health service is determined by considering the nature and extent of client goal attainment and satisfaction in relationship to the cost for the particular service. The following formula is helpful in evaluating the value of proposed services for clients (Chambliss, 2000):

$$\text{value} = \frac{\text{desired outcomes} - \text{adverse outcomes}}{\text{cost}}.$$

As Chambliss (2000) notes, both the numerator and denominator must be addressed if the value of a service is to be demonstrated. However, in practice, it is much easier to demonstrate reduction in cost than it is to provide definitive evidence regarding the quality of clinical outcomes. Thus, most managed care case managers have concentrated on the denominator.

Managed care, then, is a general term used to describe a constellation of businesses, organizations, and practices that arrange for the financing and delivery of mental health services (Lawless, Ginter, & Kelly, 1999; Phelps, Eisman, & Kohout, 1998). Generally speaking, the term *managed care* is commonly used to refer to a range of programs and policies that control access to care, the types of care delivered, and the cost of care (Morrissey, 1999). Managed care organizations (MCOs) have instituted several specific mechanisms for the purpose of cost containment. Generally, these mechanisms either reduce the overall utilization of mental health services or reduce the average price per unit of service.

When these mechanisms are organized and implemented in a coherent manner, various types of managed care programs emerge. Health maintenance organizations (HMOs) are the most common form of managed care systems (Broskowski & Marks, 1992; Chambliss, 2000). Clients are assigned a primary care provider who provides services on a prepaid, capitated fee basis. The physician also acts as a gatekeeper and makes referrals to specialists based on medical necessity. In contrast, preferred provider organizations (PPOs) are "networks of providers that collectively provide comprehensive health care coverage or an array of specialty care, such as mental health or substance abuse (Broskowski & Marks, 1992). Providers of care are invited to join a PPO based on quality of work, geographic location, or ability to provide specialty service. Preferred provider organization providers tend to be reimbursed at a discounted rate after services are rendered. The network of providers becomes managed care when authorization and review procedures are implemented. Finally, community mental health centers are increasingly fitting the definition of managed care organizations (Gaver, 2000; Uttaro, Vali, Horwitz, & Henri, 1998).

PROCEDURES FOR REDUCING UTILIZATION

Managed care organizations use several procedures to reduce utilization of mental health services and thereby limit the total cost of mental health services to third-party reimbursers. These include pretreatment authorization of treatment, concurrent utilization reviews, incentives for efficient providers, and increased employer/user cost sharing.

Pretreatment Authorization of Treatment.   The goal of pretreatment authorization of treatment is to ensure that any treatment initiated has been determined to be medically necessary and appropriate (Feldstein, Wickizer, & Wheeler, 1988). This requires that the counselor calls a review organization and gains approval for treatment prior to providing direct service to the client. Occasionally, a case manager of the MCO assists in assessing clients' needs, the degree of medical necessity, and the best provider of services.

Typically, the basis for determining "medical necessity" is the valid diagnosis of the client using *DSM-IV* criteria. Furthermore, authorization of treatment requires that the techniques used and frequency and quantity of sessions be appropriate for the specific diagnostic category. Counselors must show the scientific basis for the specific treatment approach selected and demonstrate their capacity to promote therapeutic gains for the particular client (Chambliss, 2000). In this way, managed care serves a gatekeeping function in the contemporary mental health care environment.

With the authorization of treatment, counselors usually receive assurance that they will be reimbursed for services rendered, provided that a valid claim is submitted (Broskowski & Marks, 1992). Although counselors are not necessarily limited to provision of authorized treatment, they may risk not being reimbursed for any service delivered that is not authorized.

Concurrent Utilization Reviews. Concurrent utilization reviews answer the primary question, "To what extent is it necessary for the client to continue in treatment beyond the original limits authorized?" (Broskowski & Marks, 1992). In the past, the answer to this question was based on the judgment of the counselor made in collaboration with the client. In the contemporary treatment setting, however, the counselor collaborates with a reviewer to justify continuation of treatment. For example, to extend a patient's hospital stay, counselors working in inpatient settings must provide the reviewer with objective evidence that the patient remains a clear danger to self. Counselors working with a depressed client in an outpatient program, are required to demonstrate that additional sessions using specific techniques are necessary for the client to reach an acceptable level of functioning. In either case, an independent reviewer employed by the managed care organization serves as a consultant and assists the counselor in making treatment decisions and discharge plans (Broskowski & Marks, 1992). Counselors must have relevant data to support their request for an extension of the original authorization and clearly communicate this rationale to the reviewer. Thus, the concepts of medical necessity and appropriateness of treatment are relevant throughout the entire therapeutic process.

To function adequately in the contemporary mental health setting, mental health counselors must possess a variety of foundational appraisal and research skills. At the very least, mental health counselors must possess a working knowledge of basic research methodologies that can be applied in clinical settings to measure client progress. They must also be well read on the vast range of appraisal instruments available and skilled in their administration, scoring, and interpretation.

Several benefits of pretreatment authorization and concurrent utilization review processes have been noted (Chambliss, 2000). First, it is generally acknowledged that these procedures save a great deal of money by reducing the length and frequency of hospitalizations and outpatient treatment. In addition, some believe that these procedures have led to improved efficiency and effectiveness of treatment by forcing mental health professionals to apply a technical eclecticism in determining what will work best and for whom.

Incentives for Efficient Providers. As noted in the preceding discussion, managed care is built around principles that encourage the efficient provision of service. There are specific policies that provide incentives for practitioners to incorporate these principles into their practice. For example, MCOs screen prospective providers to determine if they meet company standards as providers of service. If it is determined that they meet these established standards, mental health professionals can be placed on the organization's list of accepted providers of service (provider panel).

To be placed on a panel, several things must be demonstrated. First, there must be a need for additional panel participants in a given geographic region. Managed care organizations estimate that one provider of mental health services is needed for every 1,000 people they insure (Polkinghorne, 2001). If a particular area is oversaturated with providers, the MCO has no need to recruit new counselors. In such situations, an appropriately credentialed counselor will not be eligible to receive reimbursement from that particular MCO. However, if the demand for counseling services increases, more providers may be recruited. Thus, gaining a position on provider lists is a competitive process. Unfortunately, members of various mental health professions become pitted against one another to attain provider status.

Second, mental health professionals must show that they follow acceptable diagnosis and treatment procedures and are willing to accept reduced fees (Polkinghorne, 2001). Counselors who do not abide by the protocols of the MCO or do not achieve the desired outcomes with their clients may be dropped from the provider list. The key incentive is that providers on specific panels receive a consistent flow of referrals from the MCOs in which they are members. Theoretically, then, this can become a win-win situation for the mental health provider and third-party reimburser.

Third, the net effect of pretreatment authorization and concurrent utilization review is to encourage the use of therapeutic approaches that are brief and goal oriented. The very nature of managed care requires that counselors address presenting problems through brief, problem-solving techniques (Bistline, Sheridan, & Winegar, 1991). Doing so helps to ensure that clients will attain identified goals and objectives of treatment within the timeframes approved through the authorization process. In addition, being a provider of efficient, time-limited services is an important factor in becoming a member of provider lists.

Increased Employee and User/Client Cost Sharing. Managed care organizations distribute the financial risk among employees, users/clients, providers, employers, and the MCO itself (Broskowski & Marks, 1992). Doing so helps to lower total costs and makes health care more affordable.

Increasingly, though, the burden of these cost-sharing efforts has moved to employees and clients. Employees are paying increased insurance premiums, regardless of whether or not they use the medical or mental health benefit (Broskowski & Marks, 1992). In addition, copayments and deductibles distribute financial risk by placing increased responsibility on users of services. Typically, a maximum limit for the financial risk of users (i.e., the amount of money paid out in copayments and deductibles) is set, beyond which the MCO and provider share the remaining risk.

PROCEDURES FOR CONTROLLING PRICE PER UNIT

In addition to limiting utilization and increasing cost sharing, managed care seeks to lower total costs by exerting control over the cost per unit of service. Procedures used to accomplish this purpose include capitation, use of less expensive but equally effective treatment approaches, and retrospective claims reviews.

Capitation. Under capitation reimbursement procedures, counselors contract with the MCO to be reimbursed at a fixed rate for all medically necessary mental health services to be provided for 1 year for one health plan enrollee (Staton, 2001). Under such a reimbursement plan, a counselor's income is based on the number of persons enrolled in the plan rather than the type or frequency of service provided (Kongstvedt, 1996). For example, a managed care organization using a capitation framework might reimburse a practitioner at a rate of $0.55 per member per month regardless of the quantity or type of sessions conducted. Assuming that 2,500 persons carry the specific insurance plan, each becomes a potential client for the practitioner. In this example, the practitioner would receive $1,375 (.55 $\times$ 2,500) in monthly reimbursement from the MCO. However, the counselor's rate of reimbursement per session under capitation depends on the actual utilization of the service. Thus, if the counselor sees 15 clients who are covered by the plan in a given month, reimbursement per session is ($1,375 $\div$ 15) $91.67. However, if 25 clients are seen in that month, reimbursement per session is $55.00. To maintain a profitable practice/organization, practitioners working under such arrangements are influenced by an implicit incentive to withhold treatment and thus increase business/organizational profits (Staton, 2000).

Capitation, then, can have advantages for both the MCO and the counselor. For the MCO, costs for service become more predictable. A specific rate of reimbursement for each person covered by the plan is set. Regardless of actual types and frequencies of service rendered, each practitioner is reimbursed, typically on a monthly basis, according to the negotiated rate. Practitioners are guaranteed steady incomes under capitation. There is an obvious downside, though. If a significant increase in demand for service occurs, the mental health professional receives decreased income.

Less Expensive But Equally Effective Treatment Approaches. Managed care promotes the use of treatment approaches that cost less but have an outcome comparable to more expensive alternatives. This has been achieved in several ways. First, MCOs have tended to hire master's-level practitioners because they can be reimbursed at a lower rate than doctoral-level psychologists. Furthermore, a number of studies (e.g., Smith & Glass, 1977; Strupp & Hadley, 1979) have concluded that the efficacy of treatment was unrelated to the therapists' credentials or level of academic degree. As a result, mental health counselors, master's-level social workers, and marriage and family therapists are now the primary providers of mental health services.

Second, managed care has promoted the use of medication over talking therapies when it can be demonstrated that no significant difference exists in the efficacy of treatments. In many cases, medication proves to be a less expensive alternative and is increasingly used for conditions for which psychotherapy and counseling have traditionally been viewed as viable alternatives.

Retrospective Claims Reviews. In retrospective claims reviews, an independent reviewer audits the clinical chart after the client's termination of treatment. The purpose of such reviews is to determine if the treatment authorized and submitted for reimbursement was, in fact, rendered. Although used infrequently, a retrospective review is used when insurance fraud or abuse is suspected (Broskowski & Marks, 1992).

IMPACT ON THE PRACTICE OF MENTAL HEALTH COUNSELING

Managed care has caused "an upheaval in the practice community" (Acuff et al., 1999, p. 563). It is unlikely that mental health service providers will ever return to a simple fee-for-service structure. Changes have occurred in the nature of treatment, how it is delivered, and how business practices of mental health are managed. As a result, the emotional reactions of counselors and other mental health professionals have been, at times, intense (Beier & Young, 1998; Danzinger & Welfel, 2001, p. 394). Although such intense reactions from professionals can spill over into the counseling process, our primary focus is on how counselors have coped with and adapted their practice in light of the mental health revolution.

Responding to managed care is complicated by the fact that the relationships between service providers and MCOs are dynamic systems that are constantly changing as a result of the interaction of consumer needs, the business needs and financial risks of employers, national and state legislation, and the shifting landscape of managed care (Lawless et al., 1999). Managed care organizations also feel under attack on many fronts and are experiencing enormous economic pressures (Davis, 1999). Price competition is fierce and the administrative and network management overhead costs are enormous. In addition, MCOs organizations are beginning to feel a strong backlash from consumers who charge that medically necessary care has been inappropriately limited under the current system (Davis, 1999).

Thus, the source of the stress is a moving target. Mental health professionals and MCOs relate to one another in a context of ongoing uncertainty. Counselors are required to be especially vigilant in these changing times and landscapes of managed care. The continued existence of their professional practice may depend on it.

Beier and Young (1998) borrow from Karen Horney's terminology in describing the responses of mental health professionals to the advent of managed care (Horney, 1945). The responses can be described as either "moving toward, moving away from, or moving against the changes in the system" (Beier & Young, 1998, p.198). For counselors moving toward managed care, few are running forward with open arms eagerly seeking to embrace a good friend. Rather, these counselors are doing what they have to do to survive in the current delivery system environment. Certainly, the activities of the AMHCA fit into this category. As if playing in a high-stakes card game, the professional organization is making a concerted effort to play with the cards it has been dealt. While working actively to lobby legislators and confront the disparity among service providers, AMHCA has collaborated with some of the largest MCOs in shaping credentialing criteria (Davis, 1999). If the profession is to survive and flourish, it must play according to the rules that presently set the parameters of how the "game" is played. Many counselors have integrated the various policies and procedures of managed care into their professional practice. For some professionals, obtaining multiple licenses has become a way of increasing the number of claims that are reimbursed (Geisler, 1995). In an unpublished study, Gerig (1999) surveyed members of the Indiana Mental Health Counselors Association to determine their rate of reimbursement success. He found that a number of LMHCs in the state were using other credentials in addition to the LMHC to meet the credentialing criteria of the specific MCO.

Another group of counselors can best be described as moving away from the system. For many counselors in this category, pursuing third-party reimbursement is an option that is bypassed. Gerig (1999) found that of those members of the Indiana Mental Health Counselors Association who were providing direct service to clients, about 50% were billing clients for services directly and completely bypassing the third-party reimbursement option. Various reasons for maintaining a fee-for-service system abound. Zimpfer (1995) found that a number of licensed professional clinical counselors (LPCCs) in Ohio erroneously concluded that they were simply ineligible for insurance reimbursement and did not submit claims. Others expressed uncertainty regarding the prospect of attaining success in collecting claims. A third group professed to be "afraid to try." As Zimpfer (1995) notes, such beliefs are patently false because the results of his study give "credence to the status of counselors as eligible providers" (p. 109). In his study (Zimpfer, 1995), 78% of the individual claims submitted were declared as reimbursed.

Another reason not to seek reimbursement from MCOs concerns how the process conflicts with the nonmedical model that is an underlying philosophy of the mental health counseling profession. Diagnostic categorization of clients is contrary to a developmental emphasis on mental health and strength. Counselors who work on a fee-for-service basis are able to provide services regardless of whether or not clients fit the identified symptoms of a disorder as specified by *DSM-IV-TR*. In addition, such counselors are able to better integrate a wellness model into their practice.

A third group of professional counselors can be described as going against the managed care revolution. These are the ones who are fighting the system and actively seeking its overthrow. Many perceive MCOs as seeking to pay the smallest fees by using the least expensive service providers and obstructing client care by requiring pretreatment authorizations, capping the number of sessions, and blocking client access to qualified professionals by setting limits on provider lists (Beier & Young, 1998). Some mental health professionals have chosen to go on the offensive and engage in head-to-head combat with managed care. Unhappy about the extent to which HMOs have cut into their income and autonomy, psychologists from one state recently affiliated with the American Federation of Teachers, an organization of 140,000 members, to increase their lobbying clout (Talan, 2000). In 2000, the California Medical Association filed a federal suit against four of the state's largest health plans, claiming that these organizations had crippled the physicians businesses and 'cheated' their patients (Benko, 2000). Others are choosing to file legal suits against MCOs one at a time (Talan, 2000). Clearly, the fight is on. No one is sure, at this point, who is winning. But it is likely that this match will likely go to the final rounds. Too many see the profession and their livelihoods hanging in the balance.

SURVIVING IN THE ERA OF MANAGED HEALTH COUNSELING

All professional counselors are affected by managed care in some way. A number of counselors are attempting to cope with the contemporary situation. This can be likened to the fight or flight response to an identified stressor (Beier & Young, 1998). Others are discovering novel ways of adapting to the demands placed on them by managed care and are proceeding with varying degrees of resignation. But many are thriving in the current mental health care environment. How can mental health counselors survive and even thrive in the context of managed care?

First, counselor self-care skills are critical. The ability to cope with emotional reactions to managed care and its demands is necessary for counselors if they are to avoid the high risk of burnout. For private practitioners, the fight for survival breeds an ongoing uncertainty and fear, which become the "ground" on which the pressures and frustrations of day-to-day demands of doing business with MCOs become the "figure." Counselors do well to implement and maintain a balanced lifestyle that promotes personal wellness. A regimen of stress management techniques can be integrated into the professional's daily routine.

Second, surviving and thriving as a mental health counselor requires a working knowledge of the "ins and outs" of doing business in the managed care environment. Lawless and colleagues (1999) correctly note that two types of questions confront mental health counselors to which both knowledge and skill acquisition are prerequisites for the construction of adequate responses. Questions such as "Can you explain what capitation means?" or "How do I respond to utilization review in such a way as to gain maximum services for my clients?" call attention to the need for continuing education, accurate assessment of current skill levels, and recognition of regional variations in the operation of MCOs (Lawless et al., 1999).

Third, counselors also need specific knowledge skills if they are to conduct direct negotiations successfully with MCOs (Anderson, 2000). For example, as noted earlier, counselors frequently work with a case manager or reviewer employed by the MCO for preauthorization of services and concurrent review of services. Establishing a positive and collaborative relationship based on mutual respect ensures that the welfare of the client will be primary. Second, skills in diagnosis and treatment planning are prerequisites not only for effective clinical practice but also for communicating goals and objectives of treatment and how they are to be attained through recommended intervention. The clear, precise use of language increases the likelihood that the case manager will understand and approve the counselor's recommendations. Finally, successful relations with MCOs are enhanced when correct procedural codes are used in completing paperwork and communicating to the case manager (Anderson, 2000; Puente, 1997).

Fourth, mental health counselors must possess a thorough knowledge and understanding of their code of ethics (i.e., AMHCA, 2000; ACA, 1995), how they interact with the policies and practices of managed care, and the process of ethical decision making (Danzinger & Welfel, 2001). Basic ethical considerations for counselors include the primacy of the client's welfare, counselor competence, confidentiality, and informed consent (Glosoff, Garcia, Herlihy, & Remley, 1999).

Fifth, mental health counselors may be required to make a paradigm shift from older, traditional models of service delivery. Cummings (1995) suggests that a catalyst model be followed if a practitioner is to succeed under the new system. This model includes the following characteristics (Polkinghorne, 2001):

1. Many clients are seen for brief episodes of treatment, frequently in nontraditional modes.
2. A brief and intermittent counseling process occurs throughout the lifespan of the client.
3. Counselors serve as catalysts for client change.
4. Healing resources from the community are mobilized.
5. Capitation and other reimbursement arrangements free counselors to provide services as needed regardless of client's ability to pay.

What Cummings (1995) refers to as a catalyst model appears to have much in common with presuppositions that underlie the profession of mental health counseling. As has been noted throughout this book, professional counselors see their practice as being developmental and emphasizing mental health as well as mental illness. Mental health counseling is also guided by ecological theory (Bronfenbrenner, 1979), which supports the counselor's approach to assessment, treatment, and utilization of client support systems.

Thus, although other mental health professions may be facing significant adjustments in how they conceptualize their work, mental health counselors have a theoretical base that enables them to interact with clients as well as the current market forces in constructive ways. Generally speaking, then, mental health counselors possess a foundation for successful professional practice in the managed care environment.

DISCUSSION QUESTIONS

1. Define *managed care*. What is its goal and, generally speaking, how does it seek to attain that goal?
2. What specific procedures does managed care use to contain costs of mental health services? To what extent would you feel comfortable working within a managed care system? What specific skills would you need to work within such a setting?
3. To what extent do you see managed care as (a) a necessary correction of a system that was not working, (b) a necessary evil, or (c) an unethical system that does not have client welfare in mind? Explain your response.

4. As you consider your response to managed care, which of the following categories best fits your current position: moving toward, moving away, or moving against? Why?
5. To what extent do you believe that professional counselors have adequate preparation and skills to work within managed care environments?

SUGGESTED ACTIVITIES

1. Organize and conduct a panel discussion. Invite several LPCs or LMHCs to class and explore their experiences in working in a managed care environment.
2. Conduct a survey of various mental health professionals in your region. Include psychiatrists, psychologists, clinical social workers, professional counselors, and marriage and family therapists. Explore the extent to which their practice or the agencies in which they work have been influenced by managed care. Consider getting on provider lists, working with reviewers, and obtaining reimbursement for services. Then compare variables across the various professional groups.
3. Visit the Web sites of several MCOs. Compare and contrast the services provided, criteria for inclusion on provider lists, procedures for preauthorization, concurrent review, and so on.
4. Interview an LMHC working at a community mental health center. Review the types of documentation (i.e., paperwork) required by Medicaid or other relevant MCOs. In what ways are these documents necessary to demonstrate that mental health services provided are in full compliance with organizational standards?

11

The Changing Face of Community Mental Health

OUTLINE

Community mental health is a phrase and concept that members of the mental health profession use repeatedly. Yet I wonder the extent to which we really grasp its meaning and implications. We may refer to the community mental health center or say that we work in community mental health, but are we really meaning what we say or saying what we mean? To what extent does our training model reflect a community mental health orientation? Furthermore, to what extent do we *do* community mental health, even those of us who work in CMHCs?

The pursuit of mental health involves both the person's quest toward optimal human functioning and a simultaneous movement away from emotional distress, dysfunction, and mental illness. These aspects of mental health may be viewed as lying within two distinct but interacting dimensions. If we add to this the idea of *community*, we see that we have entered the realm of interacting systems.

The comprehensive mental health counseling model clearly reflects this perspective. The ecological perspective is foundational to the training and practice of mental health or community counselors. The theoretical and practical issues related to defining *mental health*, as noted in chapter 3, significantly increase in number and complexity when the descriptor *community* is added. Thus, community mental health is ecological by definition, and the mental health counseling profession should therefore be on the cutting edge of related theory making and practice by virtue of its theoretical foundation and training. This chapter explores the extent to which the delivery of community mental health services has been successful in maintaining an ecological focus.

This chapter discusses how services are delivered to individuals who seek to resist or overcome mental illness and pursue optimal levels of functioning. First, the history of care for the mentally ill is summarized. Second, a general model of mental health care delivery systems is presented. Third, several contemporary trends and approaches to service delivery are described. Finally, the chapter explores how specific mental health concerns are being addressed in the community.

The attainment of community mental health does not occur simply through the provision of services to individuals. The whole is truly greater than the sum of its parts. Thus, effective programs mobilize community resources to facilitate and maintain personal and community mental health. The relationship is dynamic and reciprocal.

The community mental health movement in the United States is often seen as commencing with the Community Mental Health Centers Act of 1963. However, the movement has actually been a "slow train running" with origins dating back to the mid-1800s (Cutler, 1992; Suppes & Wells, 2003). Perhaps the most famous early advocate was Dorothea Dix, who in 1843 began to draw public attention to the deplorable living conditions of the mentally ill. Systematically documenting their plight, Dix presented a report to the Massachusetts legislature that became the impetus for the state funding of hospitals to treat persons with mental illness (Suppes & Wells, 2003).

Unfortunately, resulting development of mental hospitals failed to influence significantly the condition of the mentally ill in the United States. The federal government's first major move toward addressing the needs of the mentally ill was the National Mental Health Act of 1946 (Public Law 79-487). Through this Act, NIMH was established and became the federal think tank and financial resource for innovative mental health programs through the 1970s (Cutler, 1992). The Act also established a number of research and training programs that continue to this day.

As was noted in chapter 2, flaws in the existing mental health service delivery system were being exposed by the mid-1950s. The population in mental hospitals peaked in 1955, when over 558,000 patients were being housed in prolonged care hospitals for the mentally ill (Torrey, 1997). Up to this point, the guiding principle for the treatment of mental disorders was to move the disordered person from normal family, social, and community settings to a sheltered institutionalized environment. But in recent years, the underlying philosophy has shifted toward community-based treatment, support, and rehabilitation. This philosophy is central to the concept of *deinstitutionalization,* which refers to the practice of transferring formerly institutionalized individuals to sheltered community environments or to homes in the community (Barry, 1998). By 1995, the inpatient population had decreased to 71,619 (Torrey, 1997).

However, average daily census data (as noted in Torrey, 1997) may not necessarily reflect the activity level of inpatient facilities. For example, there were approximately 2 million admissions to inpatient treatment services in 1997 (Milazzo-Sayre et al., 2001). Decreased patient counts as shown in daily census data are also a reflection of current clinical practice and economic considerations that have reduced length of stay and increased patient turnover (Levine, Perkins, & Perkins, 2005).

The locus of residential treatment has moved to community outpatient settings. In 1997, according to Milazzo-Sayre et al. (2001), 5.5 million more patients were admitted to outpatient care and an additional 171,000 admissions to community-based residential care. If we sum the total admissions to inpatient (2 million), community-based outpatient care (5.5 million), and community-based residential care (171,000), we find a total of 7.67 million persons admitted for mental health treatment annually.

Several forces have played important roles in shaping this shift (Barry, 1998). First, the development of a number of medications provides practitioners with effective means for decreasing the symptoms of major psychiatric disorders such as schizophrenia, bipolar disorder, and depression. Second, economic resources no longer support long-term, inpatient care for the mentally ill. Instead, emphasis has shifted to community models of outpatient care. Third, given the supply of mental health professionals from a variety of disciplines, multidisciplinary team approaches can be offered that provide a more comprehensive approach to outpatient mental health care than was previously available.

Other out-of-home settings must be considered as we attempt to comprehend the nature of and need for community mental health. The elderly comprise a frequently overlooked and underserved population. Although the population of persons housed in nursing homes has decreased in recent years due to improved community and in-home services, it is estimated that approximately 340,000 residents of nursing homes are in need of mental health services for psychiatric conditions (Levine et al., 2005). In addition, the criminalization of the mentally ill has been well documented, and a large number of persons with mental illness are housed in jails and prisons. In 2000, more than 128,000 adolescents were housed in public and private juvenile justice facilities. Furthermore, nearly 542,000 children and adolescents resided in foster care, many of whom were victims of abuse or neglect (U.S. General Accounting Office, 1993; National Clearinghouse on Child Abuse and Neglect, 2003).

The focus of our discussion thus far has been the treatment of diagnosable populations. However, it is important for mental health and community counselors to understand the distinction between mental illness and problems in living (Levine et al., 2005). As noted in chapter 3, placing diagnosable emotional/subjective distress and mental illness on the same continuum as mental health is an artifact of the medical model. But according to the comprehensive model of mental health counseling, the single-dimensional view directs us to conceptualize mental health interventions in terms of treating disorders rather than taking into consideration wellness and solution-focused approaches that are systemically based. In addition, by limiting our focus to persons with diagnosable conditions, we lose sight of other significant mental health concerns in communities. These include homelessness, substance abuse, dually diagnosed populations, victims and perpetrators of abuse, education-related problems, problems in living for those with chronic illness and sexually transmitted diseases (STDs), crisis intervention and disaster relief, and addressing the special needs of rural/isolated communities and the underserved. Finally, we must add to our list issues related to normal human development or transitions and family living, such as vocational stress and decision making, relational enhancement, timely and untimely pregnancy, abortion, adoption, infant mortality and birth defects, foster care, divorce, remarriage, blended families, and personal loss/grieving.

Certainly, the listed concerns represent a mere sampling of potential issues present in any given community. For community mental health services to be truly effective, programs and interventions must target real needs. According to the U.S. Surgeon General (2001), the mental health service delivery system consists of four sectors: the specialty mental health sector (psychiatrists, psychologists, mental health counselors), the general medical/primary care network (family physicians and general medical practitioners, nurses, medical specialists), the human services sector (juvenile/criminal justice system, family services and social welfare, faith-based and charitable services), and voluntary services (self-help groups and organizations). In addition to being front-line providers of mental health care, mental health and community counselors bring to the table an ecological focus and working knowledge of needs assessment and program evaluation. Thus, the mental health counseling profession is well positioned to take leadership roles in a variety of community mental health–related settings.

It is clearly beyond the scope of this introductory text to cover the vast territory described in the preceding paragraphs. The remainder of this chapter presents a general model of human service delivery systems and relates it to program development and evaluation. Several contemporary trends in the provision of community mental health services are described. Finally, the chapter discusses several models of mental health service that have been applied effectively to some of the community mental health concerns mentioned in this section.

A MODEL OF MENTAL HEALTH DELIVERY SYSTEMS

Effective community mental health programs share a number of essential elements that operate in a fully integrated manner for the purpose of delivering services that meet specific needs of persons and systems living in an ever-changing environment. In their classic text *People in Systems: A Model for Development in the Human-Service Professions and Education,* Egan and Cowan (1979) present a model that responds to the question, On what logic is an effectively designed and functioning system based? The essential components of their model are described in the following sections. Figure 11.1 displays the manner in which these components interact to create an effective, dynamic service delivery system.

ASSESSMENT OF THE NEEDS AND WANTS OF SERVICE RECIPIENTS

Prior to developing and implementing a program to meet the purported mental health needs of a given population, effective service delivery systems carefully identify who are potential service recipients living in the particular locality. Needs are best viewed as an existing state in persons or communities that is the result of the difference or discrepancy between a "what is" condition and the "what should be" condition (Altschuld & Witkin, 2000 p. 7). Needs assessment, then, is a set of procedures applied for the purpose of gathering valid and reliable data on the nature of problems affecting the particular population so that specific means can be designed and implemented to decrease or eliminate the needs.

MISSION

Mental health professionals providing service in effective programs know what their program is all about (i.e., its reason for being). Effective programs are characterized by an overarching sense of purpose and vision that is expressed in a mission statement. Such statements communicate a general purpose of the service delivery system, its underlying philosophy, and the nature of products and services delivered. Program development follows directly from an accurate needs assessment.

GOALS

Effective mental health care delivery systems translate general mission statements into specific goal statements, whose attainment represents the fulfillment of the identified

FIGURE 11.1 A Model of Mental General Health Delivery System

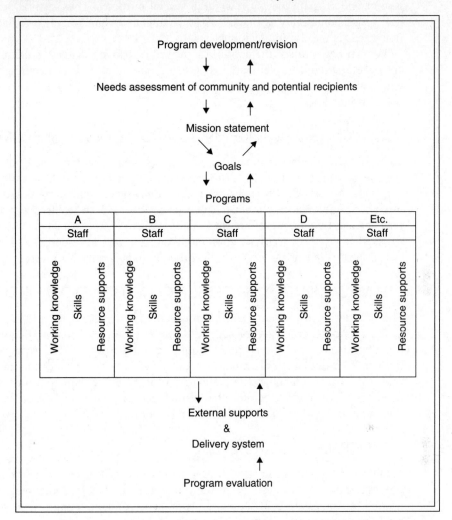

needs of recipients. Goals should be stated in terms that are measurable, realistic, worthwhile, and adequate. Failure to create objective, measurable goals often results in the development of mediocre programs, ones that have face validity but do not fulfill the expectations or needs of recipients.

PROGRAMS

Programs are the step-by-step means by which each specified goal is achieved. Sometimes there may be a one-to-one correspondence among an identified need, related goal, and program. For example, a crisis management program might be developed to meet the emergency mental health needs of clients, the general public, and community organizations. In other instances, several programs might be designed to fulfill a specific goal or one program may, in fact, fulfill several purposes. Thus, mental health, public health, and community assistance programs might combine resources to meet the multiple needs of the chronically homeless.

We can begin to see the continuity in well-developed delivery systems. Programs are developed and implemented to assist clients in attaining specific goals that fit within the general mission of the organization and were identified directly from the needs assessment.

WORKING KNOWLEDGE, SKILLS, AND RESOURCE SUPPORTS

To be effective, the leadership and professional/support staff must have both a working knowledge and requisite skills to conduct the program. For example, a particular knowledge base and set of skills is necessary if the delivery of a parenting skill development program to adult referrals from Child Protective Services is to be effective. Adequate staff selection and training procedures must be in place to ensure that all persons responsible for the delivery of services have appropriate preparation and resources (e.g., time, financial supports, credentials, etc.) to deliver the program contents as intended.

ENVIRONMENTAL SUPPORTS: TECHNOLOGY AND FACILITY

The best designed programs can fail miserably if little or no attention is paid to the backup supports necessary for successful program implementation. Required technical supports such as PowerPoint,™ liquid crystal display (LCD) projectors, and participant resource materials must be readily available as needed. Furthermore, the physical facility must be adequate to support the specific program needs and demands. These include comfortable seating, accessible location, available transportation, adequate parking, and appropriate room décor.

PROGRAM EVALUATION

Finally, managers of mental health programs seek confirmatory evidence gathered via program evaluation to ensure that the program is operating as intended and that the desired outcomes are being attained. Approaches to conducting formative and summative program assessment were discussed in chapter 7. These are vital feedback mechanisms that ensure that programs stay on target in ever-changing recipient and environmental conditions.

FUNDING PROGRAMS THROUGH GRANTS

Tight budgets, decreased federal and state support, and strict financial accountability of managed care greatly affect how community mental health agencies develop, implement, and maintain programs. In response, many organizations engage in a continual search for external funding sources to assist in provision of their programs and development of their facilities (Smith & McLean, 1988).

The process of successful grant writing involves six basic steps (Smith & McLean, 1988). First, the individual or agency seeking external funding has identified needs or developed ideas that become the focal point of the proposal. Most fundable projects are related to a clearly documented need and an innovative solution that is cost effective. Second, an appropriate funding source is identified. Generally, the primary sources for external funding are public, private, or community foundations; for-profit businesses and corporations; and federal and state government foundations. Third, a grant proposal is prepared. The sections of a standard grant proposal include

1. A two- to three-sentence summary.
2. A two- to three-paragraph description of the organization.
3. A statement of the existing problem, need, or description of specific situation. In this section, the grant writer defines the issue and communicates that the specific organization is uniquely qualified to tackle the problem.
4. Working goals and plan. A clear and concise statement is made regarding what the organization plans to do about the problem. This section clearly identifies the intended audience, who is to deliver the program, and when and where the program delivery will take place.
5. Measurable outcomes and impact. Here the funding source is informed of what specific difference or change will take place as a result of successful program implementation. It is important to specify outcomes that are relevant, meaningful, and measurable.
6. Funding. Other sources of funding being pursued and how the continuation of the proposed program will be financially supported are described.
7. Budget. An accurate, detailed budget is provided that includes an itemized list of all expected expenses and income.
8. Supplementary materials. The funding source may ask for specific materials, such as a letter declaring tax exempt status, a list of the organization's board of directors, or an organizational financial statement (Grantseeking in Minnesota, 2004).

Fourth, the proposal is submitted. It is extremely important that the submission instructions are followed meticulously. Any deviations from the stated protocol can greatly decrease the likelihood that the grant proposal will be accepted. Fifth, the proposal is either accepted or rejected. Finally, the grant is administered according to plan. If the original grant is not accepted, it is sometimes possible to revise the original proposal and resubmit it to the funding source.

How does one learn the art and science of successful grant writing? Frequently, courses in grant writing are offered for credit through colleges and universities. In addition, numerous grant-writing seminars or continuing education experiences abound. However, the best way to learn grant writing is through engaging in the actual writing process under the guidance of an experienced mentor (Longo & Schubert, 2005). Such opportunities are often available for graduate assistants or in large community mental health or human services organizations. In the contemporary mental health care environment, grant-writing skills have become vital for the mental health counselor who seeks to develop innovative ideas into effective programs.

CONTEMPORARY TRENDS IN COMMUNITY MENTAL HEALTH

A number of contemporary trends can be identified that interact with and influence the structure and delivery of programs in community mental health. These function as contextual factors that influence the particular shape and direction that mental health delivery systems are taking. Among these are the post-deinstitutionalization era and least restrictive treatment environment. In response, traditional programs have shifted toward increased application of case management models, such as assertive community treatment, and increased consumer self-help.

THE POST-DEINSTITUTIONALIZATION ERA

Contemporary mental health delivery systems operate in the post-deinstitutionalization era. The decline in the rates of psychiatric patients treated in inpatient facilities was discussed in an earlier section. This decline can be attributed in part to shifts in treatment philosophy (Levine, 1981). Changes in funding and reimbursement policies are related to increased emphasis on more cost-effective alternatives. In addition, changes in the law make it more difficult to commit and retain patients in hospitals involuntarily.

Providing adequate care for persons who formerly would have been serviced in inpatient facilities continues to present challenges for community mental health systems. Previously protected by the controlled environment of mental institutions, many are increasingly vulnerable to substance abuse and dependence, which has necessitated the development of effective programs for treating dually diagnosed populations. Furthermore, a large number of chronically mentally ill with minimal supports have found independent living difficult. Some are homeless and live as street people. Many do not clearly see their need for or the benefits of receiving mental health services. Still others, while recognizing their need for services, find the service delivery experience aversive and prefer to avoid it (Levine et al., 2005).

Clearly, creative approaches to mental health programming and delivery are required to fill the gaps in service provision in the post-deinstitutionalization era. In the sections that follow, unique approaches to service are described that avoid the "one size fits all" approach that too often characterized community mental health programs in the past.

LEAST RESTRICTIVE TREATMENT

A foundational concept supporting contemporary mental health services is *least restrictive treatment*. Basically, the idea is to match the prescribed treatment's level of intensity to the severity of the client's condition in such a way that restrictions to the client's personal freedom are minimal. Treatment is guided by the minimum sufficiency principle, wherein clients participate in programs exerting the least restriction necessary for the provision of desired outcomes.

In the contemporary mental health service environment, this concept has been applied by dramatically decreasing clients' average lengths of stay in hospitals. Lengths of stay in state mental hospitals were 421 days in 1969 and 189 and 1978. Presently, the average hospital stay for psychiatric conditions is less than 8 days (Levine et al., 2005). Rather than emphasizing delivery of intense therapy, the contemporary goal of hospitalization is client stabilization. Once stabilized, clients are released to the care of community-based agencies and practitioners, where appropriate outpatient treatment plans are devised and implemented.

These shorter stays have given rise to the "revolving-door" phenomenon. Some clients are admitted, stabilized, released to outpatient care, and readmitted. Too often, this becomes a repetitive cycle for clients and a burden not only for the service delivery systems but also for patients' families, who formerly found respite in more lengthy hospital stays. For successful service delivery in the contemporary environment, interagency networking and communication is a prerequisite.

ASSERTIVE COMMUNITY TREATMENT PROGRAMS

Persons with severe mental illness frequently require a variety of services such as general medical care, mental health treatment, substance abuse treatment, housing services, and vocational rehabilitation. Many of these services were more centrally available at long-term-stay mental institutions and are fragmented in community settings. Those in most need for services demonstrate limited ability to advocate for themselves, initiate provider contact, or coordinate the complex scheduling demands when referred to or seeing multiple service providers. As a result, the chronically mentally ill have difficulty receiving desirable or necessary services (Mechanic, 1991).

A case management model has emerged as a primary way to assist clients in accessing, coordinating, and integrating different services. Assertive community treatment, often referred to as ACT programs, is perhaps the most comprehensive case management approach (Drake, 1998). Assertive community treatment is a team approach designed to treat persons with serious and chronic mental illness. A team of professionals representing the professions of counseling, social work, nursing, rehabilitation, and psychiatry provide comprehensive, community-based treatment, rehabilitation and support to clients who have not historically responded well to traditional outpatient treatment. Often, clients served by ACT teams have co-occurring problems such as homelessness, substance abuse, or involvement in the correctional/judicial system.

In general, ACT programs share six common elements: (1) low case manager to client ratios, (2) community-based treatment, (3) shared caseloads, (4) continuous coverage 24 hours a day, 7 days a week, (5) a majority of services provided by the ACT team, and (6) time-unlimited services (Mueser, Bond, Drake, & Resnick, 1998). The team's caseload is small and responsibility is shared among team members. This allows wrap-around services to be as flexible and intensive as needed. With services such as medication delivery, rehabilitation, and behavioral training in basic adaptive living skills delivered in community living settings, the problems of nonattendance and lack of transportation are avoided. Numerous studies attest to the effectiveness of this model (Lehman, Steinwachs, & Co-Investigators of the PORT Project, 1998; Mueser et al., 1998; Salkever et al., 1999; Santos et al., 1993).

CONSUMER MOVEMENT AND SELF-HELP

Consumers of mental health services have become an increasingly influential group in shaping mental health policies and services (Kaufmann, 1999). Underlying this movement is the strong desire and effort of mental health consumers with chronic mental illness to develop appropriate control of psychiatric treatment and put an end to the oppressive stigma that accompanies such diagnostic classifications. Several notable consequences of the consumer movement include consumer-developed and managed systems of care, self-help groups, and advocacy organizations.

The Sunshine Clubhouse, a day treatment program of Madison Center, South Bend, Indiana, illustrates a consumer-managed mental health program. Building on psychosocial rehabilitation clubhouse models such as New York's Fountain House program (Carling, 1995), participants in the Sunshine House are referred to as *members* rather than patients or clients. Officers are elected and members are assigned specific roles within the organization. For example, several members serve on a menu committee and assist in meal planning and ordering of food. Another group prepares meals for members and staff of Madison Center. Furthermore, other members plan activities and make arrangements for transportation. The professional staff relates to members more as peers or friends and provides guidance as needed. But for the most part, they are clearly in the background of the program's management and might be best viewed as coparticipants with the members.

Other mental health programs have helped consumers develop and maintain after-hour helplines and drop-in centers. For example, consumers who demonstrate stability might be trained in fundamental communication skills and telephone interviewing. They then operate a hotline service that is utilized not only by other consumers of mental health services but members of the community who seek information about mental health, available services, or who simply need to talk to someone. It is critical that helpline staff are trained in recognizing clinical emergencies, making referrals, and identifying available community resources. Drop-in centers provide a place to go and participate in a variety of activities in a nonstigmatizing environment. Such centers are especially helpful for consumers who are living in the community but feeling lonely and isolated.

The number of self-help groups increased rapidly throughout the last quarter of the 20th century (Levine et al., 2005). Putnam (2000) notes that the growth of the self-help movement has occurred at a time when membership in other types of social organizations, such as churches, political organizations, and even traditional neighborhoods, has decreased. The number of Alcoholics Anonymous (AA) groups has increased from around 50 in 1942 to well over 50,000 in the United States. Parents Without Partners started in 1957 with one group consisting of two women. Today, it claims more than 50,000 members and more than 400 clubs. The National Self-Help Clearinghouse has been formed to communicate information about the activities of the more than 500,000 self-help groups currently operating in the United States (Katz, 1993; White & Madara, 2002). Self-help groups focus on a wide array of issues including addictions, abuse, bereavement, mental illness, physical disability, parenting, and other specific life stressors (White & Madara, 2002).

In addition to consumer-managed programs and self-help groups, a variety of consumer support groups have emerged to assist clients and their families as they deal with the symptoms and various consequences of mental illness (Fristad & Sisson, 2004). Frequently, these groups appear to meet three vital family needs: support, education, and empowerment (Marsh, 1996). Through these groups, families find assistance in mobilizing available resources and managing complex emotional reactions as they support family members with mental illness. Furthermore, such consumer groups are vehicles for advocacy efforts to improve standards of professional practice and care. For example, the National Alliance for the Mentally Ill (NAMI) is a self-help support and advocacy organization whose members are consumers, families, and friends of persons diagnosed with severe mental illness (National Alliance for the Mentally Ill, 2005). It consists of over one thousand local affiliates and 50 state organizations. The advocacy efforts of NAMI seek increased funding for research, housing, jobs, rehabilitation, and suitable health insurance.

SPECIFIC ISSUES IN COMMUNITY MENTAL HEALTH

Having discussed several contemporary trends in community mental health, we can now consider how community-based agencies, organizations, and mental health centers address a variety of specific mental health–related concerns. These include homelessness, chronic mental illness, dual diagnosis, corrections, and AIDS/HIV. As we shall see, some of these issues are addressed through the services of community mental health centers. In addition, other community agencies and organizations have stepped up to meet the challenges of enhancing the mental health of specific community populations.

COMMUNITY MENTAL HEALTH AND THE HOMELESS

The problems of mental illness and homelessness present significant and challenging issues for communities at large and community mental health in particular (Torrey, 1997; Yanos, Barrow, & Tsemberis, 2004). Although the existence of the problem is well recognized, identification of specific mental health needs and interventions is hampered by several factors (Bachrach, 1992). First, how is homelessness defined? Although the term refers simply to an absence of housing or permanent residence, common usage implies more significant deprivation. The population under concern is not simply those whose homes have burned down or been destroyed in a hurricane. Rather, the concern is for those persons who lack community ties and resources. In addition, there are difficulties assessing the mental health needs and prevalence of mental illness within the population. Second, is abuse of substances considered a mental illness? Third, at any given time, the homeless population in a particular area overlaps with other populations, such as those being housed in jails and other correctional facilities. Finally, it is difficult if not impossible to speak of homeless persons as comprising a stable population because they tend to be a transient group. Thus, the vague and moving target further confounds efforts toward accurate needs assessment.

There is consensus, though, that homeless persons with severe mental illness often present complex psychosocial histories. Compared to domiciled adults with severe mental illness, the homeless, severe mentally ill are more likely unemployed (Pickett-Schenk et al., 2002), display more severe psychiatric symptomatology, and have higher rates of inpatient admissions. In addition, there is a higher frequency of alcohol and chemical abuse among the homeless mentally ill (Caton et al., 1994, 1995; Drake et al., 1991). Other studies have found that the needs of homeless women and their families differ from the homeless mentally ill and include histories of domestic violence, life circumstance–related emotional distress, multiple residence moves prior to homelessness, and inadequate social support systems (Khanna, Singh, Nemil, Best, & Ellis, 1992; Vostanis, Grattan, & Cumella, 1998). In addition, the needs of homeless women differ from those of homeless men (North & Smith, 1993). Such studies suggest a need for services that provide job-seeking and job-retention skills, on-the-job social skill development, and ready access to mental health services and relevant community resources. The importance of adequate assessment, treatment planning, and implementation of programs is apparent.

There are several barriers to the provision of mental health services to homeless populations that must be overcome if adequate service delivery is to occur. Counselors may mistakenly believe that the problems of the homeless are not treatable, their problems are too complex and time consuming, or they simply would rather live a life on the streets than seek help (Friedman & Levine-Holdowsky, 1997). Furthermore, the policies and procedures within agencies and working relationships between agencies can prevent collaborative program development and implementation (Rowe, Hoge, & Fisk, 1996). The difficulties of connecting potential consumers who are homeless and living on the street to available mental health services and accompanying institutional barriers necessitate the development and implementation of innovative programs.

In many communities, the services required for the adequate treatment of issues presented by homeless clients are fragmented. Thus, case management has become a primary approach when working with homeless, mentally ill clients. Two common case management approaches are brokered case management and assertive community treatment (Wolff et al., 1997). In the brokered case management model, the case manager assesses the needs of the client and arranges for provision of services by purchasing service contracts from various service providers. Mental health services are provided through traditional outpatient programs. The case manager plays the key role in integrating the various treatment components into a coherent service delivery plan. In contrast, assertive community treatment staff provide a wrap-around service to homeless clients that includes 24-hour emergency services, medication and money management, and assistance with daily living (Wolf et al., 1997). The mental health counselor functions as a member of the ACT team rather than as a contracted service provider.

Numerous programs have been designed to meet the specific needs of the homeless. Some of these are very focused, whereas others are comprehensive and offer a wide range of services. The Thresholds of Chicago has established an assertive outreach for the homeless experiencing serious mental illness. Licensed clinicians work on the streets, in shelters, and wherever the homeless may be. Their goal is to get the homeless mentally ill off the street and into necessary services that help them regain stability in their lives. A mobile assessment unit actually cruises the streets, seeking out persons in need for services. Sometimes team workers bike through public parks in response to crisis calls. Based on the assessment, persons in need of services may be hospitalized, provided with temporary shelter, or connected to long-term supportive programs.

The Center for the Homeless of South Bend, Indiana (CFH) is a model program that provides shelter, food, and comprehensive life-building services for as many as 200 guests each day. It utilizes a *continuum of care model* of integrated services ranging from crisis treatment and assessment to education, job training, supportive housing, and home ownership. Through the partnership of more than 30 area organizations, the

CFH offers comprehensive educational, medical, and mental health services to homeless adults and their children. Upon assessment, guests applying to stay for more than 30 days are assigned to one of three tracks: Starting Over, Work Plus (for guests already working in stable employment), and Health First (for mentally and/or physically ill or disabled guests). These programs consist of the following combinations of services: individual, group, and family counseling; job and social skill building; job seeking and retention skill building; and transitional housing and employment referrals. For guests who remain in the program and successfully complete their track, the potential outcomes include stable housing with personal home ownership or permanent supportive housing.

COMMUNITY MENTAL HEALTH AND THE CHRONIC MENTALLY ILL

As noted, a policy of deinstitutionalization has been foundational to United States' mental health agenda for over 4 decades. Propelled by revelations of inhumane conditions in state hospitals, the development of psychotropic medications, expanded third-party reimbursement options, and legal restrictions on the specific criteria for involuntary commitments, community-based mental health services became the primary service delivery system for persons with chronic mental illness (Dickey, Fisher, Siegel, Altaffer, & Azeni, 1997). Treatment delivery to this population now takes place primarily in the network of residential settings, community outpatient clinics, other community-based programs, and community general hospitals. The assumption is that a systematic mix of community-based services can demonstrate effectiveness equal to or greater than institutionalization.

Morrissey (1999) notes that persons with acute mental health needs and milder conditions have generally benefited from this transition. It has been less beneficial for persons with chronic and severe mental illness. These persons present complex clinical pictures and require not only psychiatric treatment, but often social rehabilitation, housing, health care, supportive employment services, social supports, and substance abuse counseling (Rosenblatt & Attkisson, 1993). Many human service agencies are organized around a single-problem focus, so it is challenging to pull together a comprehensive treatment plan to address the multifaceted goals of the chronic mentally ill. The key to adequate treatment involves the capacity to integrate services into a coherent treatment package.

Until recently, consumers of community mental health services with severe mental illness were typically viewed as clients who participated in various services offered along the continuum of care. Thus, clients were prepared for more effective lives in the community by being fit into "program slots" (Carling, 1995). A community integration approach is emerging that emphasizes practical supports, coping strategies, self-determination, and personal strengths and capacities. Two models using this approach are referred to as (a) the comprehensive community support systems model, and (b) the "framework for support" model (Carling, 1995). The former emphasizes professional support whereas the latter emphasizes a self-help orientation.

Community mental health centers are the primary providers and offer a cluster of services, including emergency, inpatient, outpatient, day treatment, and partial hospitalization services in single-stop locations (Morrissey, 1999). Mental health services include assessment and diagnosis, supportive and clinical counseling for psychiatric and substance abuse problems, and medication management services. Although ongoing contact with clients prevents most crises, crisis intervention and stabilization services, including 24-hour hotlines, walk-in crisis services, mobile outreach, and community residential options, are offered to clients and family members. Frequently, peer support is offered through self-help groups, drop-in centers, and social clubs. These are consumer-defined, -controlled, and -operated programs and activities that typically supplement those services delivered by mental health professionals.

To ensure that chronic clients receive all necessary services to remain and function optimally in the community, many community mental health programs utilize ACT. On occasion, former consumers of services have become staff of ACT teams (Holloway & Carson, 2001). Dewa and colleagues (2003) point out that the unique elements of ACT require informal inputs of time, which can place high demands on team members and increase potential for burn-out. Drake (1998) reports that extensive study of ACT programs has yielded "robust evidence" of its effectiveness in reducing hospitalization, increasing stability of housing, and increasing client satisfaction (p. 173).

COMMUNITY MENTAL HEALTH AND THE DUAL-DIAGNOSED CLIENT

Mental health and community counselors frequently lament that basic research on mental disorder and its treatment does not always relate well to the types of problems presented by clients in the real world. One area that is sometimes shortchanged in academic preparation is the possibility of comorbidity (i.e., two conditions existing concurrently). The term *dual diagnosis* or *dually diagnosed client* refers to clients who present with both substance-related and psychiatric conditions.

Seligman (1998) notes that as many as two-thirds of clients presenting with substance abuse disorders have another coexisting condition. Regier and colleagues (1990), in reporting the results of the Epidemiologic Catchment Area Study, note that 29% of all persons with mental disorders met the criteria for a substance abuse disorder. In addition, experiencing a mental disorder increases the likelihood of having a substance abuse disorder by 2.7 times. A related problem occurs with multiple substance abuse and dependence, in which cases the client meets the diagnostic criteria for two or more substances (Yalisove, 2004).

A "chicken or the egg" dilemma occurs when we attempt to determine the specific etiology of the disorders. Which came first—the mental illness or the substance abuse/dependence disorder? There is some inferential evidence that the psychiatric conditions tend to precede the substance-related disorder (Yalisove, 2004). This sequence appears to be common in adolescents and in women more than men. Also, personality disorder does not appear to be induced by alcohol abuse. However, Verheul and colleagues (2000) have shown that symptoms of anxiety and mood disorders may be caused by excessive alcohol use.

According to Ryglewicz and Pepper (1992), much of the impetus in developing programs for dually diagnosed persons stems from the failure of existing delivery systems to achieve treatment success with this population. The contemporary consumer of mental health services, as a member of the post-deinstitutionalization generation, is more vulnerable to substance abuse and dependence than previous institutionalization generations, who in experiencing longer inpatient hospital stays were more insulated from the influences of our drug-infested culture. Furthermore, seeing the mentally ill and addict or alcoholic as distinct groups, programs and treatment approaches were designed to address the presenting concerns of each distinct population with little or no concern for symptom overlap. Finally, mental health and substance abuse programs were often housed in either different departments or different organizations. As a result, basic questions in case formulation and treatment planning revolved around the following concerns: Should removal of the substance-related disorder take place prior to implementation of treatment for the co-occurring emotional disorder? Or will the client be better served by entering an inpatient chemical abuse treatment program prior to receiving treatment in the mental health setting?

Traditional approaches to treatment tend to take the linear approach by first moving the person toward recovery from substance abuse/dependence. Thus, the client is initially admitted to an inpatient or outpatient chemical abuse treatment program. Then, as sufficient progress is noted, referral or transfer is made to the mental health agency. In most urban settings, community mental health centers have substance abuse *and* psychiatric treatment programs. However, this tendency toward linear treatment persists for several reasons. First, attempts at integrating treatment are often complicated by poor communication between or among programs and staff. For example, the substance abuse and mental health units of a community mental health center are so disconnected in practice that staff from one program rarely have an opportunity to conduct joint staffing of cases for the purpose of case planning and monitoring. In such settings, it is unlikely that a truly integrated treatment plan can take place. Treatment in such a context often proceeds with the right hand of treatment not knowing what the left hand is doing. Second, the working knowledge of the assessment and treatment of mental illness and substance-related disorders varies among staff of the respective programs, further complicating staff and interagency communication and the coordination of treatment planning, implementation, and ongoing assessment. Third, the funding mechanisms, eligibility requirements, geographic boundaries, and administrative policies of the mental health and substance abuse treatment systems inhibit coordinated and effective treatment to dually diagnosed populations (Young & Grella, 1998).

Several approaches to the treatment of dually diagnosed clients have emerged in recent years. Inpatient dual-diagnosis programs are typically housed in psychiatric hospitals (Stevens & Smith, 2005). The substance abuse and psychological condition of the client must be assessed independently and in relation to each other. The goals are to withdraw clients safely from substances, establish physical and emotional stability, and identify and treat the coexisting disorders. In addition to the delivery of mental health interventions, the treatment plans may include psychopharmacological interventions, such as antidepressants, antianxiety, or mood-stabilizing medications. Mental health counselors working in these settings assist in assessment and treatment planning, provide psychoeducational components to clients and families, cofacilitate counseling and skill-building groups, and conduct individual and family counseling. Certification as a chemical abuse counselor is sometimes required or highly preferred.

Evans and Sullivan (2001) describe a modified 12-step program that integrates treatment of both substance-related and psychological disorders. They recognize an underlying process that is shared by AA and mental health counseling. Their model uses the 12 steps as a foundation and builds in cognitive-behavioral interventions at each specific step. The goal is recovery from both the mental illness and substance abuse/dependence.

Aaron Beck and his associates (Beck et al., 1993) conceptualize the dually diagnosed client within a cognitive framework. Particular childhood experiences give rise to underlying cognitive schema characterized by dysfunctional beliefs, assumptions, and rules. When activated in specific situations, chemical use is viewed as a compensatory strategy to decrease personal emotional discomfort. The goal of the cognitive treatment is to provide alternative cognitive and behavioral strategies to release clients from the vicious cycle of craving and relapse that characterizes their pattern of behavior.

COMMUNITY MENTAL HEALTH AND CORRECTIONS

Increasingly, our nation's correctional facilities are serving significant numbers of persons with moderate to severe mental illness who violate the law. According to Bureau of Justice Statistics (1999), an estimated 283,800 mentally ill offenders were held in the nation's correctional facilities at midyear 1998. In addition, approximately 547,800 mentally ill persons were on probation in the community. Seven percent of federal inmates and 16% of persons incarcerated in state prisons and local jails or probation stated that they either had a mental illness or had been treated for mental conditions.

Hiday (1999) categorizes these persons into three subgroups. Mentally ill offenders in the first group are arrested for misdemeanor offenses, some of which would not result in arrest of nondisordered offenders. These persons break the law not so much as a function of their mental condition, but because their social background interacts with their mental illness in ways that place them as marginal and on the fringes of society (Hiday, 1999, p. 525). Common offenses for this group include loitering, disturbing the peace, shoplifting, or failing to pay restaurant bills.

Hiday (1999) identifies a second group in contact with the criminal justice system who have co-occurring personality and substance abuse disorders. These persons are aggressive and threatening and have histories of violent behavior. They are arrested and incarcerated for threatening behavior, abusive and assaultive acts, and public intoxication. Often, their uncooperative behaviors limit the extent to which they engage in available mental health services in their communities.

A third group identified by Hiday (1999) is the smallest of the three and consists of the severely mentally ill who are the stereotyped raging "madman out of control" (p. 525). These persons are driven by psychotic symptomatology to commit criminally violent acts. Although fewest in number, these persons receive extensive media attention.

Although the entire correctional system is strained by the increased numbers of incarcerated persons with mental illness, the onus for the vast majority of these offenders is on the local jails and communities. In June 1998, somewhere between 41,472 and 53,322 of the 592,462 detainees in local jails were severely mentally ill (Lurigio, Fallon, & Dincin, 2000). It is assumed that higher percentages of the jailed mentally ill are found in urban centers.

The characteristics of the mentally ill housed in local jails reveal why this population presents a complex problem for community mental health and other human service delivery systems (Bureau of Justice Statistics, 1999). In the year prior to their incarceration, 30% of the mentally ill found in jails reported periods of homelessness and 47% were unemployed in the month prior to their arrest. Sixty-five percent of the mentally ill and 57% of others incarcerated in local jails reported being under the influence of alcohol or drugs at the time of their offense. Among jail inmates identified as mentally ill, 41% had received some form of mental health service since their admission. The majority of those receiving treatment had been given medication. Only 16% in local jails, in contrast to 44% in state prisons, received counseling.

A number of obstacles can be identified that limit the availability of mental health services in jails. Landsberg (1992) notes that jail construction has not kept up with needs, and existing facilities are outdated and overcrowded. The designs of many jail facilities do not facilitate conducting assessments or counseling on the premises. For example, the local city lock-up may have no conference rooms or empty cells available. When called to conduct lethality checks on persons being held, the mental health counselor may be required to assess the person in a cell reserved for prisoners held in solitary confinement. Furthermore, correctional staff is not trained with adequate sophistication to observe, classify, or treat mentally ill inmates (Kupers, 2000, P. 242). Although conducting counseling is clearly beyond the scope of correctional officers' training, they receive little training in recognizing indicators of mental illness or lethality. If symptoms are recognized, jail staff are ill equipped to intervene. Rapid turnover in the inmate populations further limits the logic of using jails as sites for more than crisis intervention. Finally, release of inmates into the community often takes place without an adequate follow-up plan for mental health services. Clearly, articulation agreements between correctional facilities and community mental health and other human service agencies are required if the multiple needs of this population are to be met.

Morris and Steadman (1997) investigated the mental health services provided in 1,027 United States jails. Using surveys and site visits, they found that an average of 10.3% of inmates was receiving mental health services at the time of their study. The percentages served and number of services provided varied greatly according to the size of the jail. The administrators of larger jails perceived their mental health services to be more effective than did the administrators of smaller jails. Of the jails surveyed, 88% conducted initial screening of inmates for mental health needs, 69% conducted follow-up evaluations, and 79% provided suicide prevention services. Much less common were counseling services and discharge planning, and only 32.9% and 26% of the jails, respectively, had such services available.

Several innovative programs have demonstrated the ability to deliver effective community-based treatment to the incarcerated mentally ill. Several such programs provided parental skill and behavioral management training to incarcerated fathers (Harrison, 1997; Landreth & Lobaugh, 1998). The goals are to prevent or limit the disruption that occurs in the lives of their children. Baugh (1994) describes the efforts of staff at Dauphin County Prison, Harrisburg, Pennsylvania, to reduce violence against women by developing a psychoeducational program, Men Establishing New Directions (MEND). This group format focuses on changing the attitudes and behavior of male offenders. In the first phase, interventions are directed toward breaking down inmate resistance and denial and helping inmates identify alternative, nonabusive behaviors. The second phase concentrates on developing communication skills and conflict management techniques and learning to reappraise anger cues.

Other programs intervene at the point of the person's release from jail. Roskes, Feldman, Arrington, and Leisher (1999) describe a modified brokered case management approach that established a network between the probation officer and community mental health center. A Mental Health Specialist position was designed to provide offenders with appropriate supervision and case management upon their release from prison. Substance abuse and treatment for dually diagnosed persons were the most common issues requiring treatment following incarceration. When a prisoner is scheduled for release, the probation officer makes arrangements for an appointment for the offender to be seen by a counselor and psychiatrist that same day. Success of this program is attributed to the close, collaborative relationship established between probation officers and the mental health providers. ACT teams have also been used successfully to provide case management and provide mental health and drug treatment, health education, medical care, employment assistance, family support, and advocacy for mentally ill offenders upon their release.

COMMUNITY MENTAL HEALTH AND AIDS/HIV

The human immunodeficiency virus (HIV) and acquired immunodeficiency syndrome (AIDS) have generated enormous mental health needs and posed challenges to mental health professionals since the 1980s. Mental health and community counselors can play central roles in HIV/AIDS psychoeducational efforts, prevention, treatment, and advocacy. However, they must be trained for this role if their efforts are to make a difference in the lives of those infected by the disease. Thus, mental health and community counselors must have a working knowledge of the cognitive, behavioral, and affective factors that accompany HIV/AIDS and be prepared to offer services to persons and related systems at all stages of the disease (Knox, 1998).

Knox (1998) presents a list of common psychological stressors faced by HIV-infected persons. These include

- social isolation and stigmatization resulting from public revelation of diagnosis, sexual orientation or drug use
- estrangement from family
- death of friends from AIDS
- personal (or ever-present anticipation of) losses (e.g., job, housing, savings, physical and mental abilities, personal autonomy)
- guilt over lifestyle and past behaviors
- uncertainty about progression of disease
- increased frequency of infections and sickness (p. 5)

The psychological stress can negatively influence the person's immune system, potentially leading to even greater vulnerability to infections and sickness.

The consequences of being notified that one is HIV positive can be best understood by applying a *crisis paradigm* (Hoff, 1995). The crisis is precipitated when the person learns that he or she is HIV positive. HIV is a progressive and fatal illness. This awareness raises immediate concerns revolving around sexual identity/lifestyle issues and the specter of premature death. Frequently, loss of familial and social supports occurs. The crisis manifests in emotional, cognitive, and behavioral ways. Common mental health problems associated with HIV/AIDS include adjustment disorders, depression, anxiety/panic disorders, substance abuse, organic mental disorders, and the exacerbation of preexisting mental conditions (Knox, 1998).

FIGURE 11.2 Continuum of Potential HIV-Related Service Recipients

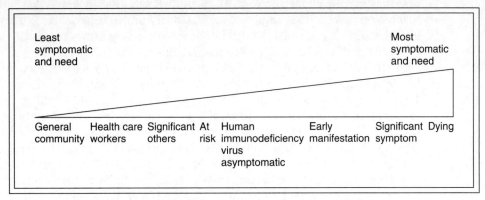

Source: Adapted from Knox, Davis, & Friedrich, 1994 and Knox, 1998

Mental health and community counselors can provide services to a broad spectrum of persons affected or possibly affected by HIV+/AIDS. The continuum shown in Figure 11.2 is an adaptation of a hierarchical model presented by Knox, Davis, and Friedrich (1994) and Knox (1998). Groups of persons who can benefit from mental health counseling interventions are arranged along a continuum, beginning with noninfected members of the general population who are psychologically affected by the disease. Beyond this initial group, the impact of the disease becomes more direct. Moving from least to most directly influenced, affected groups who may benefit from mental health interventions include health care workers, significant others of the HIV+/AIDS infected, at-risk groups, HIV positive asymptomatic patients, persons with early manifestations of HIV, persons experiencing significant symptoms, and, finally, person dying of AIDS. The need for medical and counseling services increases as movement along the continuum progresses from left to right.

Specific mental health interventions should focus on the unique needs presented by each group. For example, consultation and psychoeducational programs can be presented to the general public to increase awareness, change negative attitudes and behaviors toward persons infected by HIV+/AIDS, and reduce risk-taking behaviors (Knox, 1998).

HIV prevention utilizes individual and group modalities and can be directed toward all ecological levels of the adolescents' sphere of development. Adolescents with psychiatric disorders are highly at risk of HIV/AIDS (Brown, Danovsky, Lourie, DiClemente, & Ponton, 1997). Useful interventions may include the following:

- increasing the adolescent's personalized concern regarding the threat of HIV
- developing more adaptive thoughts to support safe sexual behaviors and mature attitudes toward intimacy
- increasing assertiveness skills
- adapting peer norms and activities

Other preventive approaches can be directed toward specific networks associated with HIV-related behaviors. For example, Latkin, Mandell, Vlahov, Oziemskowska, and Celentano (1996) describe a self-help, network-centered, psychoeducational approach to reduce risk of HIV/AIDS to injection drug users. Development of assertiveness skills, decision-making techniques, and role-playing were used to promote risk-reducing behaviors in network members. An 18-month follow-up survey found that participants in the experimental group displayed decreased HIV-related behaviors (e.g., sharing needles, sharing cookers, and decreased frequency of injecting heroin and cocaine).

Mental health and community counselors provide vital services to persons infected with HIV/AIDS. Strength-based and empowerment strategies are particularly useful for decreasing the client's attention to the pathological aspects of the disease and accompanying stigma (Orsulic-Jeras, Shepherd, & Britton, 2003; Walker, 2002). As medical advances are made, it is critical that mental health and community counselors working with this population keep abreast on new treatment approaches (Britton, 2000). In addition, working with HIV/AIDS clients raises challenging ethical and legal dilemmas related to professional responsibilities, duty to warn, competence, and confidentiality (Hughes & Friedman, 1994). Mental health and community counselors must have a clear grasp of the specific ethical and legal issues, statues, and standards if they are to deliver services in an appropriate, sensitive, and effective manner.

CONCLUSION

This chapter provided an overview of community mental health by first reviewing the history of the mental health movement in the United States; then presenting a model for understanding, developing, and evaluating mental health care delivery systems; and finally describing selected issues confronting contemporary delivery systems.

Although the chapter provided only a glimpse of what is presently happening in the field of community mental health, I hope it whetted your appetite for the exciting possibilities for mental health counseling professionals. As you reflect on the underlying philosophy and training model for the profession, mental health and community counselors have a great deal to offer clients and their service providers.

It would seem that vast numbers of opportunities knock on the doors of newly trained mental health counselors in the 21st century. Yet despite the increased professional recognition and visibility mental health counselors we have achieved in the past several decades, we continue to be a profession whose potential is substantially unrealized. Yes, mental health counselors are finding excellent jobs and making creative contributions in the contemporary milieu. But we have much work ahead of us, as a profession, if we are to become all that we can be.

What is the future of mental health counseling? What must occur if we are to become highly respected among those who identify professionally with the allied mental health professions? In the final chapter of this text, we turn to this important topic.

DISCUSSION QUESTIONS

1. Consumers of mental health services are playing significant roles in the delivery of mental health service. In what ways can consumers benefit when trained peers

participate in crisis lines or intervention services? What biases do you have regarding mental health consumers taking increased responsibility for their recovery?

2. List and discuss the unique problems presented when attempting to provide comprehensive service to dually diagnosed populations (i.e., persons who are diagnosed with severe mental illness and substance abuse/dependence). Why do you think traditional delivery systems have not been successful in treating this population?

3. Apply the comprehensive mental health counseling model to guide you in identifying the unique mental health needs of homeless populations. Specify a set of goals for this population.

4. Explore the Web sites of several community mental health centers. Discuss the various types of programs provided and the potential roles for mental health and community counselors.

5. To what extent is the comprehensive mental health counseling model (see chapter 3) relevant for the treatment of persons with severe mental illness?

SUGGESTED ACTIVITIES

1. Identify a particular mental health service that you would like to deliver. Assume that you have been given a large budget to create such a mental health program. Examples might include parent skill training, stress management, suicide prevention, or a mobile crisis stabilization team. Apply the model of mental health delivery systems and develop a detailed proposal of your selected program. Include the following components:
   a. needs assessment
   b. mission statement
   c. goals
   d. program
   e. working knowledge, skills, and resource supports
   f. environmental supports
   g. program evaluation

2. Take a tour of a community mental health program and learn about the variety of services provided. Suggested programs include
   a. community mental health centers
   b. centers for the homeless
   c. AIDS/HIV+ programs or ministries
   d. Private, not-for-profit mental health counseling organizations

3. Invite professionals working at juvenile detention centers to a panel discussion. Focus on the mental health, substance abuse, and family-related issues presented by the adolescents they serve. How are the mental health needs of this population currently being served? What are the roles of mental health and community counselors in corrections facilities?

4. Invite a representative from NAMI to present information about the organization and the role consumers are taking in the provision of mental health services.

12

The Future of Mental Health and Community Counseling

OUTLINE

Current Factors Influencing the Profession

Strengths of the Contemporary Mental Health Counseling Profession

The Struggles of the Contemporary Mental Health Counseling Profession

The Mental Health Counseling Model: Bringing Coherence and Direction to the Profession

Conclusion

Chapter 1 of this text attempted to answer the question, "What is a mental health counselor?" Furthermore, the path toward establishing a secure professional identity in this profession was likened to journeying through the land of confusion. I hope that reading this book has enabled you to conceptualize the geographic features that surround you as you continue down the path of mental health counseling.

This final chapter poses questions similar to those expressed in chapter 1: What is mental health and community counseling? Which road is it on? Where is it headed? It is a comprehensive profession that is multidisciplinary based. Mental health counselors are now recognized as licensed professionals in 48 states. In so many ways, the mental health profession has the potential for a bright future. Yet it also has numerous obstacles that restrict its forward movement and sometimes seem to create enough resistance to force counselors off the path.

This chapter discusses several factors that currently influence mental health counseling's direction and speed of forward progress. In addition, it presents the current strengths and weaknesses of the profession. Finally, the chapter provides several ideas that, if implemented, can help mental health counseling realize its full potential.

CURRENT FACTORS INFLUENCING THE PROFESSION

An ecological analysis of the mental health counseling profession reveals a number of factors that influence its current configuration and direction. Definitions of mental health counseling found in academic texts put forth an ideal description of its professional identity and scope of practice. Who mental health counselors are and what they do are shaped by forces many of which are beyond the practitioner's direct control. Included in this list of environmental factors is the credentialing of the allied mental health professions, the political and economic climate, the evolution of service delivery systems, and trends in treatment approaches.

One's professional identity as a mental health counselor develops through a dynamic interaction of academic training and professional experiences occurring within a specific ecological context. Thus, the configuration of one's actual professional identity will often differ by degree from the ideal definition. For this reason, mental health counselors' identification of who they are and what they do tends to differ from region to region. The following section discusses the nature of these contemporary forces.

PROFESSIONAL CREDENTIALING

As noted earlier, professional licensure has become a powerful and desirable force in helping mental health counselors establish professional recognition and professional identity. This statutory process enables LMHCs/LPCs to provide services to clients within the specified scope of practice. Thus, the visibility of the mental health counseling profession is enhanced among consumers and members of the allied mental health professions.

However, the specific form and content of each state's unique set of statutes are shaped by the definitions of the other mental health professions, which also have licensure statutes in the state's codes. In an ideal world, mental health counselors could integrate into their licensure law the unique sets of knowledge, skills, and scopes of practice that accurately reflect national definitions and training models. However, in many states, the mental health counseling professionals have been the newcomers in the passage of their licensure laws. Thus, their codified professional definitions and scopes of practice are shaped in ways that conform to the contours of the language that defines the identity and practice of the professions that have existing licensure laws in the states' codes. In some states, the counselor licensure laws are also a reflection of the political processes that were required to ensure passage of the licensure law.

This can be a source of dissonance for newly licensed counseling professionals, who discover that the professional identities that they were establishing throughout their graduate education do not conform to the parameters established by legal statutes in the states where they practice. For example, graduate students may learn through their academic training that the diagnosis of mental and emotional conditions is one of the core components of mental health counselor identity. However, in the specific state where they seek to become licensed, the ability to diagnose independently upon licensure is not included in the list of skills and techniques in the codified scope of practice.

Unfortunately, the process of revising or adapting the profession's identity and scope of practice as stated in licensure laws is not an easy task. The ability of the mental health counseling profession to actualize its full potential is hindered to the extent that licensure laws do not fully reflect the knowledge and skills specified in the CACREP training model (Gale & Austin, 2003). Resolution of this dissonance will require persistent professional advocacy, lobbying, and the demonstration of professional excellence.

POLITICAL AND ECONOMIC CLIMATE

A second factor influencing the mental health counseling profession is the contemporary political and economic climate. The budgetary belt has tightened greatly as the federal deficit soars. The most recent budget proposal calls for increased spending on defense and homeland security, offset by deep cuts in education and mental health program funding (Barstow, Alpert, & Campbell, 2005). Mental health leaders are concerned that the proposed cuts will significantly affect mental health and substance abuse block grants, which would further weaken public delivery service systems ("Funding Tops Issues," 2005). In response to budget deficits, it is feared that the Medicaid program, a major reimburser for publicly funded mental health services, will be scaled back considerably.

Decreases in federal funding have been accompanied by an increased burden on state and local governments to provide and oversee community mental health care. This has led to further disintegration and fragmentation of publicly funded programs and delivery systems. Many privately owned and operated agencies have stepped in to fill the gap. Faith-based ministries (frequently funded through individual donations), local congregations, denominations, and grants are viewed increasingly as viable means of providing mental health services to underprivileged, rural, and underserved populations (Laurie, 1997; Richardson, & June, 1997; Voss, 1996). Furthermore, the efforts of very small but persistent and focused advocacy groups have been successful in increasing the flow of resources from the state to local mental health systems (Wentz, 2004).

NEW MODELS AND DELIVERY SYSTEMS

Agencies and mental health professionals have responded to the aforementioned factors by developing and implementing new models of intervention and service delivery. A number of these have been mentioned earlier in this text. Given the time restraints placed on outpatient services by third-party reimbursers, many of the traditional theories and techniques of counseling are deemphasized. Taking their place are a number of brief, solution-focused, and evidence-based approaches. This trend is duly noted by the profession of psychology. Levant (2005) notes that the current zeitgeist requires mental health professionals to base their practice as much as possible on evidence. He challenges psychologists to define evidence-based practice in psychology or face the likelihood that it will be defined *for* them.

Furthermore, fewer practitioners are able to maintain viable full-time private practices. The privacy and autonomy afforded by setting out one's shingle is rapidly becoming a thing of the past. Increased numbers of mental health counselors are engaging in multidisciplinary small group practices and networks. Granted, such systems provide less freedom for the practitioner. But for many, a measure of autonomy is retained while increasing their professional economic viability and providing expanded opportunities. For example, Aitken and Curtis (2004) describe integrated care as an emerging trend in which mental health counselors work in the same offices with primary health providers. A wider array of integrated services can be offered in a variety of areas: family practice, internal medicine, obstetrics, pediatrics, oncology, and cardiology.

Finally, mental health practice has taken to the road in forms such as in-home therapy, ACT, and service provision on the Internet. We expect to see even more rapid increases in the development of innovative practices as these creative delivery systems mature and newer ones emerge.

STRENGTHS OF THE CONTEMPORARY MENTAL HEALTH COUNSELING PROFESSION

There are many reasons to view the future as bright for the mental health counseling profession. First, its underlying philosophy, theoretical base, and training model equip the profession to meet the needs and demands of contemporary society. As we have noted, mental health counselors are trained to view the human condition through lenses emphasizing the following:

- normal human developmental processes across the lifespan
- viewing the person as a holistic being—fully integrating the physical, cognitive, social, emotional, and spiritual characteristics and processes
- viewing human functioning as occurring within a unique ecological context
- a strength-based and wellness orientation that supports prevention, the promotion of optimal mental health, and the solution-focused treatment of psychopathology

Second, legislators, policymakers, and third-party reimbursers increasingly see the mental health counseling profession as an important contributor of services. Recognition as a licensed provider of mental health services in 48 of the 50 states has made a significant impact. In addition (and perhaps as a consequence), working relationships have been established between AMHCA and powerful organizations such as the Carter Center, National Governors Association, National Mental Health Association, National Association of State Mental Health Program Directors, and National Health Council (AMHCA Joins National Health Council, 2003; Wheeler, 2003). The ACA and AMHCA are actively pursuing a legislative agenda and are making significant gains toward inclusion in key federal and state programs. In addition, the results of recent empirical studies support the claim that mental health counselors are experiencing increased success in service claims reimbursement from a variety of third parties (Smith, 1999; Zimpher, 1995).

Third, mental health counselors are finding numerous job opportunities in mental health–related professions. The *Occupational Outlook Handbook,* 2006–2007 edition, states that the overall demand for counselors is expected to grow faster than the average for all occupations through 2014 (Bureau of Labor Statistics, U.S. Department of Labor, 2006). These increased job opportunities are attributed to the following factors: (a) increased funding to improve treatment of individuals, adolescents, and families with serious emotional disturbances; (b) expanded insurance coverage of services offered by mental health counselors; (c) increased number of employee assistance programs that provide mental health and drug and alcohol services; and (d) a mental health emphasis that enhances personal well-being and helps persons control stress related to job and family responsibilities.

THE STRUGGLES OF THE CONTEMPORARY MENTAL
HEALTH COUNSELING PROFESSION

Although the profession is increasingly recognized externally, significant internal incoherence may be the most significant apparent barrier in the profession's attempt to move to the next level. This incoherence is expressed in several ways.

First, although the rapid passage of 48 licensure laws has provided the profession with legal title and practice rights, the variance among the specific statutes makes it difficult to speak of the profession as a unified entity. We can point to the strengths of the training model. But our advocacy efforts are weakened when state requirements vary significantly from national definitions and standards. For example, we state that we are trained to diagnose using the *DSM-IV-TR*, but a number of LPCs or LMHCs are restricted from doing so by the statutes of their specific licensure law. In other states, licensed counselors, although trained in psychometrics and the use of a variety of psychological tests, are not allowed to use these skills in practice. Finally, the grand-parenting clauses in several states diluted the profession by allowing many persons into the profession who were not trained according to the CACREP standards for the mental health or community counseling specializations.

Second, it is troubling that the specialization of mental health counseling receives only token mention in many of the ACA publications and counseling textbooks in use. Certainly, the relationship between the ACA and AMHCA has been marked with tension throughout recent decades. But it sometimes seems as though ill feelings between professional organizations are evident when the organizations act out of sync or duplicate efforts in ways that do not always benefit of the profession as a whole. Is there underlying bitterness and misunderstanding within the professional associations and between the ACA and AMHCA that hinders the advance of the mental health counseling profession?

Third, although a clear strength of the profession is the CACREP training model, the model is also the source of some professional confusion. How are we to conceptualize the differences between community counselors and mental health counselors? On the one hand, they are identified as distinct specializations, and these specializations become the basis for academic structures in graduate programs. In many ways, the training model promotes a professional identification with the specialization and academic program. Less emphasis may be placed on developing and supplying the pipeline feeding AMHCA, the ACA division that represents the interests of the profession. One possible outcome is that licensed counseling professionals may tend to identify with their specific license type and not see membership in ACA and AMHCA as vital to their professional development and survival.

Finally, the profession lacks a coherent model that demarcates mental health counseling from the allied mental health professions. Again, the training model and philosophical/theoretical base have been clearly defined. But these ingredients have not been integrated into a comprehensive model that simultaneously communicates the distinctiveness of mental health counselors and puts forth a unique agenda for research and direction for the profession. Thus, counselors remain subservient to multidisciplinary foundations, none of which finds substantial origins in mental health or community counseling per se.

The remainder of this chapter advances an agenda based on the comprehensive model that is suggested in this text. It is my hope that this model proves to be a point of departure for the mental health counseling profession.

THE MENTAL HEALTH COUNSELING MODEL: BRINGING COHERENCE AND DIRECTION TO THE PROFESSION

The comprehensive mental health counseling model presented in chapter 3 has profound implications for training, professional practice, and research. What would our profession look like if it stood solidly on the foundational pillars it professes? Presently, mental health and community counselors find themselves talking a language of mental health, prevention, and wellness but engaging in professional practice in which treatment of mental illness and emotional disorders prevails.

Consider the questions and programs of research that might arise if we take our devotion to models of normal development, wellness, and human ecology and relate them to the scopes of practice presently contained in counselor licensure laws. Too often, we rest on concepts, theories, and techniques developed by other disciplines, integrate them into our training model, and try to convince ourselves that we are doing something unique. Unfortunately, the mental health counseling profession positioned in this manner offers little that is unique to the policymakers and powerholders. For the profession to be both viable and vibrant in the future, a unique vision of mental health counseling must emerge—one that is primarily of our own making.

Imagine (perhaps dream) of a strong discipline of mental health counseling that promotes a perspective sufficiently unique that it captures the attention of the allied mental health professions on the basis of its applications and implications. How refreshing and stimulating it might be if the mental health counseling profession came to the table with a truly unique perspective on the human condition and its positive promotion. What unique concepts, theories, and techniques might emerge if we seriously pursued the application of wellness principles and techniques to those we serve, both the mentally ill and those of relative mental health alike? Could we be a profession that does not merely strive to remediate or limit the expression of psychopathology but also facilitate personal growth within zones of proximal development (Vygotsky, 1962) and enhance the well-being of persons-in-situations?

To accomplish such an ambitious task, mental health counselors as well as counselor educators and supervisors must expend more efforts in primary research. Applying our expertise of measurement and evaluation, a new family of assessment skills and tools for mental health counselors might be developed to provide a valid and reliable appraisal of wellness. Dimensions relevant to professional practice would include the following areas:

- individuals diagnosed with mental illness or emotional disorders
- individuals displaying varying degrees of mental health and wellness
- primary relationships of clients
- unique network of relationships presently or potentially operating in the client's life
- formal institutions and interactions among them in relation to the client
- general societal and cultural influences

Appraisal of clients through systematic application of the model is a useful adjunct to the traditional *DSM* diagnosis. And perhaps it suggests an alternative paradigm for conceptualizing the problems that clients present. For example, it provides the mental health practitioner with a framework for identifying concurrent dysfunctions occurring in the person, his or her primary relationship, and his or her network of relationships (e.g., the client's particular community). It is the future task of practitioners and counselor educators to hypothesize and test the many appraisal-related research questions that can be derived as the implications of this model are considered.

Furthermore, we might ask, "What would mental health counseling theory and practice look like if the ecological and mental health foundations were more central?" Could the application of the mental health model help practitioners create more holistic conceptualization of the client's presenting condition? Several approaches previously discussed fit within our model. First, we would continue to place within our model interventions aimed at prevention. Second, we might expand on the manner in which ACT, the self-help/consumer movement, and day treatment social clubs build on a true mental health model. Third, mental health counselors could work closely with the existing programs and formal institutional supports to facilitate the mental health and wellness of persons and their communities within the specific ecological milieu. For example, mental health counselors might extend outreach efforts to the clergy and programs of African American churches to promote mental health and wellness across multiple ecological levels.

Finally, the mental health counseling model lends itself to applications in primary health care settings. The mental health needs of children, adolescents, and adults experiencing major health crises are well documented. Many such patients may exhibit co-occurring psychiatric conditions that complicate the treatment of their medical condition. Other patients may experience significant levels of emotional distress with no significant emotional disorder present. For example, numerous studies have found that cancer patients experience a variety of distressing feelings and emotions that may interfere with their abilities to cope with the disease (American Cancer Society, 2004). The wide range of emotions that can be experienced includes powerlessness, sadness, fear, depression, and anxiety. Unfortunately, the presence of distress in cancer patients may go undetected and untreated by primary care physicians (Fallowfield, Ratcliffe, & Saul, 2001). Clearly, the comprehensive model of mental health counseling provides a useful template for the assessment and treatment of such patients in their particular ecological setting.

CONCLUSION

The ideas presented in this final chapter should not be construed as a plea for exclusivity in theory and practice. The multidisciplinary nature of our profession must be retained. It is a strength. What I am advocating is an invitation for the mental health counseling profession to live up to the theoretical base it professes and actively pursue a research program that solidly reflects this foundation. I believe the stature of the profession would increase significantly if it were to give ourselves more permission to act autonomously in matters of mental health–related research and theory making.

The profession of mental health counseling is truly at a crossroads. The training received in community and mental health counseling specializations prepares master's-level practitioners for service in a wide variety of settings. I cannot think of profession practitioners have been better trained to do what they proclaim to do—counsel.

I am excited about the profession and am optimistic about the future. The challenges are apparent and it is within the profession's grasp to recognize and capitalize on its strengths and move to the next level. We can look from whence we have come with professional humility and pride. Drawing on these strengths, we can proceed confidently down the long and winding path of professional development and identity formation.

Carpe diem!

DISCUSSION QUESTIONS

1. In your opinion, how will the profession of mental health counseling change over the next 10 years? What steps would you take to prepare for that future?
2. List what you see as the primary strengths and weaknesses of the mental health counseling profession. What specific areas should be the focus of your advocacy efforts?
3. How strong is the professional identity of licensed mental health or community counselors in your state? What efforts should be expended to ensure that LMHCs and LPCs are recognized for the quality of services they provide?
4. In what specific ways is the profession of mental health counseling influenced by the contemporary political and economic environment?

SUGGESTED ACTIVITIES

1. View the Web sites of state and national counseling organizations. What vision for the future of the profession do you detect as you consider their respective mission statements and advocacy activities?
2. Develop a questionnaire that explores the extent to which mental health and community counselors in your region hold a positive view of the future of their profession.
3. Become active in the advocacy efforts of your state and national professional associations (e.g., ACA, AMHCA, and state affiliates). Ask board members what roles you can play in advancing the counseling profession.

Appendix A

National Professional Associations

American Psychological Association
750 First Street, NE
Washington, DC 20002-4242
Telephone: (800) 374-2721
www.apa.org

American Psychiatric Association
1000 Wilson Boulevard
Suite 1825
Arlington, VA 22209-3901
Telephone: (703) 907-7300
www.psych.org

American Association for Marriage and Family
    Therapy
112 South Alfred Street
Alexandria, VA 22314-3061
Telephone: (703) 838-9808
www.aamft.org

American Mental Health Counselors Association
801 N. Fairfax Street, Suite 304
Alexandria, VA 22314

Telephone: (800) 326-2642
www.amhca.org

National Association of Social Workers
750 First Street, NE
Suite 700
Washington, DC 20002-4241
Telephone: (202) 408-8600
www.naswdc.org

American Association of State Counseling
    Boards (AASCB)
3-A Terrace Way
Greensboro, NC 27403-3660
Telephone (336) 547-0914
www.aascb.org

American Counseling Association (ACA)
5999 Stevenson Ave.
Alexandria, VA 22304
(800) 347-6647
www.counseling.org

Appendix B
Licensure Boards

ALABAMA

Alabama Board of Examiners in Counseling
950 22nd Street North
Suite 670
Birmingham, AL 35203
Phone: (205) 458-8717/1-800-822-3307
Fax: (205) 458-8718
Web site: **www.abec.state.al.us**

ALASKA

Board of Professional Counselors Division
of Occupational Licensing
P.O. Box 110806
Juneau, AK 99811-0806
Phone: (907) 465-2551 7:30 a.m. to 4:00 p.m.
AST
Fax: (907) 465-2974
Web site: **www.dced.state.ak.us/occ/ppco.htm**

ARIZONA

Arizona Board of Behavioral Health Examiners
1400 West Washington
Suite 350
Phoenix, AZ 85007
Phone: (602) 542-1882
Fax: (602) 364-0890
Web site: **www.bbhe.state.az.us**

ARKANSAS

Arkansas Board of Examiners in Counseling
P.O. Box 70

Magnolia, AR 71754-0070
Phone: (870) 901-7055
Fax: (870) 234-1842
Web site: **www.state.ar.us/abec**

CALIFORNIA

California Registry of Professional Counselors and
Paraprofessionals
P.O. Box 15700
Long Beach, CA 90815
Phone: (714) 284-8857
Web site: **http://www.california-registry.org**

COLORADO

State Board of Licensed Professional Counselor
Examiners
1560 Broadway, Suite 1350
Denver, CO 80202
Phone: (303) 894-7766
Fax: (303) 894-7790
Web site: **www.dora.state.co.us/mentalhealth/
lpcboard.htm**

CONNECTICUT

Professional Counselor Licensure
Department of Public Health
410 Capitol Avenue—MS # 12APP
P.O. Box 340308
Hartford CT 06134-0308
Phone: (860) 509-7603
Fax: (860) 509-8457
Web site: **www.dph.state.ct.us/**

DELAWARE

Board of Professional Counselors of Mental Health
Canon Building
Suite 203
861 Silver Lake Blvd.
Dover, DE 19904
Phone: (302) 744-4534
Fax: (302) 739-2711
Web site: **www.delaware.gov/ default.shtml**

DISTRICT OF COLUMBIA

Health Professional Licensing Administration
825 N. Capital Street NE
Suite 2224
Washington, DC 20002
Phone: (202)442-9200
Web site: **http://dchealth.dc.gov/prof_license/
services/boards_main_action.asp?strAppID=21**

FLORIDA

Board of Clinical Social Work, Marriage and
    Family Therapy, and Mental Health Counseling
4052 Bald Cypress Way
Bin # C-08
Tallahassee, FL 32399-3250
Phone: (850) 245-4444 ext. 3434
Fax: (850) 921-5389
Web site: **www.doh.state.fl.us/mqa**

GEORGIA

Georgia Composite Board of Professional
    Counselors, Social Workers, and Marriage
    and Family Therapists
237 Coliseum Drive
Macon, GA 31217-3858
Phone: (478)207-1484
Web site: **http://www.sos.state.ga.us/plb/
counselors**

HAWAII

Department of Commerce and Consumer
    Affairs—Director
DCCA-PVL
Att: MHC
P.O. Box 3469
Honolulu, HI 96801
Phone: (808) 586-3000

IDAHO

Idaho State Licensing Board of Professional
    Counselors and Marriage and Family
    Therapists
Bureau of Occupational Licenses
Owyhee Plaza, 1109 Main Street, Suite 220
Boise, ID 83702-5642
Phone: (208) 334-3233
Fax: (208) 334-3945
Web site: **http://www2.state.id.us/ibol/cou.htm**

ILLINOIS

Department of Financial & Professional
    Regulation
Division of Professional Regulation
320 West Washington Street,
Springfield, IL 62786
Phone: (217)785-0800
Fax: (217) 782-7645
Web site: **www.ildpr.com/WHO/prfcns.asp**

INDIANA

IN Social Work, Marriage & Family Therapist &
    Mental Health Counselor Board
Health Professions Bureau
402 W. Washington St., Room W066
Indianapolis, IN 46204
Phone: (317)234-2064
Fax: (317) 233-4236
Web site: **www.in.gov/hpb/boards/mhcb**

IOWA

Iowa Board of Behavioral Science
    Examiners
IA Dept. of Public Health
Lucas State Office Building
321 East 3rd Street
Des Moines, IA 50319
Phone: (515) 281-4413
Web site: **http://www.idph.state.ia.us/licensure/
board_home.asp?board=be**

KANSAS

Behavioral Sciences Regulatory Board
712 S. Kansas Avenue
Topeka, KS 66603-3817
Phone: (785) 296-3240
Fax: (785) 296-3112
Web site: **http://www.ksbsrb.org**

KENTUCKY

Kentucky Board of Licensed Professional
    Counselors
P.O. Box 1360
Frankfort, KY 40602
Phone: (502) 564-3296 ext 226
Fax: (502) 564-4818
Web site: **http://finance.ky.gov/ourcabinet/
caboff/OAS/op/procoun/**

LOUISIANA

Licensed Professional Counselors
Board of Examiners
8631 Summa Avenue
Baton Rouge, LA 70809
Phone: (225) 765-2515
Fax: (225) 765-2514
Web site: **http://www.lpcboard.org**

MAINE

Maine Board of Counseling Professionals
Licensure State House Station, #35
Augusta, ME 04333
Phone: (207) 624-8603
Fax: (207) 624-8637
Web site: **www.state.me.us/pfr/olr/categories/
cat13.htm**

MARYLAND

Board of Professional Counselors
4201 Patterson Avenue
Baltimore, MD 21215-2299
Phone: (410) 764-4732
Fax: (410) 358-1610
Web site: **http://www.dhmh.state.md.us/
bopc/**

MASSACHUSETTS

Board Allied Mental Health
239 Causeway Street, 5th Floor
Boston, MA 02114
Phone: (617) 727-3080
Fax: (617)727-2366
Web site: **http://www.mass.gov/reg/
boards/mh**

MICHIGAN

Michigan Board of Counseling
Bureau of Health Professionals
P.O. Box 30670
611 W. Ottawa
Lansing, MI 48909
Phone: (517) 335-0918
Fax: (517) 373-2179
Web site: **http://www.michigan.gov/mdch/
0,1607,7-132-27417_27529_27536_00.html**

MINNESOTA

Minnesota Board of Behavioral Health and
 Therapy
2829 University Ave SE
Suite 210
Minneapolis, MN 55414
Phone: (612) 617-2178
Web site: **http://www.bbht.state.mn.us/**

MISSISSIPPI

Mississippi State Board of Examiners for Licensed
 Professional Counselors
419 East Broadway
Yazoo City, MS 39194
Phone: (888) 860-7001
Fax: (662) 751-4628
Web site: **www.lpc.state.ms.us**

MISSOURI

Division of Professional Registration
Committee for Professional Counselors
3605 Missouri Boulevard
P.O. Box 1335
Jefferson City, MO 65102
Phone: (573) 751-0018
Fax: (573) 526-3489
Web site: **http://pr.mo.gov**

MONTANA

Board of Social Work Examiners & Professional
 Counselors
Department of Commerce
Professional & Occupational Licensing
 Division
301 South Park, 4th Floor
P.O. Box 200513
Helena, MT 59620-0513
Phone: (406) 841-2369
Fax: (406) 841- 2309
Web site: **http://mt.gov/dli/bsd/license/
bsd_boards/ swp_board/ board_page.asp**

NEBRASKA

Nebraska Board of Examiners in Mental Health
 Practice
P.O. Box 94986
Lincoln, NE 68509-4986
Phone: (402) 471-2117
Fax: (402) 471-3577
Web site: **http://www.hhs.state.ne.us/crl/mhcs/
mental/mentalhealth.htm**

NEVADA

There is no licensure law in Nevada at this time.

NEW HAMPSHIRE

New Hampshire Board of Mental Health Practice
49 Donovan Street
Concord, NH 03301
Phone: (603) 271-6762
Fax: (603) 271-3950
Web site: **http://www.state.nh.us/mhpb/**

NEW JERSEY

New Jersey Division of Consumer Affairs
State Board of Marriage & Family Therapy
 Examiners
Professional Counselor Examiners Committee
P.O. Box 45007
Newark NJ 07101
Phone: (973) 504-6415
Fax: (973) 648-3536
Web site: **http://www.state.nj.us/lps/ca/medical/
familytherapy.htm**

NEW MEXICO

New Mexico Counseling and Therapy Practice
 Board
2550 Cerrillos Road
Santa Fe, NM 87505
Phone: (505) 476-7102
Fax: (505) 476-7148
Web site: **http://www.rld.state.nm.us/b&c/
Counseling/ index.htm**

NEW YORK

State Board for Mental Health Practitioners
Office of the Professions
State Education Building—2nd Floor
Albany, NY 12234-1000
Phone: (518) 474-3817 ext. 180
Fax: (518) 402-5944
Web site: **www.op.nysed.gov**

NORTH CAROLINA

North Carolina Board of Licensed Professional
   Counselors
P.O. Box 1369
Garner, NC 27529-1369
Phone: (919) 661-0820
Fax: (919) 779-5642
Web site: **www.NCBLPC.org**

NORTH DAKOTA

North Dakota Board of Counselor Examiners
2112 10th Avenue SE
Mandan, ND 58554
Phone: (701) 667-5969
Web site: **www.sendit.nodak.edu/NDBCE**

OHIO

Ohio Counselor, Social Worker, & Marriage and
   Family Therapist Board
77 South High Street, 16th Floor
Columbus, OH 43215
Phone: (614) 466-0912
Fax: (614) 728-7790
Web site: **http://cswmft.ohio.gov/**

OKLAHOMA

Division of Professional Counselors Licensing
Oklahoma State Dept. of Health
1000 NE 10th Street
Oklahoma City, OK 73117-1299
Phone: (405) 271-6030
Fax: (405) 271-1918
Web site: **www.health.state.ok.us/program/lpc/**

OREGON

Oregon Board of Licensed Professional Counselors
   & Therapists
3218 Pringle Road, SE, #250
Salem, OR 97302-6312
Phone: (503) 378-5499
Web site: **http://www.oblpct.state.or.us/**

PENNSYLVANIA

State Board of Social Workers, Marriage and
   Family Therapists, and Professional
   Counselors
Department of State Bureau of Professional and
   Occupational Affairs
Penn Center
Commissioner's Office
2601 North 3rd Street
Harrisburg, PA 17110
Phone: (717) 787-8503
Fax: (717) 787-7769
Web site: **http://www.dos.state.pa.us/bpoa/cwp/
view.asp?a=1104&q=433177**

RHODE ISLAND

Board of Mental Health Counselors/Marriage &
   Family Therapists
RI Department of Health Professions Regulation
3 Capitol Hill
Providence, RI 02908
Phone: (401) 222-2828
Fax: (401) 222-1272
Web site: **http://www.healthri.org/hsr/
professions/mf_counsel.php**

SOUTH CAROLINA

Board of Examiners for Licensure of Professional
   Counselors, Marriage and Family Therapists,
   and Psycho-Educational Specialists
P.O. Box 11329
Columbia, SC 29211-1289
Phone: (803) 896-4658
Fax: (803) 896-4719
Web site: **www.llr.state.sc.us/pol**

SOUTH DAKOTA

South Dakota Board of Counselor Examiners
P.O. Box 1822
Sioux Falls, SD 57101
Phone: (605) 331-2927
Fax: (605) 331-2043
Web site: **http://www.state.sd.us/dhs/boards/ counselor**

TENNESSEE

TN State Board of Professional Counselors, Marital & Family Therapists
Department of Health
1st Floor, Cordell Hull Bldg
425 5th Ave. N.
Nashville, TN 37247-1010
Phone: (615) 532-3202/(888)310-4650
Fax: (615) 532-5164
Web site: **www.state.tn.us/health**

TEXAS

Texas State Board of Examiners of Professional Counselors
Texas Department of State Health Services
1100 West 49th Street
Austin, TX 78756-3183
Phone: (512) 834-6658
Fax: (512) 834-6789
Web site: **www.tdh.state.tx.us/hcqs/plc/lpc/ lpc_def.htm**

UTAH

Professional Counselor Licensing Board
160 E 300 South
Salt Lake City, UT 84114-6741
Phone: (801) 530-6720
Fax: (801) 530-6511
Website: **http://www.dopl.utah.gov/licensing/ professional_counselor.html**

VERMONT

Allied Mental Health Practitioners Board
26 Terrace Street
Montpelier, VT 05609-1106
Phone: (802) 828-2390
Fax: (802) 828-2465
Website: **http://www.vtprofessionals.org/opr1/ allied/**

VIRGINIA

Virginia Board of Counseling
Department of Health Professionals
6603 West Broad St., 5th Floor
Richmond, VA 23230
Phone: (804) 662-9912
Web site: **www.dhp.state.va.us/ counseling**

WASHINGTON

Washington State Registared Counselor Program
Health Professionals Quality Assurance Division
P.O. Box 47869
Olympia, WA 98504-7869
Phone: (360) 236-4700
Fax: (360) 236-4918
Web site: **doh.wa.gov**

WEST VIRGINIA

West Virginia Board of Examiners in Counseling
P.O. Box 129
Ona, WV 25545
Phone: (800) 520-3852
Web site: **www.wvbec.org**

WISCONSIN

Marriage and Family Therapy, Professional
  Counseling, and Social Work Examining
  Board
Bureau of Health Service Professional Licensing
P.O. Box 8935
Madison, WI 53708
Phone: (608) 266-0145
Fax: (608) 267-0644
Web site: **www.drl.state.wi.us**

WYOMING

Mental Health Professions Licensure
  Board
First Bank Plaza
2020 Carey Avenue, Suite 201
Cheyenne, WY 82002
Phone: (307) 777-7788
Fax: (307) 777-6005
Web site: **http://plboards.state.wy.us/**
mentalhealth/index.asp

Ackerman, N., & Sobel, R. (1950). Family diagnosis: An approach to the preschool child. *American Journal of Orthopsychiatry, 20*, 744–753.

Acuff, C., Bennett, B. E., Bricklin, P. M., Canter, M. B., Knapp, S. J., Moldawshy, S. et al. (1999). Considerations for ethical practice in managed care. *Professional Psychology Research and Practice, 30*, 563–575.

Aiken, L. R. (2003). *Psychological testing and assessment* (11th ed.). Boston, MA: Allyn and Bacon.

Ainsworth, M. D. S., Blehar, M. C., Waters, E., & Wall, S. (1978). *Patterns of attachment*. Hillsdale, NJ: Erlbaum.

Aitken, J. B., & Curtis, R. (2004). Integrated health care: Improving client care while providing opportunities for mental health counselors. *Journal of Mental Health Counseling, 26*, 321–331.

Albee, G. W. (1959). *Mental health manpower trends*. New York: Basic Books.

Allen, V. B. (1986). A historical perspective of the AACD Ethics Committee. Special issue: Professional Ethics. *Journal of Counseling and Development, 64*, 293.

Altschuld, J. W., & Witkin, B. R. (2000). *From needs assessment to action: Transforming needs into solution strategies*. Thousand Oaks, CA: Sage.

American Association of Marriage and Family Therapy. (2001). *AAMFT code of ethics*. Alexandria, VA: Author.

American Cancer Society. (2004). *Distress: Treatment guidelines for patients* (Version I). National Comprehensive Cancer Network and the American Cancer Society. Retrieved April 3, 2005, from http://www.cancer.org/docroot/CRI/content/CRI_2_4_7xNCCN_Distress_Treatment_Guidelines_for_Patients.asp.

American Counseling Association. (1995). *ACA code of ethics and standards of practice*. Alexandria, VA: Author.

American Counseling Association. (2005). *Code of ethics*. Alexandria, VA: Author.

American Counseling Association (ACA) Governing Council. (1997). *Definition of professional counseling* . Alexandria, VA: Author.

American Counseling Association (ACA). (2003). *Counselor licensure legislation: Protecting the public*. Retrieved August 27, 2003, from http://www.counseling.org/site/PageServer?pagename=resources faqs.

American Counseling Association Governing Council. (2003). *Policies and procedures for processing complaints of ethical violations*. Alexandria, VA: Author, Retrieved October 25, 2004, from //www.counseling.org/Content/NavigationMenu/RESOURCES/ETHICS/Final_D.

American Counseling Association. (1999). *ACA ethical standards for internet on-line counseling*. Alexandria, VA: Author.

American Mental Health Counselors Association. (2000). *Code of ethics of the American Mental Health Counselors Association – 2000 revision*. Alexandria, VA: Author.

AMHCA Joins National Health Council. (2003, *September*). *The Advocate, 26*(8), 8.

American Mental Health Counselors Association (AMHCA). (2004, September) Hawaii becomes 48th state to license mental health counselors. *The Advocate, 27*(8), 12.

American Psychiatric Association. (2000). *Diagnostic and statistical manual of mental disorders* (4th ed.-text revision). Washington, DC: Author.

American Psychological Association. (2003). *Ethical principles of psychologists and code of conduct*. Washington, DC: Author.

American Psychological Association. (2004). Guidelines on multicultural education, training, research, practice, and organizational change for psychologists. *American Psychologist, 58*, 377–402.

American Psychological Association. (Winter 2002). Survey provides snapshot of young members' practices and priorities. *Practitioner Focus, 14*(1), 10–11.

American Psychological Association. Committee on Training in Clinical Psychology. (1947). Recommended graduate training programs in clinical psychology. *American Psychologist, 2*, 539–558.

Ancis, J. R. (1998). Cultural competency training at a distance: Challenges and strategies. *Journal of Counseling and Development, 76*, 134–142.

Anderson, C. E. (2000). Dealing constructively with managed care: Suggestions from an insider. *Journal of Mental Health Counseling, 22*, 343–353.

Anderson, N. B. (2003). *Unraveling the mystery of racial and ethnic health disparities: Who, what, when, where, how and especially, why?* Boston, MA: Institute on Urban Health Research, Northeastern University.

Angel, R. J., & Williams, K. (2000). Cultural models of health and illness. In I. Cuéllar, & F. A. Paniagua (Eds.), *Handbook of multicultural mental health* (pp. 25–44). San Diego, CA: Academic Press.

Arrendondo, P., & Toporek, R. (1996). Operationalization of the multicultural counseling competencies. *Journal of Multicultural Counseling and Development, 24*, 42–79.

Arrendondo, P., & Toporek, R. (2004). Multicultural counseling competencies – ethical practice. *Journal of Mental Health Counseling, 26*, 44–55.

Arrendondo, P. (1992). *Latina/Latino counseling and psychotherapy: Tape 1. Cultural consideration for working more effectively with Latin Americans*. Amherst, MA: Microtraining and Multicultural Development.

Arrendondo, P. (1999). Multicultural counseling competencies as tools to address oppression and racism. *Journal of Counseling and Development*, 77, 102–108.

Association for Specialists in Group Work. (2000). Professional standards for the training of group workers. *Journal of Specialists in Group Work*, 25, 327–342.

Atkinson, D. R., Morten, G., & Sue, D. W. (1998). *Counseling American Minorities* (5th ed.). Boston, MA: McGraw-Hill.

Axinn, J., & Levin, H. (1997). *Social welfare: A history of the American response to need* (4th ed.). New York: Dodd-Mead.

Ayllon, T., & Azrin, N. (1968). *The token economy: A motivational system for therapy and rehabilitation*. New York: Appelton-Century-Crofts.

Bachrach, L. L. (1992). What we know about homelessness among mentally ill persons: An analytical review and commentary. In H. R. Lamb, L. L. Bachrach, & F. I. Kass (Eds.), *Treating the homeless mentally ill: A report of the task force on the homeless mentally ill*. Washington, DC: American Psychiatric Association.

Barker, R. L. (1987). *The social work dictionary*. Silver Springs, MD: National Association of Social Workers.

Barry, P. D. (1998). *Mental health and mental illness* (6th ed.). Philadelphia, PA: Lippincott.

Barstow, S., Alpert, D., & Campbell, C. (2005, March). Budget proposal calls for tax, spending reductions. *Counseling Today*, 47(9), 1, 12–13.

Baugh, S. (1994 August). County prison combats domestic violence with MENDS Program. *Corrections Today*, 56(5), 84–86.

Baumrind, D. (1967). Child care practices anteceding three patterns of preschool behavior. *Genetic Psychology Monographs*, 75, 43–88.

Baumrind, D. (1991). Parenting styles and adolscent development. In J. Brooks, R. Lerner, & A. C. Petersen (Eds.), *The encyclopedia of adolescence*. (pp. 758–772). New York: Garland.

Beamish, P. M., & Navin, S. L. (1994). Ethical dilemmas in marriage and family therapy: Implications for training. *Journal of Mental Health Counseling*, 16, 129–143.

Beauchamp, T. L., & Childress, J. F. (1989). *Principles of biomedical ethics* (3rd ed.). Oxford, England: Oxford University Press.

Beck, A. T. (1967). *Depression: Clinical, experimental, and theoretical aspects*. New York: Harper & Row.

Beck, A. T. (1976). *Cognitive therapy and emotional disorders*. New York: International Universities Press.

Beck, A. T., Rush, A. J., Shaw, B. F., & Emery, G. (1979). *Cognitive therapy of depression*. New York: Guilford Press.

Beck, A. T., Steer, R. A., & Brown, G. K. (1996). *Manual for the Beck depression inventory* (2nd ed.). San Antonio, TX: psychological Corporation.

Beck, A. T., Wright, F. D., Newman, C. F., & Liese, B. S. (1993). *Cognitive therapy of substance abuse*. New York: Guilford.

Becvar, D. S., & Becvar, R. J. (1999). *Family therapy: A systemic integration* (4th ed.). Boston, MA: Allyn and Bacon.

Beers, C. W. (1908). *A mind that found itself*. Garden City, NY: Longman Green.

Beier, E. G., & Young, D. M. (1998). *The silent language of psychotherapy* (3rd ed.). New York: Aldine de Gruyter.

Bemak, F., & Espina, M. R. (1999, Winter). Professional counseling licensure: Going from state to state. *ACES Spectrum*, 60, 4–6, 11.

Benko, L. B. (2000 July 10). Managed care under siege. *Modern Healthcare*, 30(28), 34–36.

Bertolino, B., & O'Hanlon, B. (2002). *Collaborative, competency-based counseling and therapy*. Boston, MA: Allyn and Bacon.

Bistline, J. L., Sheridan, S. M., & Winegar, N. (1991). Five critical skills for mental health counselors in managed health care. *Journal of Mental Health Counseling*, 13, 147–152.

Bloom, J., Gerstein, L., Tarvydas, V., Conaster, J., Davis, E., Kater, D., et al. (1990). Model legislation for licensed professional counselors. *Journal of Counseling and Development*, 68, 511–523.

Bowen, M. (1960). A family concept of schizophrenia. In D. D. Jackson (Ed.), *The etiology of schizophrenia*. New York: Basic Books.

Bragman, J. L. (1994). Letter to the editor. *Psychological Bulletin*, 29(1), 58–59.

Britton, P. J. (2000). Staying on the roller coaster with clients: Implications of the new HIV/AIDS medical treatments for counseling. *Journal of Mental Health Counseling*, 22, 85–95.

Broderick, P. C., & Blewitt, P. (2003). *The life span: Human development for helping professionals*. Upper Saddle River, NJ: Merrill Prentice Hall.

Bronfenbrenner, U. (1979). *The ecology of human development*. Cambridge, MA: Harvard University Press.

Bronfenbrenner, U. (1989). Ecological systems theory. *Annals of Child Development*, 6, 187–249.

Brooks, D. K., & Gerstein, L. H. (1990). Counselor credentialing and interprofessional collaboration. *Journal of Counseling and Development*, 68, 477–484.

Brooks, D. K., & Weikel, W. J. (1996). Mental health counseling: The first twenty years. In W. J. Weikel, & A. J. Palmo (Eds.), *Foundations in mental health counseling* (2nd ed.). (pp. 5–29). Springfield, IL: Charles C. Thomas.

Broskowski, A., & Marks, E. (1992). Managed mental health care. In S. Cooper, & T. H. Lentner (Eds.), *Innovations in community mental health*. Sarasota, FL: Professional Resource Press.

Brown, L. (1994). *Subversive dialogues: Theory in Feminist therapy*. New York: Basic Books.

Brown, L. K., Danovsky, M. B., Lourie, K. J., DiClemente, R. J., & Ponton, L. E. (1997). Adolescents with psychiatric disorders and the risk of HIV. *Journal of the American Academy of Child and Adolescent Psychiatry*, 36, 1609–1618.

Bruner, J. S., & Tagiuri, R. (1954). The perception of people. In G. Lindzey (Ed.), *Handbook of social psychology* (2 vols.), Cambridge, MA: Addison-Wesley.

Bureau of Justice Statistics. (1999, July). *Mental health and treatment of inmates and probationers* (Publication No. NCJ-174463). Retrieved March 3, 2005 from Http://www.ojp.usdoj.gov/bjs/pub/press/nhtip.pr.

Bureau of Labor Statistics, U.S. Department of Labor. (2002). *Occupational outlook handbook*, 2006–07 ed.. Counselors. Retrieved February, 24, 2006. from http://www.bls.gov/oco/ocos067.htm.

Bureau of Labor Statistics, U.S. Department of Labor. (2003). *Occupational outlook handbook*, 2002–03 ed.. Counselors. Retrieved October 24, 2003, from http://www.bls.gov/oco/ocos067.htm.

Burns, D. D. (1999). *The feeling good handbook*. (revised ed.). New York: Plume.

Cangemi, J. P., & Kowalski, C.J. (1993). Does a hierarchy of significance exist in psychology and the mental health disciplines? *Education*, *113*, 489–497.

Cardemil, E. V., & Battle, C. L. (2003). Guess who's coming to therapy? Getting comfortable with conversations about race and ethnicity in psychotherapy. *Professional Psychology: Research and Practice*, *34*, 278–286.

Carling, P. J. (1995). *Return to community: Building support systems for people with psychiatric disabilities*. New York: Guilford.

Carson, R. C., & Butcher, J. N. (1992). *Abnormal psychology and modern life* (9th ed.). New York: HarperCollins.

Carson, R. C., Butcher, J. N., & Mineka, S. (1996). *Abnormal psychology and modern life* (10th ed.). New York: Harper Collins.

Carson, R. C., Butcher, J. N., & Mineka, S. (2002). *Fundamentals of psychology and modern life*. Boston, MA: Allyn and Bacon.

Casselberry, W. S. (1935). The psychologist in private practice. *Psychological Exchange*, *4*, 57–58.

Caton, L. M., Shrout, P. E., Dominguez, B., Eagle, P. F., Opler, L., & Cournos, F. (1995). Risk factors for homelessness among women with schizophrenia. *American Journal of Public Health*, *85*, 1153–1156.

Caton, L. M., Shrout, P. E., Eagle, P. F., Opler, L., Felix, A., & Dominguez, B. (1994). Risk factors for homelessness among schizophrenic men: A case-control study. *American Journal of Public Health*, *84*, 265–270.

Chambliss, C. H. (2000). *Psychotherapy and managed care: Reconciling research and reality*. Boston, MA: Allyn and Bacon.

Citron, M., Solomon, P., & Draine, J. (1999). Self-help groups for families of persons with mental illness: Perceived benefits of helpfulness. *Community Mental Health Journal*, *35*, 15–30.

Cohen, E. D. (1997). Confidentiality, HIV, and the ACA code of ethics. *Journal of Mental Health Counseling*, *19*, 349–364.

Commission on Accreditation for Marriage and Family Therapy Education. (1997). *Manual on accreditation*. Washington, DC: COAMFTE.

Corey, G. (2001). *Theory and practice of counseling and psychotherapy* (3rd ed.). Monterey, CA: Brooks/Cole.

Corey, G., Corey, M. S., & Callanan, P. (2003). *Issues and ethics in the helping professions* (6th ed.). Pacific Grove, CA: Brooks/Cole.

Cormier, S., & Hackney, H. (1999). *Counseling strategies and interventions* (5th ed.). Boston, MA: Allyn and Bacon.

Cormier, S., & Nurius, P. S. (2003). *Interviewing and change strategies for helpers: Fundamental skills and cognitive behavioral interventions* (5th ed.). Pacific Grove, CA: Brooks/Cole.

Corsini, R. J. (1995). Introduction. In R. J. Corsini, & D. Wedding (Eds.), *Current psychotherapies* (5th ed.). Itasca, IL: F. E. Peacock Publishers.

Cottone, R. R., & Claus, R. E. (2000). Ethical decision-making models: A review of the Literature. *Journal of Counseling and Development*, *78*, 275–283.

Council for the Accreditation of Counseling and Related Educational Programs (CACREP). (2001). *CACREP accreditation manual: 2001 standards*. Alexandria, VA: Author.

Crane, L. (1925). A plea for the training of psychologists. *Journal of Abnormal and Social Psychology*, *20*, 228–233.

Cuellar, I. (2000). Acculturation and mental health: Ecological transactional relations of adjustment. In I. Cuellar, & F. A. Paniagua (Eds.), *Handbook of multicultural mental health: Assessment and treatment of diverse populations* (pp. 45–62). New York: Academic Press.

Cummings, N. A. (1990). The credentialing of professional psychologists and its implication for the other mental health disciplines. *Journal of Counseling and Development*, *68*, 485–490.

Cummings, N. A. (1995). Impact of managed care on employment and training: A primer for survival. *Professional Psychology: Research and Practice*, *26*(1), 10–15.

Cushman, P. (1990). Why the self is empty: Toward a historically situated psychology. *American Psychologist*, *45*, 599–611.

Cushman, P. (1995). *Constructing the self, constructing America: A cultural history of psychotherapy*. Reading, MA: Addison-Wesley.

Cutler, D. L. (1992). A historical overview of community mental health centers in the United States. In S. Cooper, & T. H. Lentner (Eds.), *Innovations in community mental health* (pp. 1–22). Sarasota, FL: Professional Resource Press.

D'Andrea, M. (2000). Postmodernism, constructivism, and multiculturalism: Three forces reshaping and expanding our thoughts about counseling. *Journal of Mental Health Counseling*, *22*, 1–16.

Danzinger, P. R., & Welfel, E. R. (2001). The impact of managed care on mental health counselors: A survey of perceptions, practices, and compliance with ethical standards. *Journal of Mental Health Counseling*, *23*, 137–150.

Das, A. K. (1995). Rethinking multicultural counseling: Implications for counselor education. *Journal of Counseling and Development*, *74*, 45–53.

Davis, J. (1999 July/August). Annual managed care trends report: From chaos to opportunity. *The Advocate*, *22*(4), 1,4–5.

Day, S. X. (2004). *Theory and design in counseling and psychotherapy*. Boston, MA: Houghton Mifflin.

Degges-White, S., Myers, J. E., Adelman, J. U., & Pastoor, S. A. (2003). Examining counseling needs of headache patients: An exploratory study of wellness and perceived stress. *Journal of Mental Health Counseling*, *25*, 271–290.

Dell, P. F. (1980). The Hopi family therapist and the Aristotelian parents. *Journal of Marital and Family Therapy*, 123–129.

Deutsch, A. (1948). *The shame of the states*. New York: Harcourt, Brace.

Deutsch, C. J. (1984). Self-reported sources of stress among psychotherapists. *Professional Psychology: Research and Practice, 15,* 833–845.

Dewa, C. S., Horgan, S., McIntyre, D., Robinson, G., Krupa, T., & Eastabrook, S. (2003). Direct and indirect time inputs and assertive community treatment. *Community Mental Health Journal, 39,* 17–32.

Dickey, B., Fisher, W., Siegel, C., Altaffer, F., & Azeni, H. (1997). The cost and outcomes of community-based care for the seriously mentally ill. *Health Services Research, 32,* 599–625.

Dinkmeyer, D. (1991). Mental health counseling: A psychoeducational approach. *Journal of Mental Health Counseling, 13,* 37–42.

Dinkmeyer, D. Jr, & Sperry, L. (2000). *Counseling and psychotherapy: An integrated, individual psychology approach* (3rd ed.). Upper Saddle River, NJ: Prentice-Hall.

Donnelly, J. W., Eburne, N., & Kittleson, M. (2001). *Mental health: Dimensions of self-esteem & emotional well-being*. Boston, MA: Allyn and Bacon.

Dougherty, A. M. (2000). *Psychological consultation and collaboration in schools and community settings* (3rd ed.). Belmont, CA: Wadsworth/Thomson Learning.

Downie, R. S., Fyfe, C., & Tannahill, A. (1990). *Health promotion: Models and values*. Oxford: Oxford University Press.

Drake, R. E. (1998). Brief history, current status, and future place of assertive community treatment. *American Journal of Orthopsychiatry, 68,* 172–175.

Drake, R. E., Wallach, M. A., Teague, G. B., Freeman, D. H., Paskus, T. S., & Clark, T. A. (1991). Housing instability and homelessness among rural schizophrenic patients. *American Journal of Psychiatry, 148,* 330–336.

Drummond, R. J. (2004). *Appraisal procedures for counselors and helping professionals* (5th ed.). Upper Saddle River, NJ: Pearson Prentice Hall.

Egan, G., & Cowan, M. A. (1979). *People in systems: A model for development in the human-service professions and education*. Monterey, CA: Brooks/Cole.

Ellis, A. (1962). *Reason and emotion in psychotherapy*. New York: Lyle Stuart.

Ellis, A. (1996). A social constructionist position for mental health counseling: A reply to Jeffrey T. Guterman. *Journal of Mental Health Counseling, 18,* 16–28.

Engels, D. W., Minor, C. W., Sampson, J. P., & Splete, H. H. (1995). Career counseling specialty: History, development, and prospect. *Journal of Counseling and Development, 74,* 134–138.

Enns, C. Z. (1997). *Feminist theories and feminist psychotherapies: Origins, themes, and variations*. New York: Haworth.

Erikson, E. (1968). *Identity, youth, and crisis*. New York: Norton.

Erk, R. R. (1997). Multidimensional treatment of attention deficit disorder: A family oriented approach. *Journal of Mental Health Counseling, 19,* 3–22.

Erskine, R. G. (1998). Psychotherapy in the USA: A manual of standardized techniques or a therapeutic relationship? *International Journal of Psychotherapy, 3,* 231–235.

Evans, K., & Sullivan, J.M. (2001). *Dual diagnosis: Counseling the mentally ill substance abuser* (2nd ed.). New York: Guilford.

Evans, M. P., Valadez, A. V., Burns, S., & Rodriquez, V. (2002). Brief and nontraditional approaches to mental health counseling: Practitioners' attitudes. *Journal of Mental Health Counseling, 24,* 317–329.

Evans-Pritchard, E. (1962). *Social anthropology and other essays*. New York: Free Press.

Eysenck, H. (1952). The effects of psychotherapy: An evaluation. *Journal of Consulting Psychology, 16,* 319–324.

Fall, K. A., Levitov, J. E., Jennings, M., & Eberts, S. (2000). The public perception of mental health professions: An empirical examination. *Journal of Mental Health Counseling, 22,* 122–134.

Fallowfield, L., Ratcliffe, D., & Saul, J. (2001). Psychiatric morbidity and its recognition by doctors in patients with cancer. *British Journal of Cancer, 84,* 1011–1015.

Fancher, R. T. (1995). *Cultures of healing: Correcting the image of American mental health care*. New York: W. H. Freeman.

Farber, B. A. (1983). Psychotherapists' perceptions of stressful patient behavior. *Professional Psychology: Research and Practice, 14,* 697–705.

Faulkner, E. J. (1960). *Health insurance*. New York: McGraw-Hill.

Feldstein, P., Wickizer, T., & Wheeler, J. (1988). Private cost containment: The effects of utilization review programs on health care use and expenditures. *New England Journal of Medicine, 318,* 1310–1314.

Fiske, S. T., & Taylor, S. E. (1991). *Social cognition* (2nd ed.). New York: McGraw-Hill.

Foos, J. A., Ottens, A. J., & Hill, L. K. (1991). Managed mental health: A primer for Counselors. *Journal of Counseling and Development, 69,* 332–336.

Friedman, B. D., & Levine-Holdowsky, M. (1997). Overcoming barriers to homeless delivery services: A community response. *Journal of Social Distress and the Homeless, 6,* 13–28.

Friedman, D., & Kaslow, N. (1986). The development of professional identity in psychotherapists: Six stages in the supervision process. In E. W. Kaslow (Ed.), *Supervision and training models, dilemmas and challenges* (pp. 29–50). New York: Haworth.

Fristad, M. A., & Sisson, D. P. (2004). Creating partnerships between consumer groups and professional psychologists. *Professional Psychology: Research and Practice, 35,* 477–480.

Funding tops issues of concern for SA, MH leaders. (2005, January 31). *Alcoholism and Drug Abuse,* 1–4.

Gale, A. U., & Austin, B. D. (2003). Professionalism's challenges to professional counselors' collective identity. *Journal of Counseling and Development, 81,* 3–10.

Garcia, J. G., Cartwright, B., Winston, S. M., & Borzuchowska, B. (2003). A transcultural integrative model for ethical decision making in counseling. *Journal of Counseling and Development,* *81,* 268–277.

Gaver, K. (2000). Mental health care delivery systems. In P. Rodenhauser (Ed.), *Mental health care administration: A guide for practitioners.* Ann Arbor: University of Michigan Press.

Geisler, J. (1995). The impact of the passage of a counselor licensure law: One state's experience. *Journal of Mental Health Counseling, 17,* 188–199.

Geisler, J. S. (1995). The impact of the passage of a counselor licensure law: One state's experience. *Journal of Mental Health Counseling, 17,* 188–199.

Gendlin, E. (1981). *Focusing.* New York: Bantam Books.

George, R. L., & Cristiani, T. S. (1986). *Counseling theory and practice* (2nd ed.). Upper Saddle River, NJ: Prentice Hall.

Gerig, M. (1999). *Third-party reimbursement and the experiences of members of the Indiana Mental Health Counselors Association,* Unpublished manuscript.

Gerig, M. S. (2004). Receiving gifts from clients: Ethical and therapeutic issues. *Journal of Mental Health Counseling, 26,* 199–210.

Gibson, R. L., & Mitchell, M. H. (2003). *Introduction to counseling and guidance* (6th ed.). Upper Saddle River, NJ: Merrill Prentice Hall.

Gillman, P. B. (2004 February). A new era of documentation in psychiatry: Advice on psychotherapy, progress notes. *Behavioral Healthcare Tomorrow, 13*(1), 48–50.

Ginter, E. J. (1996). Three pillars of mental health counseling – watch in what you step. *Journal of Mental Health Counseling, 18,* 99–107.

Gladding, S. T. (2003). *Group work: A counseling specialty.* Upper Saddle River, NJ: Merrill Prentice Hall.

Gladding, S. T., & Newsome, D. W. (2004). *Community and agency counseling* (2nd ed.). Upper Saddle River, NJ: Pearson Prentice Hall.

Glosoff, H. L., Garcia, J., Herlihy, B., & Remley, T. P. (1999). Managed care: Ethical considerations for counselors. *Counseling and Values, 44,* 8–16.

Goldin, E. C. (1997). Interprofessional cooperation concerning counselor licensure: A survey of American Mental Health Counselor Association branch presidents. *Journal of Mental Health Counseling, 19,* 199–205.

Gopaul-McNicol, S., & Brice-Baker, J. (1998). *Cross-cultural practice: Assessment, treatment, and training.* New York: John Wiley & Sons.

Gordon, P. A., Feldman, D., Crose, R., Schoen, E., Griffing, G., & Shankar, J. (2002). The role of religious beliefs in coping with chronic illness. *Counseling and Values, 46,* 162–174.

Grantseeking in Minnesota. (2004, February 25). *Writing a successful grant proposal.* Retrieved October 31, 2005, from http://www.mcf.org/mcf/grant/writing.htm.

Guerney, B. G. Jr. (1977). *Relationship enhancement: Skill-training programs for therapy, problem prevention, and enrichment.* San Francisco: Jossey-Bass.

Guterman, J. T. (1994). A social constructionist position for mental health counseling. *Journal of Mental Health Counseling, 16,* 226–244.

Hackney, H. (2000). *Practice issues for the beginning counselor.* Needham Heights, MA: Allyn and Bacon.

Hadley, R. G., & Mitchell, L. K. (1995). *Counseling research and program evaluation.* Pacific Grove, CA: Brooks/Cole.

Hall, A. S., & Lin, M. (1995). Theory and practice of children's rights: Implications for mental health counselors. *Journal of Mental Health Counseling, 17,* 63–80.

Hanna, F. (1992). Reframing spirituality: AA, the 12 steps, and the mental health counselor. *Journal of Mental Health Counseling, 14,* 166–179.

Hanna, F. J., & Bemak, F. (1997). The quest for identity in the counseling profession. *Counselor Education and Supervision, 36,* 194–207.

Hansen, J. T. (2002). Postmodern implications for theoretical integration of counseling approaches. *Journal of Counseling and Development, 80,* 315–321.

Hansen J. (2003). Including diagnostic training in counseling curricula: Implications for professional identify development. *Counselor Education and Supervision, 82,* 131–138.

Harrison, K. (1997). Parental training for incarcerated fathers: Effects on attitudes, self-esteem, and children's self-perceptions. *Journal of Social Psychology, 137,* 588–594.

Hartwig, H. J., & Myers, J. E. (2003). A different approach: Applying a wellness paradigm to adolescent female delinquents and offenders. *Journal of Mental Health Counseling, 25,* 57–75.

Haynes, D. T., & White, B. W. (1999). Will the 'real' social work please stand up? A call to stand for professional unity. *Social Work, 44,* 385–392.

Hendrix, D. H. (1991). Ethics and intrafamily confidentiality in counseling children. *Journal of Mental Health Counseling, 13,* 323–333.

Herlihy, B., & Corey, G. (1996). *ACA ethical standards casebook* (5th ed.). Alexandria, VA: American Counseling Association.

Hernandez, M., Isaacs, M. R., Nesman, T., & Burns, D. (1998). Perspectives on culturally competent systems of care. In M. Hernandez, & M. R. Isaacs (Eds.), *Promoting cltural competence in children's mental health services.* Baltimore, MD: Paul H. Brooks Publishing.

Hershenson, D. B. (1992). The operation was a success, but the patient died: Theoretical orthodoxy versus empirical validation. *Journal of Mental Health Counseling, 14,* 180–186.

Hershenson, D. B., & Berger, G. P. (2001). The state of community counseling: A survey of directors of CACREP-accredited programs. *Journal of Counseling and Development, 79,* 188–193.

Hess, H. F. (1980). Procedures, problems, and prospects. *Professional Practice of Psychology, 1,* 1–10.

Hettler, B. (1986). Strategies for wellness and recreation program development. In F. Leafgren (Ed.), *Developing Campus Recreation and Wellness Programs.* San Francisco: Jossey-Bass.

Hiday, V. A. (1999). Mental illness and the criminal justice system. In A. V. Horwitz, & T. L. Scheid (Eds.), *A handbook for the study of mental illness* (pp. 508–525). Cambridge, UK: Cambridge University Press.

Hill, L. K. (1991). Macrostrategies: Creating paradigm – versus – paradigm thinking. *Journal of Mental Health Counseling, 13*, 43–50.

Hinkle, J. S. (1999). Psychodiagnosis for counselors: The DSM-IV. In J. Scott Hinkle (Ed.), *Promoting optimum mental health through counseling: An overview.* Greensboro, NC: ERIC/CASS.

Hinterkopf, E. (1994). Integrating spiritual experiences in counseling. *Counseling and Values, 38*, 165–175.

HIPAA. Here's what to do if you missed the extension deadline [Electronic version] (2003, January). *Psychotherapy finances.* Retrieved October 25, 2004, from http:www.psyfin.com/articles/030101.htm.

Hoff, L. A. (1995). *People in crisis: Understanding and helping* (4th ed.). San Francisco: Jossey-Bass.

Hollis, J. W. (2000). *Counselor preparation 1999–2001: Programs, faculty, trends* (10th ed.). Philadelphia, PA: Taylor and Francis.

Hollis, J. W., & Dodson, T. A. (2000). *Counselor preparation 1999–2001: Programs, faculty, trends* (10th ed.). Philadelphia, PA: Taylor & Francis and Greensboro, NC: National Board for Certified Counselors.

Holloway, F., & Carson, J. (2001). Case management: An update. *International Journal of Social Psychiatry, 47*, 21–31.

Holroyd, J. C., & Brodsky, A. M. (1977). Psychologists' attitudes and practices regarding erotic and non-erotic physical contact with patients. *American Psychologist, 32*, 843–849.

Horney, K. (1945). Our inner conflicts: A constructive theory of neurosis. New York: Norton.

Hubert, R. M., & Freeman, L. T. (2004). Report of the ACA ethics committee: 2002–2003. *Journal of Counseling and Development, 82*, 248–251.

Hughes, R. B., & Friedman, A. L. (1994). AIDS-related ethical and legal issues for mental health professionals. *Journal of Mental Health Counseling, 16*, 445–458.

Hull, C. L. & Turman, L. M. 1928. *Aptitude testing,* Yonkers-on-Hudson, NY: World

Isaacs, M. L., & Stone, C. (2001). Confidentiality with mionors: Mental health counselors' attitudes toward breaching or preserving confidentiality. *Journal of Mental Health Counseling, 23*, 342–356.

Ivey, A. E. (1989). Mental health counseling: A developmental process and profession. *Journal of Mental Health Counseling, 11*, 26–35.

Ivey, A. E., & Rigazio-DiGilio, S. A. (1991). Toward a developmental practice of mental health counseling: Strategies for training, practice, and political unity. *Journal of Mental Health Counseling, 13*, 21–36.

Jacobson, N. S., & Margolin, G. (1979). *Marital therapy: Strategies based on social learning and behavior exchange principles.* New York: Brunner/Mazel.

Jaffee v. Redmond. 1996 WL 315841 (U.S. June 13, 1996).

Jankowski, P. J. (2002). Postmodern spirituality: Implications for promoting change. *Counseling and Values, 47*, 69–79.

Joint Commission of Mental Illness and Health. (1961). *Action for mental health.* New York: Basic Books.

Jones, E. E., & Harris, V. A. (1967). The attribution of attitudes. *Journal of Experimental Social Psychology, 3*, 2–24.

Jones, J. M. (1997). *Prejudice and racism* (2nd ed.). New York: McGraw-Hill.

Kaplan, D. M. (2002). Celebrating 50 years of excellence. *Journal of Counseling and Development, 80*, 261–263.

Kaplan, R. M., & Saccuzzo, D. P. (2001). *Psychological testing: Principles, applications, and issues* (5th ed.). Belmont, CA: Wadsworth.

Kaplan, R. M., & Saccuzzo, D. P. (2005). *Psychological testing: Principles, applications, and issues* (3rd ed.). Belmont, CA: Wadsworth.

Kardener, R. R., Fuller, M., & Mensh, I. N. (1973). A survey of physicians attitudes and practices regarding erotic and nonerotic contact with patients. *American Journal of Psychiatry, 130*, 1077–1081.

Katz, A. H. (1993). *Self-help in America: A social movement perspective.* New York: Maxwell Macmillan International.

Kaufmann, C. L. (1999). An introduction to the mental health consumer movement. In A. V. Horwitz, & T. L. Scheid (Eds.), *A handbook for the study of mental health: Social contexts, theories, and systems* (pp. 493–507). Cambridge, UK: Cambridge University Press.

Kazdin, A. E. (1986). Comparative outcome studies in psychotherapy: Methodological issues and strategies. *Journal of Consulting and Clinical Psychology, 57*, 138–146.

Kelly, E. W. (1995). *Spirituality and religion in counseling and psychotherapy.* Alexandria, VA: American Counseling Association.

Kelly, K. R. (1996). Looking to the future: Professional identity, accountability, and change. *Journal of Mental Health Counseling, 18*, 195–199.

Khanna, N., Signh, N., Nemil, M., Best, A., & Ellis, C. R. (1992). Homeless women and their familiesL Characteristics, life circumstances, and needs. *Journal of Child and Family Studies, 1*, 155–165.

King, N. J., & Heyne, D. (2000). Promotion of empirically validated psychotherapies in counseling psychology. *Counselling Psychology Quarterly, 13*, 1–13.

Kitchener, K. S. (1984). Intuition, critical evaluation and ethical principles: The foundation for ethical decisions in counseling psychology. *The Counseling Psychologist, 12*(3), 43–55.

Knox, M. D. (1998). HIV-related community mental health services. In M. D. Knox, & C. H. Sparks (Eds.), *HIV and community mental health care* (pp. 3–18). Baltimore, MD: John Hopkins Press.

Knox, M. D., Davis, M., & Friedrich, M. A. (1994). The HIV mental health spectrum. *Community Mental Health Journal, 30*, 75–89.

Kongstvedt, P. R. (1996). *The managed health care handbook* (3rd ed.). Gaithersburg, MD: Aspen Publishers.

Koop, V. (2004 Spring). The search for Christian integrity. *The CAPS Report*, 33(1), 5.

Korchin, S. J. (1976). *Modern clinical psychology: Principles of intervention in the clinic and community*. New York: Basic Books.

Kottler, J. A. (2003January). Learning to surf. *Counseling Today*, 25, 27.

Kral, R., & Hines, M. (1999). A survey study on the developmental stages in achieving a competent sense of self as a family therapist. *Family Journal*, 7, 102–112.

Kreutzer, J. S., West, M., Sherron, P., Wehman, P. H., & Fry, R. (1992). Computer technology in vocational rehabilitation. *Journal of Head Trauma Rehabilitation*, 7, 70–80.

Kunda, Z., & Thagard, P. (1996). Forming impressions from stereotypes, traits, and behaviors: A parallel-constraint-satisfaction theory. *Psychological Review*, 103, 284–308.

Kupers T. A. (2000, July). How are problems of mental illness being handled in the prison system? *Harvard Mental Health Letter*, 17, 8.

Kurpius, D. J., & Fuqua, D. R. (1993). The consulting process: A multidimensional approach. *Journal of Counseling and Development*, 71, 601–607.

Landreth, G. L., & Lobaugh, A. F. (1998). Filial therapy with incarcerated fathers: Effects on parental acceptance of child, parental stress, and child adjustment. *Journal of Counseling and Development*, 76, 157–165.

Landsberg, G. (1992). Developing comprehensive mental health services in local jails and police lockups. In S. Cooper, & T. H. Lentner (Eds.), *Innovations in community mental health* (pp. 97–124). Sarasota, FL: Professional Resource Press.

Latkin, C. A., Mandell, W., Vlahov, D., Oziemskowska, M., & Celentano, D. D. (1996). The long-term outcome of a personal network-oriented HIV prevention intervention for injection drug users: The SAFE study. *American Journal of Community Psychology*, 24, 341–365.

Laughlin, P. R., & Worley, J. L. (1991). Roles of the American Psychological Association in the development of internships in psychology. *American Psychologist*, 46, 430–436.

Laurie, J. R. (1997). Samaritan counseling centers extend congregational ministry. *Journal of Psychology and Christianity*, 16, 108–114.

Lawless, L. L., Ginter, E. K., & Kelly, K. R. (1999). Managed care: What mental health counselors need to know. *Journal of Mental Health Counseling*, 21, 50–65.

Lawrence, G., & Kurpius, R. S. E. (2000). Legal and ethical issues involved when counseling mnors in nonschool settings. *Journal of Counseling and Development*, 78, 1360–1136.

Leahey, T. H. (1980). *A history of psychology: Main Currents in psychological thought*. Englewood Cliffs, NJ: Prentice-Hall.

Leahy, M. J., & Szymanski, E. M. (1995). Rehabilitation counseling: Evolution and current status. *Journal of Counseling and Development*, 74, 163–166.

Lee, C. C. (1998). Counselors as agents of social change. In C. C. Lee, & G. R. Walz (Eds.), *Social action: A mandate for ccounselors* (pp. 3–14). Alexandria, VA: American Counseling Association.

Lefrancois, G. R. (1999). *The lifespan* (6th ed.). Belmont, CA: Wadsworth.

Lehman, A. F., Steinwachs, D. M., & Co-Investigators of PORT Project. (1998). Translating research into practice: The schizophrenia Patient Outcomes Research Team (PORT) treatment recommendations. *Schizophrenia Bulletin*, 24, 1–10.

Levant, R. F. (2005 February). Evidence-based practice in psychology. *Monitor on Psychology*, 36(2), 5.

Levine, M. (1981). *The history and politics of community mental health*. New York: Oxford University Press.

Levine, M., Perkins, D. D., & Perkins, D. V. (2005). *Principles of community psychology: Perspectives and applications* (3rd ed.). New York: Oxford University Press.

Lewis, J. A., Lewis, M. D., Daniels, J. A., & D'Andrea, M. J. (1998). *Community counseling: Empowerment strategies for a diverse society*. Pacific Grove, CA: Brooks/Cole.

Lewis, J. A., Lewis, M. D., Daniels, J. A., & D'Andrea, M. J. (2003). *Community counseling: Empowerment strategies for a diverse society* (3rd ed.). Pacific Grove, CA: Brooks/Cole.

Lippitt, G., & Lippitt, R. (1986). *The consulting process in action* (2nd ed.). La Jolla, CA: University Associates.

Locke, D. C. (1992). *Increasing multicultural understanding: A comprehensive model*. Newbury Park, CA: Sage.

Locke, D. C. (2001). ACES at its best: Celebrating the human spirit. *Counselor Education and Supervision*, 40, 242–251.

Longo, D. R., & Schubert, S. (2005). Learning by doing: Mentoring, hands-on experience keys to writing successful grants. *Annals of Family Medicine*, 3, 281. &

Lourie, I. S. (2003). A history of community child mental health. In A. J. Pumariega, & N. C. Winters (Eds.), *The handbook of child and adolescent systems of care: The new community psychiatry*. San Francisco: Jossey-Bass.

Lurigio, A. J., Fallon, J. R., & Dincin, J. (2000). Helping the mentally ill in jails adjust to community life: A description of a postrelease ACT program and its clients. *International Journal of Offender Therapy and Comparative Criminology*, 44, 532–548.

Lyddon, W. J., & Adamson, L. A. (1992). Worldview and counseling preference: An analogue study. *Journal of Counseling and Development*, 71, 41–47.

Lynch, R. K., & Maki, D. (1981). Searching for structure: A trait-factor approach to vocational rehabilitation. *Vocational Guidance Quarterly*, 30, 61–68.

Mahalik, J. R., Worthington, R. L., & Crump, S. (1999). Influence of racial/ethnic membership and 'therapist culture' on therapists' worldview. *Journal of Multicultural Counseling and Development*, 27, 2–18.

March, P. A. (1999). Ethical responses to media depictions of mental illness: An advocacy approach. *Journal of Humanistic Counseling, Education and Development*, 38, 70–80.

Marcia, J. E. (1966). Development and validation of ego identity status. *Journal of Personality and Social Psychology*, 3, 551–558.

Marcia, J. E. (1980). Identity in adolescence. In J. Adelson (Ed.), *Handbook of adolescent psychology* (pp. 159–187).

Markus, H., & Wurf, E. (1987). The dynamic self-concept: A social psychological perspective. In M. R. Rosenzweig, & L. W. Porter (Eds.), *Annual review of psychology*. Palo Alto, CA: Annual Reviews.

Markus, H. (1977). Self-schemata and processing information about the self. *Journal of Personality and Social Psychology, 35,* 63–78.

Marsh, D. T. (1996). Families of children and adolescents with serious emotional disturbance: Innovations in theory, research, and practice. In C. A. Heflinger, & C. T. Nixon (Eds.), *Families and the mental health system for children and adolescents: Policy, Services, and research*. Thousand Oaks, CA: Sage.

Martin, D. G. (2000). *Counseling and therapy skills* (2nd ed.). Prospect Heights, IL: Waveland Press.

Mason, J. L., Benjamin, M. P., & Lewis, S. A. (1996). The cultural competence model: Implications for child and family mental health services. In C. A. Heflinger, & C. T. Nixon (Eds.), *Families and the mental health system for children and adolescents: Policy, services, and research*. Thousand Oaks, CA: Sage.

McAuliffe, G. J., & Eriksen, K. P. (1999). Toward a constructivist and developmental identity for the counseling profession: The context-phase-stage-style model. *Journal of Counseling and Development, 77,* 267–280.

McGoldrick, M. (1999). History, genograms, and the family life cycle. In B. Carter, & M. McGoldrick (Eds.), *The expanded family life cycle: Individual, family, and social perspectives* (3rd ed.). Boston: Allyn and Bacon.

McGovern, C. M. (1985). *Masters of madness: The social origins of the American psychiatric profession*. Hanover, NH: University Press of New England.

McKay, M., & Paleg, K. (1992). *Focal group psychotherapy*. Oakland, CA: New Harbinger.

Mead, M. A., Hohenshil, T. H., & Singh, K. (1997). How the DSM is used by clinical counselors: A national study. *Journal of Mental Health Counseling, 19,* 383–401.

Meara, N. M., Schmidt, L. D., & Day, J. D. (1996). Principles and virtues: A foundation for ethical decisions, policies, and character. *The Counseling Psychologist, 24*(1), 4–77.

Mechanic, D. (1991). Strategies for integrating public mental health services. *Hospital and Community Psychiatry, 22,* 797–801.

Meichenbaum, D. (1977). *Cognitive-behavior modification: An integrative approach*. New York: Plenum Press.

Mental health counseling training standards. (1987, June). *AMHCA News, 10*(6), 6.

Midgette, T. E., & Meggert, S. S. (1991). Multicultural counseling instruction: A challenge for faculties in the 21st century. *Journal of Counseling and Development, 70,* 136–141.

Milazzo-Sayre, L. J., Henderson, M. J., Manderscheid, R. W., Bokossa, M. C., Evans, C., & Male. A. A. (2001). *Persons treated in specialty mental health care programs*, United States, 1997. Retrieved December 30, 2004, from http://www.mentalhealth.org/publications/allpubs/SMA01-537?chapter15.asp.

Miller, W. R., & Rollnick, S. (2002). *Motivational interviewing: Preparing people for change* (2nd ed.). New York: Guilford Press.

Millon, T. (2003). It's time to rework the blueprints: Building a science for clinical psychology. *American Psychologist, 58,* 949–961.

Minister of National Health and Welfare. (1988). *Mental health for Canadians*. Ottawa: MNHW.

Mirin, S. M., & Sederer, L. I. (1994). Mental health care: Current realities, future directions. *Psychiatric Quarterly, 65,* 161–175.

Moline, M. E., Williams, G. T., & Austin, K. M. (1998). *Documenting psychotherapy: Essentials for mental health practitioners*. Thousand Oaks, CA: Sage.

Montgomery, L. M., Cupit, B. E., & Wimberly, T. K. (1999). Complaints, malpractice, and risk management: Professional issues and personal experiences. *Professional Psychology: Research and Practice, 30,* 402–410.

Morris, S. M., & Steadman, H. J. (1997). Mental health services in United States jails: A survey of innovative practices. *Criminal Justice and Behavior, 24,* 3–20.

Morrissey, J. P. (1999). Integrating services for severe mental illness. In A. V. Horwitz, & T. L. Scheid (Eds.), *A handbook for the study of mental health: Social contexts, theories, and systems* (pp. 449–466). Cambridge, UK: Cambridge University Press.

Mueser, K. T., Bond, G. R., Drake, R. E., & Resnick, S. G. (1998). Models of community care for severe mental illness: A review of research on case management. *Schizophrenia Bulletin, 24,* 37–74.

Murphy, L. L., Plake, B. S., Impara, J. C., & Spies, R. A. (Eds.), (2002). *Tests in print VI*. Lincoln, NE: University of Nebraska Press.

Myers, D. G. (2000). The funds, friends, and faith of happy people. *American Psychologist, 55,* 56–67.

Myers, D. G. (2002). *Social psychology* (7th ed.). New York: McGraw-Hill.

Myers, J. E. (1995). Specialties in counseling: Rich heritage or force for fragmentation? *Journal of Counseling and Development, 74,* 115–116.

Myers, J. E., & Gibson, D. M. (Fall, 1999). Report of technology interest network survey. *ACES Spectrum, 60*(1), 3–4.

Myers, J. E., Sweeney, T. J., & Witmer, J. M. (2000). The wheel of wellness counseling for wellness: A holistic model for treatment planning. *Journal of Counseling and Development, 78,* 251–266.

Myers, J. E., Sweeney, T. J., & White, V. E. (2002). Advocacy for counseling and counselors: A professional imperative. *Journal of Counseling and Development, 80,* 394–402.

National Alliance for the Mentally Ill. (2005, February 16). *About NAMI*. Retrieved from http://www.nami.org/Content/NavigationMenu/Inform_Yourself/About_NAMI/About_NAMI.htm.

National Association of Social Workers. (1999). *Code of ethics of the National Association of Social Workers*. Washington, DC: Author.

National Board of Certified Counselors. (n.d.). *General information – The national certified counselor (NCC) credential.*
Retrieved May 4, 2005, from http://www.nbcc.org/
cert/ncc.htm.

National Clearinghouse on Child Abuse and Neglect
Information. (2003). *Foster care national statistics.* Retrieved
on May 2, 2005, from http://nccanch.acf.hhs.gov/
pubs/factsheets/foster.pdf.

Neukrug, E., Milliken, T., & Walden, S. (2001). Ethical complaints made against credentialed counselors: An updated
survey of state licensing boards. *Counselor Education and
Supervision, 41,* 57–70.

Newberg, A., D'Aquili, M. D., & Rause, V. (2001). *Why God
won't go away: Brain science and the biology of belief.* New
York: Balantine Books.

Nichols, M. P., & Schwartz, R. C. (1998). *Family therapy:
Concepts and methods* (4th ed.). Boston, MA: Allyn and Bacon.

Nielsen, S. L. (1994). Rational-emotive behavior therapy and
religion: Don't throw the therapeutic baby out with the holy
water. *Journal of Psychology and Christianity, 13,* 312–322.

North, C. S., & Smith, E. M. (1993). A comparison of homeless men and women: Different populations, different needs.
Community Mental Health Journal, 29, 423–431.

Nugent, F. A. (2000). *Introduction to the profession of counseling*
(3rd ed.). Upper Saddle River, NJ: Prentice-Hall.

Numbers, A. (1984). *Compulsory health insurance.* New York:
Basic Books.

Nutbeam, D. (1997). Promoting health and preventing disease:
An international perspective on youth health promotion.
Journal of Adolescent Health, 20, 396–402.

Okonski, V. O. (2003). Exercise as a counseling intervention.
Journal of Mental Health Counseling, 25, 45–56.

Onstad, K., & Banks, B. (1997 September). Oedipus clicks.
Canadian Business, 70(11), 14.

Orsulic-Jeras, S., Shepherd, J. B., & Britton, P. J. (2003).
Counseling older adults with HIV/AIDS: A strength-based
model of treatment. *Journal of Mental Health Counseling, 25,*
233–244.

Oyserman, D., Coon, H. M., & Kemmelmeier, M. (2002).
Rethinking individualism and collectivism: Evaluation of
theoretical assumptions and meta-analyses. *Psychological
Bulletin, 128,* 3–72.

Palmo, A. J. (1996). Professional identity of the mental health
counselor. In W. J. Weikel, & A. J. Palmo (Eds.), *Foundations
of mental health counseling* (2nd ed.). Springfield, IL:
Charles C. Thomas.

Panos, P. T., Panos, A., Cox, S. E., Roby, J. L., & Matheson, K. W.
(2002). Ethcial issues concerning the use of videoconferenc-
ing to supervise international social work field practicum
students. *Journal of Social Work Education, 38,* 421–437.

Parsons, F. (1909). *Choosing a vocation.* Boston, MA: Houghton
Mifflin.

Pearson, B., & Piazza, N. (1997). Classification of dual relationships in the helping professions. *Counselor Education and
Supervision, 37,* 89–99.

Pedersen, P. (1991). Multiculturalism as a generic approach
to counseling. *Journal of Counseling and Development, 70,*
6–12.

Pedersen, P. (1994). *A handbook for developing multicultural
awareness* (2nd ed.). Alexandria, VA: American Counseling
Association.

Pennington, D. A. (2003, June). Licensure for all 50 states
nearing reality. *Counseling Today, 45,* 1, 10, 14, 44–45.

Perry, C. L. (1999). *Creating health behavior change: How to
develop community-wide programs for youth.* Thousand Oaks,
CA: Sage.

Perry, C. L., & Jessor, R. (1985). The concept of health promotion and the prevention of adolescent drug abuse. *Health
Education Quarterly, 12,* 169–184.

Perry, S., Francis, A., & Clarkin, J. (1985). *A DSM-III casebook
of differential therapeutics: A clinical guide to treatment planning
selection.* New York: Brunner/Mazel.

Phares, E. J. (1991). *Introduction to personality* (3rd ed.).
New York: HarperCollins.

Phelps, R., Eisman, E. J., & Kohout, J. (1998). Psychological
practice and managed care: Results of the CAPP practitioner study. *Professional Psychology: Research and Practice,
29,* 31–36.

Pickett-Schenk, S. A., Cook, J. A., Grey, D., Banghart, M.,
Rosenheck, R. A., & Randolph, F. (2002). Employment his-
tories of homeless persons with mental illness. *Community
Mental Health Journal, 38,* 199–211.

Pirodsky, D. M., & Cohn, J. S. (1992). *Clinical primer of psychopharmacology: A practical guide* (2nd ed.). New York:
McGraw-Hill.

Pistole, M. C., & Roberts, A. (2002). Mental health counseling:
Toward resolving identity confusions. *Journal of Mental
Health Counseling, 24,* 1–19.

Plake, B. S., Impara, J. C., & Spies, R. A. (Eds.) (2003), *The
fifteenth mental measurements yearbook.* Lincoln, NE: Buros
Institute of Mental Measurements, University of Nebraska.

Plato, No Date. *The laws* (Vol. 5). (G. Burges, Trans.). London:
George Bell & Sons.

Polanski, P. J. (2002). Exploring spiritual beliefs in relation
to Adlerian theory. *Counseling and Values, 46,* 127–136.

Polkinghorne, D. E. (2001). Managed care programs: What do
clinicians need? In B. D. Slife, R. N. Williams, & S. H.
Barlow (Eds.), *Critical issues in psychotherapy: Translating new
ideas into practice.* Thousand Oaks, CA: Sage.

Polvan, N. (1969). Historical aspects of mental ills in Middle
East discussed. *Roche Reports, 6*(12), 3.

Powell, B. (2003 June). Licensed professional counselors are
named in the child healthcare crisis relief act. *The Advocate,
26*(6), 8.

Prochaska, J. O., & DiClemente, C. C. (1984). *The transtheoretical approach: Crossing traditional boundaries of treatment.*
Homewood, IL: Dow Jones-Irwin.

Prochaska, J. O., & Norcross, J. C. (1999). *Systems of psychotherapy: A transtheoretical model* (4th ed.). Pacific Grove,
CA: Brooks/Cole.

Puente, A. E. (1997). Reimbursement for professional psychological services. *Journal of Psychopathology and Behavioral Assessment, 19,* 91–99.

Putnam, R. D. (2000). *Bowling alone: The collapse and revival of American community.* New York: Simon and Schuster.

Regier, D. A., Farmer, M. E., Rae, D. S., Locke, B. Z., Keith, S. J., Judd, L. J., et al. (1990). Comorbidity of mental disorders with alcohol and other drug abuse: Results from the Epidemiologic Catchment Area (ECA) Study. *Journal of the American Medical Association, 264,* 2511–2518.

Remley, T. P., & Herlihy, B., (2005). *Ethical, legal, and professional issues in counseling* (2nd ed.). Upper Saddle River, NJ: Pearson Education.

Remley, T. P. Jr. (1991 August). On being different. *Guidepost,* 2.

Resnick, R. J. (1997). A brief history of practice – expanded. *American Psychologist, 52,* 463–468.

Rest, J. R. (1983). Morality. In J. H. Flavell, & E. M. Markman (Eds.), *Handbook of child psychology: Vol. 3. Cognitive development* (pp. 556–629). New York: Wiley.

Richardson, B. L., & June, L. N. (1997). Utilizing and maximizing the resources of the African American church: Strategies and tools for counseling professions. In C.C. Lee (Ed.), *Multicultural issues in counseling: New approaches to diversity* (pp. 155–170). Alexandria, VA: American Counseling Association.

Riemer-Reiss, M. L. (2000). Utilizing distance technology for mental health counseling. *Journal of Mental Health Counseling, 22,* 189–203.

Ritchie, M. H., Piazza, N. J., & Lewton, J. C. (1991). Current use of the *DSM-III-R* in counselor education. *Counselor Education and Supervision, 30,* 205–211.

Ritchie, M., Partin, R., & Trivette, P. (1998). Mental health agency directors' acceptance and perceptions of licensed professional counselors. *Journal of Mental Health Counseling, 20,* 227–237.

Robinson, T. L. (2005). *The convergence of race, ethnicity, and gender: Multiple identities in counseling.* Upper Saddle River, NJ: Pearson Education.

Rogers, C. (1942). *Counseling and psychotherapy.* Boston: Houghton Mifflin.

Rogers, C. R. (1961). *On becoming a person.* Boston: Houghton Mifflin.

Rosenblatt, A., & Attkisson, C. (1993). Assessing outcomes for sufferers of severe mental disorder: A conceptual framework and review. *Evaluation and Program Planning, 16,* 347–363.

Roskes, E., Feldman, R., Arrington, S., & Leisher, M. (1999). A model program for the treatment of mentally ill offenders in the community. *Community Mental Health Journal, 35,* 461–472.

Rossi, P. H., Freeman, H. E., & Lipsey, M. W. (1999). *Evaluation: A systematic approach* (6th ed.). Thousand Oaks, CA: Sage.

Rowe, M., Hoge, M. A., & Fisk, D. (1996). Critical issues in serving people who are homeless and mentally ill. *Administration and Policy in Mental Health, 23,* 555–565.

Russell, M. (1984). *Skills in counseling women.* Springfield, IL: Charles C. Thomas.

Ryglewicz, H., & Pepper, B. (1992). The dual-disorder client: Mental disorder and substance abuse. In S. Cooper, & T.H. Lentner (Eds.), *Innovations in community mental health* (pp. 73–96). Sarasota, FL: Professional Resource Press.

Salkever, D., Domino, M. E., Burns, B. J., Santos, A. B., Deci, P. A., Dias, J., et al. (1999). Assertive community treatment fror people with severe mental illness: The effect on hospital use and costs. *Health Services Research, 34,* 577–579.

Sanchez, A. R. (2001). Multicultural family counseling:Toward cultural sensibility. In J. G. Ponterotto, J. M. Casas, L. A. Suzuki, & C. M. Alexander (Eds.), *Handbook of multicultural counseling* (2nd ed.). Thousand Oaks, CA Sage.

Sands, T. (1998). Feminist counseling and female adolescents: Treatment strategies for depression. *Journal of Mental Health Counseling, 20,* 42–55.

Santos, A. B., Hawkins, G. D., Julius, B., Deci, P. A., Hiers, T. H., & Burns, B. J. (1993). A pilot study of assertive community treatment for patients with chronic psychotic disorders. *American Journal of Psychiatry, 150,* 501–504.

Santrock, J. W. (1997). *Life-span development* (6th ed.). Madison, WI: Brown & Benchmark.

Santrock, J. W. (2004). *Lifespan development* (9th ed.). Madison, WI: Brown & Benchmark.

Santrock J. W (2006) Lifespan development (10th ed.) New york: McGraw Hill.

Sarason, S. B. (1984). If it can be studied or developed, shouldn't it be? *American Psychologist, 39,* 477–485.

Schlossberg, N. (1981). A model for analyzing human adaptation to transition. *The Counseling Psychologist, 9,* 2–18.

Schmidt, J. J. (1999). Two decades of CACREP and what do we know? *Counselor Education and Supervision, 39,* 34–46.

Seiler, G. (1990). *Shaping the destiny of the new profession: Recollections and reflections on the evolution of mental health counseling. In G. Seiler (Ed.), The mental health counselor's sourcebook* (pp. 85). New York: Human Sciences Press.

Seiler, G., & Messina, J. J. (1979). Toward professional identity: The dimensions of mental health counseling in perspective. *American Mental Health Counselors Journal, 1,* 3–8.

Seligman, L. (1998). *Selecting effective treatments: A comprehensive, systematic guide to treating mental disorders.* San Francisco: Jossey-Bass.

Seligman, L. (1999). Twenty years of diagnosis and the DSM. *Journal of Mental Health Counseling, 21,* 229–239.

Seligman, M. E. P., & Csikszentmihalyi, M. (2000). Positive psychology: An introduction. *American Psychologist, 55,* 5–14.

Sharf, R. S. (2000). *Theories of psychotherapy and counseling: Concepts and cases* (2nd ed.). Belmont, CA: Wadsworth.

Sherer, R. A. (2002 March). Surgeon general's report highlights mental health problems among minorities. *Psychiatric Times, 19*(3). Retrieved August 9, 2004, from http://www.psychiatrictimes.com/p020301a.html.

Sherman, A. C., & Simonton, S. (2001). Assessment of religiousness and spirituality in health research. In T. G. Plante, & A. C. Sherman (Eds.), *Faith and health: Psychological perspectives*. New York: Guilford.

Sherman, R., & Fredman, N. (1986). *Handbook of structured techniques in marriage and family therapy*. New York: Brunner/Mazel.

Slife, B. D., & Reber, J. S. (2001). Eclecticism in psychotherapy: Is it really the best substitute for traditional theories? In B. D. Slife, R. N. Williams, & S. H. Barlow (Eds.), *Critical issues in psychotherapy: Translating new ideas into practice*. Thousand Oaks: Sage.

Slovenko, R. (1998). *Psychotherapy and confidentiality: Testimonial privileged communication, breach of confidentiality, and reporting duties*. Springfield, IL: Charles C. Thomas.

Smart, D. W., & Smart, J. F. (1997). DSM-IV and culturally sensitive diagnosis: Some observations for counselors. *Journal of Counseling and Development, 75*, 392–398.

Smith, H. B. (1999). Managed care: A survey of counselor educators and counselor practitioners. *Journal of Mental Health Counseling, 21*, 270–284.

Smith, H. B., & Robinson, G. (1995). Mental health counseling: Past, present, and future. *Journal of Counseling and Development, 74*, 158–162.

Smith, H. B., & Robinson, G. P. (1996). Mental health counseling: Past, present, and future. In W. J. Weikel, & A. J. Palmo (Eds.), *Foundations of mental health counseling* (2nd ed.). (pp. 38–50). Springfield, IL: Charles C. Thomas.

Smith, M. L., & Glass, G. V. (1977). Meta-analysis of psychotherapy outcome studies. *American Psychologist, 32*, 752–760.

Smith, S. H., & McLean, D. D. (1988). *ABCs of grantsmanship*. Reston, VA: American Alliance for Health, Physical Education, Recreation, and Dance.

Sokal, M. M. (1992). Origins and early years of the American Psychological Association, 1890–1906. *American Psychologist, 47*, 111–122.

Staton, R. D. (2000). The national healthcare economic context of psychiatric practice. In P. Rodenhauser (Ed.), *Mental health care administration: A guide for practitioners* (pp. 1–31). Ann Arbor: The University of Michigan Press.

Staton, R. D. (2001). The national health care economic context of psychiatric practice. In P. Rodenhauser (Ed.), *Mental health care administration: A guide for practitioners*. Ann Arbor: University of Michigan Press.

Steinberg, L., Darling, N. E., & Fletcher, A. C. in collaboration with Brown, B. B., & Dornbusch, S. M. 1995). Authoritative parenting and adolescent adjustment: An ecological journey. In P. Moen, G.H. Elder Jr, & K. Luscher (Eds.), *Examining lives in context: Perspectives on the ecology of human development* (pp. 423–466). Washington, DC: American Psychological Association.

Stein, R. H. (1990) Ethical issues in counseling Buffalo, NY: Prometheus.

Steinberg, L., Lamborn, S., Darling, N., Mounts, N. S., & Dornbusch, S. M. (1994). Over-time changes in adjustment and competencies among adolescents from authoritative, authoritarian, indulgent, and neglectful families. *Child Development, 65*, 754–770.

Stevens, M. J., & Morris, S. J. (1995). A format for case conceptualization. *Counselor education and supervision, 35*, 82–94.

Stevens, P., & Smith, R. L. (2005). *Substance abuse counseling: Theory and practice* (3rd ed.). Upper Saddle River, NJ: Pearson Prentice Hall.

Strupp, H. H., & Hadley, S. W. (1979). Specific versus nonspecific factors in psychotherapy. *Archives of General Psychiatry, 36*, 1125–1136.

Sturdivant, S. (1980). *Therapy with women*. New York: Springer.

Sue, D. W. (1981). *Counseling the culturally different*. New York: Wiley.

Sue, D. W., & Sue, D. (2003). *Counseling the culturally diverse: Theory and practice* (4th ed.). New York: John Wiley & Sons.

Sue, D. W., Arrendondo, P., & McDavis, R. J. 1992). Multicultural counseling competencies and standards: A call to the profession. *Journal of Counseling and Development, 70*, 477–483.

Super, D. E. (1955). Transition: From vocational guidance to counseling psychology. *Journal of Counseling Psychology, 2*, 3–9.

Suppes, M. A., & Wells, C. C. (2003). *The social work experience: An introduction to social work and social welfare* (4th ed.). Boston: McGraw-Hill.

Sweeney, T. J. (1995). Accreditation, credentialing, professionalization: The role of specialties. *Journal of Counseling and Development, 74*, 117–125.

Talan, J. (2000 Jan./Feb.) Fighting with care. *Psychology Today, 33*(1), 11.

Tarasoff v. Board of Regents of the University of California. (1976). 17 Cal. 3d 425,551.

Thomas, K. R., & Weinrach, S. G. (2004). Mental health counseling and the AMCD multicultural counseling competencies: A civil debate. *Journal of Mental Health Counseling, 26*, 41–43.

Thorne, B. M., & Henley, T. B. (2001). *Connections in the history and systems of psychology* (2nd ed.). Boston: Houghton Mifflin.

Throckmorton, W. (1998). Managed care: "It's like deja-vu, all over again". *Journal of Psychology and Christianity, 17*, 131–141.

Tidwell, R. (2004). The "no-show" phenomenon and the issue of resistance among African-American female patients at an urban health care center. *Journal of Mental health Counseling, 26*, 1–12.

Torrey, E. F. (1997). *Out of the shadows: Confronting America's mental illness crisis*. New York: John Wiley and Sons.

Tudor, K. (1996). *Mental health promotion: Paradigms and practice*. New York: Routledge.

U.S. General Accounting Office. (1993). *Foster care. Services to prevent out-of-home placements are limited by funding barriers*. Washington, DC: Author.

U.S. Census Bureau. (2000). *Population profile of the United States: 2000*. Retrieved July 24, 2004, from http://www.census.gov/population/pop-profile/2000/chap16.pdf.

U.S. Census Bureau. (2003). *People: Race and ethnicity*. Retrieved July 24, 2004, from http://factfinder.census.gov/jsp/saff/SAFFInfo.jsp?pageId=tp9_race_ethnicity.

U.S. Surgeon General. (2001). *Mental health: A report of the surgeon general*. Retrieved on December 30, 2004, from http://www.mentalhealth.samhsa.gov/cmhs/surgeongeneral/.

Uttaro, T., Vali, F., Horwitz, A. V., & Henri, W. F. (1998). Primary therapists' views of managed care. *Psychological Reports, 82*, 459–464.

Vacc, N. A., & Loesch, L. C. (2000). *Professional orientation to counseling* (3rd ed.). Philadelphia, PA: Brunner-Routledge.

Vacc, N. A., Loesch, L. C., & Guilbert, D. E. (1997). The clientele of certified clinical mental health counselors. *Journal of Mental Health Counseling, 19*, 165–170.

Van Hesteren, F., & Ivey, A. E. (1990). *Counseling and development* : Toward a new identity for a profession in transition. *Journal of Counseling and Development, 68*, 524–533.

Van Hesteren, F., & Ivey, A. E. (1990). Counseling and development: Toward a new identity for a profession in transition. *Journal of Counseling and Development, 68*, 524–528.

VanZandt, C. E. (1990). Professionalism: A matter of personal initiatives. *Journal of Counseling and Development, 68*, 243–245.

Velasquez, M. M., Maurer, G. G., Crouch, C., & DiClemente, C. C. (2001). *Group treatment for substance abuse*. New York: Guilford.

Verheul, R., Kranzler, H. R., Poling, J., Tennen, H., Ball, S., & Rounsaville, B. J. (2000). Axis I and Axis II disorders in alcoholics and drug addicts: Fact or artifact. *Journal of Studies on Alcohol, 61*, 101–110.

Vessey, J., & Howard, K. (1993). Who seeks psychotherapy. *Psychotherapy, 30*(4), 546–553.

Viney, W., & King, D. B. (2003). *A history of psychology: Ideas and context* (3rd ed.). Boston: Allyn and Bacon.

Voss, S. L. (1996). The church as an agent in rural mental health. *Journal of Psychology and Theology, 24*, 114–123.

Vostanis, P., Grattan, E., & Cumella, S. (1998). Mental health problems of homeless children and families: Longitudinal study. *British Medical Journal, 316*, 899–903.

Vygotsky, L. S. (1962). *Thought and language*. Cambridge, MA: MIT Press.

Walborn, F. S. (1996). *Process variables: Four common elements of counseling and psychotherapy*. Pacific Grove, CA: Brooks/Cole.

Walden, S. L., Herlihy, B., & Ashton, L. (2003). The evolution of ethics: Personal perspectives of ACA ethics committee chairs. *Journal of Counseling and Development, 81*, 106–110.

Walker, J. (2002). Rural women with HIV and AIDS: Perceptions of service accessibility, psychosocial, and mental health counseling needs. *Journal of Mental Health Counseling, 24*, 299–316.

Weikel, W. J. (1996). The mental health counselors association. In W. J. Weikel, & A. J. Palmo (Eds.), *Foundations of mental health counseling* (2nd ed.). Springfield, IL: Charles C. Thomas.

Weikel, W.J., & Palmo, A.J. (1996). *Foundations of mental health counseling* (3rd ed.). Springfield, IL: Charles C. Thomas.

Weikel, W.J., & Palmo, A.J. (1989). The evolution and practice of mental health counseling. *Journal of Mental Health Counseling, 11*, 7–25.

Weinrach, S. G., & Thomas, K. R. (2002). A critical analysis of the multicultural counseling competencies: Implications for the practice of mental health counseling. *Journal of Mental Health Counseling, 24*, 20–35.

Welfel, E. R. (1998). *Ethics in counseling and psychotherapy: Standards, research, and emerging issues*. Pacific Grove, CA: Brooks/Cole.

Wentz, D. L. (2004 November/December). A David and Goliath story of mental health advocacy. *Behavioral Health Management, 26*(6), 30–32.

Wheeler, B. (2003 June). A time for thanks and reflection. *The Advocate, 26*(6), 12.

White, B. J., & Madara, E. J. (2002). *The self-help group sourcebook: Your guide to community and online support groups* (7th ed.). Cedar Knolls, NJ: American Self-Help Group Clearinghouse.

White, M., & Epston, D. (1990). *Narrative means to therapeutic ends*. New York: Norton.

Whiteley, J. M. (1984). A historical perspective on the development of counseling psychology as a profession. In S. Brown, & R. Lent (Eds.), *Handbook of counseling psychology* (pp. 3–55). New York: John Wiley.

Wieling, E., Negretti, M. A., Stokes, S., Kimball, T., Christensen, F. B., & Bryan, L. (2001). Postmodernism in marriage and family therapy training: Doctoral students' understanding and experiences. *Journal of Marital and Family Therapy, 27*, 527–533.

Wiersma, W. (2000). *Research methods in education: An introduction* (7th ed.). Boston: Allyn and Bacon.

Wiggins, J. G. (1988). Psychology's inclusion in health benefits planning. *Psychotherapy in Private Practice, 6*(2), 129–134.

Williams, B. (2003). The worldview dimensions of individualism and collectivism: Implications for counseling. *Journal of Counseling and Development, 81*, 370–374.

Williams, M. (2005, April). Licensure portability nears enactment. *The Advocate, 28*(4), 1–10.

Williams, R. N. (2001). The biologicalization of psychotherapy: Understanding the nature of influence. In B. D. Slife, R. N. Williams, & S. H. Barlow (Eds.), *Critical issues in psychotherapy: Translating new ideas into practice* (pp. 51–68). Thousand Oaks, CA: Sage.

Williamson, E. G. (1939). *How to counsel students: A manual of techniques for clinical counselors*. New York: McGraw-Hill.

Witmer, L. (1896). Practical work in psychology. *Pediatrics, 2,* 462–471.

Witmer, J. M, & Sweeney T. J (1992). A holistic model for wellness and prevention over the lifespan. Journal of Counseling and Development, 71, 140–148.

Wolff, N., Helminiak, T. W., Morse, G. A., Calsyn, R. J., Klinkenberg, W. D., & Trusty, M. L. (1997). Cost-effectiveness evaluation of three approaches to case management for homeless mentally ill clients. *American Journal of Psychiatry, 154,* 341–348.

Wolpe, J. (1958). *Psychotherapy by reciprocal inhibition.* Stanford, CA: Stanford University Press.

Woody, R. H., Hansen, J. C., & Rossberg, R. H. (1989). *Counseling psychology: Strategies and services.* Pacific Grove, CA: Brooks/Cole.

Wrenn, C. G. (1962). The culturally encapsulated counselor. *Harvard Educational Review, 32,* 444–449.

Yalisove, D. (2004). *Introduction to alcohol research: Implications for treatment, prevention, and policy.* Boston, MA: Allyn and Bacon.

Yanos, P. T., Barrow, S. M., & Tsemberis, S. (2004). Community integration in the early phase of housing among homeless persons diagnosed with severe mental illness: Successes and challenges. *Community Mental Health Journal, 40,* 133–150.

Young, J. S., Cashwell, C., Wiggins-Frame, M., & Belaire, C. (2002). Spiritual and religious competencies: A national survey of CACREP-accredited programs. *Counseling and Values, 47,* 22–33.

Young, N. K., & Grella, C. E. (1998). Mental health and substance abuse treatment services for dually diagnosed clients: Results of a statewide survey of county administrators. *Journal of Behavioral Health Services and Research, 25,* 83–88.

Zimet, C. N. (1989). The mental health care revolution: Will psychology survive? *American Psychologist, 44,* 703–708.

Zimpfer, D. G. (1992). Psychosocial treatment of life-threatening disease: A wellness model. *Journal of Counseling and Development, 71,* 203–209.

Zimpfer, D. G. (1995). Third-party reimbursement experience of licensed clinical counselors in Ohio. *Journal of Mental Health Counseling, 17,* 105–113.

Zunker, V. G. (1998). *Career counseling: Applied concepts of life planning* (5th ed.). Pacific Grove, CA: Brooks/Cole.

A

ACA *Code of Ethics,* 86, 164, 190–194, 197, 199
ACA Governing Council, 6
ACA Policies and Procedures Manual, 12
Academy of Certified Social Workers (ACSW), 3, 16
Acculturation, 174–176
Achievement tests, 144–145
Ackerman, Nathan, 32
Acquisition, 70
Actualizing tendency, 76
Acuff, C., 211
Adamson, L. A., 42
Addiction counseling, 12–13
Adelman, J. U., 84
Adler, Alfred, 67–69
Adlerian therapy, 67–69
Advocacy, 126
Advocates, 125
Agency mental health centers, 129–130
Aiken, L. R., 143, 145–146
Ainsworth, M. D. S., 152
Aitken, J. B., 241
Allen, V. B., 188
Alpert, D., 241
Altaffer, F., 229
American Association of Marriage and Family Counselors (AAMFC), 30
American Association of Marriage and Family Therapists (AAMFT), 16, 30, 92, 103, 190
American Association of Pastoral Counselors (AAPC), 5
American Association of State Counseling Board's (AASCB), National Credential Registry, 105
American College Counseling Association (ACCA), 9
American College Personnel Association (ACPA), 8, 30
American College Testing Program (ACT), 145–146

American Counseling Association (ACA), 4–6, 8–11, 12, 46, 86, 92, 103–104, 149, 157, 164, 181, 185, 190–191, 243
American Counselor Education and Supervisor's Technology Interest Network, 86
American Federation of Teachers, 212
American Institute of Family Relations, 28
American Medical Association (AMA), 23
American Medico-Psychological Association, 24
American Mental Health Counselors Association (AMHCA), 4, 6, 8–11, 34–35, 101, 103–104, 126, 148, 157, 164, 185, 190, 242, 243
American Mental Health Counselors Association Journal, 34
American Nursing Association, 35
American Personnel and Guidance Association (APGA), 8, 30, 33, 34–35
American Philosophical Association, 25
American Psychiatric Association, 15, 24, 35, 103, 112, 116–117
American Psychological Association (APA), 5, 15, 24–25, 35, 92, 103, 163, 180–181, 190
American Rehabilitation Counseling Association (ARCA), 9
American School Counselor Association (ASCA), 9
Ancis, J. R., 860
Anderson, C. E., 213
Angel, R. J., 168
Antidepressants, 31
Anxiety, 64
APGA Guidepost, 34
Appraisal, 102, 140–150
  categories of techniques, 143–148
  concepts and principles in, 141–143
  ethical practice in, 148–150
  test uses, 140–141

Aptitude Testing (Hull and Terman), 28
Aptitude tests, 145–147
Arbitrary inference, 74
Arredondo, P., 175–177, 180–181
Arrington, S., 233
Ashton, L., 188
Assessment, expansion of, 28–29
Association for Adult Development and Aging (AADA), 9
Association for Assessment in Counseling and Education (AACE), 9
Association for Counselor Education and Supervision (ACES), 9, 30, 34
Association for Counselors and Educators in Government (ACEG), 9
Association for Creativity in Counseling (ACC), 9
Association for Gay, Lesbian and Bisexual Issues in Counseling (AGLBIC), 9
Association for Multicultural Counseling and Development (AMCD), 9, 176, 180
Association for Specialists in Group Work (ASGW), 9, 121
Association for Spiritual, Ethical, and Religious Values in Counseling (ASERVIC), 9
Association of Medical Superintendents of American Institutions for the Insane (AMSAII), 23–24
Atkinson, D. R., 47, 165–166, 173
Attention deficit disorder (ADD), 123
Attkisson, C., 229
Austin, B. D., 240
Austin, K. M., 111
Autonomy, 189
Axinn, J., 25
Azeni, H., 229

B

Bachrach, L. L., 227
Bandura, Albert, 74
Barker, R. L., 15